OKLAHOMA!

OKLAHOMA!

The Making of an
American Musical

TIM CARTER

YALE UNIVERSITY PRESS   NEW HAVEN & LONDON

Published with assistance from the foundation established in memory of
Philip Hamilton McMillan of the Class of 1894, Yale College.

Set in Electra Roman by Tseng Information Systems, Inc.

Printed in the United States of America.

Library of Congress Cataloging-in-Publication Data
Carter, Tim, 1954–
Oklahoma! the making of an American musical / Tim Carter.
p.   cm.
Includes bibliographical references (p.   ) and index.
ISBN 978-0-300-10619-0 (cloth : alk. paper) 1. Rodgers, Richard, 1902–1979.
Oklahoma! 2. Musicals—Production and direction—New York (State)—
New York. I. Title.
ML410.R6315C37 2007
792.6′42—dc22
2006024628

A catalogue record for this book is available from the British Library.

The paper in this book meets the guidelines for permanence and durability
of the Committee on Production Guidelines for Book Longevity of the
Council on Library Resources.

10 9 8 7 6 5 4 3 2 1

For Annegret, with love

Contents

Illustrations

TABLES

MUSIC EXAMPLES

Preface

On 31 March 1943 Richard Rodgers and Oscar Hammerstein 2nd's *Oklahoma!* had its Broadway premiere at the St. James Theatre. Based on Lynn Riggs's play *Green Grow the Lilacs* (1930), it was the first collaboration by a composer and librettist who were to dominate the musical theater for the next two decades. The show had experienced its trials and tribulations since their work began in summer 1942 under the auspices of the Theatre Guild, led by Lawrence Langner and Theresa Helburn. Even if the tryouts in New Haven and Boston, where the show was rewritten and retitled, were more successful than has often been assumed, many Broadway panjandrums thought that "Away We Go!"—as it was then called—would not last long. "No legs, no jokes, no chance" was the report to the theater columnist Walter Winchell. But after a triumphant opening, *Oklahoma!* stayed on Broadway for five years and (beginning in 1947) in London's West End for three. A second company toured the show in the United States for almost ten years nonstop, and there were international tours to South Africa, Australia, and elsewhere. *Oklahoma!* also gained a second life on the silver screen, with the release of the film version in 1955. The show quickly achieved landmark status, such that accounts of the Broadway musical often divide into pre- and post-*Oklahoma!* phases. It still receives more than six hundred productions per year.

The early impact of *Oklahoma!*—and what might be viewed as the creation of various *Oklahoma!* "myths"—are easily documented by way of contemporary newspapers. For example, the 31 March 1943 issue of *PM* contained a one-page spread captioned "'Oklahoma!' New Musical, Plays Up

Homespun U.S.A." Four publicity shots of the show, each with a caption, surround three paragraphs of uncredited text. The photos show Ado Annie in her trademark frills and Ali Hakim in his checkered suit in a head-to-head shot; a family pose of Aunt Eller at her needlework in a rocking chair, with Laurey and Curly leaning over her; and two images from the dream-ballet, one of Laurey's "wedding" and another of one of "Jud's postcards." The captions tell their own story: Ado Annie and Ali Hakim are "screwball characters" who provide "most of the comedy" in the show; the dream sequence is a "fair example of Agnes de Mille's dances," incorporating "caricatured solemnity" (for the wedding) and "this fancy lady of the early 1900s" ("one of five such gals") in burlesque style; and as for Aunt Eller, Laurey, and Curly, "The cast has plenty of talent, but no big name stars." The text of the article, on the other hand, establishes a number of themes that would regularly appear in subsequent commentary on *Oklahoma!*

> Something a little different in the way of musical comedy is due here tonight with the opening at the St. James Theater of *Oklahoma!* the Theatre Guild's musical version of the Lynn Riggs play, *Green Grow the Lilacs.* For though the results were aimed straight for Broadway and most of the people connected with the enterprise are old hands at show business, the production has such unusual features as a 28-piece orchestra (very large for a musical comedy), a generous sprinkling of graduates of the Juilliard School of Music and various ballet schools, and such people as the ballet's Agnes de Mille plotting the choreography and the movies' Rouben Mamoulian directing.
>
> What Richard Rodgers, who wrote the music, Oscar Hammerstein II, who wrote the book and lyrics, and Mamoulian are trying to do is to concoct something approaching a folk operetta. The book has a hero-heroine-villain, "curse you, Jack Dalton," kind of plot that leaves plenty of room for wild West square dances, gittar playing, and fights to the death. It also allows for the colorful, Grant Woodsy sets by Lemuel Ayers and costumes by Miles White that play up petticoats and ten gallon hats.
>
> *Oklahoma* opened out-of-town on March 11 and comes to New York after a "try-out" of only 20 days—something of a record for a big musical show. And that, as the wise birds on Shubert Alley will tell you, is a good sign.

The headline of the *PM* article, playing on "homespun U.S.A.," emphasizes the folksy American quality that has often drawn both praise and blame for *Oklahoma!* This is captured still further in the photo of Aunt Eller, Laurey, and Curly diagonally above one of the Western-style dancing

'Oklahoma!' New Musical, Plays Up Homespun U. S. A.

Something a little different in the way of musical comedy is due here tonight with the opening at the St. James Theater of *Oklahoma!* the Theatre Guild's musical version of the Lynn Riggs play, *Green Grow the Lilacs*. For though the results were aimed straight for Broadway and most of the people connected with the enterprise are old hands at show business, the production has such unusual features as a 28-piece orchestra (very large for a musical comedy), a generous sprinkling of graduates of the Juilliard School of Music and various ballet schools, and such people as the ballet's Agnes de Mille plotting the choreography and the movies' Rouben Mamoulian, directing.

What Richard Rodgers, who wrote the music, Oscar Hammerstein II, who wrote the book and lyrics, and Mamoulian are trying to do is to concoct something approaching a folk operetta. The book has a hero-heroine-villain, "curse you, Jack Dalton," kind of plot that leaves plenty of room for wild West square dances, guitar playing, and fights to the death. It also allows for colorful, Grant Woody sets by Lemuel Ayers and costumes by Miles White that play up petticoats and ten gallon hats.

Oklahoma opened out-of-town on March 11 and comes to New York after a "try-out" of only 20 days—something of a record for a big musical show. And that, as the wise birds on Shubert Alley will tell you, is a good sign.

Most of the comedy in *Oklahoma!* is supplied by these two screwball characters – Ado Annie (Celeste Holm) and Ali Hakim (Joseph Buloff).

Sitting on the porch of their Oklahoma ranch house are the show's three principals (l. to r.): Aunt Eller (Betty Garde), her niece, Laurey (Joan Roberts) and Laurey's boy friend, Curly (Alfred Drake). The cast has plenty of talent, but no big-name stars.

A fair sample of Agnes de Mille's dances is this dream sequence, in which the heroine has a nightmare about her forthcoming wedding. Katharine Sergava, at left in the bridal gown, dances the dream version of Laurey. The three dancers at right represent Laurey's friends "marching" down the aisle of the church with hands folded in caricatured solemnity.

Photos by Graphic House

This "fancy lady" of the early 1900s is one of five such gals who also appear in Laurey's dream. Kate Friedlich dances the role.

1. The text and images of "'Oklahoma!' New Musical, Plays Up Homespun U.S.A.," published in *PM* on 31 March 1943, reflect the media management of the Theatre Guild press office, establishing a good number of the *Oklahoma!* "myths." The front dancer in midair in the lower left picture is Bambi Linn, who also danced Louise in *Carousel*.

in the dream-ballet. The tactic is obvious enough, if a little odd in the context of the play on which *Oklahoma!* was based. Lynn Riggs's *Green Grow the Lilacs*, produced on Broadway by the Theatre Guild in 1931, was a product of the Depression, and while Riggs certainly felt a pastoral nostalgia for the qualities of life in his native territory, he painted it warts and all, with its violence, lawlessness, and hardship. When adapting the play, Hammerstein gradually tempered Riggs's vision—the process is clear in the surviving drafts of the libretto—turning a rather grim text into something much more cozy. The reasons are clear: first, what might work in a play would not necessarily be appropriate for a musical; and second, by 1943 America was at war. Images of all that was good in rural America, and patriotic praise of the land that is "grand," would have appealed even to cynical New Yorkers, not to mention the servicemen en route to and from the battlefields of Europe who formed a significant part of the sold-out audiences each night. As contemporary documents make clear, *Oklahoma!* was easily construed as a morale-boosting part of the war effort.

While the Western-themed photographs reinforce one message about *Oklahoma!* their opposites present another. At top left we see the "screwball" Ado Annie and Ali Hakim, and at bottom right a "fancy lady" showing a good part of her leg under a louche costume. Reviewers at the New Haven and Boston tryouts had already pointed out one of the oddities of *Oklahoma!*: its apparent refusal to conform to Broadway stereotypes. The opening was seen as emblematic: it starts, like Riggs's play, with an offstage voice singing some type of folk song ("Oh, What a Beautiful Mornin'"). Where was the chorus of long-legged dancing girls? Clearly, *PM* sought to reassure New York audiences that if they paid good money to see *Oklahoma!* they would get something of what the genre typically promised: humor and sex.

The claim that "the cast has plenty of talent, but no big-name stars" rings another important note. It would become a recurring theme in accounts of *Oklahoma!* that during the casting process, Rodgers, Hammerstein, and the Theatre Guild sought individuals who could act as well as sing, and who would work together on a new kind of show. But that is not quite what the Guild originally intended. Theresa Helburn's initial plans for *Oklahoma!* incorporated revue-style specialty acts with a Wild West theme. When it became clear that Rodgers and Hammerstein wanted something different, Helburn and Langner took another tack to draw in the crowds, making concerted efforts to recruit big-name Hollywood stars. Those who ended up playing *Oklahoma!* may have formed a successful team, but for a while there was considerable doubt about whether they would be sufficient. However, *PM* turned the absence of big-name stars into a plus rather than a minus: as with the missing dancing-girls, *Oklahoma!* was not to be your run-of-the-mill Broadway show.

According to *PM*, this was "something a little different in the way of musical comedy." The "little" is significant: enough to tempt, but not so as to frighten people away. *PM* assures its readers that the show is "aimed straight for Broadway and most of the people connected with the enterprise are old hands at show business," but goes on to note the twenty-eight-piece orchestra, the classical training in voice or dance of a "generous sprinkling" of the cast, and the involvement of a serious choreographer, Agnes de Mille, and of a director, Rouben Mamoulian, known for his powerful work on stage and screen. Clearly, this was meant to be a high-class offering. And the reason for this slant soon becomes clear: Rodgers, Hammerstein, and Mamoulian are trying "to concoct something approaching a folk operetta."

This is perhaps the most frequent claim made for *Oklahoma!* and also the most significant: it was no mere musical comedy, nor even, as it was billed, a "musical play," but it tended toward the operatic. The Theatre Guild had long been interested in developing theatrical genres that might be perceived as inherently American, providing an alternative to the standard European dramatic imports that dominated Broadway. The most obvious example was their involvement as producers in George Gershwin's "folk opera" *Porgy and Bess* (1935), also directed by Mamoulian and based on a play previously staged by the Guild. *Porgy and Bess* was revived on Broadway in early 1942 and was much on Theresa Helburn's mind throughout the preparations for *Oklahoma!* And another "classic" piece of musical Americana kept pushing itself to the front of Hammerstein's thoughts: in 1942 he was hoping for a revival of the musical that had made his name with Jerome Kern, *Show Boat* (1927). Thus *Oklahoma!* was to join the small but select group of works that were serving to define a uniquely national musical theater. *PM* does not overplay its hand, however: immediately after the "folk operetta" reference, readers are reassured that *Oklahoma!* is not so highfalutin as to deny its role as entertainment: "The book has a hero-heroine-villain, 'curse you, Jack Dalton,' kind of plot that leaves plenty of room for wild West square dances, gittar playing, and fights to the death," plus comfortably familiar sets and costumes. (*Curse You, Jack Dalton* was a comic melodrama [1936] by Wilbur Braun under his pseudonym Alice Chadwicke.) In the end, it is clear that *Oklahoma!* is no oper(ett)a, just as it is easy to disprove its oft-presumed "operatic" integration of drama, music, and dance. Yet regardless of what *Oklahoma!* was, what many claimed it to be remains important.

But who is doing the claiming here? The discerning reader will already have noticed something odd about the *PM* article on *Oklahoma!*: it appeared on the afternoon of the Broadway premiere, well before the curtain rose that evening. This is not postperformance comment; rather, it is preperformance advertising. The reporter may or may not have seen the show in rehearsal or during the out-of-town tryouts, but clearly he had received a good deal of information about it. He was also persuaded to write at much greater length, and to express more opinion, than was usual in a standard opening notice (the *New York Times* of 31 March, for example, gave only a 131-word factual statement of the show's opening). The *PM* article is less media response than media manipulation.

None of this is unusual: Broadway was adept at handling the news. What is more surprising, however, is just how much of what *PM* says about *Oklahoma!* became repeated in subsequent reviews and commentary. The origins of the text lie in an obvious source: the Theatre Guild's press office, headed by Joseph Heidt. While *Oklahoma!* suffered the trials of its out-of-town tryouts, Heidt was frantically spinning stories about a would-be hit, sending out regular press releases about the status of the show—first without the exclamation point in the title and then with (*PM* uses both)—and placing the chaos of the New Haven and Boston rewrites in a far more positive light (hence the claim in *PM* that only twenty days of tryouts marked a record). Heidt was in turn guided by Theresa Helburn, who had prepared a list of notes on *Oklahoma!* for the press emphasizing the "American" quality of the show, its new use of music within a drama made sensitive to its needs, the fresh, unjaded cast of actors first and singers second, and indeed, the twenty-eight-piece orchestra. *PM* followed the brief quite closely: Heidt must have been delighted with the result. Whether we should believe it is another matter altogether.

A mountain of material survives to document the genesis and performance history of *Oklahoma!* ranging from personal reminiscences (autobiographies, memoirs, oral histories) through contemporary reports in newspapers and journals to administrative documents and draft, fair, and final copies of the words and the music. These sources, and my handling of them, are described further in Appendix B. They permit a thorough narrative of the creation of the show from its inception in spring 1942 through the rehearsals and tryouts up to the New York opening, and then through its first ten years (until Rodgers and Hammerstein purchased the show outright in 1953) and, as a brief coda to my story, the making of the film version released in 1955. The result is the most detailed account of *Oklahoma!* to date, and far more than is common in work on the Broadway musical. It is so not just because of my fascination for the "what," "where," "when," and "how" of historical artifacts that still have resonance today, but also because the "why" that must be the ultimate goal of any historical inquiry rests upon the detail that can support, modify, or undermine the generalizations upon which interpretation might rest. In this light, some of the wilder claims made of *Oklahoma!* at its time and in the subsequent literature clearly become untenable; others, however, remain surprisingly secure.

This material has remained untapped in any systematic way, although Max Wilk trawled through some of the Theatre Guild documents in the Beinecke Rare Book and Manuscript Library, Yale University, and they were consulted by David Mark d'Andre for his dissertation on *Carousel*. Thus far, Wilk has done the best work on the show: his *Ok! The Story of "Oklahoma!"* (New York: Grove, 1993) was revised as the first half of his *Overture and Finale: Rodgers and Hammerstein and the Creation of Their Two Greatest Hits* (New York: Back Stage, 1999)—the second "greatest hit" is *The Sound of Music*—and then reissued in a further revised form as *Ok! The Story of "Oklahoma!": A Celebration of America's Most Loved Musical* (2002), linked to the appearance on Broadway of Trevor Nunn's 1998 production for London's Royal National Theatre. Wilk is a distinguished author of popular books on the stage, film, and television: he drew extensively on interviews with the leading participants in *Oklahoma!* still alive when he did his background research, plus memoirs and autobiographies, journalism, and part of the Theatre Guild archive.

However, as one works closely through the narratives presented by Wilk and his predecessors (Deems Taylor, Hugh Fordin, Frederick Nolan, and Ethan Mordden, among others), problems soon appear. Quite apart from the inevitable hagiography, dates do not coincide, different stories do not jibe, and events of distant times and places are viewed through rose-tinted spectacles. It is not that these and other commentators gloss over the creative and financial difficulties that dogged *Oklahoma!* prior to its opening: indeed, telling of the bad times as much as the good is part of the mythmaking. But they write a story where the happy ending is a given from the outset: we know for sure that everything turned out right on the night. A second problem is that their accounts are often drawn from contemporary journalism (distorted, as we have seen), or based on anecdotes provided by individuals who fashioned their memories according to the best of their achievements (as do we all), embroidering as suited their fancy (ditto), and with nary a source note for corroboration. A third is that even the more scholarly treatments of the popular musical theater often tend to downplay the significance of documentary studies of the kind assayed in the present book, preferring to focus, instead, on broader cultural, stylistic, or thematic issues. Clearly, there is another story of *Oklahoma!* waiting to be told.

This is not to say that any better-documented account of *Oklahoma!* will necessarily move away from myth and closer to historical "truth." Archival work is necessarily serendipitous—there is always more to be found—and it is also a fact of archival life that documents cannot always be relied upon. Even leaving aside the fallibility of human error (a wrong date, a misplaced word, a misremembered name), a memoir, a letter, or even an account sheet is only as "true"—or as accurate, or as comprehensive—as its creator intended, was required, or was able to make it be, and when documents coincide with or corroborate each other (hence seeming to validate their content), this may often be attributable to channels of communication rather than to factual accuracy. Nor should one lose sight of the main lesson to be drawn from reading *PM*: that in the context of reception history, even the untrue contains its truths. How a work came about melds with what it came to be, with processes of genesis and reception inextricably intertwined, and with fact and fiction blending in richly textured ways. This poses some familiar but still fundamental questions about how we make and unmake our histories.

A large number of individuals have aided my transition from being a British musicologist working on the operas of Monteverdi and Mozart to one now living in the United States and engaging with the very different (but in the end, not so different) world of the Broadway musical. I am grateful to Stephen Banfield, Geoffrey Block, and my colleague Jon Finson for their close reading of my draft and a host of corrections and insights; to George J. Ferencz, Kim Kowalke, James Lovensheimer, and Jeffrey Magee for sharing material and ideas; to Katherine Axtell (Eastman School of Music/University of Rochester) for sending me her fine graduate paper "'You're Doin' Fine, Oklahoma!': The Making of an Icon, 1943–2003"; and to Maryann Chach of the Shubert Archive for her help on the ownership of "Shubert" theaters. Materials in the Theatre Guild Collection and from Lawrence

Langner's *The Magic Curtain* are quoted by kind permission of the Theatre Guild; I am grateful to Philip Langner for his support. Passages from *Oklahoma!* and from other documents associated with Rodgers and Hammerstein (as detailed in the list on pages 309–12) are quoted by kind permission of the Rodgers and Hammerstein Organization, which has supported this endeavor from the start and saw it through to the finish: I warmly thank Theodore Chapin, Bert Fink, and Bruce Pohomac for their support, and Kara Darling and Robin Walton for their help with gaining permissions to reproduce copyright material. The librarians and curators of the collections which I have consulted were unstinting in their assistance, and I benefited significantly from the wisdom and experience of Mark Eden Horowitz in the Music Division of the Library of Congress, Washington, D.C. My students at the University of North Carolina at Chapel Hill have seen this material grow from its earliest stages, teaching me about America as much as I may have taught them about its representation. I am enormously grateful to colleagues at Yale University Press for bringing this book to fruition, including my editor Keith Condon, and Dan Heaton for his impeccable copyediting. And as always, my wife, Annegret Fauser, remains my most devoted supporter and my fiercest critic: this book is dedicated to her.

OKLAHOMA!

CHAPTER 1

Setting the Stage

W HY WRITE A BOOK ON *OKLAHOMA!?* — BECAUSE IT IS A LAND-
mark in the Broadway musical, because it is a glorious show, and
because it raises important issues about the genre, the theater,
and its times. Why write a scholarly book on *Oklahoma!?* — because it has
never been done, and because musicals are no less worthy of serious treatment than any other art form. The question for the moment, however, is
where a history of *Oklahoma!* might best begin.

The Theatre Guild

The formation of the Theatre Guild from the Washington Square Players
in 1919 marked a new direction in the New York theater immediately after
World War I.[1] Its chief founder, Lawrence Langner (1890–1962), soon
formed a partnership with Theresa Helburn (1887–1959), who became the
Guild's executive director. Their aim was to leaven what they perceived as
the usual Broadway dross by offering professional performances of high-class
plays in strong productions presented by a cohesive acting ensemble; the
emphasis on the last, as distinct from box-office stars, had the double advantage of keeping costs down and professing artistic integrity. Cash flow,
brand identity, and venture capital were secured by offering a subscription
series for each season (which in principle ran from Labor Day to Memorial
Day), both in New York and on tour to the major East Coast and midwestern
cities: the Guild promised its subscribers six productions per year. In seasons

when subscription levels were high, any Guild play could be guaranteed at least a six-week run on its main stage—initially the Garrick Theatre but then, beginning in 1925, its own newly built theater at 252 West Fifty-second Street at Broadway—plus a decent tour. The Guild also used other Broadway theaters to continue longer runs of its offerings, often by arrangement with the Shuberts. Eventually, the system emerged of preceding a New York run with one or more out-of-town tryouts, normally in New Haven and/or Boston (and often in Shubert-associated theaters).

Lawrence Langner was a leading patent attorney and a playwright of some achievement, with performances on and off Broadway and in London in the 1920s and early 1930s. He was passionate about the stage: in addition to leading the Theatre Guild, he founded the Westport Country Playhouse and the Shakespeare Festival Theatre in Stratford, both near his country home in Connecticut. He worked half-time and was often away on business, although he would take leave to oversee Guild matters when needed. The Guild's powerhouse, however, was Theresa (Terry) Helburn, in charge of the day-to-day running of the office, and also of devising and presenting creative strategies to the management board. She was educated at Bryn Mawr and Radcliffe (in George Pierce Baker's "47 Workshop"), and then by the almost obligatory trips to France, one a longer stay (1913–14) when she came to know the likes of Gertrude Stein and Isadora Duncan. On her return, Helburn continued to pursue what she later admitted were limited skills as a poet, writer of short stories, and playwright—the Washington Square Players did her *Enter the Hero* in 1917, and B. Iden Payne produced her *Crops and Croppers* (the title was later changed to *Alison Makes Hay*) the next year—moving in New York literary circles and acting as drama critic for the *Nation*.[2] According to her autobiography (published posthumously in 1960), in 1919 the "two most important events in my life took place": she met her future husband, the English teacher John Baker Opdycke (known as Oliver), and she joined the administration of the Theatre Guild, which took over her professional life.[3] Whatever her own literary abilities, she became renowned as a theatrical force, selecting plays, advising authors, auditioning cast members, and minding the Guild's artistic standards. She claimed in her autobiography that she had always harbored dreams of a new kind of theater, where drama, music, and ballet would work together to forward a plot. Everyone lauded her skills and vision. At her funeral, on 20 August 1959, Oscar Hammerstein 2nd said:

A producer is a rare, paradoxical genius . . . hard-headed, soft-hearted, cautious, reckless. A hopeful innocent in fair weather, a stern pilot in stormy
weather, a mathematician who prefers to ignore the laws of mathematics
and trust intuition, an idealist, a realist, a practical dreamer, a sophisticated
gambler, a stage-struck child. That's a producer. That was Theresa Helburn.
. . . She seemed never to be still, never to be letting you or anyone else alone.
Always prodding like a very small shepherd dog, pushing you relentlessly to
some pasture, which she had decided would be good for you.[4]

By the mid-1920s the Guild had gained a reputation as the foremost
repertory theater in New York, chiefly by way of inspired literary connections
—it had the rights to American performances of George Bernard Shaw's
plays—and of daring choices, such as Ferenc Molnár's *Liliom* (1921). To
counter criticisms that they were focusing too much on European repertory
at the expense of native theater, Helburn and Langner cultivated relationships with American playwrights, most notably Eugene O'Neill and, later,
S. N. Behrman and Philip Barry; they also explored American themes, as
with Dorothy and DuBose Heyward's *Porgy* (1927) and Lynn Riggs's *Green
Grow the Lilacs* (1930–31). Langner himself also contemplated writing a
play "to deal with the opening up of Oklahoma, especially the Cherokee
Strip," no doubt influenced by the fact that his wife, Armina Marshall, whom
he married in 1925 and who later became involved in the Guild administration, was half Cherokee and brought up on the Strip. Meanwhile, *Porgy* also
had the distinction of bringing African-American actors to the Guild stage,
a trend that Langner wished to continue with his proposed foundation of
an American Negro Ballet in 1928.[5]

By the 1930s the Depression was taking its toll on audience figures, and
the Guild was afflicted with personal rivalries. In 1931 Harold Clurman,
Cheryl Crawford, and Lee Strasberg broke away to form the Group Theatre,
seeking greater political radicalism, and in 1938 a group of American writers
forsook the Guild's protection to start the Playwrights' Company. The Guild
responded to the competition, and to the financial pressures that ensued,
by basing artistic choices on more commercial considerations, and also by
making a greater effort to recruit Broadway and Hollywood stars; both strategies may have been realistic, but they involved a repudiation of principles
for which the Guild had stood for more than a decade. Nevertheless, the
mid-1930s brought a series of disastrous production choices and a run of
flops at the same time that the Guild was losing its best artists to Holly-

wood—or, in the case of the husband-and-wife pair Alfred Lunt and Lynn Fontanne, to other producers. (The Lunts joined Noël Coward in a management partnership.) The 1938–39 season promised to be a disaster, with the Guild in serious debt and only two plays to offer. Helburn and Langner sought to counter the decline by seizing greater control of the Guild from its board and running things themselves. They were also rescued by Philip Barry's offer of his new play *The Philadelphia Story* to fill out the season: with Katharine Hepburn in the lead, it became a smash hit. Helburn and Langner then inaugurated a revival series at reduced prices—presenting repeat productions of Guild classics—and attempted a more effective compromise between the needs to maintain high artistic standards and to secure enough box-office success to ensure financial stability. But matters remained so tenuous during the war period that the mood of the Guild staff in late 1942 and early 1943 was at a low ebb. All that was to change with *Oklahoma!* which far exceeded even *The Philadelphia Story* as the Guild's financial lifesaver.

The Guild had already displayed some interest in music and dance, encouraging sometimes quite extensive use of incidental music in plays, as in *Liliom*, Ibsen's *Peer Gynt* (1923; music by Grieg), *Green Grow the Lilacs*, Philip Barry's *Liberty Jones* (1941; Paul Bowles), and Sheridan's *The Rivals* (1942; Macklin Marrow). Langner had hoped to tempt Agnes de Mille with the choreography for his verse translation with Arthur Guiterman of Molière's *L'Ecole des femmes* as *The School for Husbands* in 1933 (music by Edmond W. Rickett), but she was in Europe and unavailable. The Guild also used Martha Graham to choreograph scenes to incidental music in its 1934 production of Maxwell Anderson's *Valley Forge*.[6] It was probably for less "artistic" reasons that Langner and Helburn occasionally turned to the money-earning formula of the revue (new "editions" of which could be brought out in successive years) with the *Garrick Gaieties* chiefly by Rodgers and Hart: it first appeared in the 1924–25 season (performed by the Guild Studio), with revisions in 1925–26 and a new version (without Rodgers and Hart) in 1929–30. The Guild did another review, *Parade*, in 1935. Their most extensive musical production, however, was the reworking of *Porgy* as George Gershwin's *Porgy and Bess*, which opened at the Alvin Theatre in New York on 10 October 1935 after a tryout at the Colonial Theatre in Boston.[7] The obvious precedent was Virgil Thomson's and Gertrude Stein's all-African-American musical, *Four Saints in Three Acts* (1934); perhaps surprisingly, only one cast member overlapped (Edward Matthews as St. Ignatius in *Four Saints* and Jake in *Porgy and Bess*), although Eva Jessye directed the chorus in both works.[8] But *Porgy and Bess* was to be the first of a number of attempts by Helburn and Langner to revive plays staged by the Guild in a new musical format. That it was something of an experiment was clear from their apparent nervousness about crossing the boundaries between theater and opera: before the Boston tryout, there was a concert performance at Carnegie Hall before an invited audience. *Porgy and Bess* was well regarded by those in the know but was not a box-office success: it had only 124 performances before beginning a standard (for the Guild) tour of cities judged capable of accepting "high art"—Philadelphia, Pittsburgh, Chicago, Detroit, Washington—that ended on 21 March 1936. However, it sparked significant critical interest, and in subsequent years Langner and Helburn recalled it with some pride. Even before *Oklahoma!* established itself on the New York stage, there were attempts to associate it with the cachet earned by Gershwin's "folk opera."

Helburn had not been involved in the premiere of *Porgy and Bess*—she was in California exploring a potential career in Hollywood with Columbia Pictures—although she became interested in the search for some kind of successor. Her first thoughts for an "operetta" concerned Molnár's *Liliom*, which the Guild had staged in 1921. In late 1936 or early 1937 Helburn started discussions with Kurt Weill about turning it into a musical. Weill, an exile from Nazi Germany, had recently arrived in the United States with a reputation for abrasive political theater gained from his collaborations with Bertolt Brecht on *Mahagonny* (1927, revised in 1930 as *Aufstieg und Fall der Stadt Mahagonny* [*Rise and Fall of the Town of Mahagonny*]) and *Die Dreigroschenoper* (*The Threepenny Opera* [1928], after John Gay's *The Beggar's Opera* of 1728). He was also coming into demand after the *succès d'estime* of his antiwar musical play (with Paul Green) *Johnny Johnson*, which ran on Broadway from 19 November 1936 to 16 January 1937. Weill pursued the *Liliom* initiative enthusiastically in a series of letters written from Hollywood from February to May 1937. Even before his first letter, he had spent some time considering Helburn's proposal. After outlining various plans to work on Broadway, he continued:

> But what interests me much more than all this, is your idea of doing *Liliom* as a musical show. The more I think about this idea, the more I feel that it

would be absolutely ideal. I have now very definite ideas about it, I know what to do with the book, how to introduce songs, in what style I would write and what form I would give it. The record of *Mahagonny* which I sent you, will give you a little idea how I would conceive a musical version of *Liliom*: with all kinds of music, spoken scenes, an orchester [*sic*] of not more than 16 pieces, no chorus, good singing actors (or good acting singers).

I would like very much to know what you have found out about the rights and if you think that the Guild would be interested in this project. When we talked about it, you mentioned also the possibility of doing it in collaboration with another producer. And here I had an interesting experience. I met [Erik] Charell, he was very pleased with my successes on Broadway, and suddenly he said: "I know exactly what you should do next: *Liliom*. It could be a success like *Dreigroschenoper* and I would very much like to do it with you." He seemed terribly excited about it. What would you think of such a combination? But if you don't like it, I am sure there are many possibilities. Burgess Meredith for instance would be crazy to do it and he has a charming voice. Charell, by the way, thinks I should do it with Francis Lederer (which is not a bad idea).

I don't like to bother you, dear Terry, because I know how busy you are. On the other side I have to make up my mind within the next 4 weeks what I am going to do next and I feel very strong that here is a unique chance of a success. I would have plenty time out here to work on the book and I am sure I could find here the man who could write the lyrics.

I don't know anything about the rights, but if it is difficult for you, I could easily get in touch with Molnár directly.

Please let me know how you feel about the whole affair.[9]

Weill further outlined his plans for "not an opera, but a play with songs and music, like 'Three Penny Opera'" (20 March 1937), and for the casting (he suggested Jimmy Cagney as Liliom) and for a collaborator (15 March): "The ideal situation would be to find a 'poet' or 'lyric writer' with a good sense of theatre, with whom together I could make the adaptation, for I know pretty well how the music should fit in and how the musical scenes should be rewritten." Lorenz Hart was also a possibility, he said, although Weill did not know how exclusive was his current relationship with Richard Rodgers. Helburn, in turn, was less than keen on Charell as a possible director and suggested instead Rouben Mamoulian, who had directed *Porgy and Bess* and other Guild plays.

Weill was not being entirely truthful: Helburn had to wheedle out of him the information that five years before (in fact, seven), he had tried to get permission from Molnár to produce a musical work based on *Liliom* but had failed on account of the author's refusal to accept offers from any composer (including Puccini, Lehár, and Emmerich Kalman).[10] And although Weill claimed to dislike Hollywood intensely, toward the end of the exchange he noted an offer for "a very interesting musical picture which Fritz Lang wants to do with me for Paramount" (5 May 1937)—probably *You and Me* (1938)— and also that he was working on a "musical show" for Max Gordon (perhaps *Knickerbocker Holiday* [1938], although Weill did not work with Gordon until *The Firebrand of Florence* [1945]). The chief problem facing the *Liliom* project, however, was Molnár's continuing reluctance to release his play. On 20 March, Weill suggested making to him the argument that musical adaptations of plays had a distinguished lineage, including Verdi's *La traviata*, Berg's *Wozzeck*, and Richard Strauss's *Salome*. On 8 May, however, Helburn informed Weill of Molnár's outright refusal (conveyed by Edmund Pauker, Molnár's agent) to have his play set to music. She later said that it was Molnár's seeing a performance of *Oklahoma!* (in October 1943, it seems) that prompted a change of mind when the Guild once more took up the idea, leading to Rodgers and Hammerstein's *Carousel* (1945).[11]

Helburn continued thinking about a possible musical for the Guild, impressed, no doubt, by the success of Rodgers and Hart's venture into Shakespeare in *The Boys from Syracuse* (1938), based on a play (*The Comedy of Errors*) that, oddly enough, had never been staged on Broadway. Weill also remained in the frame. In February 1939 Helburn approached him about an adaptation of Eugene O'Neill's *Marco Millions*, produced by the Guild in 1928. (The Guild had already proposed it to Rodgers and Hart that January.) O'Neill was enthusiastic—as he said to Helburn he was about turning other of his plays into musicals in the manner of *Porgy and Bess*—but plans stalled because Hammerstein and Kern were reported to be developing a different show about Marco Polo.[12] In April and May 1939 Weill was considering a work to star the Lunts based on George Bernard Shaw's *The Devil's Disciple* (staged by the Guild in 1923), which would be, Weill wrote to Helburn on 15 April, "a mixture of romantic operetta and satyrical musical comedy. . . . What I would try to do would be a new step toward a musical theatre for 'singing actors.' You know that I started this type of theatre with the 'Three Penny Opera' and that I continues [*sic*] it with different kinds of shows in Europe." This meshes with Helburn's own ambitions for a musical version of the same Shaw play some time between 1931 and 1933 (the year in which *The Threepenny Opera* was staged on Broadway), as she was "groping my way toward a new type of music, not musical comedy, not operetta in the old sense, but a form in which the dramatic action, music, and possibly ballet could be welded together into a compounded whole, each helping to tell the story in its own way (this was the idea which finally crystallized years later in *Oklahoma!*)." Shaw had then turned her idea down because of his bad experience with *The Chocolate Soldier* (a musical adaptation of *Arms and the Man*).[13]

In July 1939 Weill was considering two other O'Neill adaptations even as he was also working with S. N. Behrman on another Helburn suggestion, *The Pirate* (also for the Lunts). Discussion on the latter went on until December 1939, when the project was dropped, chiefly, it seems, because of resistance from the Lunts. Helburn revived the idea, but now as a straight play, in January 1942, and Weill briefly reentered the picture in March–May, although it opened on 25 November 1942 with incidental music by Herbert Kingsley (and choreography by Felicia Sorel). In June 1940 Russel Crouse suggested to Helburn the idea of a musical with Weill based on Shakespeare's *Much Ado About Nothing*—*The Boys from Syracuse* had closed the previous year— although the Guild eventually turned it down for the 1940–41 season because it was already planning to stage *Twelfth Night*. (Helburn did suggest holding Crouse's idea over to 1941–42.) In early September 1943 Langner continued the quest for a Weill collaboration, with a musical version of Jaroslav Hašek's *The Good Soldier Schweik* (a source for *Johnny Johnson*) and also of *The Pursuit of Happiness* by Alan Child and Isabelle Louden (pseudonyms for Langner and Armina Marshall; 1933). "You liked this idea at one time," he wrote of *Pursuit*: "What do you think about it for today?" Weill answered that "the plot of the play is so strong and so full of suspense" that there was no room for music. Langner replied rather sniffily on 19 November: "Thanks for yours of November 12th. It was the dramatic quality of *Green Grow the Lilacs* which made it a good play under the title of *Oklahoma!* However, I am not pressing the matter, so let's forget it." At least in Langner's mind, Weill had missed the boat.[14]

Lynn Riggs's *Green Grow the Lilacs*

By November 1943 Langner could speak of *Green Grow the Lilacs* in glowing terms, given the phenomenal success of *Oklahoma!* However, it is not clear that he would have said the same when the Guild first produced Riggs's play some thirteen years before. Indeed, he hardly mentions the play at all in his autobiography, seeming to regard it as nothing more than a run-of-the-mill Guild production.

Nevertheless, *Green Grow the Lilacs* was part of a growing trend for home-grown drama. On 10 October 1940, Van Wyck Brooks spoke at Hunter College, New York:

> Europe . . . has lost the charm for us that it once possessed. It has thrown us back upon ourselves, and America has risen immensely in its power to charm us. Thousands of novels, biographies, and histories, published in recent years, have shown us what multifarious strivings and failures and what multifarious victories lie behind us; and young writers now are settling in the remotest regions, determined to find them interesting or make them so. You never hear now of Greenwich Village, which used to be a haven for the exiles from Alabama and Kansas. They are founding schools in Iowa City and writing novels about Montana, and some are poet farmers in Vermont. They are cultivating their roots where the seeds were sown, and where they are sure to yield their flowers and fruit.[15]

The context clearly is the promotion of an American art of the people by the Roosevelt-inspired Federal Arts Project (1935–43), but Brooks could well have been speaking of the Oklahoma playwright Lynn Riggs. Born on 31 August 1899 on a farm near Claremore, and part Cherokee, Rollie Lynn Riggs left home for Chicago, then New York and Los Angeles—with a number of jobs, including that of film extra—before returning to Tulsa and the University of Oklahoma in 1920, then moving to Santa Fe. His poetry, then plays, attracted the attention of the New York literary scene, including Eugene O'Neill and Lionel Barrymore. His first play on Broadway, *Big Lake* (it opened at the American Laboratory Theatre on 11 April 1927), received some critical attention but not popular success, and *Roadside* (1930) fared little better. By now, however, he had caught the interest of the Guild, which spent some time working with him on *Green Grow the Lilacs*. The play had its New York premiere at the Guild Theatre on 26 January 1931, after the usual out-of-town tryouts, and ran for a respectable sixty-four performances before going on a reasonably successful tour. It was his best-known play that also found favor with local companies. *The Russet Mantle* (1936) also did quite well on Broadway, although the Guild rejected a good number of Riggs's later submissions, and he found more fortune in Hollywood, contributing to the screenplays for *The Garden of Allah* (1936) and *The Plainsman* (1937) and achieving minor celebrity status in the gay-friendly circles of the movie industry. He was also well known on the university circuit, having long-standing connections with Paul Green at the University of North Carolina at Chapel Hill (where he spent the opening night of *Green Grow the Lilacs*), and teaching a course on playwriting at Baylor University in Waco, Texas. His was a rather peripatetic life, reaching a low point during his military service (chiefly working on army training films) in Dayton, Ohio; he claimed to be happiest in Santa Fe, and then in his home on Shelter Island, New York. He died of cancer in New York on 30 June 1954.

Although Riggs was certainly not one of the Greenwich Village set, neither was he entirely the country bumpkin: *Green Grow the Lilacs* was written while he was on a Guggenheim Fellowship in France in 1928–29. It was one of a number of his plays that dealt with life in the Oklahoma Territory, including several from the mid-1920s—*Sump'n Like Wings*, *A Lantern to See By*, *The Lonesome West*, and *Rancor*—and the Indian play *Cherokee Night* (1930; first performed 1932). Clearly these plays had a strong autobiographical element, and it was later claimed that the characters and situations in *Green Grow the Lilacs* had their roots in Riggs's own childhood. Riggs's cousin Howard McNeill, a resident of Chanute, Kansas, gave an interview to the *Chanute Tribune* (published on 27 June 1998) at the grand old age of eighty-six. He said that Aunt Eller, Laurey, Ado Annie, and Curly all had their real-life counterparts, including McNeill's grandmother (and Riggs's aunt) Mary Riggs Thompson; McNeill's mother, Laura; and his aunt Willie Thompson. Moreover, "McNeill vividly remembers seeing the creep who became Curly's archenemy Jud. 'His name was Jeeter Davis and I remember him just like it was yesterday,' McNeill said. 'He was a farmhand, but one of these guys who would get drunk on Saturday and thought he was a whiz with the women and . . . he was just a dirty old boy.'" We also have a comment from Riggs's nephew Leo Cundiff on the real-life Jetar Davis (1889–1958), a contemporary of Riggs's who was also half Cherokee and the town drunk, while other events in the play (including fire raising and murder) can be linked to specific events in Riggs's early life.[16]

Oklahoma fascinated Riggs for other reasons, too. As he wrote to Walter Campbell of the *Southwest Review* on 13 March 1929, while writing *Green Grow the Lilacs*:

> You know yourself how much concerned I am about poetry and the rhythms of speech. That's the reason I continue to write about Oklahoma people, and especially backwoods or unlettered people. Or *part* of the reason, at

least—for I find it difficult to give up using that flavorous, that lustrous imagery, the beautiful rhythmic utterance. The main reason, of course, is that I know more about the people I knew in childhood and youth than many others. But it so happens that I knew mostly the dark ones, the unprivileged ones, the ones with the most desolate fields, the most dismal skies. And so it isn't surprising that my plays concern themselves with poor farmers, forlorn wives, tortured youth, plow hands, peddlers, criminals, slaveys—with all the range of folk victimized by brutality, ignorance, superstition, and dread. And will it sound like an affectation (it most surely is not) if I say that I wanted to give voice and a dignified existence to people who found themselves, most pitiably, without a voice, when there was so much to be cried out against?[17]

This Oklahoma was not a land that was "grand," it seems from his letter of 17 December 1928 to the Theatre Guild's Barrett H. Clark, the eventual dedicatee of *Green Grow the Lilacs*, from Cagnes-sur-Mer, where Riggs spent the winter:

> I can't make—in drama or poetry—the quality of a night of storm, for instance, in Oklahoma, with a frightened farmer and his family fleeing across a muddy yard (chips there, pieces of iron, horseshoes, chicken feathers)—to the cellar, where a fat bull snake coils among the jars of peaches and plums.
>
> I can't begin to say what it is in the woods of Dog Creek that makes every tree alive, haunted, fretful. I can't tell you what dreadful thing happened last Christmas—when a son and his wife stumbled drunkenly into his mother's house; the words that came out of brazen tortured throats, the murderous hints, threats—and all the time a little sick child, radiant, great-eyed, sat up in her bed and saw and heard and wept at something foul in her presence for the first time, life with venoms beyond her comprehension. And most of all—after sorrow, fear, hate, love—I can't even begin to suggest something in Oklahoma I shall never be free of: that heavy unbroken, unyielding crusted day—morning bound to night—like a stretched tympanum overhead, under which one hungers dully, is lonely, weakly rebellious, and can think only clearly about the grave, and the slope to the grave.

Yet in typical pastoral mode, Oklahoma remained a land of bygone splendor. When Riggs requested (28 December 1928) of Henry Moe of the Guggenheim Foundation an extension to his fellowship to complete *Green Grow the Lilacs*, he (inevitably) cast things in a positive light: "The play itself is the most ambitious I have tried; and I hope it will be my best. It's a play about a vanished era in the Middle West—an era a little more golden than the present one; a time when people were easier, warmer, happier in the environment they had created. Song flourished. There were the usual human anguishes, of course. But there was *wholeness* in the people, there was great endurance. And in spite of ignorances and darknesses, there was a cool wisdom our radios and autos have banished forever."

Riggs adopted a similar tack in a letter about the play to his publisher, Samuel French and Co. (6 July 1929): "This is my first poem for the theatre. This is more nearly the way I should like to write for the theatre—if I can find more people in my mind somewhere who lived lives rich enough, complete enough. I hope it will get a sensitive production, one with real heartiness, real gaiety."[18] A poetic nostalgia is also prominent in the preface to the 1931 printed text (p. vii): "It must be fairly obvious from reading or seeing the play that it might have been subtitled *An Old Song*. The intent has been solely to recapture in a kind of nostalgic glow (but in dramatic dialogue more than in song) the great range of mood which characterized the old folk songs and ballads I used to hear in my Oklahoma childhood— their quaintness, their sadness, their robustness, their simplicity, their hearty or bawdy humors, their sentimentalities, their melodrama, their touching sweetness."

Ballads, cowboy songs, and dances (authentic and invented) take a large part in the play's six scenes and their interludes (save the intermission between scenes 3 and 4). Riggs also claimed to be doing away with conventional plot types and action: he sought, instead, to "try to exhibit luminously, in the simplest of stories, a wide area of mood and feeling" (p. vii). "In the interests of this design, I thought of the first three scenes as *The Characters*, the last three scenes as *The Play*." In scene 1 (the front room of the Williams farmhouse) we meet the handsome cowboy Curly McClain, who enters singing to an aging Aunt Eller Murphy (who later describes herself as bald, with a wooden leg); then a "fair, spoiled, lovely young girl about eighteen" (p. 12), Laurey Williams, who has been brought up by her aunt after the death of her parents; then, if briefly, the hired-hand Jeeter Fry, a "bullet-colored growly man 'th the bushy eyebrows" (p. 19). The bulk of the action here, save setting the scene and mood, concerns Laurey's decision to go to the party that evening at Old Man Peck's house with Jeeter, despite Curly's description of a surrey he has hired for the occasion. In scene 2 (Laurey's bedroom), we encounter a rather plain and stupid Ado Annie Carnes, and also an exotic Syrian Peddler (the character type also appears in Riggs's comedy *Knives from Syria* [1925], where he runs off with a farm girl called Rhodie). Scene 3, which is coterminous with scene 2, has Curly and Jeeter in the smokehouse, where we discover Jeeter's boiling resentment against life and his lust for Laurey. They are joined by the Peddler, who tries to tempt Jeeter to buy naughty postcards, but Jeeter is more interested in a "frog-sticker," a long knife, while Curly contemplates buying a set of brass knuckles.

Scene 4 is set on the porch of Old Man Peck's house, where a party is in full swing: Curly arrives with Aunt Eller, and Laurey, with Ado Annie in tow, arrives with Jeeter, who tries to force himself upon her. She fires Jeeter from the farm, calls for Curly, and accepts his proposal of marriage. Scene 5 (a hayfield) is set a month later, as Curly and Laurey return to the Williams farm from what they have hoped is a secret wedding, but they are treated to a raucous shivaree (the original title of the play), disrupted by Jeeter's having set fire to the hayfield. Jeeter enters with a flaming torch; he and Curly fight; Jeeter falls on his knife and dies; and Curly surrenders himself to the federal marshal (Cord Elam in the 1931 script). In Scene 6 (the front room, three nights later), Aunt Eller, Ado Annie, and Laurey are musing on events when Curly appears, having escaped from jail and being pursued by a posse. He bids farewell to Laurey, but Aunt Eller badgers his pursuers into letting him stay the night before surrendering himself in the morning. The play ends as we hear Curly singing from the bedroom a song he had sung in scene 1 on being cast aside by Laurey, with the refrain "Green grow the lilacs, all sparkling with dew . . ."

Much of this is familiar from *Oklahoma!* although Hammerstein significantly expanded and developed the roles of Ado Annie—to provide a comic foil to Laurey (and a second female lead)—and also the Peddler. He also added Will Parker (Hammerstein originally called him Bud Meakins), who is named in the play but does not appear, and Ado Annie's father, Andrew Carnes. However, his cuts to the play reduced the role of Jeeter Fry, making his malevolence much less strong. In terms of the action, Hammerstein added the auction at the box social and, as we shall see, revised the events of scenes 5 and 6, in part to try and deal with the "problem" of Jeeter's death. Finally, given the wartime circumstances, he had to refocus the play's messages. The violence and hardships of life on the land are softened, and Aunt Eller's berating of the posse charged with recapturing Curly clearly would not stand up to scrutiny in 1943 (p. 161):

> All right, 'f you won't listen to me, I plumb warsh my hands of all of you. I
> thought you was a fine bunch of neighbors. Now I see you're jist a gang of
> fools. Tryin' to take a bridegroom away from his bride! Why, the way you're
> sidin' with the federal marshal, you'd think us people out here lived in the
> United States! Why, we're territory folks—we ort to hang together. I don't
> mean *hang*—I mean *stick*. Whut's the United States? It's jist a furrin country
> to me. And *you* supportin' it! Jist dirty ole furriners, ever last one of you!

These are the words of an alienated outsider, as we might wish Lynn Riggs—
a half-caste, gay, semifailed author—to have been.[19] Hammerstein may well
have felt that "territory folk should stick together"—so we learn in "The
Farmer and the Cowman"—but he had to put this in a very different context.

The Guild, too, had concerns about the ending of Riggs's play when
first considering it for performance. When she received the text, Helburn
reported to Langner (14 June 1929), "We are none of us tremendously enthusiastic about *Green Grow the Lilacs*. [*sic*] but we feel it has quality and
would like your reaction."[20] There seems to have been (a plan for?) a production in summer 1929 at Rochester, New York, and on 1 October, Riggs
signed a contract with the Guild to stage the play on or before 1 April 1930
(the contract was reissued on 1 October 1930). However, Helburn also made
requests for, and no doubt suggestions of, changes; this was typical of Guild
practice, where Helburn and her board of managers often intervened extensively to knock a play into shape.[21] On 16 April 1930 she acknowledged
receipt of a revised text, saying that she felt the text much improved, but "We
still feel that you haven't quite succeeded with the last act, and I hope you
won't stop thinking about it. If you can get a last act as good as the other four,
you will have a pretty fine piece of work; not that we expect violent theatre
in the last act, but anything that will help sustain the suspense will be of real
value."[22] On his own copy of this letter, Riggs added in the margin next to
Helburn's comment about "the other four," "she means *five*," although it is
still unclear what shape the play had in the copy sent to Helburn. However,
he accepted the criticism and submitted another revised text on 30 April.
Riggs's undated "A Note on the Principal Revisions made in *Green Grow the
Lilacs*" must also come from around this time.[23] Most of the changes were
to scenes 4–6. In scene 4 Jeeter had now been brought back in at the end
"so that the elements of the dramatic conflict . . . are fore-shadowed"; the
scene "ends in foreboding now." For scene 5, Riggs strengthened Laurey's
response to Jeeter's death, and he refocused the ending of scene 6 (from
what is unclear) so that although Curly must go back to jail, there was no

doubt that he would be freed. Riggs also listed less substantial changes to scenes 1–3:

1. Curly represents one relation to the soil; Jeeter another. That is clarified.
2. The dramatic scene in the smoke-house pointed emotionally, so that it's a real conflict, and a temporary victory for Curly. But the inquiry of Jeeter about the frog-sticker is a sign that the conflict is not ended.
3. Curly's and Laurey's similar rich make-up strengthened and pointed out.
4. I've cut out "Will Rogers"—in favor of "Will Parker." Although completely naturalistic and possible, it seemed self-conscious.
5. I've changed *dog-house* to *smoke-house*. The former sounded too much like a kennel.

The reference (point 4) to Will Rogers becoming Will Parker is of course intriguing, given that Hammerstein turned the name into an actual character. The play's scene 3 (p. 62) contains what seems to have started as a rather feeble joke, as Curly asks Jeeter, "You know Will Parker?" and Jeeter replies "Never heared of him." Curly goes on to explain that he is "Ole man Parker's boy up here by Claremore," who "can shore spin a rope" (the context is Curly's testing of the rope from which Jeeter might hang himself). Will Rogers (1879–1935), born in Oolagah, Indian Territory (now Oklahoma), was a famous cowboy star on stage and film who had started out as a trick roper.

Early plans for a director for *Green Grow the Lilacs* included Rouben Mamoulian and then George Abbott, before the Guild settled on Herbert Biberman. On 8 May 1930 Biberman, true to his Stanislavskian principles, wrote to Riggs asking how best to see life on a ranch, and on the 14th he sought guidance from the Rodeo Association at Madison Square Garden on where he might travel in the West to experience a rodeo at first hand. Riggs pooh-poohed such ideas on 13 May as being somewhat irrelevant, given that his was "primarily a play set in a golden farm period which had almost entirely supplanted ranch life. . . . Of course, Curly is a cowboy, with the mixture in him of the amazingly-varied characteristics cowboys had. He is adventurous, humourous, dashing, sentimental, waggish, a little stupid, quite romantic and entirely engaging. I've known dozens of cowboys—my father was one."[24]

The *New York Times* had announced on 27 April 1930 that *Green Grow the Lilacs* was to be the first play in the Guild's 1930–31 season (which opened, in fact, with a repeat of the *Garrick Gaieties* that had concluded the previous season), although by 6 July it was listed as the second, and by 9 September it had been moved to "later in the season" (it became the fifth). The opening had been pushed back because, as we read on 14 September, Riggs was occupied with the staging of his *Roadside* (which opened on 26 September at the Longacre Theatre, for just eleven performances), and because the Guild feared a clash with its other "romantic play" of the season, *Elizabeth the Queen* (by Maxwell Anderson, which opened on 3 November). Riggs submitted the play to the Library of Congress for copyright purposes on 30 August 1930, and there were plans to open out of town in mid-October, but the play did not go into rehearsal until November, with a dress rehearsal on 4 December 1930.[25] It opened in Boston on 8 December, then played in Philadelphia, Baltimore, and Washington before its New York premiere on 26 January 1931, staying on Broadway until 21 March before going on another tour that ended in Detroit on or about 23 May. Even in Boston, Riggs seems to have been rewriting, providing a new first scene and once again revising the last, in part, it seems, because of negative audience reactions.[26]

Green Grow the Lilacs was moderately well received, though more for the overall production than for the play itself. In his review in the *American* on 27 January 1931, Gilbert Gabriel likened it to *Porgy* for its local color.[27] Brooks Atkinson, in the *New York Times* on 27 January, was ambivalent. He felt that the play was "not merely a refreshing contribution to the lore of an American theatre but stimulating entertainment, full of sunshine and the tingle of the open air." However, "Mr. Riggs is so immersed in the life about which he is writing that he has none of the true dramatist's shaping point of view. You feel in his attitude a lack of perspective. Like so many folk plays, *Green Grow the Lilacs* is satisfied to collect a handful of colorful characters and native customs. It has no interest in the dramatic significance of its material. In fact, it has no philosophy." Nevertheless, the play eventually attracted some interest from Hollywood studios wanting to buy an option on the script. Following negotiations beginning at least in January 1934 (and with several studios) Riggs assigned the film rights to RKO Pictures on 10 September 1935, and they were transferred to MGM on 10 March 1936; RKO viewed it as a potential vehicle for Richard Dix, while MGM had in mind Franchot Tone (the original Curly).[28] There were a decent number of amateur performances of the play, plus various plans for professional revivals in the 1930s (it is not clear whether they ever came to fruition), and it was broadcast on the radio in Philadelphia in June 1941, although after the opening of *Oklahoma!* restrictions were placed on further productions.[29] The play also seems to have spurred Riggs to contemplate projects with composers: in the mid- and late 1930s he had ideas for working with Gershwin on something similar to *Porgy and Bess*, and with Aaron Copland to make an opera out of *Cherokee Night*, and in 1946 he was planning a collaboration with Lukas Foss. In 1945–46, Copland also started work on a "dramatico-musical," *Tragic Ground* (based on Erskine Caldwell's novel), to a libretto by Riggs and with choreography by Agnes de Mille.[30] But had *Green Grow the Lilacs* not been taken up by Rodgers and Hammerstein, it would no doubt have lapsed gently into obscurity.

Rodgers and Hammerstein before "Rodgers and Hammerstein"

The Theatre Guild claimed a long-standing association with Richard Rodgers, having given him and Lorenz Hart (1895–1943) their first real break on the professional stage with *Garrick Gaieties* (1925). Rodgers's story is well known. Born on 28 June 1902, the son of Dr. William A. Rodgers (formerly Rogansky) and Mamie Levy, Russian-Jewish emigrés to the United States, he had displayed significant musical talent as a child. His partnership with Hart began in 1919 and led to twenty-six Broadway shows and nine films. The Rodgers and Hart shows on Broadway fall into two groups. The first, from the late 1920s (and mostly to books by Herbert Fields), included *A Connecticut Yankee* (1927), *Present Arms* (1928), and *America's Sweetheart* (1931). From 1931 to 1935, they worked mostly in Hollywood on such favorites as *Love Me Tonight* (1932; directed by Rouben Mamoulian) and the Al Jolson vehicle *Hallelujah! I'm a Bum* (1933). They then returned to Broadway with *Jumbo* (1935), followed by a long sequence of hits (many directed by George Abbott) that became standards: *On Your Toes* (1936), *Babes in Arms* (1937), *I Married an Angel* (1938), *The Boys from Syracuse* (1938), *Too Many Girls* (1939), *Pal Joey* (1940), and *By Jupiter* (1942). However, Hart was subject to severe depression and alcoholism: their last collaboration was a revival of *A Connecticut Yankee* that opened on 17 November 1943, five days before Hart died. Rodgers's partnership with Hammerstein marked what he called his "second" career, with a string of musicals on a two-year cycle (more or less) until Hammerstein's death: *Oklahoma!* (1943), *Carousel* (1945), *Allegro* (1947), *South Pacific* (1949), *The King and I* (1951), *Me and Juliet* (1953), *Pipe Dream* (1955), *Flower Drum Song* (1958), and *The Sound of Music* (1959). They also wrote for Hollywood (*State Fair*, 1945) and for television

(*Cinderella*, 1957). Only three shows were relatively unsuccessful: *Allegro*, *Me and Juliet*, and *Pipe Dream*. Rodgers continued writing for the stage until his death on 30 December 1979, recognized as the patriarch of the Broadway musical.

Pursuing Helburn's quest for a musical in the late 1930s, the Guild had written to Lorenz Hart on 31 January 1939 to solicit a Rodgers and Hart musical play for the 1939–40 season: "After having tried a book of Shake-speare and George Abbott in *The Boys from Syracuse* we suppose that noth-ing less than the great classics would really appeal to you as being worthy of your mettle." The sources suggested in this letter and in another of 2 Feb-ruary (probably from Helburn) include a translation of Aristophanes' *Lysis-trata*, Philip Moeller's *Sophie*, Congreve's *Love for Love* combined with *The Way of the World*, Robert Sherwood's comedies *The Road to Rome* and *Reunion in Vienna*, an unattributed *Memorandum for Kings*, and Eugene O'Neill's *Marco Millions*; Helburn later claimed that she had "bombarded" Rodgers and Hart with suggestions given "my obsession: plays combined with music."[31] The 2 February letter adds in a postscript: "I have an idea for the adapting of *Marco Millions*, which would eliminate the death of the Princess and make a romantic ending. We considered it when we were thinking of its picture possibilities." The notion of removing a death here to make a "romantic ending" is striking in the context of the eventual refusal to remove a death from the end of *Green Grow the Lilacs*. But even though plans for *Marco Millions* came to naught (Helburn soon proposed it to Kurt Weill), probably because work was under way on *Pal Joey*, Rodgers and Hart were at the top of at least one list for adapting *Green Grow the Lilacs*, and later, Langner was to recall his eagerness to get Rodgers back on the Guild stage:

> Terry and I had long admired the musical genius of Dick Rodgers, and often tried to persuade him to write a musical play for the Guild. About four years earlier we had called on him at his home and suggested that *Lysistrata* by Aristophanes would make an excellent musical, and might be suited to the talents of the redoubtable Ethel Merman. Dick turned down the idea on completely practical grounds, but I remember remarking at the time, "Dick, I think you ought to write something for posterity," to which he replied, "I'd like to, Lawrence, but I have a family to support."[32]

In the *New York Times* on 1 August 1943, Rodgers also noted that Lang-ner and Helburn had been pursuing him since the 1925 *Garrick Gaieties*:

"Until 1942 I never saw them without receiving a mild sort of scolding. They would tell me: 'The work you're concerned with is too trivial. You must find a subject-matter of more importance. Get something truly American, something that will have lasting quality.'"

Oscar Hammerstein 2nd (born 12 July 1895; died 23 August 1960) was a somewhat more unusual choice for *Oklahoma!* Born into a theatrical family (his grandfather, Oscar Hammerstein 1st, was an opera impresario in New York), he knew Rodgers by way of Columbia University connections: Rodgers later claimed that he first met Hammerstein when he was fourteen and Hammerstein twenty-one, introduced by Rodgers's elder brother Mortimer, who was in Hammerstein's fraternity at Columbia.[33] They also collaborated on songs for the Columbia varsity show in 1919 and 1920, and their paths cross sporadically thereafter. In the 1920s Hammerstein worked on a string of operettas, including Rudolf Friml's *Rose-Marie* (1924) and Sigmund Romberg's *The Desert Song* (1926) and *New Moon* (1928). His best-known achievement, however, was his collaboration with Jerome Kern on *Show Boat*, which ran from 27 December 1927 to 4 May 1929, then was revived in 1932. *Show Boat* was soon regarded as a landmark because of its subject and its integrated approach; Hammerstein and Kern briefly considered a sequel in 1931, and they were closely involved in the production of the film version (1936).[34] Then Hammerstein's career faltered: after the success of *Oklahoma!* he famously took out a New Year's advertisement in *Variety* (4 January 1944) offering his holiday greetings and listing his failures, including *Free for All* (music by Richard A. Whiting, 1931), *Very Warm for May* (Kern, 1939), and *Sunny River* (Romberg, 1941), plus two shows seen at London's Drury Lane, *Ball at the Savoy* (Paul Abraham, 1933) and *Three Sisters* (Kern, 1934) — "I've done it before and I can do it again!"[35] Other of his 1930s shows had been marginally more successful, including Kern's *Music in the Air* (1932) and Romberg's *May Wine* (1935), while the revue *Hellzapoppin*, with songs to lyrics by Hammerstein, had a long run (1,404 performances) from 1938 to 1941. He also worked in Hollywood in the 1930s: *High, Wide, and Handsome* (1937), with songs by Hammerstein and Kern, may have had some impact on *Oklahoma!* given its related themes, and also gave Hammerstein a chance to work with Rouben Mamoulian and to continue his indirect association with the orchestrator Robert Russell Bennett, who worked on several Kern scores (and who was to arrange the music for *Carmen Jones*). *High, Wide, and Handsome* deals with pioneers (in the Pennsylvania oilfields in 1859) and with stock characters: a powerful but kindly grandma, a proud but stubborn hero (Randolph Scott), a slightly rebellious heroine (Irene Dunne) who needs to find her place, a villain within the community, a loose woman who turns out to have a heart of gold (Dorothy Lamour), and a dodgy foreigner (in this case an Italian, played, however, by Akim Tamiroff). It also has a circus caravan, two barn dance scenes (one at a wedding, another broken up by a fight), and six songs (plus some cunning reprises), with Hammerstein in Western and sentimental veins: "The Folks Who Live on the Hill" is the best known.[36]

Kern had moved finally to Hollywood in 1939, leaving Hammerstein at something of a loose end. The first documented hint we have of a potential partnership with Rodgers comes from mid-1941, when both Rodgers and Edna Ferber, who had provided the source for *Show Boat*, approached Hammerstein to provide the book for a musical version of Ferber's new novel *Saratoga Trunk*, with Hart to write the lyrics.[37] Although this came to nothing—Hammerstein declined because of his current efforts to revive *Show Boat*, and Rodgers lost interest because of difficulties with Ferber and also over the film rights—it seems to have been part of a broader strategy from Rodgers to find an alternative to the increasingly unreliable Hart while avoiding the accusation of betraying his long-standing collaborator. After *Oklahoma!* Hammerstein partnered exclusively with Rodgers, save for an adaptation on which he had already been working of Bizet's *Carmen* as *Carmen Jones*, which opened on Broadway on 2 December 1943 after the usual out-of-town tryouts. They were loyal associates and also formed a production company for plays—John Van Druten's *I Remember Mama*, 1944; Anita Loos's *Happy Birthday*, 1946; Norman Krasna's *John Loves Mary*, 1947; Samuel Taylor's *The Happy Time*, Graham Greene and Basil Dean's *The Heart of the Matter* (which closed during its tryout in Boston), and John Steinbeck's *Burning Bright*, all in 1950—and musicals, with a revival of *Show Boat* (1946), Irving Berlin's *Annie Get Your Gun* (1946; originally planned for Kern), and their own shows from *South Pacific* (1949) on.[38]

Just how Rodgers and Hammerstein first sealed their relationship remains unclear, no doubt deliberately so, given that none of the participants wanted to give the impression of betraying Hart. Despite Hammerstein's winning (with Kern) an Academy Award in 1942 for "The Last Time I Saw Paris" (in *Lady Be Good*), his Broadway career was in something of a slump after the failure of the Romberg-Hammerstein "operetta" *Sunny River*, which had just thirty-six performances between 4 December 1941 and 3 January 1942 after being panned by the critics. Max Gordon, its producer,

2. With *Oklahoma!* Richard Rodgers and Oscar Hammerstein 2nd, seen here watching an onstage rehearsal for the show, formed a partnership that dominated Broadway in the 1940s and 1950s. (John Swope)

was clear on the lesson Hammerstein should learn, writing on 2 January to explain his decision to close: "I noted the receipts last night, Thursday, following New Year's and, while business is terrible all round, we know that the situation is hopeless. *Sunny River* belongs to yesterday. Now, what are we going to do tomorrow? For one thing, I want you to keep your courage because you and I will still do great things in the theatre together but they won't be musical comedies. It is just silly to risk a hundred thousand dollars on what six men are going to say about it in the paper the next day." Hammerstein was best advised to find a play to direct or write, but "You cannot afford to waste your time any more with musical shows and I cannot afford to produce them." Gordon added in a postscript: "I know this must be a tough blow to Rommie [Romberg] and I tried to soften it by writing him a letter of explanation. I do wish you would tell him my position regarding the critics and why I will no longer be interested in musical plays." He relented slightly in a handwritten note shortly after: "This follows my other letter about not doing musical shows. There is one type I will do. If you can write a play with

music for six outstanding players three of which would have to be stars I'm
for that. We could keep that kind on the road indefinitely." He repeated the
advice on 10 January, after Hammerstein had told him of his intention to
write a patriotic song for the war effort: "Your idea to try to write the great
War Song is a good one and I hope you make it. Keep after that idea of the
small musical play with the stars. Of course, I would rather have you write a
straight play and forget this musical show nonsense, but I will take the other
if you decide to do it."[39] Gordon also became involved in the financing of
Oklahoma! but not as extensively as was hoped at the time.

Hammerstein was not one to give up so easily. With remarkable stub-
bornness bordering (his friends no doubt thought) on the obtuse, he set new
plans in motion. On 2 February he told Leighton Brill: "I have two items
that I know will be of interest to you. One: The success of the revival of *Porgy
and Bess* has stimulated interest in *Showboat.* Two producers are on my neck
and aggressively clamoring for revival rights. One is Cheryl Crawford, who
did *Porgy and Bess*, and the other is Shubert." Hammerstein was particularly attracted by the fact that the *Porgy* revival was clearing $7,000 a week.
"The second item of interest is that Billy Rose took a trip to Saratoga two
weeks ago, picked up a volume of *Saratoga Trunk* and went nuts. Negotiations are under way—and progressing very smoothly—whereby Jerry [Kern]
and I will acquire the rights and Billy Rose will produce it. All this is without regard to when the picture will be released. We have agreed to take our
chances on that." The notion of making a musical from Ferber's *Saratoga
Trunk* revived the idea originally pursued by Rodgers and Hart, with Hammerstein in the wings. On 16 February, Vinton Freedley wrote to Jerome
Kern in very negative terms about the possibilities, finding the book weak,
with nowhere near the richness of *Show Boat*; on 21 March, Hammerstein
told Angelo Rossitto, who had asked for a role, that "at the moment I have
not progressed sufficiently with my adaptation to make any decision about
this part"; and by 2 April he wrote to Brill that the idea had collapsed.[40]
The hopes to revive *Show Boat* on Broadway lasted through the spring and
summer. On 3 March, Max Gordon refused to finance it (although he said
he would support a new musical with picture rights attached), but Hammerstein was still pursuing Cheryl Crawford in May, and a potential deal
with MGM for both a Broadway production and a film emerged in mid-
May, if not before. However, *Show Boat* was performed only in St. Louis in
August.[41]

In March, Hammerstein was also concerned with helping the producer Irving Caesar rescue a show out of town (it was abandoned), and then with plans for a London production of *Sunny River*. More important, his thoughts turned to finding a producer and cast for *Carmen Jones*, on which he had been at work since January 1942, although he did not finish act 2 until late June, and act 3 some time in mid-July.[42] To judge by his correspondence, he had plenty on his plate and was not desperate for work. Nor was he poor: his estimated annual earnings from royalties were a very respectable $35,000: $15,000 from ASCAP (for radio and nightclub performances), and the rest from sheet music and recordings.[43] Something else must have attracted him to the *Green Grow the Lilacs* project. But equally, one can see why Helburn's interest might have been whetted once he came into the picture. First, he was well known for insisting on writing both lyrics and the book for any given show, contrary to the usual practice of separating the two tasks. Second, he had already made clear his views on the "integrated" musical. In an article in the *Theatre Magazine* (May 1925) linked to the opening of *Rose-Marie*, Hammerstein passionately argued the case for "the musical play with music and plot welded together in skillful cohesion."[44] *Show Boat* was just such a "musical play" that some musical critics even likened to a new form of American opera. At one stage, too, the Guild had hoped to turn *Porgy and Bess* into an even more tangible successor to *Show Boat* by using the same creative team of Kern and Hammerstein (who withdrew when they heard that Gershwin already had the project in mind).[45] Now Helburn may have sensed another opportunity.

Two Predecessors

Hammerstein's plans to stage *Show Boat* on Broadway in 1942 did not come to fruition, but Cheryl Crawford's revival of *Porgy and Bess* seems continually to have made its presence felt; it opened at the Majestic Theatre on 22 January 1942, following a preview on 13 October 1941 in Maplewood, New Jersey, and a three-week run in Boston. Compared with the original, this had a reduced cast, smaller orchestra, and dialogue replacing most of the recitative. It ran for 286 performances before closing on 26 September 1942 to go on tour until 8 April 1944, briefly returning to Broadway from 13 September to 2 October 1943.[46] Kurt Weill had mixed feelings, writing to Lotte Lenya on 5 February 1942: "Yesterday I saw *Porgy*. They have done quite a good job. It is much more of a show now and less of an opera. They have a wonderful cast and the whole thing is very alive and refreshing. The songs are still magnificent, but the rest of the score pretty bad. I listened to the first dream of *Lady [in the Dark]* in the evening and decided that it was much better music." Hammerstein, however, was enthusiastic, writing to Ira Gershwin on 2 February 1942: "The people had heard that there was something good in town,—a musical effort that did not consist of a lot of songs, burlesque bits, and comedy specialities thrown together—and it is my belief that they have been starving for quality of this kind."[47]

Helburn, too, cannot have been unaware of the impact of the *Porgy and Bess* revival, especially as her own thoughts turned seriously toward a musical based on *Green Grow the Lilacs* that would, in effect, become the Guild's successor to Gershwin's "folk opera." Certainly, Helburn made the association on several occasions, as when writing to Lynn Riggs on 18 May 1942:

> I wonder have you heard from Garrett Leverton yet about our hope and plans to get an operetta based on *Green Grow the Lilacs?* He tells me he had already discussed it with you and had even approached Kern at one time and that you were entirely in favor. So we are going ahead with our preliminary work and hope to have something definite to report very shortly.
>
> I believe it will make a grand operetta—and should do for its locale what *Show Boat* and *Porgy [and Bess]* did for theirs. Here's hoping! If you have any pet ideas of your own about it, do write me.[48]

(There is no other evidence for Riggs's approach to Kern.) This is one of the earliest documents we have concerning Helburn's plans for *Oklahoma!* and her use of the term *operetta* is significant, as is her notion that it might do for the Southwest what *Show Boat* did for the Mississippi River and *Porgy and Bess* for Charleston, South Carolina. But these plans seem to have been stewing for some time. On 15–20 July 1940 *Green Grow the Lilacs* played at the Westport Country Playhouse, a theater owned by Lawrence Langner and Armina Marshall near their country home in Connecticut that offered summer seasons, and also sometimes acted as an experimental laboratory for new talent, whether playwrights or actors.[49] John Wayne was to have played Curly, and John Ford was to have been the director, but neither showed up. Instead, Ward Bond took the role, John Haggott directed (he was to be the production manager for the run-up to the premiere of *Oklahoma!*), and Gene Kelly choreographed the dancing. (Kelly was currently playing in the Guild production of William Saroyan's *The Time of Your Life*, which ran from 25 October 1939 to 6 April 1940, and then from 23 September to 19 October; he was to take the lead in Rodgers and Hart's *Pal Joey*, which opened on 25 December.) Elaine Anderson, the assistant stage manager for the Westport production (and also for *Oklahoma!*) later recalled that after a performance, Helburn (who also had a country home near Westport) went back to congratulate the cast, saying, "This would make a good musical!" Again according to Anderson, Richard and Dorothy Rodgers were also invited to Westport ("After all, Dorothy and Dick were right nearby, up the road in Fairfield"), and shortly after, he, Helburn, and Langner discussed Helburn's idea of a musical adaptation, of which Rodgers approved, also hinting that he was already thinking of Hammerstein as a collaborator because, in his view, the play would not interest Hart.[50] Langner, too, associated the inception of *Oklahoma!* with Rodgers's purchase of a home in Connecticut and with the Westport revival, although the chronology does not quite bear this out: Rodgers moved to the house on Black Rock Turnpike in Fairfield only in June 1941—that is, the year after the production of Riggs's play.[51] But a visit from the city is not implausible, and the fact that Langner, Helburn, and Rodgers were near-neighbors in the country at least from mid-1941 would support the notion of some kind of regular contact among them. It later became something of a pattern for the Guild to revive plays at Westport that might be suitable for subsequent musical treatment: Molnár's *Liliom* was staged there in summer 1941, and in 1952 the same was done for Shaw's *Pygmalion* (first staged by the Guild in 1926), which the Guild was trying to persuade Lerner and Loewe to adapt into a musical (as they eventually did with *My Fair Lady*, but not under Guild auspices).

Elaine Anderson may or may not have remembered things correctly: in Rodgers's autobiography (1975) he gives the impression that he had not encountered *Green Grow the Lilacs* until Helburn gave him the play to read in June 1942, while in hers (1960), Helburn says of *Green Grow the Lilacs*, "I don't remember when I became convinced that this was what I had been looking for."[52] Nor do we know whether Hammerstein saw the Westport *Green Grow the Lilacs*. But clearly he knew the play. In the text of an interview with Hammerstein prepared by the Guild for a press release in anticipation of the Boston tryout of *Oklahoma!* Hammerstein tells of how he had been considering *Green Grow the Lilacs* as a musical even before Rodgers telephoned to say that the Guild was thinking of doing it. He also notes what he thought made it such a success. "I had a good time with this script":

It's a long time since any musical has had such an American flavor as this one. That kind of show is my pet. That's one reason why *Show Boat* is my favorite of all the musicals I've done.

Of course, like any musical *Away We Go!* had its problems, and some of them were tough. The art of this thing is to get in and out of the numbers so smoothly that the audience isn't aware that you are jumping from dialogue to singing. The art, you understand, is not to jump but to ooze.

The reason that's so important in this show is that it demands a much greater reality than the ordinary musical comedy. The play has a good and a realistic story, so every song and dance has to be motivated and placed so well in the story that it's completely natural for the people to be singing and dancing wherever they are.

That's the main thing we've been after. That, and to keep the flavor, the lusty spirit of the original script. *Green Grow the Lilacs* was so beautifully written it fairly shouted for a musical adaptation.[53]

Again, these were remarks for the press, so it is not surprising to find here some of the themes that would recur repeatedly in the subsequent reception of *Oklahoma!*: the "American" essence of the work, the connection with *Show Boat*, the search for integration (oozing from dialogue to song), the greater realism and naturalness, and the literary and artistic quality of the play and therefore of the musical. However, Hammerstein's comments resonate with something more than mere journalistic platitudes: he seems genuinely to have felt that *Green Grow the Lilacs* was intriguing, challenging, and indeed somehow different.

CHAPTER 2

Contracts and Commitments

THE VARIOUS ARTISTIC AND FINANCIAL PROBLEMS FACING THE
Theatre Guild in the 1930s and early 1940s provide an important
backdrop for decisions made (and overturned) as *Oklahoma!* began
to take shape. For more than a decade, Lawrence Langner and Theresa Helburn had negotiated the difficult path between the Scylla and Charybdis
of artistic worth and commercial success, had contemplated the merits of
American versus European theater, had considered the need for their dramas to focus as much on social "relevance" as on universal themes, had
wavered on the issue of whether to bring in star performers or to rely instead on an integrated acting ensemble, and had considered musicals that
would be performed by "singing actors." The outcome of those debates for
Oklahoma! and the rhetoric that ensued were established early in the show's
immediate reception history: either the Guild had come down firmly on
one side and not the other (*Oklahoma!* was truly "American"; it had avoided
using stars altogether) or it had achieved some kind of ideal compromise
(the show was both an artistic and a commercial success; its themes were
universal and yet it also had an immediate social relevance). Indeed, the fact
that *Oklahoma!* was often seen to have achieved a golden mean, so success-
fully reconciling all the different demands facing the Broadway stage in the
early 1940s, was essential not only to its critical success but also to Helburn's,
Langner's, Rodgers's, and Hammerstein's perceptions of their achievement.
It is by no means clear, however, that such a reconciliation was even in the
cards as work began on turning Riggs's *Green Grow the Lilacs* into what

was variously called an "operetta," a "musical comedy," and, eventually, a "musical play."

There is broad consensus that much of the impetus for *Oklahoma!* came from Theresa Helburn. Writing to Rodgers on 11 August 1943, Langner said that "Terry is entitled to about 99.9% of the credit for *Oklahoma!*"; and in his autobiography he admitted, "To Terry goes the full credit for having conceived the idea of producing *Oklahoma!* and for bringing together these two artists to create the work." Hammerstein was also eloquent on Helburn's role in all aspects of its creation. In part, this was because of her executive position within the Theatre Guild, but the show also became her passion: on 27 March 1947 she wrote to Mary Martin (whose young daughter was sick with measles), "My baby, *Oklahoma!* celebrates its fourth birthday Saturday night. I wish you could come to its birthday party back-stage at the St. James. The child is still strong and lusty, and bids fair to outlive its younger sister, *Carousel*. It was my baby, you know." She also noted in her autobiography that *Oklahoma!* was a "fulfillment of my dream, the production of a totally new kind of play with music, not a musical comedy in the familiar sense but a play in which music and dancing would be aids to and adjuncts of the plot itself in telling the story." For Langner, however, it was "Helburn's Folly."[1]

We have seen that the Guild had been exploring possibilities for musicals since 1936. Proposals became more frequent still in 1942—whether generated in-house or by external submissions—suggesting some kind of commitment to the genre, perhaps as a solution to the Guild's financial difficulties. Moreover, the 1942–43 season was to be of some importance, since it was being billed as a twenty-fifth anniversary (the Guild had opened at the tail end of the 1918–19 season). Even though Langner eventually played down the celebrations—"First, because we are too busy, and secondly, because this is no time for celebrations"—Helburn may have wanted something special.[2] John Gassner, the Guild's chief play reader, commented on *Camilla*, an adaptation of Offenbach's *La Périchole* by Oriana Atkinson, Samuel Barlow, and Louis Simon (22, 28 January 1942); an anonymous *Enchanted Lady* (6 February 1942); Richard Wright's book and lyrics for "a Negro musical" (29 May 1942; suggested as a showcase for Ethel Waters); and Sylvia Regan-Ellstein's *Marianne* (22 July, 4 August 1942).[3] As for *Oklahoma!* Helburn appears to have begun serious planning in late April 1942: the earliest reference to it appears in a memo from Warren Munsell, the Guild's business manager, of 5 May (see the timeline in Appendix A, which also provides references for the documents discussed below). Here Munsell noted Marcus Heiman and Lee Shubert's readiness to support the Guild's 1942–43 production costs: "They are also willing to finance a musical show if you want to make one out of *Green Grow the Lilacs.*" At a meeting of the American Theatre Society (linked to the touring arm of the Guild) on 15 May, "Miss Helburn said she was working on a project to make a musical play out of *Green Grow the Lilacs.*" To judge by other examples, this was late within, but not outside, the time frame for planning a production for the end of the following season. The other Guild offerings for 1942–43 were to be, in order, Philip Barry's *Without Love* (starring Katharine Hepburn), Ketti Frings's *Mr. Sycamore,* S. N. Behrman's *The Pirate* (in association with The Playwright's Company), and Konstantin Simonov's *The Russian People* (translated by Clifford Odets).

Given the past negotiations between the Guild and Kurt Weill, including discussions about *The Pirate,* it is not surprising to find Weill included at the end of an undated list of potential composers for *Green Grow the Lilacs* that also has Rodgers and Hart (at the head), Jerome Kern, Paul Bowles (who did the music for the Guild production of Philip Barry's *Liberty Jones* in 1941), Irving Berlin, and Cole Porter.[4] The same list suggests a number of individuals for the book, including Russel Crouse, Ira Gershwin, Ben Hecht, S. N. Behrman, Moss Hart, John Latouche, and others. These kinds of lists, whether typed or handwritten, appear frequently in Helburn's papers, and they appear to be the result of individual or collective brainstorming that might or might not generate some type of action. In this case, it seems not so much a detailed plan as a jotting of Broadway luminaries of the early 1940s. There is some hint that Helburn did indeed approach Weill over *Green Grow the Lilacs* in May 1942, and Ira Gershwin was later quoted as having been asked by Rodgers to write the lyrics. She certainly invited Russel Crouse to a meeting at the Guild on 18 May 1942, before which she had already suggested to him that he might write the book for her new musical. Crouse had started his writing career while working in the press office of the Theatre Guild, and was well known for his work with Cole Porter (*Anything Goes,* 1934; *Red, Hot and Blue,* 1936) and Howard Arlen (*Hooray for What!* 1937), as well as for his long-running hit play (with Howard Lindsay), *Life with Father* (1939).[5] He wrote to Helburn that morning:

It is going to be impossible for me to get in to see you this afternoon. . . . I agree with you that *Green Grow the Lilacs* will make a swell operetta. I disagree with you when you say it is an easy job. It means close collaboration between the composer and the librettist, and tedious, hard, detailed work.

As I told you, Howard [Lindsay] and I are just finishing a play which we hope to put into production very soon [their *Strip for Action* opened on 30 September 1942]. We have another one beyond that, and in view of the hard work I have just outlined, I am afraid that it eliminates me entirely from the picture.

Sorry, it would be fun working together again, but it is impossible. Good luck with it, and I will pop in and see you soon, just for a visit.

Helburn tended to be both organized and systematic in her business dealings. On the same day as that proposed meeting with Crouse (and others?), a Monday, she wrote to Riggs about her plans for an "operetta" based on his play, and she or her secretary also typed up some notes (from the meeting?). At their head is the observation "The two best places for comedy are in the Peddler scenes and at 'Peck's Party'" (*Green Grow the Lilacs*, scene 4), preceding a list of possible peddlers (W. C. Fields, Bobby Clark, Ned Sparks, Jimmy Savo, Teddy Hart), and of specialty acts for Peck's Party, including Bob Burns, Spivy's Ventriloquist, Andy Devine, Judy Canova, and Zeke Manners. Of the possible peddlers, Savo and Hart had played the two Dromios in *The Boys from Syracuse*, Bobby Clark was Bob Acres in the Guild's 1942 production of Sheridan's *The Rivals* and was soon to star in Michael Todd's revue *Star and Garter* (opened 24 June 1942), and Fields and Sparks had not been on Broadway since 1930–31 and 1921, respectively, although both had distinguished careers in Hollywood as comedians in the 1930s.[6] For the "leads," Helburn's list included Roy Rogers, Eddie Albert (Sr., also in *The Boys from Syracuse*), and Ray Middleton (who had been in Weill's *Knickerbocker Holiday*). For the "Music and Book," she suggested Paul Bowles, Woody Guthrie (composer of "This Land Is Your Land"), Tex Ritter, Richard Hageman, Bucky (Russel) Crouse, Nunally Johnson, and Mortimer Offner. The mismatch (save for Bowles and Crouse) between Helburn's two different lists for the music and the book—the undated list with Broadway luminaries, and the notes of 18 May—is striking. Of course, we cannot tell whether one was a reaction to the other (nor do we know which came first). However, it does seem that on 18 May 1942, at least, Helburn had a particular vision for *Green Grow the Lilacs* that involved comic interludes and specialty acts, that played up the cowboy theme, and that involved composers and writers unlikely to produce standard musical-comedy fare. Both Roy Rogers and Tex Ritter, for example, were famous "singing cowboys" at the annual Madison Square Garden rodeo and on film.[7] All this seems to lighten the tone of the play, and also to suggest an entertainment at least with episodes containing elements of a revue.

Helburn's Western theme continues in a penciled addition to her 18 May notes: "Announcer from Mad[ison] Sq[uare] Dance Festival" (perhaps J. R. Hickisch, whom Helburn later approached in 1943 for square-dance calls). This presumably refers to the National Folk Festival, held at Madison Square Garden on 11 May 1942, which was a huge success according to the next day's report in the *New York Times*:

> Certainly riches and variety were manifest on all sides. Indians from up-State Oklahoma and New Mexico; cowboys, lumberjacks, sailors, anthracite miners in their own songs and dances; regional dance groups from Tennessee and North Carolina, Negro choirs and choruses, a boys' harmonica band from West Virginia, traditional ballads of English and French origin current in this hemisphere, national groups representing traditional cultures of France, Poland, Lithuania, Mexico, Italy, Russia, India, Peru, Palestine, and some of May Gadd's stunning massed English dances, give only a modest cross-section of what took place. . . .
>
> The National Folk Festival, which concluded four days of these activities at Constitution Hall in Washington last week, is now in its ninth year. It is late in making its New York bow, but the unquestionable success of its first venture here should secure its becoming an annual event in this sophisticated but folk-conscious metropolis.[8]

The experience may well have encouraged Helburn to think about reviving a particularly national folk play.

Finding the right approach, and therefore the right composer, still took some time. On 27 May, Gassner wrote in a memo to Helburn and Langner: "Have you, Terry, heard Earl Robinson's music, which he wanted to play for you? A good man for *Green Grow the Lilacs* would be Aaron Copland, if you have ruled out Kurt Weil[l] for some reason." The reason for his mentioning Robinson becomes clearer in Gassner's memo of 12 June:

> Re *Green Grow the Lilacs*, if you want a really original music-drama, Roy Harris or Aaron Copland is your man. If you want someone merely to weave cowboy lyrics together, and there are many fine ones that were not used in the original production, I suggest Paul Bowles. However, it might also be a good idea to include at least one strong number,—a song on the American democratic spirit as evoked by the West. In that case, Earl Robinson could probably contribute one or two really stirring and original numbers; as you

know, he has great force, even if he is not the man to handle *Green Grow the Lilacs* as a whole.

In this memo, Gassner then excised Copland's name (had the composer already turned it down?) and added in ink in the margin "Ferde Groffe" (Grofé), best known for his arrangement for Paul Whiteman of Gershwin's *Rhapsody in Blue* (1924). Robinson and Bowles were each known for punchy political songs for the left-wing theater, and it seems unlikely that they would have endorsed "the American democratic spirit as evoked by the West," even if Gassner's notion of "at least one strong number" would be prophetic.

Helburn appears to have heard Robinson before 29 May, when Gassner urged, "Don't you, Terry, want to write to Earl Robinson a little note after listening to his music, even if you commit yourself to nothing[?]" But by the date of Gassner's second memo of 12 June, she already seems to have started moving ahead with other ideas. Even after fixing on Rodgers and Hammerstein, however, her own rather mixed vision of what might be made of *Green Grow the Lilacs* appears to have persisted. On 8 October 1942 she suggested that they might usefully attend the Madison Square Garden rodeo (which ran from 7 to 25 October); and even in February 1943 she was seeking square-dance calls and rope spinners. The *Oklahoma!* that eventually emerged was very different, although tensions between Rodgers and Hammerstein's ambitions and Helburn's May 1942 plans would surface as it headed toward the premiere.

Rodgers and Hammerstein (and Hart?)

In May 1942 the Guild seems to have had three relatively distinct notions of how best to handle *Green Grow the Lilacs*: as a "serious" musical venture (with Copland, Harris, or Weill), as something in the vein of a musical comedy (with one or other Broadway luminary), or as a folkloristic entertainment with patriotic overtones. In her autobiography Helburn inevitably painted a clearer picture, saying that her immediate thought for adapting the play was Rodgers and Hart. Rodgers also said that when representatives of the Guild approached him, they were not aware that he had stopped working with Hart. He later wrote that shortly after *By Jupiter* opened (on 3 June 1942), "Terry asked me to read the script of a play that the Guild had produced eleven years before. It was *Green Grow the Lilacs*, by Lynn Riggs, and I only had to read it once to realize that it had the makings of an enchanting musical. Set in the Southwest shortly after the turn of the century, with a cast of farmers and ranchers, it was a distinct departure from anything I had done before. I promptly told Terry and Lawrence that I wanted very much to write the score."[9]

The first actual documentation we have of Rodgers's becoming directly involved in Helburn's plans for Riggs's play is probably his letter of 16 June 1942 to Joshua Logan enclosing an unnamed script, presumably *Green Grow the Lilacs*: "Terry Helburn and I have ideas for it. I'll talk to you about it the first time I see you."[10] Logan later associated this with a request to direct the show—he had done the same for Rodgers and Hart's *I Married an Angel* (1938), *Higher and Higher* (1940), and *By Jupiter*—and explained that he turned it down because of his imminent draft into the army. But he had also collaborated (with Gladys Hurlbut) on the book for *Higher and Higher*, so Rodgers may have had a different task in mind. Clearly, however, some conversations must have occurred between Helburn and Rodgers before 16 June to bring Rodgers on board (or back on board if we are to believe the accounts of Rodgers in Westport in 1940), even if he would not have had much time to think about new projects while getting *By Jupiter* on the stage. Indeed, he was presumably out of town during the three-week tryout of the show (titled *All's Fair*) at the Shubert Theatre in Boston, which began on Monday 11 May.

The striking omission from Helburn's lists is, of course, Oscar Hammerstein. He, too, was out of town in May 1942, visiting Hollywood to work with Jerome Kern on the proposed MGM film of *Very Warm for May* and a revival of *Music in the Air*. It is very odd, however, that on that visit he should have discussed with Kern the idea of turning *Green Grow the Lilacs* into a musical, and still more so that he may have done so precisely on 18 May. (Did Kern receive a telephone call or cable from Helburn that day, based on his presence on her luminary list?) Kern seems to have known the play already—Helburn said that Garrett Leverton had approached him on Lynn Riggs's behalf—and he reportedly pooh-poohed Hammerstein's suggestion on the grounds that it had not been a success, and that the second act was hopeless.[11] Hammerstein later made some capital of the situation, while (inevitably) leaving Kern out of the reckoning: "It is one of those strange coincidences of show business that while Miss Helburn was mulling over the project on her Connecticut farm I was reading Riggs's play in a California patio and wondering whether it would make a good musical. The difference between us was that I just kept on wondering while the more decisive duo who guide the Guild's destinies took immediate action. Miss Helburn and Mr. Langner phoned Mr. Rodgers—all three of them live in Connecticut—and the first 'conference' was held."[12] Certainly, this was a convenient "coincidence," granting, by way of the telling, some kind of inevitability not just to *Oklahoma!* but also to a partnership between Rodgers and Hammerstein.

Of course, things were more complicated, not least the matter of Rodgers's prior relationship with Lorenz Hart, which created a number of diplomatic difficulties that various individuals sought to negotiate, and also fudge, in their accounts of the genesis of *Oklahoma!* Rodgers and Hammerstein's decision to work together seems to have been reached over lunch at the Barberry Room some time in July (four days after Hammerstein had completed *Carmen Jones* in one telling): Rodgers broached the topic and suggested that Hammerstein read the play, but Hammerstein said that he knew it already, and he agreed to the project on the spot.[13] The chronology and other details remain somewhat fuzzy. On 2 July, Hammerstein told his Hollywood agent, Frank Orsatti, that he would finish *Carmen Jones* on 15 July, and that between then and rehearsals starting on 1 September, he would be available to work on a story treatment for Arthur Freed at MGM.[14] On 17 July, Helburn's secretary sent Dorothy Hammerstein a copy of *Green Grow the Lilacs*, and Rodgers and Hammerstein may have had their first lunch on the 19th or 20th (if this lunch was indeed four days after the completion of *Carmen Jones*). Certainly some kind of agreement had been reached before 22 July, although Hammerstein's precise role still remained unclear: on 23 July the *New York Times* reported that on the 22nd the Theatre Guild had announced that "Richard Rodgers, Lorenz Hart, and Oscar Hammerstein 2d will soon begin work on a musical version of Lynn Riggs's folk-play *Green Grow the Lilacs* . . . which is replete with scenes and songs of the frontier." (A similar notice appeared in the *Daily News* the same day.) To add to the confusion (or to the duplicity), on the day of the Guild announcement, Rodgers also cabled John O'Hara (who wrote the book of *Pal Joey*) asking for his phone number so that he could speak with him. It is not clear what this was about, although it is odd that it is filed in a sequence of miscellaneous correspondence concerning *Oklahoma!* By 28 July, however, Hammerstein was acknowledging his involvement to his own correspondents: on that day he wrote to bandleader Artie Shaw hoping that he would be able to write a lyric for him even though "I am juggling three shows at once at the moment"—*Carmen Jones*, the *Show Boat* revival, and now the Guild musical.

The Rodgers-Hart-Hammerstein collaboration proposed here has echoes of the 1941 plans for Edna Ferber's *Saratoga Trunk*. Although this came to nothing, it allowed Rodgers to express his enthusiasm for working with Hammerstein in the future: as Rodgers wrote, "I can say this, however, I was delighted and warmed by several things in your letter. Even if nothing further comes of this difficult matter it will at least have allowed us to approach each other professionally. Specifically, you feel that I should have a book with 'substance' to write to. Will you think seriously about doing such a book?"[15] No doubt Rodgers was hedging his bets. Hart's worsening alcoholism and bohemian lifestyle were making it harder to guarantee any successful collaboration—1941 was the first year without a new Rodgers and Hart musical since 1935 (*Jumbo*)—even though Rodgers persisted in trying to protect his longtime partner. Hammerstein was supportive: for the next project proposed (in September 1941) for Rodgers and Hart, a show based on stories in the *New Yorker* by Ludwig Bemelmans about a fictional Hotel Splendide, he promised to step in as a silent collaborator should Hart be unable to complete the task.[16] Rodgers's search in 1941 for another possible partner also extended to Ira Gershwin, whom he had already contacted in 1938 or 1939, and who was later quoted as saying that Rodgers had approached him with the idea of *Green Grow the Lilacs* while on a trip to California.[17] Hart's binge drinking worsened still more during the writing and rehearsals for *By Jupiter* in early 1942, leading to periodic admittance to the Doctors' Hospital in Manhattan. Rodgers needed to extricate himself from an increasingly difficult professional and personal relationship.

Rodgers later said in his autobiography that he did indeed try to interest Hart in the *Green Grow the Lilacs* project but that Hart turned him down, in part because he could not see any future in it, but also because he was exhausted after work on *By Jupiter* and wanted a vacation in Mexico. The crunch came at a meeting between Rodgers and Hart in the offices of Chappell and Co. (with Max Dreyfus in the wings): Rodgers ended up issuing an ultimatum that if Hart did not get involved, he would approach Hammerstein.[18] The date of this meeting is unknown; it may have been before or after Rodgers told Joshua Logan in June 1942 (presumably after he had sent the script on the 16th) that he and Hart had been offered *Green Grow the Lilacs*, that Hart did not wish to work any more, and that Rodgers was considering breaking up and working with Hammerstein.[19] Yet the Guild announcement on 22 July, reported on the 23rd, suggests that some hope for Hart was still in the air. This announcement must have had the approval of both Rodgers and Hammerstein, either as a way of pressuring Hart to stay in the picture or to save face. Hammerstein himself perpetuated what seems to have become a party line in his personal (if official) correspondence. On 27 August 1942, he wrote to Louella Parsons refuting a story in the *New York Journal-American* that he and Kern were writing a musical version of *Rain* (perhaps the play by John Colton based on a story by Somerset Maugham, first performed in 1922 and revived in 1935) for Marlene Dietrich: "I have already planned a very full season which includes a stage revival of *Show Boat*, a musical version of *Green Grow the Lilacs* which I am writing with Rodgers and Hart for the Theatre Guild, and a version of *Carmen* for an all-negro cast which I call *Carmen Jones*. After these three plays are produced—and following a few weeks in some quiet sanitarium—I look forward to coming out to Hollywood on a screenplay assignment which is at the moment cooking. This will be somewhere around February." The Hart story lingered on: on 31 August (a Monday), the *New York Times* noted that Rodgers, Hart, and Hammerstein had spent the previous weekend at the Rodgers home in Connecticut working on *Green Grow the Lilacs*, which seems to have been true for Rodgers and Hammerstein but cannot have been so for Hart, who was presumably in Mexico. Only on 17 September was it reported that Hart would have no hand in the project. Even then, however, efforts were being made (by whom remains unclear) to protect Hart: he had instead gone to Mexico to gather local color for a new Rodgers and Hart musical for the current season, "Muchacho."[20] Just the next day, the *New York Times* issued another correction: Hart was not in Mexico but in the Doctors' Hospital being treated for "undulant fever" contracted south of the border while planning "Muchacho." Rodgers, too, notes Hart's return from Mexico on a stretcher and leaves the matter there. According to Nanette Guilford (a musical-comedy actress), however, he continued trying to persuade Hart to take on *Green Grow the Lilacs*, phoning him in his hospital bed.[21] But by this time, his work with Hammerstein was well under way, and Helburn, who returned from California on 17 September, had some serious sorting out to do.

Rodgers's repeated efforts over Hart must have been more charitable than realistic. In fact, the triple combination of Rodgers, Hart, and Hammerstein was very unlikely indeed: Hammerstein had written both the book and the lyrics for all his main shows thus far and would continue to do so save for *South Pacific* (where Joshua Logan pressured for cocredit for the book because of his extensive rewriting) and *The Sound of Music* (book by Howard Lindsay and Russel Crouse, who had signed before Rodgers and Hammerstein became involved). But newspaper reports (and therefore press releases) on the Rodgers and Hammerstein collaboration made scant reference to a new partnership or to changed circumstances. Only a few attempted any speculation either that the show marked a permanent rift between Rodgers and Hart—the *Sunday Journal* on 17 January 1943 and the *Daily News* on 26 February were exceptions; the latter had Hart working with Jerome Kern on the score of Paul Gallico's *Circus Revue*, produced by Doc Bentler—or that they would soon reunite (*New York News*, 14 March). Even Margaret Case Harriman's profile of Rodgers and Hart written for the *New Yorker* just before Hart died on 22 November 1943 treated them as a permanent couple: "Larry Hart had no part in writing *Oklahoma!* but with a team like Rodgers and Hart, one member can disappear for a while without splitting the act." [22] The rhetoric shifted significantly only after *Oklahoma!* was established on Broadway, and after Hart's death. Thus on 25 June 1944 the *New York Times* reported, "Ever since they pooled their talents to create *Oklahoma!* the names of Rodgers and Oscar Hammerstein 2d have been linked with one project or another. The extent and anticipated duration of the union, however, was not guessed until the other day when Mr. Rodgers remarked: 'We have no plans that don't include each other.'" History was rewritten still further in the *New York Times* on 21 January 1945, where Gertrude Samuels implied by omission and elision that Rodgers and Hammerstein had begun their partnership only after Hart's death: "When Larry Hart died a year ago, after a quarter of a century of collaboration with Rodgers, many predicted the end of a 'modern Gilbert and Sullivan team' on the ground that a musical comedy writer is only as good as his lyricist. Oscar Hammerstein and *Oklahoma!* have apparently proved how wrong the prediction was."

Those not in the know in the second half of 1942 could well have been fooled. After all, *Green Grow the Lilacs* was sufficiently different from the normal Rodgers and Hart musical to enable the fiction that it was just an isolated endeavor; *By Jupiter* played strongly through 1942 and until 12 June 1943 (when Ray Bolger left the cast to entertain the troops in the South Pacific); Rodgers and Hart musicals were still being bought by Hollywood studios; and the revival of *A Connecticut Yankee* on 17 November 1943 (which Rodgers paints as an act of charity but which had 135 performances) suggested that the partnership was still alive.[23] For his part, Hammerstein tended to give newspapers the impression that the musical version of *Green Grow the Lilacs* was just one of several irons in his fire, and indeed that he had more important projects to consider. These included his long-planned

Broadway revival of *Show Boat*; a collaboration with Kern and Otto Harbach, *Hayfoot, Strawfoot* (a rewriting of *Gentlemen Unafraid*, staged in St.
Louis in 1938); and the opening of *Carmen Jones*, which he planned for
October 1942, then January 1943, then spring 1943—the *New York Times*
regularly attributed the postponements to work on *Green Grow the Lilacs*—
before being put back to the 1943–44 season.[24] The *Show Boat* project was
in fact on the rocks by mid-August 1942 (despite a positive report in the *New
York Times* on the 9th) because of casting problems (in particular, the role
of Cap'n Andy Hawkes): on 23 July, Hammerstein cabled Arthur Freed at
MGM, "I am getting desperate on the Cap[']n Andy situation. Do you think
it conceivable that I might get Frank Morgan[?] I have very little hope for
this but I have now gotten down to throwing long forward passes in the last
three minutes of play." (Morgan had played the title role in *The Wizard of
Oz*.) However, he continued to express some hope (depending on his corre-
spondent) that it would be done in the spring, and with *Oklahoma!* in the
bag, he revived the idea for summer 1943 (with a similar lack of success).
Casting difficulties were also used by Hammerstein in some official correspondence to explain the delays with *Carmen Jones*, although on 6 October
he admitted to one of the investors, Charles Brackett (whose investment was
being returned), that he was "reshuffling the cards" on the project because
of his dissatisfaction with Max Gordon as producer and thought he could
get a better deal elsewhere (as he did eventually with Billy Rose).[25] Unbe-
knownst to the *New York Times* (although Hammerstein freely admitted it
in his letters), he was also considering an extended Hollywood contract as
associate producer to Arthur Freed at MGM (to start in February 1943), although he turned it down definitively on 27 November 1942 because, he
said, of suspected tax difficulties. Even after *Oklahoma!* opened, Hammerstein was pursuing the idea of a show with Kern until he was persuaded by
Rodgers that a sole partnership was an inevitability.[26]

Certainly, Hart never figures in any official Guild documents associated
with the *Green Grow the Lilacs* project save in the initial "luminary" list.
On 30 July 1942 Howard Reinheimer (the attorney acting for Rodgers, Hammerstein, and Riggs, plus many other individuals in New York theatrical
circles), wrote to the Guild's business manager, Warren Munsell, about contractual arrangements for the adaptation (Hart is not mentioned), by which
time Munsell had also been in correspondence with Garrett Leverton about
the film rights to the play (a matter of ongoing discussion). Contracts were
drawn up in early August for Rodgers and Hammerstein (only) as the adap-

tors of the play, with the requirement "that the Book, Music and Lyrics thereof shall be written and/or composed only by the adaptors, except as to interpolations." However, these contracts were not signed, chiefly because of difficulties with the film rights. The Guild must have been getting anxious: 1 October was a standard deadline for contracts for new works for the current season. Accordingly, on 2 October, Rodgers and Hammerstein signed a "letter of agreement," while Reinheimer drew up another contract, which Munsell reviewed the next day: "I have looked over the attached contracts from Reinheimer and they all seem to be O.K. except I think possibly we ought to have a little more time to put the opera into production after receiving the finished script. I have told this to Reinheimer. The contracts cannot be completed until Reinheimer gets the Metro [MGM] agreement, which he hopes to have within the next day or so." Presumably this was the contract prepared in October 1942 (but again not signed) specifying a performance by 15 April 1943. The royalties were quite generous, with 3.5 percent of gross receipts each going to Rodgers and Hammerstein and 1 percent to Riggs; this was more than the norm (2 percent each to the composer and lyricist, and 1 percent to the writer of the book), although on a par with Rodgers and Hart's contracts.[27]

Now the chronology becomes hazy, at least within the Guild materials, in part because Helburn was out of town in August (in Maine) and September (in California). In the first half of September, Hammerstein was also in Hollywood for an ASCAP meeting and (according to the *New York Times*) to audition actors and singers for *Carmen Jones*, *Green Grow the Lilacs*, and the Broadway revival of *Show Boat* (and also, one assumes, to talk further with MGM). Toward the end of September, Rodgers was helping George Abbott rescue Johnny Green's *Beat the Band* during its Boston tryout (it opened on Broadway on 14 October 1942, with Marc Platt in the cast), for which Rodgers was a "silent" coproducer.[28] Both Langner and Helburn later claimed that Hammerstein's script was completed by late summer 1942, but this seems unlikely given that Helburn told Riggs on 28 September that act 1 was then in progress and due to be finished by mid-October.[29] On 14 October, Hammerstein declined a request for an audition for *Green Grow the Lilacs* from Millicent Hoyt McKean—"I am too busy at the moment writing a play to grant any interviews but if you will write to me again after two weeks, I shall be able to arrange one"—and on the 26th, Riggs was told (by Frank Sheil of Samuel French and Co.) that Hammerstein had completed the first act. He must have been working very hard indeed given that on

28 October he wrote to Laurence Schwab, a friend and former producer now living in Miami, "I will send you some more deathless work from my pen very soon. When I finish the book of *Green Grow the Lilacs* next week, I will send it to you if only because you seemed skeptical about the wisdom of adapting it. I don't guarantee that you will change your mind but I think I should give you the opportunity." Schwab replied on 7 November: "Shall be glad to read *Lilacs*. I think you'll make it good and throw away most of the original. At least that is what I shall say about it anyway. I think Dick Rodgers is a swell showman, and you should knock out a hit together." Hammerstein responded on the 12th, saying that he would send a copy "next week when I have more scripts made," and keeping to his schedule, he deposited a copy of the script with the Library of Congress for copyright purposes exactly one week later, on the 19th. This included the complete dialogue, outlines for the musical numbers, and a few lyrics. However, he was not finished: on 25 November he declined an invitation from Mrs. Brock Pemberton to co-chair the opening of the American Theatre Wing Merchant Seaman's Club because "I am unfortunately tied up at the moment, with a new play. I am now in the last lap of the script. When I have finished with this, I will get in touch with you because I am deeply interested in this enterprise." On the 27th Hammerstein told Arthur Freed, "I have just finished the adaptation of *Green Grow the Lilacs* for the Theatre Guild (as a matter of fact, my script has been sent out to your studio. I would like you to read it). I am now working with Dick Rodgers on the songs and we expect to go into rehearsal next month, opening in New York about Feb. 1." Similarly, the *New York Times* reported on 3 December that Hammerstein was still "wrestling" with the lyrics for *Green Grow the Lilacs*, and on the 7th, Hammerstein declined Josephine Shelton's request for advice on how to handle new songs: "At any other time I would gladly have granted you the interview you suggested but I am, at the moment, working very hard to finish up a new play and I am not breaking the days with any appointments at all." According to Helene Hanff (who had been working in the Guild press office since November 1941), it was during the opening night of Konstantin Simonov's *The Russian People* (29 December 1942) that Helburn started spreading the news to journalists—scooping her own staff in the process—that the Guild's new "opera" was finished and would be called "Away We Go."[30] But we shall see that Hammerstein still had much to do even by the second half of January 1943.

The delivery of the script for copying in early November, however, seems to have given Hammerstein and Rodgers a brief respite to consider other plans. On 17 November, Hammerstein wrote to Charles (Charlie) Ruggles:

> The last time you were in New York we had a telephone conversation in which you threw out the attractive news that you and Charlie Winninger would be receptive to a proposition of doing a show together in New York. Dick Rodgers and I have an idea for a musical play in which you and Charlie would be teamed and linked with Vera Zorina in a story which has a strong comedy basis. Because we are at the moment immersed in finishing another play which the Theatre Guild is about to produce, I won't be able to send you a scenario for this story for a few weeks. But, meanwhile, Dick and I are most interested to know whether the crack still goes and whether you think you and Charlie would be available for a play to be produced this spring.

Hammerstein also asked whether Ruggles would be willing to accept a post-Broadway season on tour, suggesting that he was thinking somewhat along the lines of Max Gordon's advice to him on the closing of *Sunny River* in early 1942 (for a compact musical with at least three stars which could also go on the road). Ruggles was a well-known comedian often remembered for *Bringing Up Baby* (1938); Winninger was a Hammerstein favorite, having played Cap'n Andy Hawkes in the original *Show Boat* (1927), the 1932 revival, and the 1936 film, and he was also in the film of Rodgers and Hart's *Babes in Arms* (1939). Both had recently starred in the serious film *Friendly Enemies* (released on 21 June 1942). Vera Zorina was a ballerina (then married to George Balanchine) who appeared in the stage version of Rodgers and Hart's *I Married an Angel* (1938) and in the film of their *On Your Toes* (1939), and who took the lead as Marina Von Minden in both the stage (1940) and film (1941) versions of Irving Berlin's *Louisiana Purchase*. The ballet connection may reflect some of the recent thinking (with or without Agnes de Mille) on *Oklahoma!* although we have no clear indication of the "scenario" being considered by Rodgers and Hammerstein. Nothing seems to have come of this, although Hammerstein did continue pursuing Ruggles in early 1943 as yet another potential Cap'n Andy for the *Show Boat* revival that never reached fruition.

The Backstage Team

The Theatre Guild would have wanted to keep Rodgers and Hammerstein focused on the matter in hand, and not planning other ventures, given the pressures on the timetable and the commitment to Guild subscribers. Although October was a busy month of writing for Hammerstein, he, Rodgers, and the Guild also had other decisions to make that would have a significant impact on the show. On 4 October, Lou Calhern wrote to the Guild saying that he had heard of the plans for *Green Grow the Lilacs* and that it was to be directed by Rouben Mamoulian (he was linked to the project in the *Daily Mirror* on 26 September), although Calhern suggested Robert Ross (who had directed the 1941–42 revival of *Porgy and Bess*). Mamoulian's involvement with the Guild went back almost twenty years: he had been associated with the Theatre Guild's Acting School, and Langner was writing cordial letters of introduction for him in 1926 and 1927 following his three-year stint at the Eastman Theatre School, where he had also directed the opera company.[31] He had directed both *Porgy* (1927) and *Porgy and Bess* (1935) for the Guild and was approached for the original *Green Grow the Lilacs* in 1930, although he was not interested in it.[32] In Hollywood, Mamoulian had directed Rodgers and Hart's *Love Me Tonight* (1932) for Paramount, and later, the Kern-Hammerstein *High, Wide, and Handsome* (1937); his other film successes included *Dr. Jekyll and Mr. Hyde* (1931). In 1937 Helburn pushed him for the *Liliom* project with Weill, and the Guild tried to tempt him with various other productions in 1939–41. However, he was not necessarily the first choice for *Oklahoma!* in part, Rodgers suggests, because of fears that an Armenian could not handle a play about the American Southwest.[33] Rodgers may or may not have intended Joshua Logan to take it on (depending on how one reads his approach in June 1942). But on 26 October, Helburn cabled Bretaigne Windust to see whether he was interested; Windust was the stage manager for the original play, and as director was currently having a run of successes on Broadway, including *Life with Father* and *Arsenic and Old Lace*.[34] On 21 November, Helburn then left a copy of Hammerstein's script to be picked up in the Guild office by Elia Kazan, asking him to keep matters confidential. Kazan cabled on 26 November: "I reread *Green Grow* carefully and I just don't click with it. I'm afraid I'd do a very mediocre job and neither of us would benefit. I'd feel so proud and honored to do a show for you, but this had better not be it."

Moving down Helburn's list, it seems, her secretary then sent Hammerstein's script plus a printed copy of Riggs's play to Mamoulian on 2 December. By 12 January 1943 Helburn included him in a list of individuals who had already agreed to be involved in *Oklahoma!* along with Agnes de Mille, Alfred Drake, Joan Roberts, Robert Russell (probably as Jud), Celeste Holm, and Betty Garde. However, save for Drake and Roberts, contracts had not

3. Rouben Mamoulian and Oscar Hammerstein review the script for *Oklahoma!*
Mamoulian directed Gershwin's *Porgy and Bess* (1935) for the Theatre Guild
and worked with Hammerstein and Jerome Kern on the film *High, Wide, and
Handsome* (1937), which prefigured a number of the show's themes. He had a
significant impact not just on the production style but also on the major
revisions to the text during rehearsals, in particular act 2, scene 3. (Vandamm)

been signed, and Mamoulian was in Hollywood for much of January. Stories
were circulating in the newspapers at least from 17 January onward that
Mamoulian had agreed to direct, and later, that a contract had been signed.
However, the final negotiations seem to have taken place in Mamoulian's
New York hotel room (the Gotham) in early February: Langner drafted a
letter of agreement on hotel paper, and it was typed up on 5 February.[35]
Mamoulian was careful to insist that he had total control over the "entire"
production, and that he be credited as such on programs and advertising,
although the "entire" never appeared in the official publicity (perhaps because of pressure from Agnes de Mille). He was offered $3,500 payable in
weekly installments of $500, starting with the first rehearsal (which the letter
says was to be on 8 February), and 1 percent of the gross, plus travel expenses
outside New York City; there were also clauses covering revivals under a different director (one-half of one percent of gross) and by different companies
(1 percent of gross).

   This late signing of contracts and letters of agreement seems to have
been typical of the preparations for *Oklahoma!* and one assumes that various
informal agreements had been in place long before, even if it remains unclear whether the late signing was due to normal administrative sluggishness

4. Agnes de Mille drew on her choreography for Aaron Copland's *Rodeo* (1942) for the dream-ballet in *Oklahoma!* in particular in terms of stylized Western gestures. Here dream-Curly (Marc Platt) struts his stuff before dream-Laurey (Katharine Sergava) with typical de Mille "cowboy" movements. (Uncredited)

or to some kind of caution on the part of the Guild. For example, Agnes de Mille's letter of agreement was typed up only on 29 January 1943, offering her $1,500 plus an agreed bonus of $500, payable in weekly installments of $50 once production costs had been paid off; the deal was a bone of contention even after it had been modified (before the New York opening) to $50 per week for the duration of the run. However, de Mille had already been involved in *Oklahoma!* since late October or early November, and she had been angling for the choreography since mid-September.

   A later remark by de Mille suggests that Robert Alton was originally in mind to take charge of the dancing in *Oklahoma!* As part of the later dispute over her recompense, she wrote to Langner and Helburn on 15 June 1948 that "You would have had to pay Bob Alton 1½ percent of the gross for all these years had you hired him as planned. It is also true that he might not have made an important contribution to an enterprise that has altered several fortunes and changed the history of dancing in this country."[36] Langner also suggests that when it came to finding a choreographer, "there was some difference of opinion as to the style of production and the kind of dance director needed."[37] Alton had worked with the Guild on the revue *Parade* (1935), and with Rodgers and Hart on *Higher and Higher* (1940), *Pal Joey* (1940), and *By Jupiter* (1942), and he choreographed the *Ziegfeld Follies* that opened in New York on 1 April 1943, the day after *Oklahoma!* Although his prolific working pattern (at least in 1938–40) was such as to be able to choreograph a new show every two or three months, he may not have been available in the second half of 1942 (when Rodgers and Hammerstein were looking for a choreographer), given that he was working on Ann Ronell's revue *Count Me In*, staged at the Ethel Barrymore Theatre from 8 October to 21 November 1942.

Rodgers's later claim that the vogue for Western ballets had been initiated by his own *Ghost Town* (1939, in collaboration with Marc Platt) is patently absurd, given the success of Aaron Copland's *Billy the Kid*, staged by Eugene Loring and the American Ballet Theatre in 1938.[38] However, it was another Copland ballet, *Rodeo*, that had a direct impact on *Oklahoma!* On 24 September 1942, de Mille wrote to Helburn:

> As you suggested in our phone conversation I am writing to ask you to keep me in mind when deciding on the dance-director for *Green Grow the Lilacs*. I have made a very deep study of American folk material and have become something of a specialist in this field. On October 16th at the Metropolitan Opera House the Ballet Russe [de Monte Carlo] will present the first performance of my new American ballet *Rodeo*—score by Aaron Copland, scenery by Oliver Smith, costumes, Kermit Love. I am dancing the lead in the première. I hope you and Mssrs. Rodgers and Hammerstein can come to this performance.
>
> In the keeping of your telephone operator is a scrap-book of mine containing press on the folk dances I staged for *American Legend*. Lynn Riggs knows my work very well, and what I am capable of doing.
>
> Please do not settle on anyone else before the 17th.[39]

Langner had known de Mille for a number of years, and he had tried to get her to do the choreography for the Guild production of Molière's *The School for Husbands* in 1933. De Mille had also approached Langner in early April 1941 about her "revue based on American folk material" (*American Legend*, premiered by the American Actors Company on 11 May), and on 13 April

1942 she asked him, "May I see you at your earliest convenience? I have something very important to discuss."[40] Her work with African-American dancers (in her *Black Ritual* [*Obeah*] of 1940, to Darius Milhaud's *La Cré-ation du monde*) may also have struck a chord with Langner. In addition, de Mille perhaps counted on other connections, given that she had known Hammerstein since 1930, when he attended her first recital.[41]

De Mille's letter of 24 September has various annotations suggesting that Helburn planned to go and see *Rodeo*, and on 30 September, Langner passed the news on to Rodgers:

> Agnes deMille [*sic*], who is an old friend of mine, asked me if I would speak to you about the possibility of her working on the dancing for *Green Grow the Lilacs*. She has done some very good comedy ballets as well as aesthetic ones. She is doing a Wild West Rodeo Ballet at the opening of the Metro-politan Ballet Season and you really should go and see this because it shows her ability to handle western material.
>
> Please give this your usual kind consideration.

Helburn, Rodgers, and Hammerstein (but not Langner) did indeed attend the premiere of *Rodeo* on 16 October 1942, with Rodgers later describing the occasion: "It had tremendous humor, easy grace, and was so good in general that it wasn't even artistic. We yipped with joy along with the rest of the audience."[42] When de Mille invited Helburn to a revival of *Rodeo* in 1948, she wrote: "Remember Oct. 16, 1942? My life changed that night at 10:28 and you were there to help. . . . I am old and fat now, but I can still dance a hoe-down."[43] De Mille met variously with Hammerstein, Helburn, and Rodgers soon after the premiere, although she claimed that they took a while to agree on her, chiefly because Rodgers had qualms; Hammerstein also arranged an interview on 25 November with Felicia Sorel, who had writ-ten on 20 November requesting a meeting to discuss her choreographing *Green Grow the Lilacs*. (She arranged the dancing for the Theatre Guild coproduction of Behrman's *The Pirate* that opened on 25 November.) There may have been some double-dealing here, given that de Mille later said that she started mapping out the dances for *Oklahoma!* while taking *Rodeo* on tour in November: "So, on the tour in my suitcase went a blank copybook labeled *Lilacs* with pages entitled 'Ballet'—'Many a New Day,' 'Cowmen [*sic*] and the Farmer,' 'Kansas City,' 'Jud's Postcards,' and as I sat happily in hotel bedrooms, I made notes."[44]

Oliver Smith, who did the sets for *Rodeo*, also proposed himself for *Okla-*

homa!, probably on 18 October, and was further recommended by Jacob Steisel, an attorney, on 6 November: Hammerstein replied on the 12th, "As a matter of fact, we have already discussed Oliver Smith, after having seen the *Rodeo* ballet, the designs of which impressed me very much. It is not at all improbable that we will have a talk with him about our show." However, the Guild once again relied on a previous contact. On 11 November 1940 Lemuel Ayers had requested an interview with Langner on the basis of their having met at Amherst College, where Langner had "seemed interested enough in my work," and he did the sets for Behrman's *The Pirate*.[45] He was not included in the list of 12 January 1943 of people enlisted for *Oklahoma!* although his name was in the frame earlier that month. On 21 January, Helburn or her secretary made a note of a telephone conversation wherein Ayers said, "I have been thinking the thing over and I think $2500 is the best I could do unless you want to give me $2000 and $1000 interest in the show"; the call also included arranging a meeting the next day, with Ayers anxious to fix a contract so that he could work on the sets while in New Haven the following week (perhaps for the tryout of Florence Ryerson and Colin Clement's *Harriet*, which he also designed). However, he signed only on 30 January. The contract was for $3,000, but fortunately for Ayers, $1,000 of that was indeed a share in the show, eventually netting him much more money. Ayers was also paid an additional $100 for devising a backdrop added late to the sets, plus a further $100 for designing the poster.[46]

For the costumes, the Guild approached Miles White, who also worked on *The Pirate* (and on the *Ziegfeld Follies* that played at the same time as *Oklahoma!*). He, too, was not on the 12 January list, and it is not clear whether Helburn's cable to him sent sometime in mid-January ("Would like to see you. When will you be back in town. Please wire") was their first point of contact concerning *Oklahoma!* If it was, he must have worked very hard to complete the sketches for the costumes by the second week of February at the latest. He signed his contract on 1 February, to which Helburn added a codicil that same day: "Referring to our contract dated February 1st, 1943, in addition to the fee of $1500 which you are to receive for designing *Green Grow the Lilacs* costumes, you are also to receive a bonus of $500, after the production costs have been paid off." This set him on a par with de Mille.

With Jerome (Jerry) Whyte appointed stage manager by 1 January 1943 —he had done the same for *The Boys from Syracuse*—the production team was officially in place by early February.[47] But there were two agreements still to be made. The first was for the orchestrator, an issue that seems to have been primarily in Rodgers's hands. His choice, Robert Russell Bennett (1894–1981), was a distinguished composer (he had studied with Nadia Boulanger in Paris) who also worked extensively as an orchestrator on Broadway and in Hollywood: in the late 1920s and early 1930s he collaborated with Jerome Kern (*Show Boat*), George Gershwin (*Girl Crazy, Of Thee I Sing*), and Cole Porter (*Anything Goes*), and he also contributed orchestrations to the Theatre Guild's 1935 revue *Parade*. Hammerstein had agreed with him to arrange and orchestrate Bizet's music for *Carmen Jones* by spring 1942, and he later did the orchestrations for a number of Rodgers and Hammerstein musicals (*Allegro, South Pacific, The King and I, Pipe Dream, Flower Drum Song, The Sound of Music*, although they had a brief falling out over *Carousel*), and many others (for example, *Annie Get Your Gun, Kiss Me, Kate, My Fair Lady, Finian's Rainbow, Camelot*).

The second remaining issue was the conductor. Rodgers seems initially to have approached Johnny Green (who conducted *By Jupiter*), who went to Hollywood instead.[48] On 30 October 1942 Hammerstein was approached by Arthur List, a conductor with extensive experience, requesting an interview; Hammerstein's secretary (Nellie Rassias) replied on 6 November, "This is to inform you that Mr. Richard Rodgers is in charge of the musical department for *Green Grow the Lilacs*." But it may have been Hammerstein who suggested Jacob Schwartzdorf (about to change his name to Jay Blackton), who had directed the Romberg-Hammerstein *Sunny River* and was also associated (like others of the *Oklahoma!* cast, including Joan Roberts and Ralph Riggs) with the St. Louis Municipal Opera (which also had a Kern-Hammerstein connection). Blackton received a letter of engagement on 9 February, and his appointment was noted in the *Morning Telegraph* on 19 February, but he seems not to have signed any contract until later.[49]

Auditions and Casting

At some point in the second half of September 1942, Lynn Riggs (by now in the army) wrote to the Guild asking for news about *Green Grow the Lilacs*. He was already feeling out of the loop if one is to believe a report in the *Monterey Peninsula Herald* on 25 August 1942: "Lynn picked up a *New York Times* in the Post library the other day and learned that the musical version of *Green Grow the Lilacs*, with music by Rogers and Hart [*sic*], will be produced in New York around Christmas time. He'd signed the contract and knew it was to be done, but no one had told him when. He had to find out by accident. The chances are he won't be there to see it, however."[50] He must have been still more confused by the reports in the *New York Times* on 17 and 18 September. Helburn replied on the 28th:

> Dick and Oscar profess to be working hard and say they will have one act ready to show us the middle of this month, but Dick has just been called out of town to help save the new Abbott show [*Beat the Band*] so that may hold things up.
>
> Casting will be a difficult problem because we really need box office names to carry the expense of a musical. I think Oscar has the right spirit towards the play and wants to keep as much of its poetic quality and charm as possible.
>
> However, if we get a script and score by November I think we will be lucky.

Helburn's claim of seeking to preserve the qualities of the play may have just been an attempt to reassure Riggs, although it does capture something of what seems to have been Hammerstein's intent. The question of "box office names," however, was more problematic, and it remained an issue until the first rehearsal call. Helburn's and Langner's opinions of the casting seems to have varied in much the same way as their views of the show in general. For a while, Helburn appears to have been unable to decide whether *Oklahoma!* was to be a simple musical expansion of *Green Grow the Lilacs* or something very different, and just as she initially considered bringing back some of the originals involved in Riggs's play if in a different capacity (Bretaigne Windust as director, Tex Ritter as composer of the music), so did she wonder about replicating at least some of its casting: thus one proposed list of possible actors included Franchot Tone to repeat the role of Curly.[51] This list also had Joan Roberts for Laurey, Roy Rogers and Eddie Albert (Sr.) for Curly, W. C. Fields and "Spivey's Ventriloquist" for the peddler (a sublist for "Peck's Party"), Ralph Riggs for Old Man Peck (Riggs eventually played Carnes), and two groups for a "singing comedy trio"; thus it bears similarities with Helburn's ideas for the show outlined on 18 May 1942. However, the Guild soon set its sights somewhat differently.

Rodgers and Hammerstein began thinking about casting fairly early on, in anticipation of an opening sooner than would actually be the case. On 12 August 1942 Hammerstein wrote to the veteran actor John Charles Thomas that "Dick Rodgers and I have a notion for a musical play that might be a great vehicle for you. The last time I spoke to you, you said you would be interested in doing a show. Is this still true? This one would be designed to open on Broadway sometime around the Christmas holidays." Thomas replied on 25 August that he was interested but booked up over Christmas. Also in early August, it seems, Hammerstein approached Charlotte Greenwood for Aunt Eller: she had played in the Kern-Hammerstein *Three Sisters* (London, 1934) and would take the role in the film version of *Oklahoma!* In September 1942 he was pursuing Mary Martin to choose between his proposed revival of *Show Boat* (as Magnolia) and Laurey. Helburn was also very keen on Martin, who in the late 1930s and early 1940s was making a name for herself in Hollywood and on Broadway (in Cole Porter's *Leave It to Me* of 1938–39). On 23 September, Martin's husband, Richard Halliday, noted to Hammerstein that she "is anxious to do a play in New York, a play for which she has enthusiasm and which she believes will help her. She is still enormously interested to know more about the adaptation of *Green Grow the Lilacs*," although she felt that *Show Boat* was not the star vehicle that she required. Reportedly, Martin ended up tossing a coin between *Oklahoma!* and Vinton Freedley's *Dancing in the Streets*, choosing the latter, which turned out to be a flop: it had its tryout in Boston during the second week of the *Oklahoma!* run there (starting on 22 March) but closed. She later took the title role in Kurt Weill's *One Touch of Venus* (which opened on 7 October 1943), although Marlene Dietrich had been planned for it. Subsequently she became closely associated with Rodgers and Hammerstein, with leading roles in *South Pacific* (she was previously in the touring company of the Rodgers and Hammerstein–produced *Annie Get Your Gun*) and *The Sound of Music*. By all accounts, however, Hammerstein was in the end glad not to have had her for *Oklahoma!* ("I am going to send you roses for a long time. Had you accepted the role, I would have written a different show.")[52]

On 2 October, Helburn suggested to Hammerstein the relatively unknown Jessica Dragonette for Laurey: "I'm told she is small, blonde, beautiful, a good actress with a superb voice. Of course the person who tells me is her lawyer[-]agent and may be prejudiced." However, by 8 December her sights were again set higher, to judge by her cable to Nate Blumberg of Universal Pictures in Hollywood: "Would you be interested in loaning Miss [Deanna] Durbin to play the lead in the Theatre Guild musical version of *Green Grow the Lilacs* for which Richard Rodgers has done the music and Oscar Hammerstein the book. Going into rehearsal in February. We suggest this because it has a fine leading part for Miss Durbin which we feel would also make a great picture role for her. If you are interested would be glad to send you script. Please let me hear from you as soon as possible." Universal

Pictures replied in the negative on 10 December. These and similar requests were presumably a matter of kite-flying, although they reflect not just issues over the nature of *Oklahoma!* and what it might need to be a success but also the complex symbiotic relationship between Broadway and Hollywood, as New York theaters tried to capitalize on film "names" while also pressuring their own players not to succumb to the siren call of the silver screen (as cast members of *Oklahoma!* were later to discover). Certainly this is how Rodgers later construed the pattern of events: "From the start, Oscar and I were determined that a musical such as ours required actors and singers who had to be right for their parts, regardless of whether or not they were box-office names. Terry Helburn, however, perhaps because of the financial plight of the Guild, felt that the only way to stage a musical was to spend little on scenery and costumes and to concentrate on established stars who could lure both backers and customers."[53]

Meanwhile, the Guild initiated the standard audition procedures for a show, comprising a brief five- or ten-minute office interview and then a possible recall for a more extended reading. According to Helburn, "Auditioning was no bed of roses. Oscar wanted people who could speak his lines. Dick wanted people who could sing. Agnes wanted people who could dance. Why, I kept asking, can't we have girls who can dance and also have pretty legs? It seemed reasonable to me. It seemed unreasonable to Agnes."[54] The first surviving appointment list for *Oklahoma!* dates from 1 October, giving meetings with Hammerstein (presumably Rodgers was still out of town working on *Beat the Band*), and it includes Alfred Drake and Lee Dixon for Curly, but Dixon seems not to have shown up (his name is crossed out in pencil). Dixon had been included in Helburn's undated cast suggestions as a "male dancing cowboy," and he eventually played Will Parker. Drake, however, appears to have caught Hammerstein's interest, and he was called back on 6 October to read Curly at the end of another series of appointments, even though he was also under consideration for a role in *Beat the Band*. This may or may not be the occasion later recounted by Drake when he was reading Curly for Hammerstein, with the text finished but the score still in progress: Hammerstein stopped him midstream to explain his thoughts about the speech where Curly describes the surrey to Laurey, which, Hammerstein said, he was going to turn into a song.[55] Onstage auditions began on 8 October (with Rodgers back in town?), in part grouped by role; these seem to have been by invitation or recommendation only, given that Hammerstein often turned down unsolicited requests. (On 14 October, he told Ruth

5. Two singers audition for Theresa Helburn and Oscar Hammerstein (who usually claimed to be relatively unmusical). This photograph appeared in the *Christian Science Monitor* on 27 February 1943 but was probably taken much earlier for the Theatre Guild; the newspaper caption refers to Hammerstein and Helburn "trying out candidates for the impending show, *Away We Go.*" Richard Rodgers was out of town for the early stages of the casting process, working for George Abbott on Johnny Green's *Beat the Band.* Helburn, however, took a close interest in all stages of a show which she called her "baby." (Philippe Halsman)

Ives, "I am not having any general auditions now.") The process ground on through November to early December. However, scripts were unavailable for distribution to likely candidates until 16 November; presumably these were carbon copies of the text that Hammerstein deposited in the Library of Congress on the 19th.

Meanwhile, theatrical agents and other interested parties were making recommendations for different roles, some of which would be passed on to Rodgers and Hammerstein for further consideration. In late August or early

September, Dorothea MacFarland, who had worked with Hammerstein on *Music in the Air*, approached him for news of auditions; Hammerstein replied on 2 September that he would see her after his return from the West Coast (after 15 September), and on 14 December he told her that he would notify her of audition dates for the chorus once they were announced — "It looks now as if we will go into rehearsal the latter part of January." On 4 October, John M. Fuhrman ("a young comedian") asked Hammerstein for an interview "in regard to some of the shows you are doing this fall," and on the 23rd, Miriam Howell of Myron Selznick Ltd. suggested the eighteen-year-old Suzanne Foster: "She has a sensational voice, having a range from G below middle C to B-flat above high C. And she has as well a very considerable degree of acting ability." The letter seems to have been passed on to Rodgers, but it contains the curt penciled note, "No." On 4 December, John Gassner suggested Valentine Grenville: "She might be just right for *Green Grow* with her colleen looks and turned up nose." Few of these introductions bore fruit. On 7 December 1942 Hammerstein told his Hollywood agent, Frank Orsatti, "There is nothing for Ilona Massey in my new show. It is too thoroughly American in its feeling." (Massey, a Hungarian and star of the 1939 film *Balalaika*, had briefly been hailed as a new Marlene Dietrich and eventually appeared in the *Ziegfeld Follies* contemporaneously with *Oklahoma!*) Similarly, Langner wrote on 8 December to Thomas Midgely, who had recommended an Andzia (no last name given): "I had a talk with Richard Rodgers and Oscar Hammerstein, Jr., about Andzia and I am sorry to say that neither of them see her for the part in *Green Grow the Lilacs*. They have in mind a different type of singer, and I personally feel that it probably would be better for Andzia's career if she was not in what, after all, is a musical comedy. I know you will be disappointed about this, but there is nothing I can do as the control of this proposition is entirely in the hands of these parties." His statement that the casting was entirely under the control of Rodgers and Hammerstein may well have been true, but it was also, of course, convenient for crafting such explanations.

Alfred Drake was known to the Guild (he had most recently played in the Guild production of Emlyn Williams's *Yesterday's Magic* in April–May 1942) and to Rodgers (he was in *Babes in Arms*), and Joan Roberts had worked with Hammerstein in *Sunny River*. Their probable casting was noted in the *New York Times* on 15 November (Drake) and 3 December (Roberts), although Drake signed a Standard Minimum Contract only on 21 December, and Helburn was yet to pursue Deanna Durbin for Laurey.[56] But after the failure to recruit Durbin—and a probably false rumor in the *Daily News* of 17 December that Elizabeth Patterson would take the lead—the Guild seems to have moved quickly to secure Roberts (she signed her Standard Minimum Contract on 22 December). By 12 January, Helburn claimed to have firmed up other agreements with Robert Russell (probably for Jud), Celeste Holm (presumably as Ado Annie), and Betty Garde, who was on an early list (somewhat implausibly) for Laurey but eventually played Aunt Eller.[57] Yet even at this late stage, the overall casting was far from fixed: Hammerstein had already expressed concern on 11 January, and another round of auditions was still to take place. Things were not yet looking as stable as the Guild might have hoped.

An article in the *New York Herald Tribune* of 17 January noted that Alfred Drake and Joan Roberts had been cast (the *Sunday Journal* of the same day added Garde, who had signed "yesterday"), and that Celeste Holm had been mentioned. Similarly, the *New York Times* of 19 January listed the casting of Drake, Roberts, Holm, and Garde, but noted, "Two other important roles, one a peddler and the other a new character recently added, are yet to be filled." In fact, the situation was more complex. That day the Guild held auditions for four roles: Will Parker (Walter Donohue, Danny Drayson, Fred Barry, Hie Thompson, Jack Blair, Marc Platt), Lotta (Lorraine de Woods), the Peddler (Joseph Buloff, Zero Mostel), and Ado Annie (Shirley Booth and perhaps Eugenia Rawls, Georgette Starr, and Ann Terry).[58] None of these characters was "recently added" (they are all present in Hammerstein's November draft libretto), although this list causes some surprise. Lotta is a Mexican vamp (removed before New Haven tryout) who pursues Will but eventually marries the peddler. For Ado Annie, the 19 January auditions make one wonder just what type of agreement had already been reached with Celeste Holm (as Helburn had said on the 12th). Although she had auditioned for Ado Annie in the period leading up to Christmas 1942, tangential references suggest that Bonita Granville, Kathryn Grayson, and others were also being considered for the role in January 1943; Holm was anyway unable to sign a contract until her current Broadway show, *The Damask Cheek*, closed (on 9 January 1943) due to Flora Robson's illness.[59] Holm was also later told that even during rehearsals, the Guild was attempting to recruit Judy Canova and Shirley Booth (again) for her role.[60] At any rate, Holm signed her Standard Minimum Contract only on 3 February. Canova (who had been included in Helburn's notes of 18 May 1942) was known for comic, hillbilly roles; Shirley Booth was a familiar comic actress

6. Although Joseph Buloff (Ali Hakim) and Celeste Holm (Ado Annie)—seen here on the set for act 1, scene 1—were recruited late for *Oklahoma!* their comic talents were one cause of its success. Buloff was the longest-running principal player, and even after leaving the cast, Holm would return for special performances. (Graphic House)

on Broadway, but she would have made an old Ado Annie (Holm, born in 1919, was twenty-one years younger).

That particular Tuesday (19 January) seems to have been a busy day in the Guild offices, for in addition to holding those auditions, Helburn and Langner were each pursuing other possibilities for the cast. That day, the Guild cabled Buster Collier (of the William Morris Agency in Beverly Hills) asking whether the script of *Green Grow the Lilacs* had arrived; Collier acknowledged receipt of the script on 30 January, and shortly thereafter, he passed it over to its intended recipient, Shirley Temple (or rather, Shirley Temple's mother). On 3 February (although the date is unclear), Collier cabled Helburn: "Mrs. Temple feels although script great part too mature and sexy for Shirley. Sorry caused you all this trouble but Mrs. Temple has definite views and ways and does not want to consider venture"; that decision was confirmed the following day. Temple was aged fourteen (to be fifteen on 23 April 1943), and of course she had scored some spectacular successes in Hollywood, most recently in *Miss Annie Rooney* (1942). In January 1943 speculation was rife about her coming to New York, and several producers were seeking to pull off the coup. According to the *New York Times* on 24 January 1943, Henry Duffy was trying to give Temple her Broadway debut (in an unnamed production), but her mother had turned him down, as she did with "many producers who have had such an idea." No part for Temple is mentioned in the Guild correspondence, although Helburn and Rodgers later said that she was approached for the role of Laurey (not Ado Annie?).[61] This smacks somewhat of desperation if the Guild was prepared to drop Joan Roberts, who had already signed a contract, been announced in the papers, and helped with the fund-raising auditions.

While Helburn was pursuing Temple, Langner had another iron in the fire concerning the peddler. Zero Mostel, who auditioned on 19 January, may have been (or have become) a first choice—he was also sent a copy of the script at an unknown date—although if so, he withdrew, perhaps because of an offer from Hollywood.[62] (He played in *Du Barry Was a Lady*, released in August 1943.) Again on 19 January, however, Langner cabled Groucho Marx: "Would you be interested playing comedy role in Theatre Guild[']s new musical *Green Grow [the] Lilacs* by Rogers [*sic*] and Hammerstein. This is to be on order of *Porgy and Bess* a very high grade proposition and part of Armenian Peddler acted fairly legitimately would be new type of work for you without responsibility for entire show. We think you would be wonderful and will gladly send you script. Rehearsals begin about three weeks. Telegraph if interested and will mail script." Rodgers did not approve of the idea: "And Oscar and I rose up, you know, and screamed. We thought this would ruin the show and it damn well would have. We . . . wanted fresh people, young people, people who hadn't been seen before."[63] But it was not as outlandish as it might seem. The Marx Brothers had in fact donated money for the building of the Guild Theatre in 1925, and Langner had been eager to get Groucho involved in a Guild production at least since early 1942, when (on 14 February), Marx wrote to Langner: "Frankly, I'm more interested in a play that is not a revival—something like Cohan's part in *Ah, Wilderness*—not necessarily *Hamlet* but, as a tour de force, it would be good if I could play in a regular comedy or even in a straight play, discarding the painted, black mustache and all the other mannerisms."[64] Langner suggested *The Beggar's Opera*, which did not interest Marx, and then a new rhymed version of Molière's *Le Bourgeois Gentilhomme*, on the lines, presumably, of the Langner-Guiterman *The School for Husbands*. As he wrote on 24 March 1942 (with the Molière in mind): "I have found just the play for you, a comedic masterpiece which we want to get going on very soon. I won't tell you what it is until you have read it. . . . Meanwhile, if anything strikes you—the *Theatre Guild wants you!*"

The exchange with Marx over the role of the peddler fit the pattern. On 20 January 1943 Marx cabled that he was interested: "The nature of the script would play an important part in my discussion please send it on." On 21 January, Langner cabled Marx: "Airmailing uncut script try and envisage it cut fifty percent but not the part of the butler [crossed out: "peddler" in pencil] which we hope will interest you." Marx replied by cable on 28 January: "Liked play a lot Peddler part good but subsidiary one not what I am seeking this is probably the reaction of an incurable ham anyway good luck regards to Dick and Oscar." The Guild replied the next day: "Sorry better luck next time." In the end, the peddler was allocated to Joseph Buloff, who was recommended on 9 December by Mildred Webber of the William Morris Agency (her letter has the penciled note, "We have thought of him") and by Sylvia Hahlo on 16 January (she also suggested Romney Brent), and who also auditioned on 19 January. Presumably these agency letters were prompted by Buloff himself, who appears to have been very keen on the role. He was recruited late, however, as also was, it seems, Lee Dixon as Will Parker; their casting was announced in the *New York Times* on 2 and 8 February, respectively, although both were included in the rehearsal call issued on 3 February.

While Temple and Marx may just have been Guild kite-flying—alternatives were waiting in the wings—another flurry of telegrams to Hollywood around this time appears to have been precipitated by a genuine crisis. Jud had originally been allocated to Robert Russell, it seems, but Russell soon disappeared from the reckoning. It was a difficult character to cast: Joan Roberts later said that every time she was called for audition, there was a different actor playing the role.[65] On 28 January John Haggott, the production manager, cabled Maxwell Arnow of United Artists Corp.: "As a favor which you do not owe me would you wire collect an honest appraisal of Ward Bond[']s singing voice as confidentially he is possibility for heavy in Rogers [sic] and Hammerstein musical Guild is doing but good singing essential." Bond had played Curly in the 1940 Westport production of Green Grow the Lilacs, and Haggott must have had a favorable response, for on 1 February he cabled Bond directly with an offer for the show, to start rehearsal on the 8th. Meanwhile, also on 28 January, Mamoulian (then in Hollywood) sent a cable to Anthony Quinn confirming the imminent arrival of a script (the one that had been sent to Marx). This also relates to a cable from Mamoulian about Quinn (same date) summarized by someone in the Guild office: "His agent is Marin of Feldman Blum who is not enthusiastic about Quinn going to New York unless part is outstanding and wants to see script. Checked Quinn who would be delighted to go into this show especially under Mamoulian if part were right. He sings." Haggott also cabled Quinn on 1 February: "Would you be interested and available to do Guild musical with rehearsals starting the eighth of this month understand you have script to read." And the same day, he sent another cable to Paul Guilfoyle about Jud: "Mamoulian directing rehearsals start nezt [sic] week part requires good singing have no idea what your siniing [sic] voice is please reply if interested."[66] There is also another undated cable from Haggott to Arthur Hunnicut (who had played in the Guild's production of Saroyan's The Time of Your Life in 1939–40) about an unnamed role in the show. Guilfoyle replied on 3 February saying that he was a baritone but no great singer, and that he was interested but needed to see the script and the music; Haggott replied (undated), "Sorry part set locally many thanks for consideration."

Haggott was not being wholly truthful, but it is clear that other arrangements were being put in place. On 1 February (it seems), he cabled the actor Howard da Silva (Howard Silverblatt), who had taken secondary roles in Hollywood and on Broadway, including the role of Larry Foreman in Marc Blitzstein's politically controversial musical The Cradle Will Rock in 1937–

38: "Would you be interested and available to do part of heavy in musical of *Greengrow* [*sic*] *the Lilacs* for the Guild Mamoulian directing with music and book by Rodgers and Hammerstein you would have two songs part follows original play closely if interested call me collect Tuesday noon your time."[67] On 4 February, Haggott attempted to send another cable: "Rodgers and Hammerstein willing to redo songs to fit your style budget is limited but Guild will pay round trip and two fifty with a three week guarentee [*sic*] and three hundred after production cost id [*sic*] paid off please reply at once." A penciled note says that this cable could not be delivered (it was misaddressed) and so was substituted by telephone calls from Helburn and Haggott. Another undated cable from Haggott suggests that da Silva's involvement was finally agreed upon by telephone: "Confirming our telephone arrangement you are to appear in our production of *Green Grow* at the following terms three hundred per week with five week guarantee fare for yourself and wife to New York and return if play runs less than total six weeks. You will be featured in all display ads. Wire how soon you can be here." On 8 February (the day rehearsals started), Haggott cabled da Silva to ask whether he had managed to make a reservation for the trip to New York: da Silva had his first rehearsal call on 10 February.

Marc Platt, who had auditioned for Will Parker on 19 January, was taken on instead as a lead dancer, playing dream-Curly and also doing specialty cowboy numbers. Auditions for the dancers were firmly in the hands of Agnes de Mille, despite her occasional tussles with the Guild and Rouben Mamoulian over skill versus good looks.[68] An audition call for dancing boys and girls (both tap and ballet), to be held on 25 January before de Mille, was issued in the *New York Post, Brooklyn Citizen, Women's Wear Daily, New York World-Telegram,* and *Daily Mirror* on 21 January, and the *New York Times* on the 22nd; a similar range of papers was used for another call on the 29th. However, she must have had some idea of her principal dancers before then. Platt, who had made his brief Broadway debut in George Balanchine's choreography for Vernon Duke's *The Lady Comes Across* (it had three performances in January 1942), was in *Beat the Band* (choreography by David Lichine), which opened on 14 October 1942 but closed on 12 December, leaving him desperate, he said, for work.[69] He had also provided the choreography for Rodgers's *Ghost Town* (1939). Kate Friedlich was in the Kern-Hammerstein *Very Warm for May* (1939) and is credited as a dancer in Duke's *Banjo Eyes* (1941)—which also included another *Oklahoma!* dancer, Ray Harrison—and in the revue *Star and Garter* (opened 24 June 1942), where she was the "première danseuse" in the spoof "Les sylphides avec la bumpe." Jack Dunphy had appeared on Broadway in Kurt Jooss's ballet *The Prodigal Son* (music by Frederic Cohen), which played with Gilbert and Sullivan's *The Pirates of Penzance* in February–March 1942. Most of the other dancers, however, were new to Broadway, including Katharine Sergava (dream-Laurey), although a good number had prior experience in classical ballet: Platt, Sergava, and Vivian Smith were members of the Ballet Russe de Monte Carlo; Sergava had been *première danseuse* in the American Ballet Theatre; and Joan McCracken had studied with Balanchine in the School of American Ballet. Sergava had also been in films in the early 1930s. The chief exception, it seems, to this classical background was George Church, who was recruited late, and perhaps more at the instigation of Rodgers and Hammerstein: he had made his debut at the Radio City Music Hall in 1933, was a Rodgers and Hart veteran, having danced in *On Your Toes* (1936; he was the villain in the ballet sequence "Slaughter on Tenth Avenue") and *The Boys from Syracuse* (1938), as well as in other Broadway shows such as the *Ziegfeld Follies of 1936* and Burton Lane's *Hold On to Your Hats* (1940; an Al Jolson vehicle), also taking a straight comedy role in Jo Eisinger and Judson O'Donnell's *What Big Ears* (1942).[70]

Most of the principals and a good number of the chorus and dancers were called on 3 February for the first rehearsal on 8 February; one version of the call list includes Merce Cunningham as dancer.[71] However, there seem to have been shortages in the chorus, and an emergency call for auditions (the second, it seems) appeared in the *New York Times* on 5 February: the *Sunday News* on 14 February reported a dearth of chorus men because of the war. Later rehearsal calls were issued for George Church ("dancer"; called for 9 February), Howard da Silva as Jud (10 February), Barry Kelley as Ike Skidmore (15 February, replacing Henry Antrim), Jack Harwood ("fancy roper"; 16 February), Sherry Britton for Lotta and Owen Martin for Cord Elam (17 February), and Jane Lawrence ("Gertie and understudy"; 20 February), plus a few replacement singers and dancers for those individuals (mostly chorus and dancers) removed from the cast on 10 February, presumably for not having turned up or for other inadequacies. Britton's signing (as Lotta) was reported in a Guild publicity tactic that seems to have backfired: the *Boston Daily Record* and other Boston papers picked up the story on and after 26 February with some prurient interest, given that she was a well-known burlesque star there. Jane Lawrence's call on the 20th seems to have been a result of second thoughts: she was in the original call for 8 February

7. Marc Platt and Katharine Sergava (dream-Curly and dream-Laurey) were two of the classically trained dancers brought from the professional ballet to Broadway to perform in *Oklahoma!* Here they pose for a publicity shot on the set for "Out of My Dreams." (Vandamm)

but had been removed from the cast on the 10th, with her role to be taken by Elaine Anderson (who would be assistant stage manager).[72] Her return may be linked to the eventual decision to remove Lotta and therefore to give Gertie a more prominent role (as the eventual wife of Ali Hakim).

This more or less fixed the cast for the New Haven and Boston tryouts and the New York opening. By this time, too, the intended salaries were fairly settled, save for some last-minute negotiations (especially as the show seemed to be emerging as a success). An undated memorandum by Helburn, probably from late February or early March 1942, lists them all. The details here for the principals appear in table 2.1; those for the chorus and dancers tended to be either $75 per week on the road and $70 in New York (for example, Joan McCracken and Kate Friedlich) or $45 and $40 (Margit DeKova, Bambi Linn), although on average, the women were paid less than the men. The figures vary slightly in different lists and do not always collate directly with those in the contracts; this seems to reflect a series of ongoing negotiations and informal agreements. Betty Garde's contract of 29 January, for example, specified $450 out of town and $400 in New York; other figures suggest that she got $500 in New Haven and Boston. Helburn's memorandum also notes the bonuses to be paid after production costs were paid off — Miles White, $500 ($250 weekly); Agnes de Mille, $500 ($50 weekly) plus an additional fee of $150 — and likewise intended salary increases for Joan Roberts and Joseph Buloff (both to $350 per week). On 8 February, Helburn had also agreed that Drake's salary would be increased to $500 per week once production costs had been met. For comparison, Gertrude Lawrence was guaranteed $2,000 per week (against gross receipts, with a potential for more) for the revival of Kurt Weill's *Lady in the Dark* on Broadway opening on 27 February 1943 (after a highly successful tour). At the other end of the scale, the lesser chorus and dancers' salaries were lower than the current Equity minimum, recently raised from $50 per week to $57.50.[73]

The total weekly salary costs according to the Helburn memorandum were $8,822.50 for New Haven and Boston, and $5,830 for New York. This is an increase on Haggott's preliminary salary list of 9 February (including $200 for Lotta), which gives totals (including conductor, stage manager and assistant, company manager, and press agent) of $6,651 in New Haven and Boston, and $5,655 in New York. The later figure for New Haven/Boston was higher not just because of additional out-of-town living costs, but also because the Guild had to pay for a concert master and players of the harp, drums, guitar, trumpet, trombone, and French horn. (The other orchestral

Table 2.1. Proposed weekly salaries of *Oklahoma!* principals

Name	New Haven and Boston	New York
Betty Garde (Aunt Eller)	550	400
Alfred Drake (Curly)	400	400
Joseph Buloff (Ali Hakim)	325	325
Howard da Silva (Jud)	300	300
Lee Dixon (Will Parker)	300	300
Joan Roberts (Laurey)	250	250
Celeste Holm (Ado Annie)	250	225
George Church (dancer)	200	200
Jerome Whyte (stage manager)	175	150
Ralph Riggs (Andrew Carnes)	175	150
Eric Victor (dancer)	150	125
Marc Platt (dancer)	125	125
Jane Lawrence (Gertie Cummings)	125	125
Barry Kelley (Ike Skidmore)	100	100
Katharine Sergava	100	100
Jack Harwood (roper)	85	75
Owen Martin (Cord Elam)	75	75

Source: Memorandum by Helburn in *NHb* TG 118/7 (undated, but probably late February or early March 1943).

members were recruited locally.) By December 1943 the weekly salaries just for the cast amounted to $6,123.06, and in May 1944 it was estimated (for the purpose of costing the reduced-price tickets for the weekly special matinee for the armed forces) that each weekday performance of *Oklahoma!* cost the Guild in total $1,837.63, and slightly more on Sundays.[74]

Once the "stars" had been excluded from the reckoning, Langner concentrated on building up the myth of *Oklahoma!* conforming to the Guild's original principles of creating an ensemble on the basis of emerging talent rather than name recognition. On 7 January 1943 the *Daily News* reported, "The cast is composed of unknowns in the hope that the Riggs-Rodgers-Hammerstein show will turn out to be another *Show Boat* and launch a lot of new stars." Early reviewers also made the point (encouraged, we have seen, by the Guild's press office), and Langner emphasized it in an internal memorandum on the publicity for the touring national company established in August–September 1943: "The play *Oklahoma!* is not a starring vehicle for anybody and does not require stars as demonstrated by the New York company, all the members of which were unknown."[75] Rodgers later adopted the same rhetoric in his autobiography. However, the original cast of *Oklahoma!* was not entirely "unknown"—for the full list, see table 2.2—and indeed, many of its members had had quite notable careers. The details of "Who's Who in the Cast" in the first New York program (31 March 1943) gives the usual thumbnail sketches of the principals. Betty Garde (Aunt Eller) had last appeared on Broadway in 1939 (in *The Primrose Path*), had been involved in the 1941 Westport production of *Liliom* (making her a "Guild alumnus"), and was also well known on radio. Alfred Drake (Curly) "is one of Broadway's most versatile performers," having started his career in Gilbert and Sullivan, then operetta on Broadway (including *White Horse Inn* in 1936–37) and musicals (*Babes in Arms* and others) and straight dramatic leads, including Orlando in *As You Like It* (1941), and *Yesterday's Magic* (1942); he is also noted as an author, currently translating Offenbach's *La Belle Hélène* for performance. Joseph Buloff (Ali Hakim) had appeared in John Crump's *Don't Look Now* (1936) and Dan Goldberg's *Call Me Ziggy* (1937) and had also been in the Guild's production of Ben Hecht's *To Quito and Back* (1937); recent comic successes included Isabel Leighton and Bertram Bloch's *Spring Again* (1941–42) and Joseph A. Fields and Jerome Chodorov's *My Sister Eileen* (1942), and his performance in the latter as Appoppolous, "the irrepressible Greek," had made him "the most sought-after comedian hereabouts." Joan Roberts (Laurey) was "a comparative newcomer to Broadway," having made her debut in 1941–42 in the Romberg-Hammerstein *Sunny River*; she also had credits for the St. Louis Municipal Opera Company and operettas in Los Angeles and Dallas, and in other summer seasons (including *No, No, Nanette*, *Girl Crazy*, *Naughty Marietta*, and *Hit the Deck*). Lee Dixon (Will Parker), originally an accountant and then a professional basketball player, had appeared in films in the 1930s and had performed on Broadway in 1940 in the Rodgers and Hart *Higher and Higher*. Howard da Silva (Jud) was formerly a member of the Civic Repertory Theatre, had appeared on Broadway in Clifford Odets's *Golden Boy* (1937–38) and with the Playwrights' Company in Robert Sherwood's *Abe Lincoln in Illinois* (1938–39) and Elmer Rice's *Two on an Island* (1940; incidental music by Kurt Weill)—the playbill entry ignores the controversial *The Cradle Will Rock*—and more recently had been in half a dozen films. Celeste Holm (Ado Annie) had just played in John Van Druten and Lloyd Morris's *The Damask Cheek*, and her other credits included two Guild productions, Saroyan's *The Time of Your Life* (1939–40) and Patterson Greene's *Papa Is All* (1942), although *Oklahoma!* was her first musical role.

Table 2.2. The original cast of *Oklahoma!*

Aunt Eller	Betty Garde
Curly [McClain]	Alfred Drake
Laurey [Williams]	Joan Roberts
Ike Skidmore	Barry Kelley
Fred	Edwin Clay[a]
Slim	Herbert Rissman[a]
Will Parker	Lee Dixon
Jud Fry	Howard da Silva
Ado Annie Carnes	Celeste Holm
Ali Hakim	Joseph Buloff
Gertie Cummings	Jane Lawrence
Ellen	Katharine Sergava[b] (dream-Laurey)
Kate	Ellen Love[a]
Sylvie	Joan McCracken[b]
Armina	Kate Friedlich[b]
Aggie	Bambi Linn[b]
Andrew Carnes	Ralph Riggs
Cord Elam	Owen Martin
Jess	George Church[b] (dream-Jud)
Chalmers	Marc Platt[b] (dream-Curly)
Mike	Paul Shiers[a]
Joe	George Irving[a]
Sam	Hayes Gordon[a]
Singers [male]	John Baum, Edwin Clay, Hayes Gordon, George Irving, Carl Nelson, Herbert Rissman, Paul Shiers, Robert Penn
Singers [female]	Elsie Arnold, Harvey Brown, Suzanne Lloyd, Ellen Love, Dorothea McFarland, Virginia Oswald, Faye Smith, Vivienne Simon
Dancers [male]	Kenneth Buffet, Jack Dunphy, Gary Fleming, Eddie Howland, Ray Harrison, Eric Kristen
Dancers [female]	Diana Adams, Margit DeKova, Bobby Barrentine, Nona Feid, Rhoda Hoffman, Maria Harriton, Kate Friedlich, Bambi Linn, Joan McCracken, Vivian Smith, Billie Zay

Source: Program issued for the New York premiere, with names given in order of appearance. The New Haven program has seventeen named characters and the Boston ones eighteen. The publicity flyer for New Haven advertised a "cast of sixty"; the real number was forty-seven. Nor do the New Haven and Boston programs list separate dancers for "Many a New Day" (in New York: Joan McCracken, Kate Friedlich, and Katharine Sergava); and in the dream-ballet, "Jud's Post Cards" are listed together (in New York, Joan McCracken, Kate Friedlich, and Margit DeKova were given separate billing). This seems to have been at least in part a result of pressure from the dancers and their agents.

The printed libretto does not include text for Ellen (save, perhaps by mistake, singing in "Out of My Dreams," and speaking in act 2, scene 3), Sylvie, Armina, Aggie, Jess, Chalmers, or Sam; all

continued

Table 2.2. Continued

---

of these are dancers save Sam, who is ordered by Aunt Eller to play the banjo at the end of act 2, scene 1. But the printed libretto does include text for Vivian (Vivienne in early typescript copies) and Virginia in act 1, scene 3 (taken by Vivienne Simon and Virginia Oswald in the chorus?), a Farmer, a Man (another farmer), Dorothy, and Tom in act 2, scene 1, and Second Girl and a Man in act 2, scene 3. Presumably, some of these names were in-house jokes, for example, Armina (Armina Marshall, Langner's wife), Aggie (Agnes de Mille), and Dorothy (the name of the wives of Hammerstein and Rodgers). Later, Gemze de Lappe, who danced dream-Laurey in London, was cast as "Terry" (Helburn).
[a] Also listed in the chorus.
[b] Principal dancers also given separate credit in individual numbers. Friedlich, Linn, and McCracken are also listed among the dancers.

Ralph Riggs (Carnes) had most recently been on Broadway in Irving Berlin's *Louisiana Purchase* (1940–41) and had played in George Gershwin's *Of Thee I Sing* (1931–32) and *Let 'Em Eat Cake* (1933–34), and Vernon Duke's *The Show Is On* (1936–37), as well as in straight drama; he, too, had credits with the St. Louis Municipal Opera. It was not a star-studded cast, but it was by no means inexperienced or undistinguished.

Finding Investors

Lawrence Langner's evident involvement in the preparations for *Oklahoma!* was somewhat unusual: he tended to spend more time in Washington working for the National Inventors Council, but he took six weeks' leave to support Helburn and later also attended the tryouts.[76] However sympathetic he might have been to "Helburn's Folly," he must also have been concerned about impending financial disaster. On 1 May 1942 Langner noted to Warren Munsell, "With the war on, the future uncertain, and a loss of over $8,000 per month since we started this season, the order of the day is economy and economy," and Helburn claimed that in early 1942 the Guild had only $30,000 left in the bank.[77] In late April or early May 1942, however, Marcus Heiman and Lee Shubert, two prominent theatrical figures, came to some kind of rescue: on 5 May, Munsell reported enthusiastically to the Guild on Heiman and Shubert's proposal to finance the entire 1942–43 season (including a musical based on *Green Grow the Lilacs*) with a 50–50 share of profits: "In special cases they will finance the amount of money that the Guild wants on a proportionate basis. . . . In some cases they might be willing to permit the Guild to have a reserve amount of investment for itself." This arrangement, which would have solved all financial problems in a stroke, seems to have operated for part of the season, but not, at least directly, for *Oklahoma!* for reasons which remain unclear. (With Rodgers on board, did the Guild view the show as warranting a gamble on a "special case" or a "reserve amount"?) But certainly, when it came to financing a musical, Helburn and Langner were out of their depth. At some time during the second half of 1942, Rodgers was asked to provide the cost sheets for *By Jupiter* to give an idea of what might need to be considered in financial terms, and at the same point, Helburn also noted hopefully that "Max Gordon said he would like to work on this play with us. He also suggested he would be able to get some more money for it."[78] Gordon had already promised Hammerstein on 23 September, "When you are ready, I will get together with you about digging up money for the show and I will personally put money into it" (which presumably refers to *Green Grow the Lilacs* unless this is the tail end of negotiations over *Carmen Jones*). He was a well-known producer, and a Broadway talent spotter for Columbia Pictures; he had also produced the Kern-Hammerstein *Very Warm for May* (1939) and the Romberg-Hammerstein *Sunny River* (1941). But in the world of theatrical investment, something "said" or "suggested" is hardly a commitment, and Gordon's own eventual financial involvement seems to have been somewhat less than direct.

The financial situation did not improve: Langner said that in late 1942 and early 1943 the Guild had just $30,000 (the same figure given by Helburn for early 1942), and Helene Hanff begins the account of *Oklahoma!* in her memoirs with the bleak financial picture in December—rumors spread of bankruptcy—particularly when it became evident that the Guild production of *The Russian People* (which opened on the 29th) would be a flop (according to Hanff, the sixteenth in a row).[79] For *Oklahoma!* the initial goal had been to raise nearly $100,000—a figure confirmed by Helburn in a memo of 8 January 1943 to Warren Munsell (now in the army and based in London)—which was far more than a normal Guild play (usually capitalized between $15,000 and $35,000, with weekly running costs of $5,000 to $7,000), but less than the $125,000 projected for Cole Porter's *Something for the Boys*, which opened on 7 January 1943.[80] The figure for *Oklahoma!* soon settled around $90,000, the contributors to which would own shares in 60 percent of the show (so a $1,500 investment "bought" 1 percent), the remaining 40 percent being owned by the Guild. Investors' return would be an apportionment of the operating profit, representing 70 to 75 percent of

gross receipts (30 percent of the weekly gross up to $20,000 went to the the-
ater, then 25 percent thereafter) less royalties, salaries, and other expenses.
Investors would similarly benefit from the sale of any rights. Investment was
not easily forthcoming, however, and by late December 1942, the Guild appears to have decided to seek external advice, entering into some kind of
relationship with David Lowe, who worked out of an office in Suite 5111, 30
Rockefeller Plaza. Lowe's letterhead does not identify the nature of his business, although an article in the *New York Times* on 15 February 1943 refers to
him as a figure in radio and an impresario from Roslyn, Long Island, seeking
to break into Broadway management. In Roslyn he managed (beginning in
1940) the Cabal Players at the Millpond Playhouse; in late 1947 he was producing on Broadway; and in 1948 he ran David Lowe Theatre Productions
(not from the same address).

Lowe's initial pitch for the task of raising funds was wholly enthusiastic. Following a meeting with Helburn on 29 December 1942 (the day *The
Russian People* opened), he wrote on the 31st that the Guild musical had
tremendous potential. It was important, he said, not to give the impression
of looking for money but, rather, to give individuals the impression of a
once-in-a-lifetime opportunity to earn a share in great theater: "The idea
of cocktail parties at Mr. Langner's residence, with the two leads singing
selections from the show, is excellent. Always, however, with this thought in
mind. The Guild does not need the money, but is willing for the first time
to accept small outside investments. In this way, it is merely one step further
than the subscription plan employed by the Guild." He felt that with an estimated $75,000 for the cost of the show, and the Guild contributing $25,000,
making the sums add up should be easy, especially if the Guild were to produce an "attractive brochure." After all, Howard Lindsay and Russel Crouse
had raised $67,000 selling shares in *Strip for Action* (opened 30 September
1942), "a show which comes no where near approaching the potentialities
of *Green Grow the Lilacs*."

After a second meeting on 4 January, Lowe adopted a more measured
approach in a letter to Helburn written the next day; it also seems to have
been agreed that he would be paid $50 per week for his services. The Guild's
commitment was now $40,000 (perhaps because of the $15,000 bond required to cushion the performers and stagehands from a flop). Lowe needed
to present a strategy: "A select list of potential investors would be prepared
from names supplied by you, Mr. Langner, Miss Williams, and myself. I will
call them as a representative of the Theatre Guild and ask for an appoint-

ment. I would explain the Guild is trying a new experiment in permitting outsiders to invest in a production, a certain portion of the production being split up into small shares for this purpose." Lowe also listed twelve major selling points of the show, including music by Rodgers, words by Hammerstein, designs by Ayers, dances by de Mille, the investment opportunities (especially if a film deal was in the offing), and the "past success of *Porgy and Bess.*" It all seemed plausible enough, and Helburn, Langner, and John Haggott put their heads together to come up with a list dated 10 January 1943, noting who might be approached personally, and who by their new "representative." It is also likely that this initiative prompted the Guild to draw up a draft contract for a limited partnership called "Oklahoma Associates" in early 1943 (which seems never to have been invoked).

When it came time for Lowe to produce his report on 17 February 1943, hard-edged reality had set in. He glumly recounted having attended two auditions arranged at the apartments of Natalie (Mrs. Vivian) Spencer, a friend of Helburn's, and of Jules Glaenzer, the head of Cartier and a friend of Rodgers's; other documents reveal that they took place on 15 and 28 January, respectively. This was no doubt part of what Rodgers described as an arduous tour of "the penthouse circuit," with Alfred Drake and Joan Roberts in tow to sing highlights from the show while Hammerstein read extracts from the libretto (and also sang with Drake in "Pore Jud Is Daid").[81] In his autobiography, Robert Russell Bennett noted, "When those of us who were to work on the production met for a hearing of the music, it was at the home of Jules Glaenzer, theater's biggest fan of the era"; anecdotal evidence also links the inception of the song "Oklahoma" to a taxi ride shared by Helburn and Hammerstein on the way to an audition at Glaenzer's (when Helburn proposed "a song about the earth—the land"); and Glaenzer hosted the first-night party for *Oklahoma!*[82] According to Lowe, six were present at the Glaenzer audition, and twelve at Mrs. Spencer's, although the latter figure was inflated by the presence of individuals whose investment was already (so it seems) guaranteed, including Herbert and Ruth Langner (Lawrence's parents) and Lemuel Ayers. There also seems to have been a larger gathering hosted by Natalie Spencer and later described by Langner: "She generously gave us a large party, inviting guests who were in the habit of backing plays, and Dick, Oscar, Alfred and Joan—like a little band of itinerant musicians—played and sang the songs while Oscar explained the story of the play. Alas, neither the songs nor the speeches were persuasive, for among all those present, only two persons were found to invest in the play, and

this only to the tune of $2,ooo."[83] These two small investors were probably
Sherman and Marjorie Ewing, while Jules Glaenzer declined, as did Lillian
Gish (who had played in the Guild's *Mrs. Sycamore* in November 1942) and
(on another occasion) Katharine Hepburn. Reactions were famously cool:
Helburn later recalled a chillingly dismissive "I don't like plays about farm
hands."[84] Lowe conscientiously provided a detailed account of his attempts
to contact those who had attended, and others on the Guild list, presenting
a woeful tale of unreturned phone calls, missed appointments, and trans-
parent excuses: it was wartime, the script was not interesting enough, and
there were not enough stars in the cast. He did note wryly, however, that he
had gained some invitations to summer residences in Florida.

Success or no, Lowe wanted compensation for his efforts. He made the
point that at least some of his contacts had borne fruit; the Guild countered
that even if Lowe knew some of the eventual investors in *Oklahoma!* their
money came by a different route. In early March 1944 the Guild asked some
of the investors for an account of how they had been moved to contribute.
On 4 March, Sherman Ewing (writing to Langner) was clear: "Mr. Oscar
Hammerstein, 2nd mentioned the project to us before he had completed
the book. Upon completion of the book he sent it to us and invited us to
an audition of the music. After the audition of the music he asked us if we
would be interested in investing and we told him that we would. As far as
I can remember no other person suggested the possibility of our investing
in *Oklahoma*[!] and certainly Mr. Hammerstein was the only person who
was in any way responsible for our decision." Jules E. Brulatour, on 8 March
1944, denied Lowe's claim of influence, saying that he had been persuaded
to invest by Max Gordon; James Stroock of Brook Costume Co. also ruled
out Lowe on 10 March 1944. These requests for information were in response to a lawsuit instituted by Lowe, who claimed not just some recompense for his fund-raising "successes" but also consultancy fees for advice
on casting, scenery sketches, script cuts, budgeting, and screen rights. He
settled for an *ex gratia* payment of $14,500 on 19 March 1946.[85]

Langner continued his own fund-raising efforts within the New York theatrical community. Harry Cohn of Columbia Pictures said that the studio
was encouraged to invest after he had heard "an audition in Carnegie Hall
during which Richard Rodgers played the score with Oscar Hammerstein 2d
interpolating continuity between songs by Alfred Drake."[86] A similar occasion is suggested in Langner's letter to the playwright Bertram Bloch of
5 January 1943:

I am sending you herewith the mss. of *Green Grow the Lilacs*. There is to be an audition of the music at Studio 520, Steinway Hall, Friday January 8th at 4 P.M. and we would very much like you to come and bring with you anyone else you think might be interested.

We are quite excited about the possibilities of this and think a deal can be worked out by which you can have an interest in the play and own the picture rights on an extremely inexpensive basis; in fact, possibly the biggest bargain that can be had for a Rodgers and Hammerstein musical.[87]

It may or may not have been a good move to hold this audition the day after Cole Porter's *Something for the Boys* opened to rave reviews. Strictly speaking, however, the picture rights were not Langner's to offer. Lynn Riggs had sold the rights to *Green Grow the Lilacs* to RKO Pictures on 10 September 1935, and RKO had passed them on to MGM on 10 March 1936; negotiations for the Guild to retrieve them began in mid-July 1942. When the Guild tried to interest MGM in investing in the show, Helburn had been hoping that the studio would provide around $75,000, but the best to be done was an option signed on 23 January 1943 to purchase back the rights either for $40,000 no later than two days before the New York premiere of *Oklahoma!* or for $50,000 within four weeks after (the option was exercised on 9 April 1943).[88] Quite apart from the financial issues, the MGM deal was necessary to enable Rodgers and Hammerstein to sign their contract with the Guild (on the same day as the MGM signing), and the lack of it had created problems with earlier fund-raising, in particular from other film companies. On 17 November 1942 Helburn had written to Warren Munsell, "Max Gordon says Columbia is interested in *Green Grow* but I'm trying to use this to force Metro's hand. So far no luck." By 29 December she was downcast: "The Metro tie-up on *Green Grow* has proved something of a boomerang as no other picture company will play ball with us under these arrangements. We will either have to buy the picture outright from Metro for quite a sum or try and raise the money entirely out of the picture business. All Max's talk has turned into hot air." The MGM deal (requiring no money up front) at least provided something of a compromise.

The details of the investors in *Oklahoma!* reveal the position in terms of the amount of money gained and the timing of its receipt (see table 2.3), even if matters are further confused by the fact that shares were subsequently transferred and subdivided.[89] Broadly speaking, the investors divide into two groups: private individuals or companies on the one hand, and what the Guild called the "pool" on the other. Two film moguls, evidently brought

in by Max Gordon, were tempted to invest: Cohn and the independent producer Jules E. Brulatour, who probably had no film interest, given that he
paid his money before the signing of the deal with MGM.[90] Sherman and
Marjorie Ewing, Ralph Friedman (a stockbroker), Lilian Riegelman (her
husband, Charles, was an attorney), and William Rose II appear to have
been private investors. However, the Ewings (New York socialites, it seems)
had been dabbling in the theater since their marriage in 1938—they also
invested in *One Touch of Venus*—and they produced plays and revues on
Broadway later in the 1940s and in the early 1950s, including Benjamin Britten's *The Rape of Lucretia*, opening at the Ziegfeld Theatre on 29 December
1948 and directed by Agnes de Mille.[91] Other investors were already linked
to the Guild, some, like Lawrence Langner's parents, by blood: Herbert
Langner's share was later transferred to his wife, Ruth. Others took their
investment in lieu of payment, whether as a gamble or because the Guild
pleaded poverty. We have seen that Lemuel Ayers accepted $1,000 of his
$3,000 fee for the stage design as a share in the show. Likewise, Brooks Cos-
tume Co. (the Guild dealt with James E. Stroock) took $5,000 off the cost
of the costumes for *Oklahoma!* and treated it as an investment: this was not
an unusual arrangement, it seems, from subsequent correspondence with
Stroock, and John Haggott later said that he tried a similar deal with Vail
Scenic Construction Co. for the sets, but they turned him down.[92] The playwright S. N. Behrman was also part of the Guild "family," as was Al Greenstone, who published and sold souvenir programs for its productions. Still
somewhat murky is the involvement of the so-called Guild Associates, represented by Joseph E. Swan, a prominent stockbroker: according to Theatre
Guild documents, this entity had contributed to production costs at least
since 1940, although it was also viewed as problematic. According to Langner, Swan and his daughter were early attendees at the Steinway Hall auditions, and he was so delighted that he decided to invest 10 percent of the
capital needed.[93] However, this may have been a cover story. By 18 March
the Guild Associates' $15,000 share had been transferred to another corpora-
tion in which Swan seems to have been involved, American Trusteed Funds
Inc. On 30 October 1943 Armina Marshall bought back (for $15,000) half
the share held by American Trusteed Funds—the rest later got assigned to
other individuals—and then almost immediately sold just under half of her
new share to Fania Marinoff. This may well suggest some kind of wheeling
and dealing in the initial funding stages.

Table 2.3. Investors in *Oklahoma!*

	Date of investment (all 1943)	Amount
"Private" investors		
J. [Jules] E. Brulatour Inc.	14 January	$5,000
Herbert Langner	29 January	1,000
Lemuel Ayers	30 January	1,000
Guild Associates Inc.	3 February	15,000
Al Greenstone	3 February	1,250
Marjorie H. Ewing	3 February	1,000
Sherman Ewing	3 February	1,000
Brooks Costume Co., Inc.	8 February	5,000
Columbia Pictures Corporation	24 February	15,000
S. N. Behrman	9 March	5,000
Lilian Riegelman	15 March	2,500
Ralph Friedman	15 March	2,500
William Rose II	17 March	2,500
"Pool"	9 March	
Select Operating Corp.		9,375
Theatre Guild Inc.		6,250
Marcus Heiman		3,125
Max Gordon		3,125
American Theatrical Co.		1,562.50
M.G. Plays		1,562.50
(Bond)		15,000
Total		97,750

Sources: Various documents in Wc TG 12, the most useful of which is a summary dated 3 April 1953 listing the names, the dates of initial agreements, and details of subsequent transactions; this can be further clarified by a summary of April 1947, which reveals how shares later changed hands. Dates of investment reflect the earliest documented indication of a commitment to give; the actual money often arrived a few days later.

These investors were insufficient to keep the show afloat during its preparatory stages, such that the Guild had to rely on what was called the "pool" in a memorandum of 9 March, two days before the New Haven opening. This memorandum appears to reflect some kind of prior agreement—the 9 March memorandum refers to an "understanding"—and may have involved a mutation of the funding arrangement described by Munsell on 5 May 1942. In effect, the Guild teamed up with Lee Shubert of the Select Operating Corp. (owner of the St. James Theatre) and Marcus Heiman (acting on behalf of Max Gordon, Gordon's M.G. Plays, and the American Theatre Co. based in St. Louis); Heiman and Shubert were also president and vice president, respectively, of the United Booking Office and had some interest in the touring arm of the Guild. They each offered $9,375 (Heiman's sum was split between him and those he represented), and the Guild $6,250 ($25,000 in total): they also guaranteed their respective portions of the $15,000 bond, which increased their percentage quite favorably. This certainly injected some much needed money—Langner called it in the next day—the need for which was even greater given that some of the "investments" (for example, from Ayers, and Brooks Costume Co.) did not, in fact, represent ready cash. It might also seem advantageous to the Guild—there is no further mention of its $40,000 investment noted to David Lowe in early January (in effect, it was supplied by the "pool," which may have been the original source of this money anyway)—although by this point one starts to suspect the nature of the financial picture being presented in the documents.[94] Even a trained accountant would have a hard time getting to the bottom of the funding for *Oklahoma!* which of course may be precisely the point. Such fudging was perhaps typical of Broadway, but had the show not turned a profit, serious questions might have been asked.

On 21 January 1943 Helburn reported to Munsell the agreement with MGM over the film rights and said that she had raised about $65,000 out of the required $90,000; on 30 January she wrote, "I really think I've got the money for *Green Grow the Lilacs* though I can't quite believe it and am planning to go into rehearsal in a week. No use asking you to keep your fingers crossed as we'll probably be on the verge of opening or closing by the time you get this." Similarly, on 25 February she wrote: "We're in the thick of *Green Grow* and believe me, it's been some job. I do hope it's going to be worth the effort. I think we've got enough money though I'm still taking in anything I can get." De Mille complained vigorously about investors being invited to, and disrupting, rehearsals.[95] On 26 February, Langner wrote to the Broadway producer and director Jed Harris (Jacob Horowitz):

> Here's the script (uncut) and most of the lyrics. Can you let me have them back in the morning?
>   I don't know how you got anything out of this afternoon, but maybe you are more imaginative than I.

This was probably the chaotic run-through of the show that Celeste Holm said took place in front of thirty potential backers ten days before the crew left for New Haven (on 7 March).[96] Neither Bloch nor Harris opened his checkbook.

Unless Helburn's claim of 30 January to have found all the money for *Oklahoma!* included the "pool" arrangement, it seems to have been exaggerated. A provisional account of the various financial issues associated with *Oklahoma!* prepared by the Guild on 6 March 1943 shows the receipt of $51,500 from investors ($5,250 more than suggested by table 2.3) and expenses of $45,717.68, which with additional disbursements brought the total expenditure to $52,284.93. Some savings had been achieved by the agreement of Max Dreyfus of Chappell and Co. to assume one-third of the costs of the orchestration.[97] But the budget was looking very tight indeed. David Lowe had estimated an initial cost of $70,875, and $11,425 per week during the run. In early February 1943 John Haggott, the production manager, estimated the likely costs of *Oklahoma!* up to the New York opening at $76,130 (the figure is modified by penciled additions to $78,630), including bonds and loss provision of $25,900. A production schedule dated 5 March 1943 gives a subtotal of $68,763, added to which are bonds and loss provision of $30,200, producing a grand total of $98,963; the bulk of the increase on the early February estimate lay in the scenery ($9,150 to $16,588) and the costumes ($13,770 to $18,890).[98] This was far and away more expensive than the standard Guild play. John Haggott started quibbling over single items in the invoices that were starting to come in, and the Guild tried to cut expenses to the bone. Matters were not helped by rumored (but probably not realized) threats from the "pool" to pull the funding after New Haven—spurred, so Helene Hanff says, by the terse pan reportedly wired to the columnist Walter Winchell: "No legs, no jokes, no chance."[99] When *Oklahoma!* opened in New York, it had in effect run out of cash.

Of course, that changed very quickly. Once the hit-status of *Oklahoma!* was realized, very soon after the premiere, the Guild could breathe more easily, and the investors started to enjoy the regular checks representing their portion of the profit, sometimes accentuating their bravado and acumen in betting on an outside chance. Al Greenstone's $1,250 investment made on 3 February 1943 was later claimed to be a last-minute purchase (of a $2,500 share) from an exasperated Max Gordon at the New Haven opening; in Boston a few days after, Greenstone was reported as owning a $25,000 share of the show.[100] Meanwhile, rueful stories started to circulate about those investors who had turned down *Oklahoma!* thereby missing the opportunity of a lifetime.[101]

Opening Schedules

Success was by no means so secure in the second half of 1942. On 9 August (according to the *New York Times*), Helburn thought that *Green Grow the Lilacs* would be ready around about Christmas, but by 17 September she accepted that it would go into rehearsal only in December. On 27 November, Hammerstein told Arthur Freed that he expected rehearsals to begin "next month" and the show to open in New York about 1 February 1943, and this schedule was repeated in the *New York Times* on 3 December, with the Guild hoping to begin rehearsals in late December or early January for a February opening. However, Sara (Sadie) Greenspan, the Guild's assistant business manager, had already noted (on 25 November) that it was getting late to reserve "booking time" on Broadway for February, and it is clear that the timetable was being pushed back once more. On 14 December, Hammerstein told Dorothea MacFarland that rehearsals would begin in the "latter part" of January, and the *New York Times* confirmed this on the 21st, with rehearsals beginning around 20 January and a New York opening in March. In fact, as we have seen, rehearsals began on 8 February. There were two chief constraints here. One was that the Guild preferred in principle to open a show before Lent (Ash Wednesday was 10 March 1943), even if that principle was often violated in practice. The second, and probably more important, was that the Guild was committed to providing its subscribers with six productions in the 1942–43 season; otherwise refunds or credit would have to be issued. On 15 November the *New York Times* noted that *Oklahoma!* was to be the penultimate production of the Guild season, with a choice still to be made between two comedies for the final one; by 31 January, however, the Guild had canceled its final play (Peggy Lamson's *Respectfully Yours*), with the result that the subscribers were indeed offered recompense.[102] This may have been galling at the time, although given the eventual success of *Oklahoma!* the Guild was not going to complain.

Greenspan's memorandum suggests that the Guild knew already that it would not use the Guild Theatre for the show, whether because it was unsuitable for a musical or because some decision had already been made about selling the lease, as occurred in February 1943. (The building was taken over by WOR Mutual Radio later that year, and it was not used for theatrical purposes again until 1950.) A report in the *New York Times* on 11 February cited Helburn's explanation for the sale that the theater, with 914 seats, was "too small for the group's more expensive undertakings"—

that is, it could not generate sufficient nightly income from ticket sales—although the rumor within the Guild offices was that the sale had been forced by straitened financial circumstances.[103] The same *New York Times* article noted that the Guild already had "a verbal understanding with the Shuberts, giving it first call on the St. James, where the Guild's next offering, the musical version of *Green Grow the Lilacs* will make its home." The St. James Theatre (246 West Forty-fourth Street) was currently being used for the first Guild play of the 1942–43 season, Philip Barry's *Without Love*, and at 1,503 seats it was a much better financial bet.[104] But as always, matters were a little more complicated.

The *New York Times* article on 11 February also corrected a report on the 7th that the Guild musical would open at the Forty-sixth Street Theatre; this theater had been dark since *Beat the Band* closed on 12 December 1942. However, the Shuberts instead transferred the Jack Yellen and Sam Fain revue *Sons o' Fun* there from another Shubert theater, the Winter Garden, on 29 March 1943; the transfer was not anticipated, given that *Sons o' Fun* was originally to move to Philadelphia, then Washington (so said the *New York Times* on 11 February). The Winter Garden Theatre then saw the opening of the Shubert-produced *Ziegfeld Follies* on 1 April. It is not clear whether the St. James was viewed by the Guild as a better or worse option than the Forty-sixth Street Theatre—the latter was slightly smaller (1,429 seats) but seems to have been in better condition—although the initiative appears to have come from Helburn, who with typical chutzpah cabled Lee Shubert about the St. James on 8 February, noting the first rehearsal of that day and claiming that the show was "perfectly enchanting"; she also did not want the "very dirty" seats in the St. James to affect audiences and requested new slipcovers. The contract for the St. James was prepared on 11 February (the same day as the *New York Times* report), although Helburn continued to haggle on the 15th over the sharing of musicians and, again, the seat covers. The Shuberts would take 30 percent of the weekly gross up to the first $20,000, and 25 percent thereafter, sharing advertising costs, and providing twenty stagehands plus twelve musicians (and sharing ten more). The contract allowed one week's notice by either side if the weekly gross dropped below $18,000.

Choosing an opening date on Broadway (and therefore, working backward, for pre-Broadway tryouts and rehearsals) was always a matter of some complexity, and still more in the case of a large-scale production such as a musical. The schedule was always squeezed at both ends: rehearsals could not start until the book, lyrics, and music were in some kind of final shape, and Actors' Equity Association rules required cast members to receive full wages in the fifth week of rehearsal regardless of whether the show had opened. The Guild must have worked everything out by the time it issued the first rehearsal call for 8 February 1943, prompting some kind of opening in the week of 8 March (the fifth week): the Shubert Theatre in New Haven was booked for 11–13 March, and the Colonial Theatre in Boston for two weeks starting on the 15th. (The schedule was announced in the *Brooklyn Citizen* on 1 February and the *New York Times* on the 10th, without giving a date for the New York opening.) Both out-of-town theaters were under the direct or indirect control of the Shuberts, suggesting some kind of (not untypical) package.[105] The contract for the St. James prepared on 11 February specified opening on 31 March, but the Guild may have been made nervous by a report in the *New York Times* on the 11th that the *Ziegfeld Follies* would open on Broadway in the week of 29 March, confirmed in the *New York Times* on 16 February as 1 April. Once again, this was unexpected: the *Follies* was trying out in Boston, then Philadelphia, where its stay was planned to extend depending on the fortunes of *Sons o' Fun* at the Winter Garden (where the *Follies* would open).[106] It seems that the Shuberts were playing both ends against the middle, using the *Follies* and (to a lesser extent) *Sons o' Fun*, in which they had a greater interest as producers (rather than just backers or theater owners) as both competition and insurance against *Oklahoma!* This was not unusual in the cutthroat world of Broadway, although the Guild may have started to feel out of its league: on 16 February, the *New York Times* carried a rumor that the Guild was undecided whether to keep *Oklahoma!* in Boston for a third week so as (it implied) to avoid the clash, and even on 16 March, when the paper again announced the intended opening of the *Follies* on 1 April, it gave no date for the Guild musical.[107] Postponement seems to have been considered seriously within the Guild offices: on 26 February, Langner (always more cautious than Helburn) noted in support of Alfred Drake's appeal against being drafted into the army that the show would open in New York in the second week of April.[108] However, a change of plan would have caused serious contractual difficulties all around. By now, the die was cast: *Oklahoma!* was more or less obliged to open on Broadway in some shape or form in the week of 29 March. The 31st was finally announced in the *New York Times* on 18 March (the third day of the Boston tryout): it is not clear whether beating the *Ziegfeld Follies* by one day was just one minor triumph in a battle that the Guild feared losing.[109]

CHAPTER 3

Creative Processes

RICHARD RODGERS WAS CLEAR ON THE MERITS OF OKLAHOMA!:

> I have long held a theory about musicals. When a show works per-
> fectly, it's because all the individual parts complement each other and
> fit together. No single element overshadows any other. In a great musi-
> cal, the orchestrations sound the way the costumes look. That's what
> made Oklahoma! work. All the components dovetailed. There was
> nothing extraneous or foreign, nothing that pushed itself into the spot-
> light yelling, "Look at me!" It was a work created by many that gave
> the impression of having been created by one.[1]

Rodgers's account of the creation of the show paints a rosy picture: once
the partnership with Hammerstein had been decided upon, the composer
and librettist were in constant contact during the summer of 1942 to discuss
their plans and to hash out ideas that, in the end, reflected a true collaboration. They also took their time putting pens to paper such that, Rodgers
suggests, by virtue of their careful preparation the actual writing process was
fairly painless and quick, at least for him. He also notes one peculiarity of the
relationship: contrary to common practice, Hammerstein insisted on writing the words of the songs before the music. This was not always true, but it
certainly suited the notion of Oklahoma! being a "new," more artistic type
of musical, and the claim grew stronger with time. As for Hammerstein, he
said that he worked harder than usual on the show (another claim serving a
purpose), although he was struck by the ease and speed with which Rodgers
could capture the essence of a lyric and produce just the "right" music at
the right time (yet another).

No less common in accounts of the genesis of *Oklahoma!* is the notion of some kind of fidelity to Lynn Riggs's play, thereby making a further appeal to artistic status. Rodgers and Hammerstein, and numerous later commentators, identified the opening of the musical as setting the show on the right path, one directly inspired by the play. Contrary to the presumed standard beginning of Broadway shows, with a chorus of long-legged dancing girls, the curtain rises on *Oklahoma!* to reveal Aunt Eller churning butter on her porch, and to the sound of an offstage tenor singing "Oh, What a Beautiful Mornin'." Rodgers claimed that this emerged only after "much thought and talk" ("We didn't want to begin with anything obvious, such as a barn dance with everyone a-whoopin' and a-hollerin'"); Hammerstein says that they considered strawberry festivals and quilting parties.[2] However, they reverted to the opening of Riggs's play, also picking up on his initial stage direction: "It is a radiant summer morning several years ago, the kind of morning which, enveloping the shapes of earth—men, cattle in a meadow, blades of the young corn, streams—makes them seem to exist now for the first time." Rodgers does not note that Riggs also begins his play with Curly's offstage singing (the well-known ballad "Whopee Ti Yi Yo, Git Along Little Dogies"); nor, for that matter, does he acknowledge the potential parallel with *Porgy and Bess*, with Clara's "Summertime" (at least after the "Jazzbo Brown" opening was cut prior to the New York premiere).[3] But all the evidence suggests that "Oh, What a Beautiful Mornin'" was indeed one of the first ideas for the show: its lyrics are included, somewhat unusually, in what seems to be Hammerstein's first surviving draft libretto (where most of the other songs are just given a title and an outline of contents).[4] This supports Rodgers's claim that this was the first lyric by Hammerstein he set in their new partnership. However, the designing and writing of the show was by no means as straightforward as Rodgers's and Hammerstein's later accounts sought to suggest.

Drafting the Text

In 1949 Hammerstein gave a quite precise account of how he worked with Rodgers:

> Dick and I stay very close together while drawing up the blueprint of a play. Before we start to put words or notes on paper, we have agreed on a very definite and complete outline, and we have decided how much of the story

shall be told in dialogue and how much in song. We try to use music as much as we can. . . .

After we have passed the blueprint stage, we then work together on the interior problems. We approach the spots we have chosen for songs and we discuss each song very carefully. It is not at all unlikely that Dick will give me valuable lyric ideas and I, on the other hand, frequently contribute important suggestions for the music. I don't mean to imply that I give him ideas for melodies. I have no melodic gift whatsoever, but I have a feeling for the treatment of a score, ideas for its structure.[5]

Clearly Hammerstein had an agenda: his remarks are designed to support his claim that a composer and a librettist must "weld their two crafts and two kinds of talent into a single expression. This is the great secret of the well-integrated musical play." We shall see that the notion of "integration" was itself strongly coded. It was also aided by the fact that Hammerstein tended to write both the book and the lyrics for almost all his musicals, although in the case of *Oklahoma!* much of the "book" was provided by Riggs's play, and anyway, the combined authorship of book and lyrics was not quite as unusual as has been assumed: Hart provided the lyrics and the book for *Babes in Arms* (1937), while both Hart and Rodgers were credited with the books for *On Your Toes* (1936; also with George Abbott), *I Married an Angel* (1938), and *By Jupiter* (1942).

An earlier account by Hammerstein of the creation of *Oklahoma!* (in the *New York Times* on 23 May 1943) fills out the picture: "Dick Rodgers and I tackled the job slowly. This was midsummer [1942]. It was hot. My home is in Doylestown, Pa. His is in Fairfield, Conn. We had lunch in New York twice a week for several weeks. We would talk over the play and then go to our respective homes in the country and think over the things we had talked about."[6] Hammerstein also claimed here that he and Rodgers were concerned about the final scenes, including the shivaree, with its "vaguely Freudian flavor in the comments and the behavior of the men"—they decided to keep a toned-down version because it was a well-known feature of the play—and then the killing of Jud and its long aftermath: it took "several discouraging conversations," Hammerstein said, before he and Rodgers hit upon the trial as an expedient conclusion.

In this same 1943 account Hammerstein dated the solution of the ending to a weekend in "late August" 1942, when he and his wife were staying with Richard and Dorothy Rodgers in Fairfield. By this time he must have been thinking quite extensively about his adaptation, given that on 20 August he

turned down a request from E. P. Conkle of the Department of Drama at
the University of Texas at Austin to read Conkle's comedy-fantasy play on
the life of the cowboy Pecos Bill on the grounds that "I am working on the
adaptation of *Green Grow the Lilacs*, which is also a cowboy play, and to
prevent future misunderstandings, I would prefer not to have any access to
the manuscript." He also wrote to Victor Roudin on 24 August declining an
invitation to a cocktail party on the 27th: "I am afraid I won't be able to come
because I am going down to Doylestown Wednesday [26th] where I expect
to do some concentrated writing for a solid week." The "solid week" was
interrupted, however, for by the weekend he was in Fairfield. He said that
he arrived that Friday evening (the 28th) with the opening lyric, "Oh, What
a Beautiful Mornin'"—after he and Rodgers had struggled "for a long time
before this" with how to open the show with a chorus—and that Rodgers set
it to music on Saturday morning: "The opening song was itself a very significant moment in the 'childhood' of the play and influenced a great many
other of its later-developed characteristics." Rodgers, in turn, claimed that
when he saw the lyric of "Oh, What a Beautiful Mornin'," "I was a little sick
with joy because it was so lovely and so right"; he also said that he composed the song in ten minutes. By May 1944 the story had changed—the
song had been written over a cold chicken sandwich at Sardi's—although
the Friday night/Saturday morning version was preferred in the speeches
and press releases celebrating the tenth anniversary of *Oklahoma!*[7]

Although the beginning and ending of *Oklahoma!* may have been fixed
in late August 1942, there was a great deal to sort out in between. The problems are clear in the draft librettos and the sketches and working copies of
lyrics that reflect the evolution of the show from August 1942 through the
rehearsals and tryouts (for their details, see Appendix B). The drafts concern
the spoken dialogue and the placement of the songs (but not, for the most
part, their lyrics). Three survive: an early version of act 1, scene 1 (*Draft1*);
a text for the complete show that Hammerstein submitted to the Library
of Congress for copyright purposes on 19 November 1942 (*Draft2*); and a
revision of *Draft2* with a new version of act 2, scene 3 (*Draft3*). For the
lyrics, we have a series of sketches by Hammerstein, plus lyric sheets given to
Rodgers (they survive with his voice-piano scores) and disseminated in various formats to other members of the production team. These latter materials
provide evidence of genesis from the earliest stages of a song's conception
to the latest fine-tuning; they sometimes give details of otherwise unknown
spoken dialogue incorporated within individual songs (as in "The Farmer

and the Cowman"); and in some cases, they also provide details in sketch or final form of songs that were dropped. But it is clear that the spoken dialogue and the lyrics were brought together into a single text only very late in the creation of the materials for the show, which was a common enough practice in this repertory.

The chronology of these drafts remains hazy. *Draft1* presumably dates from late summer or early fall 1942; certainly it precedes *Draft2*, given that the version of act 1, scene 1 in *Draft2* revises *Draft1* significantly. Presumably, *Draft1* was preceded by, and typed from, an annotated copy of Riggs's printed play, which seems to have been how Hammerstein began, given that we have little or no sketch or similar material for the dialogue.[8] *Draft2* must have been completed by early November, given that copies were being distributed by the Theatre Guild from the 16th on, and one was submitted to the Library of Congress on the 19th. Both drafts, however, may contain within them earlier versions of portions of the text, and so may each be conflations. We cannot tell when *Draft2* was revised and retyped as a more complete *Draft3*. However, the distribution of scripts on or about 4 February 1943, including one in "blue and silver covers (with new last scene)," suggests that it came quite late in the process and also was used in the first rehearsals (which started on 8 February).[9] This new last scene may well have been written in the second half of January 1943, for on 11 January, Carl E. Weininger sent Hammerstein some songs for comments, and Hammerstein replied on 2 February, apologizing for not having had time to look at them: "I would have written to you sooner and returned your manuscripts but I have been away in the country finishing my own script for rehearsal and found your letter awaiting me when I came back."

In an article in the *New York Times* on 31 March 1946, Hammerstein admitted that for him producing a libretto was difficult. "Writing comes darned hard to me," he said:

> I do most of it on our farm in Doylestown. There I have a room with one of those tall old-fashioned desks you used to see in shipping offices. It takes me a long time to get started, and even then the words come slowly. I keep walking up and down the room and when I get what I want I go over to the desk and write in longhand with a soft pencil. I often wonder how many miles an act I walk. But I keep changing what I have written all the time, and when I fill one sheet of paper, I usually have trouble deciphering my own handwriting.
>
> The lyrics are easier for me than the dialogue, but even so, they don't

write themselves. Many a time after I have sweated two or three days over some verses, the composer will turn out the tune in a few hours. I remember one night my wife and I dropped in at Dick Rodgers's house. I had a lyric with me that I had just finished. I showed it to Dick and he said "Excuse me for a few minutes." He came back in ten, with the tune for the "Oklahoma!" song.[10]

Some of these travails are apparent in the *Oklahoma!* drafts. As we have seen, Hammerstein for the most part separated the writing of the book and that of the lyrics. Thus in the drafts the spoken dialogue is presented complete, with stage directions. But with the exception of "Oh, What a Beautiful Mornin'," Aunt Eller's "I Know a Cowboy" (in I.1 in *Draft1* and *Draft2*, but then removed), the Laurey-Curly love duet (untitled in *Draft1*; "Someone Will Teach You" in *Draft2*), and the opening of "The Farmer and the Cowman," Hammerstein provides just song titles (such as "A Surrey With Fringe on the Top" [*sic*]) and an outline description of contents. Thus in the case of "Kansas City," sung by Bud Meakins (the first name for Will Parker; *Draft1*, 1-1-13), "The idea is that Kansas City's got everything—but Annie. Develop this number into a dance, featuring Bud. He exits on the number." This also appears to have been Hammerstein's standard way of working with Jerome Kern, although the presence of the song titles may reflect the closer advance planning undertaken with Rodgers.[11] Separating the lyrics squares with what we know of Rodgers and Hammerstein's working practices, and it also makes pragmatic sense: the songs might be positioned (and allocated to specific characters) early on, but it would be foolish to write or fix them too soon. Only in *Draft3* did Hammerstein bring some of the lyrics into the main text, and then not always completely.

In terms of the dialogue, the *Draft1* version of act 1, scene 1 suggests that Hammerstein started by following the play quite closely in terms of its content, speech for speech, and also its verbal mannerisms reflecting presumed Oklahoma speech patterns ("whut" for "what," "fergit" for "forget"), plus the obvious slang. It seems clear from the content that he was working from the 1931 printed "reading version" of the play, or a close copy thereof, rather than a performance text held by the Theatre Guild. His opening stage direction quotes from the play (the "It is a radiant summer morning . . ." that both Rodgers and Hammerstein claimed set the tone of their opening), although Hammerstein had already decided to set the scene outside ("In front of the porch of Laurey's farm house. Neither a deep nor shallow set—about half a 'full-stage'") rather than in the front room of the Williams farmhouse, as in the play. The shift outdoors allowed for greater freedom of action and movement. Hammerstein also removed most of the more obscure words for which Riggs had felt it necessary to provide a glossary at the end of his printed version, and he explained certain situations, such as the nature of the Box Social and also its reason, it being Union Day (this was removed in *Draft2*). Between *Draft1*, *Draft2*, and the final version, he increasingly cut down this text, removing the wordier passages and focusing the action. In general, however, Hammerstein seems to have been as yet undecided on the precise nature of Jeeter/Jud's malevolence: in *Draft1*, Laurey is more ready to go with him to the Box Social than in either the play or the final musical. Hammerstein also tried to expand (in *Draft1*, at least) on themes to be developed later in the show, as when Aunt Eller explains the reasons behind the tensions between farmers and cowmen. Further, the growth in the role of Ado Annie, with obvious consequences particularly for Will Parker and the Peddler (in *Draft1* and *Draft2* named Kalenderian Kalazian, an Armenian), occurred only gradually: in the case of *Draft1*, the position of Ado Annie's "I Cain't Say No" is unclear due to a missing page, but this draft does not contain the proposed shotgun wedding between Annie and the Peddler, and the latter character is not yet fully developed. In broader terms, one problem is that Hammerstein had already decided (by *Draft1*) to conflate Riggs's scenes 1 and 2 in his own first scene, to expand the roles of Ado Annie and the Peddler for comic effect, and to add a fiancé for Ado Annie to create a secondary love triangle. This made the scene very long (the songs would make it longer still), as it remains in the final version: Hammerstein appears to have been nervous about the result.

Draft2 is a complete script (if still mostly without lyrics) and thus provides us with the opportunity to see a first plan for the entire show. Its status remains unclear: we have no prior material for anything but act 1, scene 1, so the *stemma* for the rest of the show is obscure. For example, in *Draft2* act 1 is preceded by a list of songs, but there is no such list preceding act 2, which may therefore come from an earlier, less fixed version. However, as we shall see, there is some sense that *Draft2* was active into early 1943 and even (with the amended final scene in *Draft3*) during the early rehearsals. Certainly its survival in multiple copies suggests that it was more than just work in progress.

Comparing the first two drafts with each other and with the final version reveals the evolution not just of the book but also of the position, allocation, and content of the songs (tables 3.1, 3.2). For act 1, scene 1, *Draft2* has

Table 3.1. Proposed musical numbers in act 1, scene 1 in *Draft1* and *Draft2*

Draft1	*Draft2*
[1] Oh, What a Beautiful Mornin' [Curly]	1. Oh, What a Beautiful Mornin' (Curly, then Eller)
[2] I Know a Cowboy [Eller]	
[3] A Surrey with Fringe on the Top [*sic*] [Curly]	2. A Surrey with Fringe on the Top [*sic*] (Curly, then Laurey and Eller)
[4] She Likes You Quite a Lot [Eller]	3. She Likes You Quite a Lot (Eller, then Boys)
[5] Kansas City [Bud Meakins] *leads to dance*	4. Kansas City (Will and Boys) *leads to dance*
[?6] [I Cain't Say No (Ado Annie with Laurey)?; page missing in draft]	5. I Cain't Say No (Ado Annie with Laurey, then Will and the Boys)
[7] All That I Want [Laurey] *leads to dance*	6. Many a New Day (Laurey and Girls)
[8] I Cain't Say No [Annie and Bud; reprise?] *leads to dance* Reprise of "Oh, What a Beautiful Mornin'" *leads to dance*	
	7. I'll Be at Your Elbow (Ado Annie and The Peddler, and Chorus)
[9] [Duet for Laurey and Curly; no title given, but chorus begins "Someone Will Tell You"]	8. Someone Will Teach You (Laurey and Curly)

Note: *Draft1* song titles are abstracted from the prose descriptions in the text; *Draft2* titles and characters follow the separate list of numbers on fol. 4r.

some changes from *Draft1*. We lose Aunt Eller's first ballad, "I Know a Cowboy," intended to be "half improvised" (*Draft1*, 1-1-4), perhaps in the spirit of the folksongs in Riggs's play; her second song, "She Likes You Quite a Lot" (still present in *Draft2* and for which a draft melody by Rodgers survives), would also be dropped, and left just as a single spoken line in the final text.[12] Reportedly, the part of Aunt Eller was subject to "constant cutting" during rehearsals, whether or not because of problems with Betty Garde, who was not known for musicals, and whose vocal range is inconsistently notated (in different octaves) in "The Farmer and the Cowman."[13] The position and role of "I Cain't Say No" is clearer in *Draft2*, and the song is reworked in a reprise with Will Parker (*Draft2*, 1-1-28), the new name for Bud Meakins, where he proposes to Ado Annie, leading to a dance: "But even as WILL is leaving a group of BOYS come in, and each, dancing with her, captures

Table 3.2. Proposed numbers in *Draft2* compared with final version

Draft2	Final version (lists main songs only, excluding music for entrances and exits, and most reprises)
Act 1, scene 1	
Oh, What a Beautiful Mornin' (Curly, then Eller)	Oh, What a Beautiful Mornin' [Curly, then Laurey]
A Surrey with Fringe on the Top [*sic*] (Curly, then Laurey and Eller)	The Surrey with the Fringe on Top [Curly, Eller, Laurey]
She Likes You Quite a Lot (Eller, then Boys)	
Kansas City (Will and Boys) *leads to dance*	Kansas City [Will, Boys, Eller] *leads to dance*
I Cain't Say No (Ado Annie with Laurey, then Will and the Boys)	I Cain't Say No [Ado Annie, then Will]
Many a New Day (Laurey and Girls)	Many a New Day [Laurey, Girls] *leads to dance*
I'll Be at Your Elbow (Ado Annie and The Peddler, and Chorus)	
	It's a Scandal! It's a Outrage! [Hakim, Boys] *leads to dance*
Someone Will Teach You (Laurey and Curly)	People Will Say We're in Love [Laurey, Curly]
Act 1, scene 2	
Folks Ud Gether Around and Sing (Curly and Jud)	Pore Jud Is Daid [Curly, Jud]
All That I Want (Jud)	Lonely Room [Jud]
Act 1, scene 3	
Peddler's Pack (Peddler and Girls) [includes "When Ah Goes Out Walkin' with Mah Baby"]	
How Would It Be? (Entire Company) *leads to dream-ballet*	Out of My Dreams [Laurey, Girls] *leads to dream-ballet*
Act 2, scene 1	
The Farmer and the Cowman [Carnes, Company] *leads to dance*	The Farmer and the Cowman [Carnes, Company] *leads to dance*
Act 2, scene 2	
[reprise of "All That I Want" (Jud)]	
	All er Nuthin' [Will, Ado Annie] *leads to dance*
[untitled, unspecified duet for Laurey and Curly]	Reprise of "People Will Say We're in Love" [Laurey, Curly]

continued

Table 3.2. Continued

Draft2	Final version (lists main songs only, excluding music for entrances and exits, and most reprises)
Act 2, scene 3	
It's Still Goin' On [Will and Company]	
leads to dance	
[Untitled "barbaric Spanish song" (Lotta)]	
[reprise of "It's Still Goin' On" or perhaps new song.]	
	Oklahoma [Company]
[reprise of "The Surrey Song"]	Finale involves reprises of "Oh, What a Beautiful Mornin'" and "People Will Say We're in Love"

her interest. She winds up dancing off with all of them." The reprise was retained in the final version (but without the marriage proposal), although the dance was dropped (except perhaps in the Boston tryout).[14] Laurey's "All That I Want" in *Draft1* has now been replaced by "Many a New Day," which seems to have been intended to maintain her feistiness. *Draft2* then has a new duet between Ado Annie and the Peddler, "I'll Be at Your Elbow," reflecting the expansion of their roles in the scene (and Carnes forcing their engagement, if not yet with a shotgun), although there are obvious problems in having them sing together (and prior to the leads) if they are not intended to become a couple in the end. In the case of this duet, Hammerstein noted (*Draft2*, 1-1-35), "The girls may be a part of the number, at the end of which, all exit," which is close to what eventually happened in the replacement for "I'll Be at Your Elbow," "Its a Scandal! It's a Outrage!" For the rest of this scene, the Laurey-Curly duet was still to be refined (as we shall see), although even in *Draft1* Hammerstein had fixed the handling of Curly's subsequent exit at the end to visit Jud in the smokehouse (so Curly says; that is, for scene 2), with Laurey left alone musing on their duet and breaking down in tears.

With Riggs's scenes 1–2 conflated in Hammerstein's scene 1, Riggs's scene 3 (which plays at the same time as his scene 2) becomes Hammerstein's scene 2 (in the smokehouse). Jeeter Fry (in the play and *Draft1*) becomes Jud Fry in *Draft2*, with the consequence that a bit-part cowboy in *Draft1* called Jed is renamed.[15] This scene in *Draft2* has the basic shape of the final version. "CURLY sings a lugubrious song, describing how he would imagine Jud's 'wake' to be. In the course of this, JUD is deeply touched by the scene and sings with Curly" (*Draft2*, 1-2-3); "Folks Ud Gether Around and Sing" (a line from the play) eventually became "Pore Jud Is Daid." As Jud and Curly play cards, Curly waxes lyrical over life on the farm over the music of "Oh, What a Beautiful Mornin'." We then have a solo for Jud ("All That I Want," transferring that title from Laurey's act 1, scene 1 song in *Draft1*), although the precise content of this number (eventually, "Lonely Room") seems to have taken a while to coalesce. The shift from a more generic "All That I Want" to the specific "Lonely Room" did, however, deny Hammerstein the opportunity to present Jud's song as a reprise in act 2, scene 2 (as planned in *Draft2*), which helps explain why Jud has nothing more to sing in *Oklahoma!*

Hammerstein's scene 3 is an addition to the play, and in *Draft2* it is somewhat ill-defined. According to his description of this scene in *Draft2* (1-3-1: "This will all be done with lyrics and music"), the girls are buying the Peddler's wares, which include the "Lixir' of Egyp'" and also sheet music of popular songs:

> Spanish-American War songs like "You don't belong to the regulars you're only a volunteer" and "Coon songs" like "Bill Bailey." In fact the Peddler, who has seen these gems performed in St. Louis[,] gives a rendition of a song like "Bill Bailey," cake-walk and all, imitating Marie Cahill or whatever artist he had seen. Then a group of girls, with a sheet of music to read from[,] sing a popular, sentimental ballad of the period in soft, "Close" harmony. One of them is probably the grandmother of the Andrews Sisters, and very likely started all this kind of trouble. The purpose of the soft harmony here, however, is mainly to create a background for the following dialogue.

(The three Andrews Sisters were a highly popular close-harmony group in the late 1930s and 1940s.) This "following dialogue" includes Aunt Eller's offer to go to the Box Social with Jud in Laurey's place (so that Laurey can go with Curly), then a long-winded version of Laurey taking the Elixir of Egypt before the dream-ballet. By page 1-3-8, Ado Annie sees Curly in the surrey in the distance in front of the setting sun, reminding her of a silhouette: "That's whut I mean . . . Sil-you-ets." At least this part of this version of scene 3 seems to have remained current up to the point of Rodgers composing "Out of My Dreams": "That's what I mean . . . sil-you-ets" is given as a text cue at the head of the lyric sheet accompanying his voice-piano score. As Ado Annie leaves, Laurey starts to sing (there is no title or outline in *Draft2*): "The song will set the mood and establish the theme of a ballet to follow." According to the song list at the beginning of act 1 in *Draft2*, the dream-ballet was to have been introduced by an ensemble number, "How Would It Be?" although this does not quite square with the lead-in to the ballet in the text.

What Hammerstein gives as "Peddler's Pack" in the list of songs for act 1 at the head of *Draft2* becomes clearer in the lyric sheet accompanying Rodgers's manuscript of "When I Go Out Walkin' with My Baby."[16] Here the action already seems to have become simplified, and there is no reference to a sentimental ballad in close harmony. Instead, the Peddler just brings out his sheet music and hams up his account of the song and its performance (the rubric also cues a boy with a mandolin):

PEDDLER

He puts his hat down over his eyes like this.
(ADO ANNIE *giggles*)
And this is how it go . . . *something* like:
(*He sings, referring to the published copy now and then*)

When Ah goes out walkin' with mah baby,

(*Spoken, aside, in confidential explanation*)
Dialect.
(*Singing again*)

Stars are dancin' in mah baby's eyes! . . .

The girls (including Gertie) form an impromptu quartet, and then Fred enters to announce that the team is hitched up; Aunt Eller tells the girls to go, and that she and Laurey will follow; and the others exit singing the song and "doing impromptu cakewalk steps." The "coon song" comes from the age of blackface minstrelsy that Hammerstein presumably thought to invoke for period color—Hughie Cannon's "Bill Bailey, Won't You Please Come Home" dates from 1902—although it remained a performance practice on Broadway and in the cinema through to the mid-1940s.[17] However, Hammerstein may have decided that it was in dubious taste. The final version removed all these shenanigans and moved more quickly into the dream sequence. Rodgers did indeed compose the music for "When I Go Out

Walkin' with My Baby," but there is no indication that it was ever orchestrated for *Oklahoma!*

The version of act 2 in *Draft2* seems less well developed, perhaps because Rodgers was out of town for part of the time that Hammerstein was working on it. Its pagination is continuous (although act and scene numbers are still given), and some of the names or characters from *Draft1* (Bud, Jeeter, Jed) occasionally creep in by mistake. Also, the locations of the three scenes (the Skidmore ranch, Skidmore's kitchen porch, a hayfield by moonlight) do not square with the scene locations at the head of the act in *Draft2* (the Skidmore ranch, the kitchen, Laurey's front porch). In general, too, the reading of act 2 here is much less fixed than that of act 1, and the text is still much more closely linked to the play than would eventually be the case.

Act 2, scene 1 covers similar ground to Riggs's scene 4 (the Box Social, although the auction is Hammerstein's addition), and it seems to have been decided early on to begin it with a communal dance number; *Draft2* gives an early version of "The Farmer and the Cowman," mixing verse, spoken dialogue, and prose description; the music then carries on through the dialogue (including the auction) and even into scene 2. However, turning the Box Social into a more significant part of the action (by way of Jud's defeat in the auction) gave less opportunity for the specialty acts that Theresa Helburn initially envisaged for this part of the show. At the end of scene 1, there is no front-of-traveler scene for Will and Ado Annie (which was a later addition in *Draft3*). Hammerstein's scene 2 separates the end of Riggs's scene 4; and scene 3 conflates the play's scenes 5–6 (the shivaree and Jud's death, then Curly's escape from jail to spend the night with his bride). But as we shall see, Hammerstein had significant difficulties with the last third of the show, after the Box Social. In part, this was because of the need to bring Jud's death to a speedier conclusion and to enact the show trial within a single scene so as to provide the necessary happy ending (the play ends before any trial, with the outcome left unclear). However, it was also because of the question of how best to bring the newly developed Ado Annie–Will–Peddler triangle to some kind of resolution. These problems extended through the New Haven and Boston tryouts.

Hammerstein's acute indecision over act 2, scenes 2–3 involved more than mere cutting, and although Hammerstein had decided on the speedy show trial by *Draft2*, if not before, getting to that point took some deliberation. He was uncertain how to handle the shivaree (still a problem in the final version) and was unclear on whether Jud's attack on Curly should involve setting a haystack on fire (as in the play), setting Laurey's house on fire (in *Draft2* and *Draft3*), or just the knife fight of the final version.[18] The Jud problem went back still farther, however. In his encounter with Laurey in act 2, scene 2, *Draft2* (2-2-27) gives him a powerful reprise of his act 1 solilo- quy, "All That I Want": "JUD now starts to sing, softly, appealingly, a reprise of the song he sang at the end of the smokehouse scene in Act One. . . . As he sings[,] LAUREY looks at him, bewildered, not knowing how to cope with such earnest and overpowering emotion. After he finishes the refrain, the music continues under his next speech." Jud does not sing here in the final version, presumably because "Lonely Room" was inappropriate for a reprise. The scene then moves to a planned love-duet between Curly and Laurey: "They now sing what will be the best song in the show—when it is written" (*Draft2*, 2-2-35). This became the rather feeble "Boys and Girls Like You and Me," eventually dropped for the reprise of "People Will Say We're in Love."

Act 2, scene 3 was subject to constant revision even during the tryouts. Quite apart from how best to construct Jud's attack on Curly and Laurey, the question remained of enabling Will Parker and Ado Annie to tie their knot, while also creating a resolution for the Peddler. In *Draft2* the scene opens as follows (2-3-36): "WILL with a group of boys and girls is singing a song about the institution of marriage, called: 'It's Still Goin' On.' Another boy plays the guitar, ADO ANNIE is with Will. The singing and guitar strumming are soft and low and form a background for the dialogue." This grows to become "a big number of movement, comedy and dancing" (2-3-38). Hammerstein then has the Peddler introduce Lotta Gonzales, "a gorgeous looking Mexi- can girl" (2-3-39) who, it turns out, has had a fling with Will during his recent trip to Kansas City ("Where there's a weel [*sic*] there's a way," she says). Lotta is to sing "a barbaric Spanish song" (2-3-41): "If there is no encore, Lotta will be thrown out of the show." This may have been intended as a so-called "eleven-o'clock number" to revive the audience at a typical low point in a Broadway musical. It is also worth noting that Hammerstein had recently engaged with another exotic Hispanic female character in his reworking of Bizet's *Carmen* as *Carmen Jones*, although there were plenty of other prece- dents currently finding favor on stage and screen, including, most obviously, Carmen Miranda, the "Brazilian Bombshell." Lotta's broader function, how- ever, is to enable Ado Annie to fight for her man—distracting the crowd from Jud's entrance and the fire—and then to restore peace. Ado Annie returns with straw on her back, hair mussed, and with a contented look: "Will and me had a misunderstandin' 'bout his trip to Kansas City. But he explained it fine" (*Draft2*, 2-3-53)—a line retained in modified form in the final version ("Will and me had a misunderstandin'. But he explained it fine"), which is usually played for laughs but makes scant sense in the new context. Then in *Draft2*, the Peddler eventually carries Lotta back onstage with two black eyes and, it is implied, pairs off with her.

As for the end of the show, Hammerstein's original plan also differs from the final version (*Draft2*, 2-3-53): Laurey and Curly are brought on in the surrey, and "Others run along-side lustily shouting and heartily singing 'The Surrey Song.' The lights lower, the crowd continues to jog along—in place—and the surrey's wheels shine like silver, and so do Laurey's and Curly's eyes as they ride side by side, finally off to the gay and happy start in life they deserve." This is, he says, "A good time to leave them," which is Hammerstein's final line in *Draft2*. He and Rodgers eventually adopted the better plan of ending with reprises of "Oh, What a Beautiful Mornin'" and (for the first curtain call) "People Will Say We're in Love," both of which are more appropriate for the ensemble than "The Surrey with the Fringe on Top," while also bringing things full circle. However, for a while at least, Hammerstein seems to have regarded the "Surrey Song" (which may or may not already have been composed) as somehow thematic to the show: we shall see that he also gave it an important place in his initial outline for the dream-ballet. Rodgers may offer an explanation: "Oscar was so moved by this song that just listening to it made him cry. He once explained that he never cried at sadness in the theatre, only at naïve happiness, and the idea of two bone-headed young people looking forward to nothing more than a ride in a surrey struck an emotional chord that affected him deeply."[19]

In general, *Draft3* gets closer to the final version, with more lyrics in the text. For act 2, scene 3 the setting is now "Behind Laurey's House. A hayfield dominates the background, the moon making silver tents of the un-baled mounds of hay." The opening song is now to be "Hale and Hearty," perhaps picking up on a sentence for Aunt Eller in the play, "You gotta be hearty, you got to be," which also appears for the first time in *Draft3*. The title suggests something closer in tone to "Oklahoma," if not quite the patriotic ode that would steal the show. According to *Draft3*, "Hale and Hearty" might lead to a dance for Will, and the music would then continue under dialogue (as with "It's Still Goin' On" in *Draft2*). Lotta then enters with the Peddler and "pitches into a barbaric Spanish song" (2-3-46; a later version just gives her a reprise of "When I Go Out Walkin' with My Baby").

Meanwhile, Curly has locked Laurey in the farmhouse to prevent her being carried off in the shivaree. Flames are seen emerging from the building, and Jud enters carrying a can of kerosene; Curly and Jud fight over the key to the house, which Curly wants to throw up to Laurey and Aunt Eller so that they can escape; and Jud dies as in *Draft2*. The rest of the earliest copy of *Draft3* follows *Draft2*, with some minor additions, ending (2-3-58) as before with the "Surrey Song." This avoids the problem of how to stage the haystack fire, while Jud is also painted as more evil. Yet as we shall see, the scene was still causing problems during the rehearsals and the tryouts. As for Lotta, at least one actress auditioned for the role (Lorraine de Woods on 19 January 1942), and two seem to have been called for rehearsal (perhaps Juanita Juarez on 8 February, and certainly Sherry Britton on the 17th). However, the part was cut soon thereafter, with the Peddler's fate being sealed more neatly by his marrying Gertie Cummings and managing her father's general store in Bushyhead.

The Lyrics

Rodgers's claim that Hammerstein insisted on providing the lyrics for the songs before he wrote the music—in contrast to standard Broadway practice—may have served a purpose, but the reality appears to have been more complex. The *Christian Science Monitor* on 3 March 1943 quoted Rodgers: "No, there wasn't any set way we worked. We were flexible. Sometimes I would write a tune first, getting the idea out of the book. Then I'd give it to Oscar and he'd write the lyrics for it. Sometimes he'd hand me a completed lyric before the tune was written or thought of, and I'd write the tune then" (but Rodgers also went on to say that he liked having the lyric first because it made composing easier given the presence of a rhythm and a theme). Robert Russell Bennett later said that in the case of the song "Oklahoma," Rodgers and Hammerstein "worked out the words and music together, part of it words first and part the other way round."[20] For "The Surrey with the Fringe on Top," too, Rodgers and Hammerstein appear to have told Margaret Case Harriman of the *New Yorker* (in early 1944), that Rodgers wrote the first and last sections of the chorus with just an image in mind—turning carriage wheels—whereas the bridge came only when Hammerstein had supplied the lyrics; Harriman also claims that Rodgers wrote or partly wrote the music before the lyrics for "Kansas City," "I Cain't Say No," and "People Will Say We're in Love" (but for the other songs, she says, the lyrics came first). Such flexibility was not, in fact, unusual: Rodgers had earlier written that with Hart the process varied, with lyric first, music first, or a tossing around of ideas. Hammerstein also said in a prepremiere interview in the *Boston Morning Globe* on 14 March 1943 (also in the *New York Post* on the 29th) that he preferred to write words to preexisting music for sentimental songs, and the words first for comic ones. Harriman suggested something similar: "According to Hammerstein and Rodgers, a love song always comes out better if the music is written first and the words fitted to it later. The boys don't know exactly why this is true, but they think it may have something to do with music being the language of love."[21]

With the exceptions noted above ("Oh, What a Beautiful Mornin'," Aunt Eller's "I Know a Cowboy," the Laurey-Curley love duet "Someone Will Teach You," and the opening of "The Farmer and the Cowman"), Hammerstein left the bulk of the lyrics until he had completed *Draft2* (by early November 1943). On 27 November he told Arthur Freed that having finished the script he and Rodgers were now working on the songs, and a report in the *New York Times* on 3 December had him "wrestling" with the lyrics. He still had some way to go even toward the end of January 1943, to judge by his letter to Laurence Schwab of the 22nd of that month: "This letter is mainly to thank you for sending me the copy of *Palmetto Country* which I have not been able to read due to the necessity of getting into rehearsal the first week in February with six unwritten numbers hanging over my head. For this same reason I will not be able to read Phil Wylie's new book [*Generation of Vipers?*] for some time. In fact, the only reading I will have time for will be my own rhymes when I have written them and the only writing I will have time for is these same rhymes which is the reason why I can't make this letter any longer." By now, Rodgers and Hammerstein had already completed at least "Oh, What a Beautiful Mornin'" (composed in August 1942 and present in *Draft2*) and "The Surrey with the Fringe on Top" (described to Alfred Drake probably in early October), plus "Pore Jud Is Daid" (which Hammerstein sang with Drake on the penthouse circuit) and perhaps the other numbers for Curly and Laurey ("Many a New Day," "People Will Say We're in Love"), which seem likely to have been used for fund-raising; in addition, "When I Go Out Walkin' with My Baby," "The Farmer and the Cowman" (partially present in *Draft2*), and "It's Still Goin' On" (starting act 2, scene 3 in *Draft2*; notes for the lyric are in the sketch folder) may have been finished in some shape or form, and Hammerstein seems already to have crafted an introduction to the dream-ballet (but not yet "Out of My

Dreams"). It is impossible to say for certain which six lyrics remained, although by this reckoning they probably included "Kansas City," "I Cain't Say No," "It's a Scandal! It's a Outrage!" (or its predecessor), and "Lonely Room"—for which Rodgers and Hammerstein would probably have waited for clarity in the casting—plus the Laurey-Curly duet for act 2 and Lotta's "barbaric Spanish song." "All er Nuthin'" and "Oklahoma" probably came later still.

This chronology, as well as Hammerstein's "wrestling," is broadly confirmed by the folder of sketches for *Oklahoma!* lyrics. This contains some 108 items (I number them as they appear in the folder), some grouped in subfolders but most loose and in general not organized in any evidently systematic way; they are mostly handwritten, although a few are typed or in carbon copy. Different types of material in various states are represented here: (a) lists of rhyming words (in no. 1, for example, headed "Surrey": curry, flurry, hurry, furry, blurry, sirree, scurry, worry, chauffoury, arbitrury, sanitury, millinury, stationury, vury vury, burr we/he, blur we/he, and so on); (b) lists of synonyms (no. 69, for "fiery"); (c) aphorisms and anecdotes concerning life on the prairie (no. 85: jottings concerning food on the farm, play parties and socials, and the like); (d) memorable "poetic" images (no. 30: "Pink honeysuckle," "Blue grass," "June bugs zooming round the [illegible]/Sunlight slanting over open water"); (e) poetic lines or groups of lines representing portions of lyrics; and (f) complete drafts of lyrics either in some kind of finished (albeit rough) form, or sometimes with nonsense syllables (for example, "heigh-ho me") or blank underlines to retain temporarily the meter pending finding the right words. The folder also contains (no. 84) a map sketched out by Hammerstein, with (his imaginary) Claremore at its center and various locations and landmarks identified. The materials in categories (e) and (f) are clearly the most interesting for present purposes, although other notes here are suggestive of later developments: thus the "June bugs zooming round the . . ." in no. 30 sowed a seed for the verse of the song "Oklahoma" (Aunt Eller's "flowers on the prairie where the June bugs zoom"), while the rhyme "bloomers—rumors" (no. 42) eventually appeared in "All er Nuthin'." The songs recognizable from, if not always used in, *Oklahoma!* among these sketches are (in order of the show): "Oh, What a Beautiful Mornin'" (no. 5; carbon copy; text as in *Draft1* and *Draft2*), "The Surrey with the Fringe on Top" (nos. 1, 40), "She Likes You [Quite a Lot]" (nos. 3 [including a draft melody by Rodgers], 91), "Kansas City" (nos. 42–44, 106), "I Cain't Say No" (nos. 27, 45–53), "Many a New Day" (nos. 9,

15, 54–55, 94), "It's a Scandal! It's a Outrage!" (called "Peddler Song"; nos. 16–22, 24, 25, 73–76), "Someone Will Teach You" (no. 26; carbon copy; text as in *Draft2*), "People Will Say We're in Love" (nos. 41, 80–82, 107, 108), and "[It's] Still Goin' On" (no. 29) plus two attempts, it seems, at an introduction to the dream-ballet, "Why, Oh Why?" (nos. 2, 4, 6, 7, 8, 10, 11, 13, 57–68, 83, 87, 88, 97–105) and "You Are a Girl" (no. 14). In addition, there are notes on square-dance calls (no. 35; including "Swing your honey," "Shake yer spurs and make 'em rattle!" and the like), which may have been intended for "The Farmer and the Cowman" (although "Swing your honey" was at one time suggested as a possible title for the show), and some of the other jottings seem to hint at early thoughts about what Helburn proposed should be a "song about the earth" (that is, "Oklahoma"). Given that the folder does not include sketches for lyrics included in *Draft2* (although it has carbon copies of "Oh, What a Beautiful Mornin'" and "Someone Will Teach You"), this does indeed suggest that these materials reflect work done after *Draft2* was submitted for copying—that is, after early November 1942, and probably until mid- or late January 1943. The absence of sketches directly related to "Pore Jud Is Daid," "Lonely Room," "All er Nuthin'," "Boys and Girls Like You and Me," "Oklahoma," and Lotta's "barbaric Spanish song" may be indicative of chronology (but "Pore Jud Is Daid" was not composed late, it seems), although the preservation of these materials may also have been contingent upon where Hammerstein happened to be when working on a lyric (in Doylestown, his New York apartment or office, or Rodgers's Connecticut home) and how effectively he kept and collated his notes.

Although there is nothing in the ordering or paper types here to suggest Hammerstein's sequence of working, it is clear that he was proceeding on the basis of *Draft2*. Thus he mapped out a few lines of the text for Aunt Eller's "She Likes You Quite a Lot" (act 1, scene 1)—"If she takes the trouble to hate you/She likes you quite a lot," "If she acts like she wants to shoot [replaced with "kill"] you/She likes you quite a lot," and (for a bridge) "If she's snippy, pernickety and contrary"—and Rodgers wrote down a complete melody with a different hook responding to the "If" clause ("You can tell she's crazy for you"; ex. 3.1). Similarly, Hammerstein made a quite detailed page of notes for "It's Still Goin' On," intended to start act 2, scene 3, one line of which ("Clear as the wind that blows behind the rain") appears, again, to have found some place in "Oklahoma" ("When the wind comes right behind the rain").[22] This never seems to have reached the stage of becoming a

Ex. 3.1. Draft melody for "She Likes You Quite a Lot." Cut-off portion of music-manuscript paper, in Rodgers's hand, headed "She Likes You." (Wc HC "*Oklahoma!* sketches," no. 3)

lyric (and there is no evidence that Rodgers ever provided any music), probably because Hammerstein remained uncertain about how exactly act 2, scene 3 would play out (and "It's Still Goin' On" was replaced by "Hale and Hearty" in *Draft3*). But despite these obvious connections to *Draft2*, there is some evidence that the sketches reflect further interim discussions of which there is little other tangible evidence. For example, "I'll Be at Your Elbow" (for Ado Annie and the Peddler) does not appear here: we shall see that in an annotation to the act 1 song list in *Draft3*, it was replaced by "Together" (also not present in the sketches), which then became a lyric for Ado Annie and Will in act 2 to be replaced by "All er Nuthin'." Similarly, some collections of lines here seem to refer to songs not listed in *Draft2* (or annotations to *Draft3*) but which may have been planned at some stage in November–January: no. 12 would seem to be for Laurey ("I'd fall in love, but I'm too [replaced by "so"] busy—/Haven't got the time," with notes in the margin for rhymes with "too busy," such as "grew busy" and "who is he"). It is also hard to find a place for no. 56 save that it is clearly for a female character ("They's all kinds of clothes 'at a girl can wear . . . ," "They's all kinds of ways I can do my hair,/Roll it in a pom[p]adour or slap it down slick . . .").[23]

The sketches for "Kansas City," "I Cain't Say No," "Many a New Day," and "It's a Scandal! It's a Outrage!" reveal some of the wit involved in the creative process. In "Kansas City," Hammerstein seems to have planned some rhyming patter for the middle (no. 43): "The trolley cars go whizzin' by/And take you to the fair" plus "I ate some meat in a resterant/It tasted like coyote/They served [illegible]/And called it table dotey." In "I Cain't Say No," Hammerstein seems to have played with the idea of having Ado Annie beginning four stanzas each with the same first line and a similar second one, but leading to a different rhyme: (no. 49) "I'm in a turrible fix/turrible spot/turrible state/turrible mess." An early version of a bridge also suggests that Rodgers had not yet composed his music (given that it would not fit): (no. 50) "When a woman plays with fire/It c'n turn her awful bad/So far I ain't been turned at all/And I ain't so sure I'm glad." Hammerstein had fun with "Many a New Day"—(no. 55) "Many a good girl has tried and failed," "Never have I ever wept or wailed," "Many a new chance has come my way/Over the spilt milk of yesterday"—and he was anxious to get "Auld Lang Syne stuff" somehow in there, also writing out a list of synonyms for "Auld Lang Syne" and "bygone" (no. 94), although the obvious rhyme for the latter, "Where has last July gone" (used in the song) appears in a different sketch (no. 9). As for "It's a Scandal! It's a Outrage!" Hammerstein experimented with the Peddler's opening expletives, and his first idea was for the song to begin (no. 18) "Friends,/Out in the east,/Out in the east,/A woman's a slave./She is bought,/Rented or leased./Then she's taught/How to behave!" before continuing in a dialogue patter. Even as it started to take its final shape as "It's a Scandal for the Jaybirds" (which is what Rodgers set to music) the conclusion was not yet fixed: "It's a scandal, for the jaybirds—/When we hear our country call,/It's the men who fight for freedom,/But the women git it all!" Presumably, it was revised still further (the men sing "It's a scandal, it's a outrage!/It's a problem we must solve!/We gotta start a revolution!" to which the entering girls respond "All right boys! Revolve!") to allow for the dance, which seemingly was added during the rehearsals. (Bennett first orchestrated the song without it.)

The most obvious case of Hammerstein "wrestling" with the lyrics, at least as can be documented in the drafts and sketches, is the Laurey-Curly love duet at the end of act 1, scene 1. *Draft1* (pp. 38–40) has a piece in which Laurey and Curly each hope that the other will find the right partner:

LAUREY
(*Starting to sing, almost too light-hearted*)

> I had no self-confidence.
> My talk was timid and shy—
> But I go around now with a satisfied air
> And a smirky look in my eye.
> So just you keep yer courage up
> And some fine morning you'll see
> That the very same thing can happen to you
> Just as it happened to me.

(*Her voice loses its false gaiety. She becomes more earnest with each line*)

> Someone will tell you and then you will know
> How really important you are.
> Someone will tell you and give you that glow
> That really belongs on a star.
> Someone will kiss you and say you are wonderful.
> You'll think you're wonderful too,
> For somehow that someone will make you believe
> There's no one on earth like you.

(*She looks straight at Curly and he looks straight back at her. The music continues. Then* CURLY *sings:*)

CURLY

I c'n make out whut yer drivin' at—
You're just feelin' great!
But it may be you're far from arrivin' at
Yer very last final fate.
I don't know how to put it into words—
Maybe I should write a letter.
What I mean, don't take the first feller that comes
Some day yer shore to do better.

(*Really letting go now*)

Someone will teach you to walk down a lane
As if you were riding a cloud.
Someone will teach you and clearly explain
Why you are the cream of the crowd.

(*She turns away and now he sings with honest, lover-like intensity*)

Someone will kiss you and say you are wonderful.
You'll think you're wonderful too,
For somehow that someone will make you believe
There's no one on earth like you . . .

(*After a pause he speaks. Continue with a succeeding refrain under dialogue*)

The scene continues much as in the final version, with Curly's exit to the smokehouse and Laurey left singing "softly and tenderly" ("Wish I c'd kiss you and tell you you're wonderful/You'd think yer wonderful too./For some-how—Oh, somehow I'd make you believe/There's no one on earth like you!") before breaking down in tears and leaving Aunt Eller alone on stage (though there is no indication of whether Eller is to hum the refrain until the curtain).

Although it is clear even in *Draft1* that Laurey and Curly are using the song to woo each other, the focus of the opening, and therefore the argument of the song as a whole, is unclear. (Just who has told Laurey of her importance?) *Draft2* (1-1-38) resolves the ambiguity in a surprising direction, with Laurey "adopting a superior and motherly tone that burns him [Curly] up, as she starts to sing" a revised verse:

You're shy and you got no confidence.
You hide in a hole like a crawfish.
Folks cain't account for the way you act

And they say you act stand-offish.
I understand how you feel.
Onct I was jist like you.
Nen love come along and cured me,

(*She looks off as if she means Jud*)

And 'at's whut'll cure you, too.

(The following chorus is similar to *Draft1*, save that lines 1–2 and 3–4 are switched, as is the continuation of the song to Laurey's exit.) So overt a reference to even just a temporary "love" for Jud clearly would not do. Hammerstein therefore pondered the issue still further:

> The problem of a duet for the lovers in *Oklahoma!* seemed insurmountable. While it is obvious almost from the rise of the curtain that Curly and Laurey are in love with each other, there is also a violent antagonism between them, caused mainly by Laurey's youthful shyness, which she disguises by pretending not to care for Curly. This does not go down very well with him, and he fights back. Since this mood was to dominate their scenes down into the second act, it seemed impossible for us to write a song that said "I love you," and remain consistent with the attitude they had adopted toward each other. After talking this over for a long time, Dick and I hit upon the idea of having the lovers warn each other against any show of tenderness lest other people think they were in love. Of course, while they say all those things, they are obliquely confessing their mutual affection. Hence the title, "People Will Say We're in Love."[24]

In his sketches, Hammerstein tried out various "Don't" formulas, some of which made it into the final version: "Don't keep your hand in mine,/Your hand feels so [replaced by "too"] grand in mine," "Don't tie my ties for me," "Don't tell pretty lies for me," "Don't choose my hats for me," "Don't buy a hat for me," "Don't turn democrat for me," "Your eyes mustn't shine like mine," "[Your] cheeks mustn't glow like mine," "Don't wax poetical," "Don't hum romantic tunes," "Don't say my hands are cool/cold," and so on. He also tried out a complete chorus:

Don't praise the clothes I wear,
Don't throw bouquets at me,
Don't sigh when you gaze at me,
People will know [replaced by "say"] we're in love.
Don't walk to church with me,
Don't rush my folks too much,

> Don't laugh at my jokes too much,
> People will say we're in love.
> Don't dance all night with me
> Till the stars fade from above.
> I'll say [added in margin: "Thinking," "Knowing,"
>   "Seeing," "They'll see"] it's allright with me—
> People will say we're in love!

He also (first?) attempted a different version of the last four lines:

> Don't say good-night all night
> Till the stars fade from above.
> I may hold you tight all night—
> People will say we're in love!

The middle section of (what became) Laurey's stanza also had a slightly different cast:

> Don't start collecting things,
> Handkerchief, dance card or glove.
> Kind friends are suspecting things—
> People will say we're in love.[25]

In fact, some of these readings are rhetorically more appropriate than those adopted in the final version ("Your hand looks too grand in mine" rather than "so grand"; "Kind friends are suspecting things" rather than "Sweetheart, they're suspecting things"), and on the whole, one has the feeling that Hammerstein could not quite work out how a cowboy and a farm girl should declare their affection for each other (Laurey is much better at trading insults): bouquets, roses, and gloves smack more of urban sophistication, while Laurey, an orphan, does not have many "folks" for Curly to please.

In most cases, however, Hammerstein had a clearer sense of direction. The song outlines in *Draft1* and *Draft2* presumably reflect discussion between him and Rodgers, and they often seem to have acted as some kind of springboard for writing the lyrics. For example, the description of "The Surrey with the Fringe on Top" in *Draft1* (1-1-7–8), paraphrasing a speech given to Curly in the play (p. 14), already contains important seeds of the song itself:

> As he goes on with the song he is starting to "get" Laurey. The fringe on the top is four inches long—and yeller! And two white horses a-rarin' and

faunchin' to go. Laurey will ride like a queen settin' up in *that* carriage—feel like she had a gold crown on her head, 'th diamonds in it, big as goose eggs. Further, the rig has four side curtains, case of rain, isinglass windows to look out of. And a red and green lamp set on the dashboard, winkin' like a lightnin' bug[.]

Something similar occurs in Laurey's "Many a New Day" (*Draft2*, 1-1-30), where Hammerstein notes in his outline that "Many a new day will dawn before she loses her heart or weeps for a man. Many a red sun will set and many a blue moon will rise 'fore she wastes time or love or tears on any of 'em."

In other cases, a prompt was provided by text that Hammerstein originally intended as dialogue. Ado Annie's "I Cain't Say No," for example, was originally to be some kind of duet between her and Laurey (*Draft2*, 1-1-20):

ADO ANNIE

. . . I like it so much when a feller talks purty to me I get all shaky from horn to hoof! . . . Don't you?

(*Pause*)

LAUREY

Cain't think whut yer talkin' about.

(LAUREY *walks away from her, scowling*)

ADO ANNIE

Don't you feel kind of sorry for a feller when he looks like he wants to kiss you?

LAUREY

Never heard sich talk!

ADO ANNIE

Well, whut're goin' to do when he pets your hand all gentle and talks purty and tells you you got skin like whipped cream and lips like cherries! Whut're you goin' to do? Spit in his eye?

LAUREY

All I know is you jist cain't go around kissin' every man that asts you!

ADO ANNIE

That's whut people tell me, but nobody ever give me a good reason for not kissin' a feller.

(ANNIE *now sings of her chief difficulty in life*)

"I Cain't Say No":

(LAUREY *discusses the problem with her, in the verses,* ANNIE, *however, returns to the refrain, no matter how many people warn her she just cain't help it! When a man asks her purty she cain't say no.*)

ADO ANNIE

(*After number*)
It's like I told you. I git sorry fer them!

LAUREY

I wouldn't be sorry for any man no matter whut.

However, when it was decided to have this just as a solo number (and one that would strongly define Ado Annie's character), Hammerstein took elements of the dialogue into the song, as in the "Trio":

> Whut you goin' to do when a feller gets flirty
> And starts to talk purty?
> Whut you goin' to do?
> S'posin' 'at he says 'at yer lips're like cherries,
> Er roses, er berries?
> Whut you goin' to do?
> S'posin' 'at he says 'at you're sweeter'n cream
> And he's gotta have cream er die?
> Whut you goin' to do when he talks thet way?
> Spit in his eye?

It is also clear from the *Oklahoma!* drafts that Hammerstein's intention was to make quite extensive use of spoken dialogue over music to provide some kind of continuity through the action, and also to "ooze" between speech and song. We have already seen the technique in the *Draft2* version of act 1, scene 2 (as Curly distinguishes himself from Jud by extolling life on the farm over the music of "Oh, What a Beautiful Mornin'") and at the proposed beginnings of the final scenes of act 1 (following "Peddler's Pack") and act 2 ("It's Still Goin' On" in *Draft2*; "Hale and Hearty" in *Draft3*). Hammerstein also seems to have wanted the effect at several points in act 1, scene 1. In the play (pp. 33–43), followed by *Draft1*, Laurey and Aunt Eller have a long exchange concerning Laurey's hopes for the future ("Wish 't I lived in the White House, and had diamonds on my shoes, and a little nigger boy to fan me. . . . Er wish 't I lived in Virginia or Californie"), her love of the farm, and her fears of Jeeter Fry. When Laurey speaks of the farm and the delights of nature, Hammerstein notes (*Draft1*, 1-1-17) that "the following speech should be accompanied by music and may eventually be written in verse." Although the exchange is cut down in *Draft2* (and we lose the reference to the White House), the lyrical moment remains (1-1-15): "The following speech should be accompanied by music and will eventually be converted to verse, to be spoken, however, not sung." Something similar occurs later in the scene. In the final version, as the Peddler asks Laurey if she wants to buy something, Laurey begins to wax lyrical (p. 33):

> Me? Course I want sumpin. (*Working up to a kind of abstracted ecstasy*) Want a buckle made outa shiny silver to fasten onto my shoes! Want a dress with lace. Want perfume, wanta be purty, wanta smell like a honey-suckle vine!

In *Draft1*, this speech had been a cue for underscoring (1-1-29):

> Me? 'Course I want sump'n. Want lots of things!
> (*Music starts. She speaks the following verse in a kind of abstracted ecstasy, gradually slipping into Song as she goes on.*)

This then led to "All That I Want." But although that song had been re-moved by *Draft2* (1-1-24)—presumably because it was decided to focus on a different, more forceful side of Laurey in "Many a New Day"—Hammer-stein repeats his intention of underscoring (and a shift to spoken verse) at this moment. Rodgers and Hart had experimented with rhymed dialogue in, for example, *I Married an Angel* (1938). Hammerstein had also used underscor-ing for moments of heightened expression in his stage musicals with Jerome Kern from *Show Boat* on.[26] The technique was further developed in their film musicals—*High, Wide, and Handsome* provides some good examples—and Hammerstein may also have been influenced by his work on *Carmen Jones* given that Bizet makes prominent use of such so-called melodrama. The final version of *Oklahoma!* however, has much less underscoring—per-haps Rodgers and Hammerstein thought it too adventurous—although it does become a feature of *Carousel*.

Clearly, *Draft2* still left significant work to be done on fixing a final se-quence of songs and providing their lyrics and music. As we shall see, a good number of decisions were made during the rehearsals and even try-outs. However, something of an intermediate stage between *Draft2* and the rehearsals can perhaps be detected in penciled annotations (in an unknown hand) to the act 1 song list in the New York Public Library copy of *Draft2* that also contains the final scene of *Draft3*. (There is no act 2 song list in *Draft2*.) Table 3.3 provides a transcription. All the songs here save "She Likes You Quite a Lot" and "All That I Want" have ticks by them, suggesting that they were somehow written (if only in terms of the lyrics). The other excisions

Table 3.3. An intermediate song list for act 1

1.	Oh, What a Beautiful Mornin'	
2.	A Surrey with Fringe on the Top	
3.	<She Likes You Quite a Lot>	
4.	Kansas City	
5.	I Cain't Say No	
6.	Many a New Day	
7.	<I'll Be at Your Elbow>	Together
8.	<Someone Will Teach You>	People Will Know [*sic*]
9.	<Folks Ud Gether Around and Sing>	Pore Jud
10.	All That I Want	
11.	<Peddler's Pack>	
12.	<How Would It Be?>	

Source: Based on penciled annotations to the act 1 song list in the *NYp* copy of *Draft2* (black hard cover). Angled brackets indicate excisions; replacements, where indicated, are given in the right-hand column. All songs save nos. 3 and 10 also have penciled ticks by them. Some of these revisions are also reflected in various copies of *Draft3*.

are "Peddler's Pack" and "How Would It Be?" in act 1, scene 3. (The last would of course be replaced by "Out of My Dreams," leading to the dream-ballet.) The Laurey-Curly love duet "Someone Will Teach You" is replaced by "People Will Say We're in Love" (although the reading is that of a line in the sketches: "People will know . . ."), and "Folks Ud Gether Around and Sing" is fixed as "Pore Jud [Is Daid]." Finally, "I'll Be at Your Elbow," for Ado Annie and the Peddler, is replaced by "Together," which just before or during the rehearsals was shifted to act 2 and given to Ado Annie and Will, before being replaced by "All er Nuthin'." Some version of this list is most probably the format of act 1 as the show went into rehearsal: we cannot tell whether the substitutions had already been made, although the cuts ("She Likes You Quite a Lot," "Peddler's Pack") may have been decided by the middle of January 1943, given that the *New York Herald Tribune* reported on the 17th that the whole show contained twelve songs "in a more-or-less popular ballad style." (Table 3.3 shows twelve songs just in act 1, *Draft2* has fourteen across both acts, and the final version thirteen.) However, "Lonely Room" (or something of similar substance) must have been at least planned by the end of January given the concerns over finding someone with a good singing voice to play Jud. Also, we shall see that "When I Go Out Walkin' with My Baby" may still have been present when rehearsals began.

Quite apart from the writing of new numbers during the rehearsals and even, perhaps, the tryouts, Hammerstein was no doubt required to make ad-

justments to preexisting songs or to provide for encores. He seems to have
done both in the case of "I Cain't Say No." The lyric sheet accompanying Rodgers's manuscript has the opening verse, then the chorus, trio,
and chorus (for the *dal segno*: the last ends "Though I c'n feel the under-
tow/I never make a complaint . . ."). In the final version Hammerstein
provides a different last four lines ("I cain't resist a Romeo/In a sombrero
and chaps . . ."), and then an encore stanza ("I'm just a girl who cain't say
no/Kissin's my favorite food . . .") ending with what he planned to be the
original ending of the song ("Though I c'n feel the undertow . . ."). According to Celeste Holm, this encore stanza was provided in Boston, although
it seems to have been achieved by recombining elements that appear in an
earlier sketch for a single stanza of the song.[27]

That is normal. One case, however, is quite unusual and merits further
thought. Hammerstein seems to have worried considerably about how best
to handle Jud at the end of act 1, scene 2. *Draft2* (1-2-9–10) offers the first
indication of Hammerstein's intentions for the scene's conclusion:

PEDDLER
All right. Jist as you say, Mr. Fry. Don't want me to leave no fresh postcards?
Those I sell you last year mus' be all wore out, ain't they?
JUD
Don't want 'em. Don't want any more pitchers. Want somethin' real. You
hear me? Real! I ain't goin' to stay in this rat-hole no more. Goin' outside
an' take what I want.
PEDDLER
(*About to close the flat box*)
You—don't want nuthin' in here?
JUD
(*Shouting*)
No. Git out!
(*The* PEDDLER *goes*)
(JUD *paces the room*)
I don't want nothin' in no peddler's pocket—
(*Tearing cards*)
—or on postcards—
(*Yanking the Police Gazette cover from its nail*)
—or p'lice Gazettes! I want *her*. Her own self!
(*He starts to sing, "All That I Want," the intensity of his yearning increasing
as he sings, his voice building to a dramatic-music climax, for the scene
fade-out*)

When it came to providing lyrics for the song, however, Hammerstein seems to have been undecided on whether to focus on Jud's violent passion for Laurey ("I want *her*. Her own self!") or on his more general "yearning" for a better life implied in the title "All That I Want." The text first set by Rodgers in his manuscript (table 3.4) is in fact titled "Lonely Little Room."[28] This is not quite what one might have expected from *Draft2*: indeed, Hammerstein appears to have shifted focus. The start of the song now picks up on a hint in Riggs's stage description of the smokehouse in the play (p. 59: "the floor is full of holes; at night the field mice scurry about the room"). For the last five lines, Hammerstein, not atypically, brings in elements of his original dialogue in *Draft2* ("I ain't goin' to stay in this rat-hole no more. Goin' outside an' take what I want"). Even at this stage, however, the main thrust of the song in its middle section remained unclear. The version of the text in the lyric sheet accompanying Rodgers's manuscript contains some significant differences compared with the final one, the latter clearly written after he had composed the music to the first.

It is not entirely clear which of these texts was included in the version of the song sent to Robert Russell Bennett for orchestration: as usual, Bennett's score does not give the complete text underlay for the vocal line.[29] Here the music of the song is more or less in its final form, but some of the orchestral effects seem to respond to the first version of the text rather than the second: the flourishes on "And her long, yeller hair/Falls acrost my face" appear better suited to "In the flash of an eye/We was whizzin' through the sky." Yet the final version of the text clearly is preferable. It is also remarkable that Hammerstein managed to preserve the accentual patterns (and for the most part, the rhyme scheme) of his own previous text. The shift from a generic, even sympathetic, fantasy to a more focused, present-tense assault on Laurey cements the character of Jud much more firmly, while the greater violence here makes his downfall in act 2 all the more likely.

Crafting the Music

Richard Rodgers's *Oklahoma!* manuscripts comprise the individual songs (voice and piano accompaniment) in separate fascicles, most also with typed lyric sheets; they are clean copies, seemingly intended for sheet-music publication, and were probably produced late in the preparations for the show, albeit prior to its definitive version (see Appendix B for other details of

Table 3.4. First and final versions of "Lonely Room"

The Floor creaks	The floor creaks,
The door squeaks.	The door squeaks,
There's a fieldmouse a-nibblin' on a broom,	There's a fieldmouse a-nibblin' on a broom,
And I set by myself	And I set by myself
Like a cobweb on a shelf,	Like a cobweb on a shelf,
By myself in a lonely little room.	By myself in a lonely room.
But last night the moon passed my winder	But when there's a moon in my winder
And a beam slanted down 'crost my bed,	And it slants down a beam 'crost my bed,
And the shadder of a tree	Then the shadder of a tree
Got to dancin' on the wall,	starts a-dancin' on the wall
And a dream got to dancin' in my head!	And a dream starts a-dancin' in my head.
I bust that door from its hinges.	And all the things that I wish fer
Then I walked with a five-mile stride	Turn out like I want them to be,
Till I stood on the shoulder of a mountain	And I'm better'n that Smart Aleck cowhand
And picked out a star I cud ride!	Who thinks he is better 'n me!
When I pulled down a star	And the girl that I want
And I called to a girl	Ain't afraid of my arms,
And she hopped right up by my side.	And her own soft arms keep me warm.
In the flash of an eye	And her long, yeller hair
We was whizzin' through the sky—	Falls acrost my face,
Me on my star—with my bride . . .	Jist like the rain in a storm!
Then the floor creaked.	The floor creaks,
The door squeaked!	The door squeaks,
And the mouse started nibblin' on the broom.	And the mouse starts a-nibblin' on the broom.
Then the sun flicked my eyes,	And the sun flicks my eyes—
And I wasn't in the skies—	It was all a pack o' lies!
I was back in a lonely little room.	I'm awake in a lonely room . . .
(*His shoulders droop in defeat, then rise in protest*)	
I ain't gonna stay in this room no more,	I ain't gonna dream 'bout her arms no more!
I ain't gonna live all alone!	I ain't gonna leave her alone!
Goin' outside,	Goin' outside,
Find a star to ride,	Git myself a bride,
Git me a womern to call my own!	Git me a womern to call my own.

Source: Lyric sheet in Wc RC 12/7 ("Lonely Little Room"); Hammerstein, "*Oklahoma!*" 76–77.

the musical sources). Their format is entirely typical of the materials that Rodgers prepared for his shows (also with Hart), and they reflect common practices within the Broadway musical, such as the intended reliance on professional copyists, arrangers, and orchestrators: thus his piano accompaniments are functional (and would serve for learning and rehearsal purposes) but somewhat unpolished, he uses notational short cuts for repeated patterns and phrases, and he provides only the minimum music necessary from which the complete song could be written out. For *Oklahoma!* one assumes that Rodgers worked reasonably closely with the orchestrator, Robert Russell Bennett, who as usual deserves significant credit both for his elegant accompaniments and countermelodies (although some are present in the Rodgers manuscripts) and for much of the incidental music and the dream-ballet. Rodgers also seems to have made use of Albert Sirmay (Szirmai), a well-known editor and arranger (and sometime composer) who worked on other Rodgers and Hammerstein shows, as well as with Cole Porter and others. Sirmay is credited with editing the published (1943) vocal score, which he must have done with some knowledge of the Bennett orchestrations. No rehearsal scores survive.

It seems clear that Rodgers regarded these manuscripts as somehow marking a limit to his compositional involvement in *Oklahoma!* Certainly any competent arranger could get quite easily from here to the final score. Presumably they were preceded by other materials as the composer worked things out (and some of the preliminary sketches will be discussed further), although it is possible that, as Hammerstein and others noted, Rodgers was so fluent, and quick, that it did not take much writing down to get the songs to these "finished" states. Certainly the impression left by these materials confirms Agnes de Mille's comment that "Dick seldom revises or alters. His work is virtually complete when we go into rehearsal. Oscar, on the other hand, does considerable editing."[30] Compared with the final versions of *Oklahoma!* songs, there are minor differences in rhythm (for example, dotted patterns or not), in phrasing (the lengths of upbeats), and in the harmony, but little of any substance. The main exceptions are in songs that also seem to have caused problems in the later stages of the show's preparation, in part perhaps because of their ambitious nature. In "Lonely Room," Rodgers originally notated the middle section ("But last night the moon passed my winder") in doubled note values compared with the final version (so, the accompaniment in eighth-notes rather than sixteenths, with two measures of this part of the song becoming one measure in the vocal score); Rodgers's apparent intention to preserve a constant pulse from the opening, indicated by "L'istesso tempo" in the vocal score, was reflected, instead, in the tempo marking (from Moderato to Allegretto). In the case of "It's a Scandal! It's a Outrage!" (with the text "It's a scandal for the jaybirds . . ."), Ali Hakim is given the melody in mm. 65–73 (and later instances) rather than the rhythmically notated speech in the vocal score, which presumably plays on Joseph Buloff's manner of delivery.

The differences between the manuscript and printed versions of "Lonely Room" may reflect Rodgers's desire for notational simplicity, at least at the compositional stage. This is also apparent in the keys he chose for writing the songs (table 3.5), where he tended to prefer no more than two sharps or one flat in the key signature, whereas in the final versions, the songs range more widely. This is not to say that Rodgers was musically unsophisticated: we shall see plenty of examples to the contrary. Nor should one read too much into tonal choices in a repertory where transposition to suit circumstance was the norm. Nevertheless, Rodgers's choice of key when composing his songs presumably was not random, and likewise, there must have been some logic to fixing the keys both for the orchestrations and for the published vocal score (whatever the order in which that occurred).

The ranges of the *Oklahoma!* songs in Rodgers's manuscripts tend to span an octave plus one or two notes on either side, and rarely more than a tenth overall (save the twelfth in the final version of "It's a Scandal! It's a Outrage!" and the wider range resulting from the choral harmonization of "Oklahoma"). Such somewhat narrow ranges, and a lowish tessitura, are typical for the repertory from the mid-1930s on and reflect the use of relatively untrained singers, especially in the absence of microphones.[31] Thus the ranges are noticeably wider in *Carousel*, the cast of which was largely made up of singers with experience in light opera and operetta (compare the twelfth in "If I Loved You"). The location of this octave range will be fixed on the musical stave in terms of absolute pitch according to two criteria: first, the voice type (soprano, mezzo-soprano, baritone), and second, notational convenience, such that the melody fits conveniently on the stave without too many leger lines. When Rodgers composed a good number of these songs, he probably had little idea of his final cast save perhaps Alfred Drake (Curly) and Joan Roberts (Laurey), given that most of the roles were allocated only in January 1943. Nevertheless, he had some view of their voice types: for example, Curly and Will Parker were to be light baritones and Laurey a middle-range soprano. The striking decision at this point was to view Ado

Table 3.5. Keys and ranges of *Oklahoma!* songs

	Wc RC 12	Vocal score	Orches-tration	Original-cast recording
Oh, What a Beautiful Mornin'	D (c♯–d′)	E	E	E♭
The Surrey with the Fringe on Top	Gᵃ (c♯–d′)	A	A	A
Kansas City	F (c–d′)	A♭	A♭	G
I Cain't Say No	D (a–b′)	F	F	F
Many a New Day	C (b–d″)	D	E♭ᵇ	D
It's a Scandal! It's a Outrage!	a (a–d′)– D (b–f♯′)	b–D	b–D	b–D
People Will Say We're in Love	G (c♯/c♯′–c′/c″)– C (c/c′–e′/e″)	A–D	A–D	A♭–D♭
Pore Jud Is Daid	D (b♭–b′)	E	E♭ᶜ	E
Lonely Room	aᵈ (c–b′)	b	bᵉ	cᶠ
Out of My Dreams	F (c′–d″)	A♭	A♭	A♭
The Farmer and the Cowman	C (b–c′)ᵍ	F	E♭ʰ	F
All er Nuthin'	D (c♯/c♯′–d′/c♯″)	F (ends in E♭)	E♭	E♭
Oklahoma	C (c–e′)	D–D♭–D	D–D♭–D	D♭–Dⁱ
(When I Go Out Walkin' with My Baby)	C (c–d′)			
(Boys and Girls Like You and Me)	F (c–e′)			

ᵃ Sketch in Wc RC 12/16 is in C. Rodgers notates the chorus in G major in *Musical Stages*, 219.
ᵇ But marked to be transposed to D.
ᶜ NY*rh* has parts in F.
ᵈ Has annotation at top of p. 1: E——
ᵉ NY*rh* has parts in D minor.
ᶠ Sung by Alfred Drake.
ᵍ Equivalent range is extended downward in vocal score for Aunt Eller in mm. 228–39.
ʰ Subsequent modulations are also different from vocal score.
ⁱ Chorus only; no verse.

Annie as a relatively low mezzo-soprano role, making a clear distinction between her and Laurey: "I Cain't Say No" in its original key (D major) has a low range (*a–b′*), placing her a third below Laurey. This distance of a third between the two female leads is retained in the final versions, although both Joan Roberts (Laurey) and Celeste Holmes (Ado Annie) had higher voices than in Rodgers's original scheme, such that their songs were in most cases each transposed up a minor third in the orchestrations and vocal score (thus "I Cain't Say No" is in F major rather than D major). In the case of Laurey, transposition up a third seems to have worked in the case of "Out of My Dreams" (so her top note on the climactic "go" in mm. 113–14 becomes f'' rather than d''), but not, for some reason, in "Many a New Day": here the orchestration is up a third (E flat major rather than C major) but was marked to be transposed down a semitone to D major (the key also in the vocal score and in the original-cast recording). There is nothing in the range of the song itself to prevent E flat major; the problem, instead, may have lain with the restatement of the chorus toward the end of the dance a semitone higher than at the opening (E major rather than E flat major), which may have taken the melody too high. However, some confusion ensues. The cadential tag for the exit of the singers before the dance (mm. 90–93) is in E flat major, as befits the original key and not the transposition. This leads to a terrible introduction to the dance (in A major), which also gets confused in the orchestration. There seem to have been several other problems with this number given the alternative introductions and conclusions provided by Bennett.

Although these kinds of transpositional adjustments are standard, they can still be revealing. Rodgers seems to have come fairly close in his estimation of the voice type of his likely Curly, perhaps because he knew Drake's voice: his songs were almost consistently transposed up just a tone in the orchestrations, although two of them ("Oh, What a Beautiful Mornin'" and "People Will Say We're in Love") then seem to have been transposed down a semitone in performance. The partial exception is "Pore Jud Is Daid," which went from Rodgers's original D major to E flat major in the orchestrations (but parts also survive in F major), and to E major in the vocal score (and in the original-cast recording). However, the vocal range here is somewhat narrower than the norm for Curly (perhaps because of the intended inclusion of Jud), and so transposition is not so much an issue. But while Rodgers seems originally to have conceived Curly's and Will Parker's roles for the same voice-type, the eventual Will Parker (Lee Dixon) appears to have had a somewhat higher range. As a result, his songs go up a minor third, too ("Kansas City" and "All er Nuthin'," although "Kansas City" then went down a semitone in performance, or so it seems from the original-cast recording). However, in the case of "All er Nuthin'," the decision to give a chorus to Ado Annie toward the end created problems: Will Parker's climactic top note (f' in the transposed version) seems to have been too high for

Celeste Holm, whose voice, although higher than originally conceived by Rodgers, still lay lower than Joan Roberts's. Accordingly, the final Ado Annie chorus is presented a tone lower, in E flat major. Still more drastic problems seem to have occurred in the case of Jud's "Lonely Room." Rodgers wrote it in A minor, squeezing a remarkably expressive song into the narrow melodic range of a seventh: he must have known that any actor likely to play that type of character would probably have a limited voice. This was taken up a tone to B minor in the orchestration, but orchestral parts also survive in D minor. Presumably, this is related to the problems Howard da Silva had with the song.

The light baritone and middling soprano voices fit fairly comfortably on a treble stave (that is, one with a G2 clef, transposing down an octave in the case of the baritone); the mezzo-soprano range (for the original key of Ado Annie's "I Cain't Say No") does not. However, there is still another issue that Rodgers must have brought into play: the location of the tonic within this range. For example, a *d–d'* range can have its tonic at the outer limits (so, D major) or in the middle of the range (say, G major). To borrow the terminology applied to music in the Renaissance modes, the former represents an "authentic" division of the octave (a lower fifth plus an upper fourth, with the "final" as the lowest note of the fifth), and the latter a "plagal" one (a fourth plus a fifth, with the "final" still the lowest note of the fifth). A melody in the *d–d'* range (plus or minus additional notes) divided authentically (*d–a–d'*) will work very differently from one with a plagal division (*d–g–d'*), given that the position of the tonic (at the bottom and top of the range, or in the middle) will determine the character of the melody, not least by virtue of its cadential gestures (given that cadences tend to end on the tonic). D major (using a *d–d'* range) and C major (using a *c–c'* range) will be authentic, and G major (using a *d–d'* range) and F major (using a *c–c'* range) will be plagal, and the closing gestures—and the larger-scale melodic structures—will work very differently.[32] The consequences for Rodgers's melodic writing are clear if one compares Curly's "Oh, What a Beautiful Mornin'" and "The Surrey with the Fringe on Top": both have the same vocal range (*c♯–d'* in Rodgers's original manuscripts), but the different tonics (D and G, respectively) cause the melody to lie very differently (the fifth-plus-fourth and fourth-plus-fifth divisions are clearly apparent) and to reach different cadential goals. Moreover, songs based on an authentic division of the octave will have a tendency toward the subdominant (substituting a plagal division of the octave for the authentic one), whereas those based on a plagal division will tend to the dominant (substituting an authentic division): this is also clear in Curly's first two songs. The same is apparent in a comparison of Laurey's "Many a New Day" (*b–d″*; C major) and "Out of My Dreams" (*c′–d″*; F major).

Solving the problem of how to achieve tonal variety within the relatively narrow range of the human voice is simply part of the composer's craft—the same issues are apparent in, say, Schubert's *lieder*—but Rodgers plays with it quite neatly, and in ways that cannot have been accidental. In "People Will Say We're in Love," the two voices (an octave apart) each have the range C–E (D–F♯ in the transposed version in the vocal score and orchestration). For the verse, Rodgers identifies within this overall range the octave D–D divided plagally (so, G major); for the chorus, he instead takes as the octave C–C divided authentically (so, C major). In effect, the overall range remains constant, but it is articulated and divided in different ways, producing an effect of relaxing into the chorus (in the tonic against the verse's dominant). Something similar occurs in "The Farmer and the Cowman," where the octave C–C (F–F in the transposed version) is divided authentically for "The farmer and the cowman should be friends . . ." and "Territory folk should stick together . . . ," hence in C major (F major in the transposed version), and plagally for "I'd like to say a word for the farmer . . . ," hence in F major (B flat major). This accounts for the prominent subdominant episodes in the song.

Although Rodgers's original choice of keys is bound to be based on some reason, there are times where it seems just a default. It is probably not useful to speculate on whether he composed at the piano, in his head, or on paper, although it may be worth noting that his initial tonal choices are not always piano-friendly, in contrast to, say, Irving Berlin's oft-reported method of picking out tunes on the black notes of the piano (therefore with a preference for F sharp major and inherent pentatonicism). Rodgers seems to have been more methodical. It may seem odd, for example, that he composed "Oklahoma" in C major and not its final D major, given that this song, even in its first version, was composed relatively late (and therefore when at least some of the cast was known). However, C major, with a key signature of no sharps or flats, is a good default key for drafting songs on paper because modulations and chromatic harmonies can be worked out quite easily. That this was Rodgers's common practice becomes apparent from some of the preliminary sketches, notably "The Surrey with the Fringe on Top." The three components of the song have three separate sketches (see ex. 3.2), again in

Ex. 3.2. Sketches for "The Surrey with the Fringe on Top." (Wc RC 12/16, fol. 2v [a], fol. 3r [b], fol. 3v [c])

C major: "Surrey middle" (the bridge; "The wheels are yeller, the uphol-
stery's brown . . ."); "Verse Surrey" ("When I take you out tonight with
me . . ."); and "Surrey" ("Chicks and ducks and geese better scurry . . .").
The sketches are untexted, save for the final line at the end of the chorus,
where Rodgers has "never stop with the funny little surrey with the fringe
on the top" (the final version has ". . . shiny little surrey . . .").

   As is typical of Rodgers's sketches, the *Oklahoma!* ones are presented
on a single stave, with the melody, some indications of one or more inner
parts, and, very occasionally, roman numerals to indicate the harmony. This
squares with the report in the *New York Times* of 14 May 1944 that "usually
Rodgers writes only the melody line with chord symbols indicated (V7 for
diminished, I for tonic, IV for subdominant)." It is not always clear whether
the inner part is intended as a real inner voice or just to indicate the direction of the harmony. However, one can go farther in identifying the likely
purpose of this material. In the case of the "Surrey" sketches, the melody
seems already to have been fully composed: it is almost the same as the final
version, save some minor differences of rhythm and one note toward the
end of the verse (m. 12, the g' half-note instead of an f', which may be a
misprint). However, octave displacements are ignored (the first notes of ex.
3.2a and ex. 3.2c should be an octave apart), so this cannot be viewed as
a "final" version. Rather, the aim appears chiefly to have been to sort out
the harmony: despite the absence of a bass line, it readily becomes clear
from Rodgers's annotations for the inner voice(s). In the bridge (ex. 3.2a),
the move to IV then V is clearly established, as is the 4–3 suspension in
the final half-cadence that gets taken over into the final version. However,
Rodgers eventually abandons an inner-voice chromatic descent (in quarter-
notes) in mm. 3 and 7. This does not work well harmonically, although the
main reason for its disappearance may well be that a similar quarter-note
descent was intended as an inner voice in the first section of the chorus (see
ex. 3.2c, m. 1), perhaps as a repeating ostinato. Had Rodgers kept this ostinato (or even just the descent in the first measure), it would have made the
song very clunky, and in the final version he had the much better idea of
taking the four-note descent (c'–g) and having it instead in half-notes (thus
spanning two measures rather than one), repeated twice more before the cadence. As a result, the horses pulling the surrey may go at a brisk clip-clop,
but the wheels turn much more smoothly.[33]

   Although the harmonies and modulations in the chorus are close to the
final version, the verse seems to have caused some problems. Having I and

IV in the first measure of ex. 3.2b is very odd (the final song has the standard I–V), and the move to the somewhat unconventional VI (A major) rather than vi (A minor) in m. 3 seems to have caused some problems (Rodgers indicates a flat seventh, which at first glance would suggest some kind of further move to ii, and there seems to be some confusion about the inner voice in m. 5). Having mm. 5–8 as a sequence of mm. 1–4 (down a minor third) takes the melody from VI to ♯IV (F sharp major), and having mm. 9–10 as the start of a further sequence (again down a minor third) takes the melody from ♯IV to ♯II (D sharp major), which Rodgers notates as ♭III (E flat major). He does not indicate how he intends to get from ♭III to the cadential V6/4–5/3s in the tonic (C major) in mm. 13–14 (the final version provides a wonderful solution via V/♭III). But all this, in turn, depends on how Rodgers is construing the harmony. The verse is based on a sequential pattern, with four measures being stated three times, the second and third times each down a minor third (the melody spans g'–e' in mm. 1–4; e'–$c\sharp'$ in mm. 5–8, and by implication, $c\sharp'$–$a\sharp$ [$b\flat$] in mm. 9–12). A fourth statement on the same lines would go from $b\flat$–g, hence providing the starting note for the statement on g' in m. 13 (the same as at the opening, although it will be given a different harmony). In short, there is an elision (also providing an octave transfer to the original pitch), with Rodgers jumping from the third to the fifth statement of the sequence. The full five-statement version of this sequential pattern would divide the octave into four minor thirds to bring things back full circle, somewhat in the manner of the partitioning created by a diminished-seventh chord (hence the initial notes of the five-step sequence form a diminished seventh chord: g'–e''–$c\sharp'$–$a\sharp$ [$b\flat$] leading to g [g']). This seems to be the way Rodgers is thinking: the rather odd inner voices in mm. 3, 5, and 7 themselves suggest diminished-seventh chords, perhaps indicating not so much an intended harmonization as the guiding principles behind the overall progression.

This may appear a heavy-handed explanation of an extended moment of melodic inspiration, but it does have consequences that Rodgers needed to resolve. The partitioning of the octave by minor thirds requires an enharmonic shift to return to the starting point (the $a\sharp$/$b\flat$ noted above). Rodgers had to decide whether to notate the descending minor-third progression as I–VI–♯IV–♭III, as in his sketch, or as I–VI–♭V–♭III. He chose the latter for the final version of the song. In strict harmonic terms, this may seem counterintuitive (and it would probably not score top marks in any harmony examination)—which is why the sketch proceeds a different way—but it is much easier to sing a db' in m. 7 (recognized as the same note as the $c\sharp'$ in the preceding measures) than the chromatic half-step $g\sharp$–g in mm. 10–11. This is especially the case in the eventual transpositions of the song from the C major sketch, first into G major in the manuscript version of the song (where the chromatic half-step runs from $d\sharp$–d), and then into A major in the orchestration and published vocal score (where without the enharmonic rewriting, the chromatic half-step would run from $e\sharp$–e). In the end, Rodgers was nothing if not a pragmatist.

He was famous both for writing music quickly and for taking a detached attitude toward his songs, dropping them without compunction if they were felt not to work in a given theatrical environment: "It is often necessary to remove a particular number if it is inappropriate or slows down the action."[34] Later accounts abound of his businesslike approach to composition, as he sat in a Manhattan office (in the RKO Building on Sixth Avenue) from eleven in the morning to five in the afternoon each working day, looking for all the world like a corporate executive. His

> methods would be something of a shock to those who confuse inspiration with a picture of Beethoven in a frenzy. Rodgers' musical processes are refined to the thousandth of an inch. The musical-comedy writer works behind a long polished desk inside a suite of three offices, tastefully furnished with straight-back chairs, a couch, brass lamps, Chinese ash trays and paintings of sets from his *Connecticut Yankee*, *On Your Toes* and the current Pulitzer prize–winning *Oklahoma!* which recently celebrated its first birthday. The telephone rings as often as any busy lawyer's. The only obvious concession to the craft is the Bechstein grand near the window.[35]

Rodgers claimed for *Oklahoma!* that "most of the musical numbers presented no great problems," and his estimates of the actual composition time for the show ranged from five hours to six days, although he made it clear that this was only after months of planning. "People Will Say We're in Love" may have been an exception: Rodgers later said that he spent several days at the piano before he was satisfied with the first part of the chorus, although this was reported in the context of an article by Gertrude Samuels on how to write a hit song, where Rodgers would have been concerned to give a particular impression.[36] In general, however, it is clear that Rodgers was remarkably fluent, and that the kinds of musical issues discussed above were merely second nature. But this is not to say that they do not matter.

The Dream-Ballet

Pragmatism of a different sort has often been used to explain the dream-ballet in *Oklahoma!* Here there are a number of problems both in the sources and in the accounts of their genesis that raise some profound questions not only concerning Hammerstein's and Rodgers's working methods, but also about the myths that have been generated around the show.

One of the striking features about Hammerstein's draft librettos is the extent to which he and Rodgers incorporated opportunities for dance, which from the start (if not surprisingly) seems to have been conceived as an essential part of the show. In the case of *Draft1*, act 1, scene 1 has four proposed dance numbers: "Kansas City" (1-1-13: "Develop this number into a dance, featuring Bud"), Laurey's "All That I Want" (1-1-29: "Describe and develop ballet details later"), and the reprises of "I Cain't Say No" (see below) and "Oh, What a Beautiful Mornin'" ([1-1-]35: "Some start an impromptu waltz and dance off"). The presence of a "ballet" for Laurey following "All That I Want" is striking and in one sense sets the tone for the later dream-ballet. However, in most of these cases, the nature of the proposed dances remained somewhat inchoate, save for the clearly defined dramatic function for the reprise of "I Cain't Say No" (*Draft1*, 1-1-34): "BUD leaves to get a bag of presents for Annie *in which he shot the entire fifty dollars*! The boys come back and with successive and brief compliments, in a dance routine, capture her interest, for in fact, she cain't say no to anyone." *Draft2* keeps this reprise (in a slightly different position) but removes the dance, although its idea would be taken up again in the case of the late-added "All er Nuthin'." "Many a New Day," the replacement for Laurey's "All That I Want," does not have a dance specified in *Draft2*, but this may be an oversight; certainly it has one in the final version. However, in the case of act 1, scene 1, *Draft2* does have fewer dances than *Draft1*, which may suggest a degree of nervousness at this second stage about the intentions for the choreography. Nevertheless, *Draft2* maintains the choreographic momentum in act 2, with dance episodes in "The Farmer and the Cowman" in scene 1 and "It's Still Goin' On" in scene 3.

The place and design of the dream-ballet has proven more contentious. As we have seen, de Mille later claimed in the first part of her autobiography to have started planning the choreography for *Oklahoma!* while touring *Rodeo* in November 1942. Her notes made then, she said, included "Jud's

8. Agnes de Mille had a great deal to do in *Oklahoma!* including as well as the dream-ballet the dances for "Kansas City," "Many a New Day," "It's a Scandal! It's a Outrage!" and (shown here) "The Farmer and the Cowman," opening act 2. For the last, she enlisted the help of May Gadd of the American Country Dance Society to provide "authentic" square-dance moves. This dance sequence also included a number of specialty slots—including Eric Victor jumping up into the tree stage right—that were removed as the show was tightened during the tryouts. (Uncredited)

Postcards," although in a subsequent interview with Max Wilk, she situated their arrival at some later stage during the rehearsals: "Up till then it's been an innocuous, gingham-aprony Sunday-school sort of show. That first act, there was nothing in it, no threat, no suspense, no sex, nothing. And I told this to Oscar, who said, 'No sex?' 'No, Mr. Hammerstein,' I said. 'None. What have we done with those postcards of Jud Fry's?' And he looked at me, and then he went to the phone and called Dick. 'Dick, get over here immediately.'"[37] Such inconsistencies in accounts of, and memories of, the creation of *Oklahoma!* are not surprising, especially given that the dream-ballet soon became so iconic a feature of the show. However, it also becomes clear that de Mille had her own agendas. Her relationships with the production team on *Oklahoma!* and with Rodgers, Hammerstein, and the Theatre Guild thereafter, were famously stormy, and it rankled that she felt that she never got either the credit or the royalties due for her unique contribution to the show. The sense of injustice seems only to have increased over time. On 13 December 1979 *Oklahoma!* was revived at the Palace Theatre, New York, preceded by a press preview on 6 December (it played until 24 August 1980). Agnes de Mille, aged seventy-four, was now a living legend, and one of the few survivors of the original production; she had also made a remarkable recovery from a debilitating cerebral hemorrhage in 1975. Clearly she enjoyed the press limelight, giving interviews to a number of daily newspapers and weekly magazines, and taking full advantage to write her own version of history that could not be gainsaid. Her remarks to Rosemary Tauris of *Cue New York* are representative. They appeared in an article "Oklahoma! It's Still Okay" in the issue for the week ending 21 December 1979:

> Far worse, there was no ballet music. De Mille had written out a scenario which Rodgers "stuffed in his pocket" never to look at again. "What do I play on the piano?" wondered de Mille. "You have the songs," replied Rodgers. With that he departed. How do you create a 17-minute dream ballet without music? The orchestrator, Robert Russell Bennett, came to the rescue. As de Mille tells it, Bennett wrote what he called "hurry music" to tide her over until Rodgers changed it. Rodgers never did.
>
> More disconcerting still was Hammerstein's original idea of a circus ballet. When de Mille asked why, the librettist explained, "Well, you have to end the act with something gay and colorful and up, to send the audience out in the lobby with." De Mille protested. "Girls don't dream about the circus. They dream about horrors. And they dream dirty dreams." More important, de Mille visualized it as an anxiety dream.[38]

Two issues here demand examination. First is the question of who wrote the ballet music. In the second part of her autobiography, *Promenade Home*, de Mille gave some credit to Rodgers. Here, too, we learn that she had made the first selection of the show's songs for the ballet (Rodgers was too busy), but he then became involved, "accenting, changing keys, shaping phrases, organizing both pace and music."[39] There was no music in the songs appropriate for the "death" scene at the end of the ballet, and de Mille choreographed it to silence. Rodgers approved, but suggested putting timpani strokes underneath to cue the dancers. Then "he added a coda and the

9. De Mille deserves credit for introducing "Jud's Postcards" (from left, Joan McCracken, Margit DeKova, Kate Friedlich, Vivian Smith, Bobby Barrentine) into the dream-ballet—"Girls . . . dream about horrors. And they dream dirty dreams"—although her plot owed more to Hammerstein than she later claimed. (Vandamm)

whole piece worked out well." Clearly, her reconstruction of events in 1979 was somewhat different, and rather insensitively so (Rodgers was to die on 30 December): here Rodgers takes no active interest in the ballet, and Bennett comes to the rescue with his "hurry music."

There seems little doubt that de Mille had a significant role in choosing the songs to be used in the ballet: Jay Blackton suggested something similar: "What amazed me was how she took Dick and Oscar's lyrical songs and used them as the framework, the roots, the sperm of her choreography."[40] It is also clear that Bennett did all the work in arranging the music: this would have been standard practice, just as Trude Rittman, Agnes de Mille's rehearsal pianist and dance arranger, composed Louise's ballet in act 2 of Carousel (and gained separate credit for it, presumably because it contains a significant degree of new music not drawn from songs in the show). Bennett's orchestral score of the dream-ballet matches the published vocal score quite closely, although there is some evidence that cuts were made before that score was prepared: one significant example (there are other minor ones) is represented by a lacuna in the orchestration, where according to the measure numbers, some sixty measures disappeared before mm. 381, suggesting that the version of "I Cain't Say No" here (for Jud's postcards) originally included the song's "trio" and a repeat of the chorus.[41] Bennett drew on his orchestrations for six of the act 1 songs, varying them in terms of tempo, harmony, and scoring to fit the new scenario, and in terms of key to fit the tonal sequence. However, de Mille's 1979 interviewer seems to have misunderstood (or was encouraged to misunderstand?) her reference to "hurry music." This cannot be the ballet music as a whole, which is well enough put together, with the songs matching the action in the ballet (in a fairly obvious manner, such as "Oh, What a Beautiful Mornin'" for the bridal preparations, a slowed-down version of "The Surrey with the Fringe on Top" for the wedding march, "I Cain't Say No" for "Jud's Postcards"). Rather, the "hurry music" probably refers to one point in the ballet where Bennett was required to provide a link, just after the "wedding" is interrupted by Jud, before his dancing with Laurey to "Pore Jud Is Daid" (mm. 293–97) then diverted by the arrival of the dance-hall girls (three in the stage directions, although the original production shots show five) greeted by a wolf whistle from the assembled cowboys.[42] The music to "Pore Jud Is Daid" attempts to continue (mm. 298–99) but breaks down: the orchestration has a note in blue pencil at m. 299 (where the "Pore Jud Is Daid" quotation breaks off), "Leave one line blank in parts," presumably because it was undecided whether to continue the quotation depending on how much time was needed for the stage movement. "Pore Jud Is Daid" yields to the introduction to "I Cain't Say No" for the "bawdy" dance, which Bennett labels a "can-can."

The "hurry music" is presumably the rather static chord sequence in mm. 285–92 (between "The Surrey with the Fringe on Top" and "Pore Jud Is Daid"). Bennett labeled this "The Tides," presumably a personal joke given that, as Agnes de Mille noted in 1979, this music was to "tide her over until Rodgers changed it." The original has an additional four measures between mm. 289–90 marked to be cut, which explains why the chromatic voice-leading in the top part (in the vocal score) misses a step. This music also reappears in an abbreviated form in mm. 389–93, where, according to a note in the orchestral score, "George wrestles with Katja."[43] The chord sequence is indeed fairly functional and has a temporary feel to it, although given Rodgers's overall lack of involvement in the ballet, it was probably unreasonable for de Mille to give the impression that he should have done something about it.

De Mille's 1958 reference to a late added coda for the "death" scene is more intriguing, if still a little confusing. Music seems to have been provided up to the fight between Curly and Jud—that is, to mm. 473–74 (containing a timpani roll cued to follow a shot from Curly's imaginary pistol). Measure 475 onward presumably corresponds to the action that de Mille originally choreographed to silence (the "death" scene), and for which Rodgers then added timpani strokes to cue the dancers. Regular timpani strokes are still present in Bennett's ballet score (almost to the end of the scene), but new music has been composed (mm. 475–510) to precede the distorted version of "The Surrey with the Fringe on Top" (as Jud kills Curly and carries Laurey off) and then "People Will Say We're in Love" as real-Laurey is awakened and goes off with real-Jud, leaving real-Curly "puzzled, dejected and defeated, as the curtain falls."

Bennett's original manuscript score for the dream-ballet ends precisely at m. 473 (there is no m. 474, the second of the two-measure timpani roll). There is a separate manuscript headed "End of Act I" (pp. 1–12), covering mm. 475–520 (the new music through the distortion of "The Surrey with the Fringe on Top"; m. 521 is omitted), then another containing "New end Act I" (pp. 1–2), covering mm. 522–31 (up to the end of the act; the reprise of "People Will Say We're in Love"). Here m. 475 is preceded by two measures containing just quarter-note Ds in cello, double-bass, and timpani, marked to be cut; it also has the blue-pencil note "Start when men lock arms" (presumably, for the fight). These two additional manuscripts are presumably what contain the late-added "coda" to which de Mille refers.

The question of when this coda might have been added is answered by an article in the New York World-Telegram of 15 June 1943:

> Early on the morning of the day *Oklahoma!*, the colorful musical play now showing at the St. James, was to open in New Haven, Robert Russell Bennett was faced with one of the toughest jobs of his distinguished career. The music for the first-act curtain scene had not yet been written!
>
> But why, you ask, should Mr. Bennett have had anything to worry about? He was merely the orchestrator, wasn't he? The composer was none other than Richard Rodgers.
>
> Right you are. But Mr. Rodgers had done his part—he had supplied the

orchestrator with four chords. Now it was up to Bennett to build this frag-
ment up into suitable ballet music for Marc Platt and Katherine Sergava.

At 3 A.M. he went to work. Eight hours later he was still at it. Moreover,
practically exhausted from long effort spent on other parts of the show before starting this new grind, he began to wonder if he would be able to hold
out. Yet he must. The curtain was to rise in a matter of hours.

Recalling the incident in his office in the RKO Building the other day
the pleasant, gray-haired composer-arranger smilingly declared: "Maybe it
was a good thing I was so darned tired, at that. When I am close to exhaus-
tion is when I am best able to produce the sort of music required in this
scene. Had I been thoroughly rested the chances are it wouldn't have turned
out so well."

As it was the complete score was ready for rehearsal at 3 P.M. Nothing
stood in the way of a successful presentation that night.

"But I still get a funny feeling in the middle of my back," laughed Mr.
Bennett, "every time I think how near we came to having no first act curtain
music."[44]

The "four chords" which Rodgers gave Bennett presumably made up the sequence in mm. 507–8, which also supports Bennett's new material in mm.
491–92 and then reappears as an ostinato under the distorted restatement
of "The Surrey with the Fringe on Top." By this reckoning, in that feverish
twelve hours before the New Haven opening (on 11 March 1943) Bennett
composed and orchestrated some fifty-seven measures of music (or forty-
seven if the final reprise of "People Will Say We're in Love," in the second
separate manuscript, was a still later addition). This was not the only frantic
composing, arranging, and orchestrating done just before and after the New
Haven opening.

Thus far, de Mille's various accounts of the creation of the dream-ballet
can at least somehow be reconciled with the "facts" as we know them, allowing for the inevitable distortions of memory and invention. However, her
other main claim in 1979—that the subject matter was wholly due to her—
turns out to be very problematic indeed. Here she seems to have had a two-
pronged agenda: first, to demonstrate her unique contribution both to *Oklahoma!* and to the treatment of ballets in musicals as a whole; and second, to
claim that the idea of creating a nightmare of Laurey's sexual fantasies was
entirely hers. In her interview with Wilk, de Mille took credit for introducing "sex" into the ballet (by way of Jud's postcards), and in 1979 she reveled
in the tale of how she dissuaded Hammerstein from his idea of a "circus ballet." Certainly, Hammerstein had written shows about circuses (for example,

Sunny and *Three Sisters*), and there was a circus ballet in Kurt Weill's *Lady in the Dark* (1941; it also ran in New York from 27 February to 15 May 1943, concurrently with *Oklahoma!*). But it was never Hammerstein's intention to do the same in *Oklahoma!*

Dream-ballets were not new, and a number of features of the *Oklahoma!* one have precedents in previous musicals by Rodgers and Hart, and by others. Hammerstein had already tried out dream sequences with Kern, including those in *Three Sisters* (London, 1934), *Gentlemen Unafraid* (St Louis, 1938; with Otto Harbach), and *Very Warm for May* (1939; choreographed by Albertina Rasch and Harry Losee).[45] Rodgers and Hart's *On Your Toes* (1936) had two ballets, one of which ("Slaughter on Tenth Avenue") dealt with two men, a woman, and a murder, and *Babes in Arms* (1937) also had a dream-ballet ("Peter's Journey")—both shows were choreographed by George Balanchine—as did *Pal Joey* (1940; choreographed by Robert Alton) at the end of its act 1. The trend was confirmed by Irving Berlin's *Louisiana Purchase* (1940), and still more by Weill's *Lady in the Dark*, which had a series of dream sequences choreographed by Rasch. But while none of this necessarily denies Agnes de Mille's contribution to the genre, her claim about Hammerstein's plan for a "circus ballet" cannot be true. *Draft2* (1-3-8–10) contains Hammerstein's detailed outline of the dream-ballet that must have been completed before de Mille came in on the project: Hammerstein notes here that a dance director is still to be engaged and consulted, and therefore that his ideas remain flexible. Laurey has just taken a whiff of the "Elixir of Egypt" and, dazed, sits under a tree:

ADO ANNIE

You all right, Laurey?

LAUREY

'Course I'm all right. You and the Peddler git along and leave me by myself. I want to think clear. Beginnin' to, a'ready.

(*She closes her eyes and screws her face up in a big effort at concentration*)

PEDDLER

(*To Annie*)

C'mon and leave her be. If she believes she's thinkin' clear, well then mebbe she is.

(ADO ANNIE *joins him. They start to walk away. Then* ADO ANNIE *stops and points off.*)

ADO ANNIE

Look! Wonder who's surrey 'at is, comin' up over the rise.

PEDDLER

How c'n I tell? Mus' be a mile off.

(LAUREY *opens her eyes slowly and looks off*)

ADO ANNIE

Looks purty with the horses steppin' high, drivin' smack in front of the settin' sun, like them pitchers y'cut out with scissors.

PEDDLER

Sil-you-ets, y'call them, Ado Annie.

ADO ANNIE

That's whut I mean . . . Sil-you-ets.

(*She takes the Peddler's arm and they walk off.* LAUREY *sits still, her back against the tree, her eyes gazing far off. Music steals in softly. The lights fade down.* LAUREY *starts to sing. The song will set the mood and establish the theme of a ballet to follow.*[)]

Hammerstein then proceeds to describe the ballet:

As the lights dim further, LAUREY's voice dies off. The trunk of the tree revolves slowly and she goes round with it, out of sight. Dim figures glide on to the stage, and now a ballet is started which states, in terms of fantasy, the problems that beset Laurey. The treatment will be bizarre, imaginative and amusing, and never heavy.

The figures in the ballet, LAUREY, CURLY, JUD, etc. may be portrayed by the actors who play these roles or by Dancers who simulate them. This will depend on the talents of the cast and the judgment of the dance director.

LAUREY's contemplation of her problems will be played against the background of the world she lives in and the people she knows. AUNT ELLER appears in pink tights, dressed as a circus rider and advises Laurey to do whut's natchrel and ride to the party with Curly. ANNIE dances first with WILL and then with the PEDDLER and advises Laurey not to say no to nobody.

JUD dances on wearing a costume full of knot-holes. He says Curly shot through ev'y one of 'em and never tetched him. Curly cain't hurt him. Nuthin' can. He'll always be here, always hangin' over Laurey like a cloud. (The vocal statements may be sung or spoken by one group and interpreted by another group who dance—after the manner of "Coq D'or." At this point, however, we don't wish to adopt any inflexible ideas of approach until a dance director is engaged and consulted and is made a co-creator of this entire sequence.)

Now CURLY comes on, in the most gorgeous and glittering surrey ever seen. Yeller fringe? It's gold! And the lamps are winkin' and blinkin' like lightnin' bugs, just as he said they would. Two wonderful—though somewhat misshapen—horses trot in front of him. CURLY sits holding the reins, looking like a king. In fact, the front seat of the surrey is a throne, and there is a throne beside it—for a Queen.

CURLY jumps down lightly. LAUREY offers him her lunch basket. They may even sit under the tree and have a bite while JUD and his companion-spirits of evil dance behind them. Then CURLY asks her if she'll ride with him, of course she will! She looks like a Queen now and certainly feels like one as he leads her to the surrey. The simple melody of the "Surrey song" is now played triumphantly and with symphonic brilliance. But as CURLY is about to lift her on to the surrey—indeed he is holding her in mid-air—JUD comes in and challenges his right.

CURLY starts firing shots at JUD but they make no sound and only the blowing of Jud's coat indicates that the bullets are going through knot-holes. JUD keeps coming after Curly with a frog-sticker. The horses get frightened and bolt off, dragging the surrey after them. It looks as if Jud will kill Curly. In fact, he keeps saying he will—"Less'n Laurey goes with me, like she promises, I'll kill Curly, kill him dead!"

The only way for Laurey to save Curly's life is to pull herself out of this contemplation. All details of the final ensemble picture of the ballet are now blocked out by dimming lights as a spot "Fades up" on the center again and the trunk of the tree revolves, revealing LAUREY as we left her, except that her eyes are frightened. As the lights come slowly up, JUD'S VOICE can be heard, growing louder.

The script continues:

JUD

Laurey . . . Laurey—Where air you?—Laurey!—
(*He enters dressed in his "good suit." He probably hasn't had it on in a long time. It's too tight. His neck looks stiff in a high, starched collar, and from the way he walks, his shoes can't be very comfortable. His hair is plastered down in a flat curl—"Bartender fashion."*)
Y'ready, Laurey?—Hey, don't you hear me?—
(*Shouting*)
Laurey!

LAUREY

(*Looking around*)
Whut? Whut's the matter?—Oh, that you, Jud?

JUD

Sure, it's me. I said, air you ready? I got ol' eighty hitched to the buckboard.
(CURLY *enters. He's dressed up too, but not uncomfortably*)

CURLY

'Lo, Laurey. Look!
(*He points off.* LAUREY's *eyes follow his*)

Ain't she a beauty?
(*From the light in* LAUREY's *eyes "she" is indeed a beauty*)
Nice team too, ain't they? And can they go!

JUD

(*In a low, threatening voice*)
Air you comin' with me?
(LAUREY *turns, startled*)
Air you?

CURLY

Whut if she ain't?

JUD

Jist let her say fer herself.
(Pause)

LAUREY

(*In a small voice*)
See you at the party, Curly.
(*She goes to* JUD *who grins across at Curly.* CURLY *takes out his Bull Durham
    and starts to roll a cigarette, to appear unconcerned.* LAUREY *looks at the
    bottle of 'Lixir.*)
Ole 'Gyptian smellin' salts!
(*She flings the bottle away from her and goes off with Jud.* CURLY *looks off
    towards his Surrey, heartbroken. The "Surrey Theme," which started with
    his entrance, now swells up, but not triumphantly—A deep, beautiful cello
    and violin moan.* CURLY *never finishes rolling the cigarette. He crushes it
    in his hand and lets it all drop to the floor, tobacco, paper and all.—The
    Curtain, too, falls at about this time.*)

Hammerstein's outline may lack the strong narrative thread linking the
episodes of de Mille's version of the ballet, but the bones are there. Two
things are particularly striking. First is Hammerstein's granting of significance (once again) to the "Surrey Song," which appears at climactic points
in the ballet (as it would in the final version), and also at the end of the act
after the ballet has returned to the "real" world. Second is the reference to a
double team of performers, comprising singers/speakers and dancers/mimes
"after the manner of 'Coq D'or.'" This refers to the Metropolitan Opera's
1918 production of Rimsky-Korsakov's *The Golden Cockerel* (modeled after
the Diaghilev-Fokine version of 1914), which had singers seated at the side
of the stage and dancers and mimes enacting the plot. This pantomime production made something of a splash in New York, being done annually at
the Metropolitan in 1918–21 and 1924–28—often as part of a double bill
with *Cavalleria rusticana*; a similar version was done by the Charlotte Lund

Opera Company in 1930. It was remembered fondly through the 1930s (at least in the *New York Times*) until the "original" sung version (but with significant cuts) appeared at the Metropolitan in 1937, plus a new ballet version by Fokine, with no singing, the same year.[46] Rodgers parodied the 1918 production in his *Say It with Jazz* (1921), while in 1933, Kern cited it as a model for a new type of drama that might permit psychological exploration.[47] It is not clear whether Hammerstein's intentions reflected a concern about communicating meaning through dance or were an attempt to increase the artistic stakes for *Oklahoma!* Either way, de Mille clearly had a better idea.

Her impact certainly made itself felt not just on the scenario for the dream-ballet but also on the manner of its introduction. Once Rodgers and Hammerstein had decided on a dream-ballet (by *Draft2*), Hammerstein began to draft a text for the song for Laurey that would "set the mood and establish the theme of a ballet to follow." Although the provisional title for this song in *Draft2* was "How Would It Be" (for the "entire company"), Hammerstein instead worked extensively on a lyric variously titled "I Hear a Breeze in a Tree, Sighing" and "Why, Oh Why?" This went through numerous sketches and redactions, one of the latest of which seems to be the following:

> I hear a breeze in a tree, sighing
> Why, oh why, oh why . . .
> Seems like an echo of me sighing
> Softly sighing why, oh why, oh why
> Must I be all alone?
> I dream, but my dream's my own.
> I know a boy who must be sighing,
> Why, oh why, oh why?
> Lonely and wistful are we, sighing,
> Gazing at the sky and sighing, why
> Can't we combine our dreaming—
> Only the breeze and the boy and I?[48]

This fits the stage direction as Laurey "sits still, her back against the tree, her eyes gazing far off. Music steals in softly. The lights fade down." It is also suitably dreamy. However, it has all the hallmarks of being provisional (the repeated *sighings*), if not a disaster: the extraordinarily high number of sketches (thirty-two) reveals Hammerstein's concern even as they make one wonder why he bothered to continue.

A way out of the impasse appears to have been offered by the suggestion (presumably from Agnes de Mille) that the dream-ballet should show how "Laurey makes up her mind." Hammerstein provided a new text for which no sketches survive at all, but only a "finished" typed version (two pages), headed "Prelude to ballet":

> (*The* PEDLAR *and* ADO ANNIE *have made their exit, leaving* LAURIE [sic] *sitting under the tree with her bottle of Elixir, deep in thought. The lights change. Soft voices are heard*:)

GIRLS

> You are a girl who knows what she wants
> And you can choose
> Flowers for your easter hat
> and buckles for your shoes.
> You are a girl who knows what she wants,
> And when you find him,
> You will know the man
> Your heart has waited for,
> And when you are in his arms
> You will want no more.

ALTO'S [sic]

What do you want?

SOPRANO'S

Is it Curly?

LAURIE

Maybe so.

ALTO'S

Or—

SOPRANO'S

Ha-ha-ha!

ALTO'S

Is it Jud?

LAURIE

Oh, no.

GIRLS

No?

LAURIE

No!

GIRLS

> Laurie! Make up your mind—by yourself.
> Don't ask Aunt Eller,
> Don't ask the stars,

Don't ask the pedlar—he only guesses.
Don't ask Elixir's or 'Gyptian Princesses—

(Their voices dying off)

You are a girl who knows what she wants,
You are a girl who knows what she wants . . .

(As their voices die off, LAURIE starts to sing, her voice gaining in strength as she confesses the truth to herself for the first time:)
LAUREY [*sic*]
I am a girl who knows what she wants
And I can choose
Flowers for my easter hat
and buckles for my shoes.
I am a girl who knows what she wants,
And I have found him,
I have found the man
My heart has waited for,
And once I am in his arms
I will want no more.

(The music continues. The lights grow lower. After a moment's thoughtful silence, LAUREY speaks:)
I know what I want . . . Only—
(She looks off, frightened)
Only I'm skeered of . . . sumthin' . . . Jist the same, I'd like to go with Curly in the surrey.
(A light dawning in her eyes.)
I want to marry Curly! . . .
(The wispy figure of a bride glides on from the shadows. LAUREY gazes ahead of her, entranced in her daydream . . .)
Yes . . .
(Bridesmaids, too! Her voice goes down to a whisper.)
. . . Yes . . .
(Take it, Agnes!)[49]

Hammerstein's final instruction makes it clear that this text was written in full knowledge of Agnes de Mille's involvement, and probably in response to her ideas for the ballet: the middle section here does indeed have Laurey making up her mind, albeit in a clumsy way (presumably Hammerstein was extemporizing). It may even date from the rehearsal period, given that costumes for the girls in act 1, scene 3 were a late addition. The lyric is still somewhat pedestrian, but it anticipates significant elements of the final text, "Out of My Dreams," in terms of content ("in his arms" becomes "and into his arms"; "Laurie! Make up your mind—by yourself" becomes "Make up your mind, make up your mind, Laurey") and also structure (the ABA form, with the final A for Laurey, and the disposition of the voices). For that matter, the poetic meter for the chorus ("You are a girl who knows what she wants") is almost exactly the same (save the five syllables of the final line "You will want no more" compared with the six of "Into a dream come true"). Either Rodgers wrote his melody (for the chorus) to this text and Hammerstein then revised it into a more effective form, in a manner similar to the case of "Lonely Room," or (and perhaps more likely) Hammerstein added one set of words to a preexisting melody, then produced another.

These various materials for, and accounts of, the dream-ballet provide a number of intriguing glimpses into creative decisions and compositional processes as ideas started to coalesce and come into focus. They also serve as an object lesson for the historian seeking too simple a reading of the sources. It would be easy to take Agnes de Mille's 1979 interviews at face value; it would be equally easy, in the light of the present discussion, to dismiss them entirely. But neither strategy seems appropriate. Certainly Hammerstein wanted the dream-ballet to be "bizarre, imaginative and amusing, and never heavy" (he says in *Draft2*), and his initial scenario does not play on Laurey's "dirty dreams" that Agnes de Mille claimed were her invention: the notion of Laurey and Curly sitting down to a picnic "while Jud and his companion-spirits of evil dance behind them" is also somewhat absurd, if typically whimsical. Equally certainly, however, Hammerstein never wanted a "circus ballet," and for de Mille to suggest otherwise in 1979 seems disingenuous or worse. But perhaps memories have become so distorted by this point that de Mille really did believe what she was saying. One can see what might have triggered it: Hammerstein's outline in *Draft2* does indeed refer to Aunt Eller appearing in Laurey's dream "in pink tights, dressed as a circus rider." Here the reference is to a prior moment in act 1, scene 3 (*Draft2*, 1-3-4; developing the play, p. 54) where the Peddler is selling wares to Ado Annie, Laurey, and Eller:

LAUREY

(*Trying to lighten up*)
You buy the face-whitenin' Aunt Eller, nen you'll look as purty as them lady riders in the circus—'cept for not havin' on no pink tights.

AUNT ELLER
All right then, if it'll make me look like a circus rider.

De Mille, then, could well have taken a fragmented memory and elaborated it in ways that certainly served a purpose, but which may also have had for her some status of truth.

 CHAPTER 4

Heading for Broadway

K ONSTANTIN SIMONOV'S *THE RUSSIAN PEOPLE*, IN THE GUILD
Theatre, closed on 31 January 1943; Philip Barry's *Without Love*, the
first Theatre Guild play of the season (it had opened on 10 November 1942), closed at the St. James Theatre on 13 February (after grossing
$967,541, including $260,000 for the film rights).[1] Although the Guild's
other long-running play of the 1942–43 season, S. N. Behrman's highly popular *The Pirate*, was still playing at the Martin Beck Theatre (it opened on
25 November 1942 and closed on 27 April 1943), one assumes that thoughts
were becoming entirely focused on *Oklahoma!* save for the problems of
planning the next season.

By now, the Guild had multiple copies of Hammerstein's libretto, and
Rodgers's rehearsal pianist, Margo Hopkins, voice-piano scores of the main
songs composed thus far (another set must have been prepared for Robert
Russell Bennett to orchestrate), which presumably would have been taught
by ear to the principals and chorus. This is not to say, however, that the creation of *Oklahoma!* was in any way complete. Both the text and the music
were to be revised significantly during the rehearsals and pre-Broadway tryouts as problems were found and solved, and creative compromises were
made to get the show on the road. The issue raises important questions about
authorship and responsibility. It is also a simple fact of theatrical life.

Rehearsals

On Monday, 8 February, just over one week after *The Russian People* closed, rehearsals for *Oklahoma!* began in the Guild Theatre. After the customary speeches (from Lawrence Langner and Rouben Mamoulian), the first afternoon was devoted to Rodgers and Hammerstein running through the music. Within the next day or so, the cast was whittled down — Equity rules granted five days to confirm contracts once rehearsals had begun — with a number officially dismissed on 10 February, presumably for not showing up on the 8th or for other inadequacies.[2] Also on 8 February (coincidentally, it seems), Lynn Riggs asked for a report: "*Green Grow* seems to be in progress and I'm glad. . . . I wonder if your publicity man could send me a significant story on *Green Grow* once in a while as they come out — naturally I'd like to know who's in it, and such things. Friends report stories occasionally — but no one thinks to send me clippings!" This prompted Theresa Helburn (probably) to reply on 13 February:

> We went into rehearsal Monday and life has been chaotic since then, but the play looks good. Dick has done some lovely music and I think Oscar's book has shaped up extremely well. We've tried to keep as much as possible of the original spirit, but of course a musical entails an enormous amount of change. Unfortunately, we can't keep the title, because of the picture situation, and after much travail and agony we finally got everyone to agree on
>
> Away We Go!
>
> which I'm sure you won't like at all since *Green Grow* is in your blood, but it has action and gaiety and it is the only one that has so far gotten a majority vote from the six of seven judges involved.
>
> Alfred Drake, who plays Curly, is going to be excellent and has a lovely voice. The girl, Joan Roberts, has a fine voice though she is not as good an actress as we would like. Betty Garde is a tower of strength as Aunt Ella [*sic*]. Howard deSilva is going to be fine as Jud (your Jeeter). Buloff will, I think, be excellent as the peddler and Celeste Holm is enchanting as Ado Annie. There's a new comedy dancing boy introduced into the book — he is in love with Ado Annie — and is being played by Lee Dixon.
>
> Agnes deMille is working on the dances and I think will produce results that have both humor and beauty. We just got a new number for the last act called "Oklahoma," which I know would delight you. I'll ask Joe Heidt to send you notices from time to time. More anon.
>
> I hope you'll be able to get a furlough to see the show.

Langner also located the creation of the title song during the rehearsal period: "While *Oklahoma!* was in rehearsal at the Guild Theatre, Oscar and
Dick were writing new songs without any apparent effort during the rehearsals, whenever they were needed. Terry and John Gassner, our playreader,
suggested that some kind of rousing song of the earth would be helpful in
the second act, and one day Dick and Oscar appeared at the theatre, [and]
sat at the piano where we surrounded them on benches and chairs, while
they played for us the rousing melody of the song 'Oklahoma!'"[3]

Helburn's calm report to Riggs must have hidden a great deal. Given that
everyone was now on site for the rehearsals, we have relatively few written
records of day-to-day events. For this period, Wilk relies mainly on memoirs
by, and/or interviews with, Agnes de Mille, George Irving, Celeste Holm,
Alfred Drake, Bambi Linn, and others, which, as usual, cannot always be
reconciled with other sources or even with one another. For example, there
is nothing to confirm (or deny) the story of how Hammerstein browbeat Jay
Blackton into accepting quite late in the day the engagement to conduct
Oklahoma! However, certain stories told by the participants that might be
thought unbelievable (or at least, grossly exaggerated) can in fact be shown to
be based on fact. George Church relayed the hilarious tale of how Mamoulian wanted more spectacle for the last scene of the show, bringing in an
"honest-to-goodness cowboy from Oklahoma" who spun ropes. The idea was
for the roper to spin his lasso round Joan Roberts and Alfred Drake while
they sang "Oklahoma," but the rope caught the singers, then, in a separate attempt, Mamoulian himself, and the roper was unceremoniously dismissed.
This was presumably Jack Harwood, the "fancy roper" called for rehearsal
on 16 February, who later (on 19 November 1944) wrote asking for tickets to
the show for his doctor: "You may recall [that] I did the roping routine and
taught Alfred Drake to spin the rope in *Oklahoma*[!]"[4] It seems that Harwood was due to play in the show in New Haven and Boston (he is listed as
a "cowboy" in the programs)—we do not know whether he did—although
he had been dropped by the New York opening.

Prominent in several accounts of the rehearsals is the shabby treatment
accorded to Agnes de Mille and her dancers by Mamoulian. He had tried
to interfere in their selection, taking objection to Bambi Linn, Joan Mc-
Cracken, and Diana Adams.[5] And while he hogged the stage for the dialogue
and the songs, she and her team were relegated—in different tellings—to the
Guild Theatre's lobby, a dusty attic, or the basement, and probably all three
for simultaneous rehearsals. Just before the start of the rehearsal period, Hel-

burn still had a folk-type vision of the show. On 6 February she contacted
J. R. (Jack) Hickisch, whom she had heard calling dances at the Madison
Square Dance Festival (probably the National Folk Festival held at Madison Square Garden on 11 May 1942). She wanted to use his ideas for "a
general country dance," and anything he could offer "would be most helpful to our dance director, Miss deMille. . . . As we go into rehearsal next
week, time is of the essence." De Mille's idea may have been to repeat one
of her scenes in *Rodeo* which involving a square dance choreographed to
dance calls, clapping, and foot stamping, but no music. Hickisch responded
by sending a handwritten list of calls and a recording. On 9 March, Helburn sent an apology: "I am terribly sorry to have delayed writing to you
but I have been in the thick of the production of *Green Grow the Lilacs*,
and as the musical shaped up we found we could use no calls at all and that
the whole number would have to be done in ballet and singing." Helburn
offered to send a check to cover costs and invited him to the show ("We
expect to open in New York early in April"); Hickisch in turn requested a
donation to the Red Cross (the Guild sent $25). Presumably all this relates
to "The Farmer and the Cowman," for which de Mille instead enlisted the
help of May Gadd of the American Country Dance Society (also involved
in the 1942 National Folk Festival) to show the appropriate moves.[6] However, it was left to an out-of-town critic, Cecil Smith of the *Chicago Daily
Tribune* (1 April 1943), to point out rather mischievously that (according to
his headline) "Square dances are the rage in N.Y. musicals," following the
precedent, he said, of Cole Porter's *Let's Face It!* (which ran on Broadway
from 29 October 1941 to 20 March 1943): Smith notes the phenomenon
in connection with Porter's *Something for the Boys* (opened on 7 January
1943, with choreography by Jack Cole) and *Oklahoma!* although both were
outdone by Robert Alton's spectacular extravaganza "Swing Your Honey,
Mr. Hemingway" in the new *Ziegfeld Follies*.

Despite de Mille's claims of planning all the dancing and the dream-
ballet in November–December 1942, much of the choreography seems to
have been worked out during rehearsal. Several of the dancers (including
Bambi Linn and Marc Platt) variously recalled her technique of allowing
them to explore movement, try out gestures, and gradually build up a sequence: they also remembered with distinct fondness the sheer physicality
of the process, and shared a ferocious devotion to de Mille for her innovative,
liberating approach.[7] Kate Friedlich also told how she lost the part of the
"girl who falls down" in the "Many a New Day" ballet to Joan McCracken

because she missed two days of rehearsal on grounds of the illnesses that seem to have affected many of the cast due to the cold February weather. McCracken's agent, Audrey Wood, requested special casting credit for her during the Boston tryout.[8] In particular, the dream-ballet appears to have undergone several mutations. An early February (it seems) costume list for the show includes one for the Peddler in the dream-ballet. (He does not appear in the final version.) The costumes for the five "postcard girls" were included in the original designs, it seems (which may contradict de Mille's account that they were added during rehearsal), but there were some other costume adjustments made here as the ballet reached its final form. (Capes and hats for five girls were added later, on 24 February.) The lead-in to the ballet also appears to have been rethought: again from the costume lists, it seems that having Laurey's friends sing in "Out of My Dreams" was not in the initial plan—the veils that appear in production photographs were subsequently provided for them separately)—which suggests that its predecessor, "You Are a Girl," also came late.[9] The "Vivian" and "Virginia" included in the dialogue of act 1, scene 3 in the printed libretto, and singing in "Out of My Dreams," were probably actual chorus members (Vivienne Simon and Virginia Oswald), so this scene was almost certainly created after rehearsals began. It had been done so by 24 February, however, given that in her notes on the run-through on that day, Helburn wanted to attend to "Staging in the group around Laurey in the 'Out of your Dream' scene." According to Elaine Anderson (the assistant stage manager), the dream-ballet and one or more other dance numbers were first tried out on stage on a Sunday, probably 21 February; de Mille instead said that she put the dream-ballet together on the "second Sunday" (the 21st), and first showed it at what seems to have been a run-through on the 22nd.[10] Either way, this suggests that de Mille was close to the mark when she said that all the dances in the show were set within the first two weeks of rehearsal. Her demands appear to have exasperated Mamoulian and even, it seems, Helburn; de Mille, in turn, claimed that Rodgers was a significant source of strength.[11] According to her memoirs, she also wrote to her fiancé on 23 February that "disorganization, demoralization and confusion" had set in, although she was in a better mood the next day (after another run-through, it seems):

> Nearly all the important dances are done, only bits and pieces are left. I have never worked so fast in my life. I've set forty minutes of straight dancing in less than three weeks. The company raves. Rodgers put his head on

my shoulder this afternoon and said, "Oh, Aggie, you're such a comfort in my old age." And Marc Platt, my leading dancer, said this evening, "In all soberness, I never worked with anyone I respected more." Katya has made a hit. I've discovered two girls who are going to be sensations, my two leading men *are males* and also the stage manager, so rehearsals are lively and gay. We live in the basement. I see sunlight only twenty minutes each day. The dust from the unvacuumed Guild rugs has made us all sick, and I put away three Thermos bottles of coffee an afternoon. I look awful. Thin, old, and hard. A rumor came down from upstairs, where the grownups work, that Mamoulian (Mamoo, he is called) did something good at eleven-thirty.[12]

Even outside the dancing, the show needed a great deal of work. We have seen that *Draft3*, or something close to it, provided the text at least for the start of the rehearsals, so there must have been a great deal of rewriting and composing during February. At least some of this reworking must have been prompted by Rouben Mamoulian as he tried to get the show into shape. "When I Go Out Walkin' with My Baby" seems to have been current at least in the early stages of rehearsal, given that it is included in the lyric sheets prepared for Jerome (Jerry) Whyte, the stage manager. Also, at least one and perhaps two potential Lottas were called for rehearsal, and Miles White's original costume designs included one for the "Mexican girl."[13] Helburn's rehearsal notes following the run-through on 24 February seem to refer to the "fire" in the second act, suggesting that the last scene of the show had not yet reached its final form. But there were also problems earlier in this same act, and indeed, from the end of "The Farmer and the Cowman" on. One, not to be solved until the tryouts, was the number for Laurey and Curly. Another was the design of "Oklahoma." In addition to Mamoulian's attempt to add rope spinning, the decision to have a central tap dance episode for George Church (abandoned in Boston, as we shall see) was made after the costumes were commissioned, and probably after 20 February: on 16 March 1943, Brooks Costume Co. submitted an invoice for additional items, including $110 for "Geo. Church—for Specialty in Wedding."[14]

With or without Lotta, the Ado Annie/Will Parker subplot caused further problems. We have two sets of lyrics for *Oklahoma!* on mimeographed sheets; one was used by Jerry Whyte, and the other was sent to Lynn Riggs and kept by him in some disorder (see table 4.1).[15] This makes sense for Whyte: only partial lyrics were included in *Draft3*, so for a complete text of the show, a stage manager would have needed to refer to two separate sources. These lyric sheets correlate for the most part with those linked to

10. "Out of My Dreams," with Joan Roberts as Laurey. The women's veils were a late purchase during the rehearsals for *Oklahoma!* as the lead-in to the dream-ballet was revised to include a song for Laurey and her friends as she starts to focus on the man of her dreams. (Uncredited)

the songs in the Richard Rodgers Collection, and they seem to reflect one step further in the design of the show. The fact that most of them are mimeographed prompts the notion of a degree of fixity; equally, the use of typescript for "All er Nuthin'," "Boys and Girls Like You and Me," and (in the Rodgers Collection) "Lonely Room" suggests that they were written during rehearsal (as does the fact that they did not get entered into Whyte's set), while "It's a Scandal! It's a Outrage" (another song not included in Whyte's set) also seems to have come late.[16] This supports Hammerstein's claim (reported in the *Boston Herald* on 13 March) that some of the best songs in the show had been added in rehearsal, a line also taken on 3 March in the *Christian Science Monitor*, which describes Rodgers at what seems to have been a recent rehearsal: "He was sitting there talking to Mr. Hammerstein a short while later, when suddenly he got up and went to the piano, whis-

Table 4.1. *Oklahoma!*: Mimeographed (etc.) lyric sheets

Jerome Whyte's copy (*NHb* TG 122/1)	Lynn Riggs's copy (*NHb* Riggs 13/228; out of order)
Oh, What a Beautiful Mornin'	Oh, What a Beautiful Mornin'
The Surrey with the Fringe on Top	The Surrey with the Fringe on Top
Kansas City	
I Cain't Say No	I Cain't Say No
Many a New Day	Many a New Day
	A Scandal for the Jaybirds (It's a Scandal! It's a Outrage!)
People Will Say We're in Love	People Will Say We're in Love
Pore Jud Is Daid	Pore Jud Is Daid
When I Go Out Walkin' with My Baby	When I Go Out Walkin' with My Baby
Out of My Dreams	Out of My Dreams
The Farmer and the Cowman	The Farmer and the Cowman (two copies; one just typescript of opening)
Together	Together
	All er Nuthin' (typescript; as lyric-sheet in *Wc* RC 12/1)
	Boys and Girls Like You and Me (typescript; as lyric-sheet in *Wc* RC 12/2)
Oklahoma (chorus; no verse)	Oklahoma (chorus; no verse)

tling a little as he went. He sat down, tapped out the beginning of a melody, then began to play it. The melody grew, while the company listened. And in ten minutes, there emerged a new song, simple and charming and in the opinion of the *Away We Go!* company, one of the sure-fire hit songs of the show." (Was this "Boys and Girls Like You and Me"?)

The other surprise in these lyric sheets is the presence in act 2 of "Together," a song that at one point replaced "I'll Be at Your Elbow" for Ado Annie and the Peddler in act 1, scene 1 but was now relocated, and reallocated to Ado Annie and Will (who have no act 2 number in *Draft2*):

WILL

(*Talking to music, then singing*)

I'd like fer my wife to be true to me.

ANNIE

Bet yer life yer wife'll be true,
As long as you see that I'll alw'ys be

Right up clost to you!
(It's easier to be true,
When I'm up clost to you.)

WILL

Then tha's jist the way it's goin' to be.
I'll keep you tied to me:

BOTH

(*In close harmony*)

We'll go on together
Singin' in the sun.
You're as close to me as "B" to "A."
Two contented voices,
Blended into one,
We'll go harmonizin' on our way.
If we drift apart as people do,
I'll come harmonizin' back to you.
What's the diff'rence whether
We have rain or sun?
We'll have sun if we can sing together.

(*Music continues. They start to walk off.*)

This fits the context of the dialogue that would eventually lead up to "All er Nuthin'," although the lyric itself is rather anodyne, like the equally saccharine "Boys and Girls Like You and Me."

"Together" does not seem to have lasted very long; indeed, it is not clear that Rodgers ever wrote the music. However, its much punchier and wittier replacement, "All er Nuthin'," which is much more in character, also seems to have undergone changes. The set of lyrics sent to Riggs includes a four-page carbon copy typescript (marked "insert") paginated 2-2-11, then 2-2-11a–c.[17] The format (which seems to be typing from the Rialto Bureau) suggests that this was produced in New York and not later (so during the rehearsals), even though both Bambi Linn and Vivian Smith linked (somewhat inconsistently) the dance part of "All er Nuthin'" to frantic revisions in New Haven.[18] Page 2-2-11 contains dialogue (Will gives Ado Annie an "Oklahoma hello" and then says that she cannot continue her previous behavior with men), leading to the lyrics of "All er Nuthin'" on 2-2-11a and 2-2-11b (ending "He'd better look a lot like me!"). Page 2-2-11c is headed "Suggested dance idea":

(*Annie and Will start to dance together. Another man dances on. She looks over at him curiously and a little wistfully. Will frowns. She obediently looks back at Will, who now starts to do one of his best steps, showing off for her.*)

ANNIE

You shore c'n shake yer trotters, Will!

(*Pleased, he continues. Then another dancer, perhaps Eric, enters and starts a showy step. Annie looks at him, tries to look back at Will but is finally compelled to fasten her attention on the wonderful step Eric is doing. Will gets her shoulders and yanks her around.*)

Well they shore make it tough to look at you, Will!

(*Eric exits. Will dances away from Annie angrily. She dances after him, now she becomes crafty and feminine.*)

Trouble with you is you don't trust me. I believe you and you don't believe me. I even believe it when you say how good you was in Kansas City.

(*This strikes home. He probably wasn't.*)

I think when you love a person, you orta trust him. You orta go the whole way!

(*Singing*)

> With me it's all er nuthin'!
> Is it all er nuthin' with you?
> It cain't be "in between"
> It cain't be "now and then"
> No half and half romance will do!
> I cin [*sic*] cook like a streak,
> Biscuits er bread,
> Handy with a needle and threat [*sic*]—
> Take me like I am er leave me be!
> If you cain't give me all, give me nuthin'—
> And nuthin's whut you'll git from me!

(*She struts away*)

WILL

Oh, Ado Annie!

ANNIE

(*Making an exit*)
Nuthin's whut you'll get from me!

WILL

Come on and kiss me![19]

ANNIE

(*Coming right back out of the wings on the same step*)
Hello, Will.
(*Embrace, Oklahoma style. Blackout.*)

The pagination suggests that this comes from a typescript that numbered the pages of each scene of act 2 separately: most of the surviving draft copies of act 2 have through pagination, with scene 1 ending on 2-1-25 and scene 2 running from 2-2-26 to 2-2-35. Here, scene 2 concerns Laurey and Jud, then Laurey and Curly (leading to their as yet unwritten act 2 number); it takes up ten pages. Thus page 2-2-11 would follow Laurey and Curly's exit, suggesting that at this stage, "All er Nuthin'" was situated at the end of act 2, scene 2, where the final version has a front-of-traveler scene for the Peddler and Ado Annie (with his "Persian goodbye"), then Will with his "Oklahoma hello" (mentioned in the draft, although there is no Peddler here), allowing the change of set for scene 3. This was also its location in New Haven; it seems to have been shifted to the end of act 2, scene 1 in Boston so as to cover the previous set change and also, perhaps, to place more emphasis on the union of Laurey and Curly.

The "suggested dance idea," with two men coming on to distract Ado Annie, much to Will's annoyance, picks up on Hammerstein's original design for the reprise of "I Cain't Say No" in act 1, scene 1. The "Eric" mentioned in the plan for "All er Nuthin'" is Eric Victor, a specialty dancer whose *Oklahoma!* career was short-lived. By or during the Boston tryout, however, the "All er Nuthin'" dance was cut, then expanded to include both men and women (the latter presumably to distract Will) — or expanded, then cut, depending on the chronological order of the two Boston programs listing the dancers — and was then reduced just to two women for the New York premiere and the final version (p. 115): "Two girls come on and do a dance with WILL in which they lure him away from ADO ANNIE. ADO ANNIE, trying to get him back, does an oriental dance. WILL, accusing her, says: 'That's Persian!' and returns to the girls. But ADO ANNIE yanks him back. The girls dance off. ADO ANNIE sings." The new "oriental dance" (at m. 167 in the vocal score) required some additions and alterations to the orchestrations. Ado Annie's final stanza in "All er Nuthin'" was also changed late (in Boston, Langner said) to give a much more feisty punchline.[20]

Preparations were no less frantic behind the wings. Miles White seems to have designed the costumes in the last week of January and early February: by 11 February he had prepared a list of costumes, plus sketches, for a show that he thought was in three acts. (Act 3 was the final scene, it seems.)[21] Brooks Costume Co. was on board by 8 February (the day rehearsals began), when it agreed to reduce its charge for the costumes by $5,000 as an investment in the show, although the company provided its first estimate for the costumes only on 16 February. The shoes were provided by I. Miller and Sons, which submitted an invoice for $1,538.60 on 19 February 1943; already on 10 February, John Haggott, the production manager, had contacted the Office of Price Administration seeking exemption from rationing on shoe leather (and some concern about the issue was reported in the *New York Post* on 15 February). Lemuel Ayers seems to have worked on the sets with a time frame similar to White's, although an agreement was reached with Vail Scenic Construction Co. only on 17 February, when a first installment was paid on the costs. Ayers was originally commissioned to produce six sets for two acts, to which an additional backdrop was added (for $100) on 2 March: the extra backdrop is probably the one for which I. Weiss and Sons submitted an invoice on 4 March ($295): "One (1) framed drop, 22' high and 40' wide, consisting of trees and foliage in profile contours, completely covered in black velour as specified." This may have been the "meadow" used in act 2 in New Haven and Boston, or perhaps some rethinking of the beginning of act 1, scene 3 before the dream-ballet. Meanwhile, Haggott was haggling with the Universal Flower and Decorating Co. over the cost of foliage and cornstalks, and with I. Weiss and Sons for cloth material for the sets (for the interior of the surrey, curtains, and such).

The need to gain exemption from rationing for shoe leather was only one of several ways in which wartime stringencies impinged upon the preparations for *Oklahoma!* The first sign of problems, which cannot have been unanticipated, was on 15 February, when George Church received notice of being drafted into the army.[22] Lawrence Langner entered into what became a standard process of appeal and negotiation with the Selective Service Board. The case of Alfred Drake (Alfred Frederick Capurro), called up for 9 March 1943, was typical of a number of others in the second quarter of 1943, including Joseph Buloff, Howard da Silva, Lee Dixon (Emil Hulser), Marc Platt, and Jerome Whyte. On 26 February, Langner noted on Drake's behalf that "We have been negotiating with the above listed registrant *Alfred Frederick Capurro*, since early in November of last year to appear in our production now entitled *Away We Go*," which had gone into rehearsal some three weeks earlier. "As I have stated, the registrant is now playing the leading role in a musical production which represents an investment of over a hundred thousand dollars and supplies employment to over one hundred people." According to Langner, because the making and financing of Broadway productions was geared to the lead players, Drake was irreplaceable; not only would his being drafted damage the show, but it would also injure the backers. "We are at present scheduled to open in New York some time during the second week in April." Langner thus sought a ninety-day deferment so that the show could begin its New York run and a replacement could be trained.

The deferment was granted, but this case and others would not go away.[23] On 26 April, Haggott produced a report on the status of all the men involved in the show, and feared that the able-bodied would be drafted in June.[24] On 14 May, Langner entered another appeal for Drake on the grounds that *Oklahoma!* had cost $82,000 to produce, that box-office receipts were currently running at $30,000 per week, and that Drake was uniquely able to combine singing and acting, which is what the show required. Langner also argued that although *Oklahoma!* might not be great art, it was entertainment of a type important in time of war, and its financial success was also subsidizing other, greater works put on by Theatre Guild. By 2 November 1943 the argument had become even more directly related to military morale: "It is the first play called for by soldiers and sailors at this point of embarkation. The Guild makes a special effort to give them preference in seats. It permits twelve members of the Army, Navy and Merchant Marine to see the play free of charge each night. It sells standing room only to men in uniform. An average of 150 soldiers see the play each night." In the end, Drake seems to have avoided the draft: when he left the show in 1944, he moved to Hollywood. Langner, however, continued to play the patriotic card so as to appease the Select Service Board; one assumes that special cheap-rate *Oklahoma!* matinees for servicemen staged from June 1944 to early March 1945 were part of the same strategy.

While the first two weeks of rehearsal seem to have been focused on separate scenes—although the cast complained of being kept on call even when not needed—the pattern appears to have shifted in the third.[25] Run-throughs were held on the Monday, Wednesday, and Friday (22, 24, and 26 February, in the afternoons, it seems), with the remaining time left for rethinking, revising, and reworking the weak spots that emerged. There was a further run-through on Tuesday, 2 March, which Langner called a "dress rehearsal," although neither the costumes nor the sets were yet available to the cast; this was presumably the occasion described by Rodgers in his autobiography (a run-through in early March without costumes and scenery) after which his wife, Dorothy, noted, "This is the best musical show I have ever seen."[26] There was a "dress parade" at Brooks Costume Co. on 4 March to try on the costumes and allow for adjustments: Langner wanted to lower

the necklines of the dresses, while some of the colors needed toning down—
"'Can't you get rid of those "bitch-pink" shirts,' asked Lem Ayers. 'They're
killing my scenery.'"[27] The set was not in place until rehearsals began in the
Shubert Theatre in New Haven. As the show was packed on 6 March for
the move on the 7th, it still had a long way to go.

Not the least of the problems still to be solved was the question of the
title. *Green Grow the Lilacs* was not available because of the film rights
owned by MGM, although it was regularly used as a working title in Guild
correspondence until early February 1943, and also by Robert Russell Bennett on the orchestrations ("Lilacs"). Hammerstein's original title, *Oklahoma* (in *Draft2*) was not finding much favor, and brainstorming in the Theatre Guild had borne little fruit: attempts included "In Jig Time," "Dancin'
Party," "Singin' Pretty," "Jump for Joy," "Laurey and Me," and "Swing Your
Honey."[28] By 13 February 1943 the title had focused on a square-dance call,
"Away We Go!"—it was announced in the *New York Times* on 15 February—although in some documents, the exclamation mark is omitted, and
some draft posters used "And Away We Go." But even after this was agreed
upon for publicity and printing for New Haven and Boston, Helburn was
still looking for alternatives, as she wrote to Riggs on 2 March 1943:

> Have you got any ideas for titles that would have more quality than *Away
> We Go!* and yet a gaiety and a lightness that would suit a musical version?
> We can't use *Green Grow the Lilacs* because of the picture situation as you
> know[,] and also we don't use the "Green Grow" song in the musical. We've
> thought of a great many, including "Oklahoma" and "Sing Oklahoma," etc.,
> but people feel that "Oklahoma" is too heavy. We would like something that
> would have the quality of the earth or the sun and at the same time some-
> thing happy. It seems to me that you were very good at titles, and maybe
> you'll have some brilliant idea.

Helburn adds a postscript: "We can change the title for New York though
the paper is out for New Haven where we open on the 11th and Boston where
we open March 15th. The show gets better every day. More anon." Some
reviewers of the Boston performance noted the intended change of title to
"Oklahoma," which was also the subject of a press release issued by the Guild
just before 16 March; that title continued to be used in Guild press releases
until 22 March.[29] The exclamation mark appeared in the first display advertisement for the show in the *New York Times* on 24 March; according to

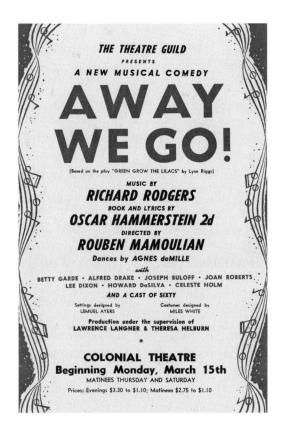

THE THEATRE GUILD
PRESENTS
A NEW MUSICAL COMEDY

AWAY WE GO!

(Based on the play "GREEN GROW THE LILACS" by Lynn Riggs)

MUSIC BY
RICHARD RODGERS
BOOK AND LYRICS BY
OSCAR HAMMERSTEIN 2d
DIRECTED BY
ROUBEN MAMOULIAN
Dances by AGNES deMILLE

with

BETTY GARDE · ALFRED DRAKE · JOSEPH BULOFF · JOAN ROBERTS
LEE DIXON · HOWARD DaSILVA · CELESTE HOLM

AND A CAST OF SIXTY

Settings designed by   Costumes designed by
LEMUEL AYERS   MILES WHITE

Production under the supervision of
LAWRENCE LANGNER & THERESA HELBURN

•

COLONIAL THEATRE
Beginning Monday, March 15th
MATINEES THURSDAY AND SATURDAY
Prices: Evenings $3.30 to $1.10; Matinees $2.75 to $1.10

11. The uncertainties over the show's title created severe problems for the Theatre Guild press office. This flyer for the Boston opening on 15 March clearly was a temporary solution; it also reflects confusion over generic labels (here, "a new musical comedy" but later, "a musical play"). The different type sizes for the show's creators (with Mamoulian given equal prominence to Rodgers and Hammerstein) was a matter of contractual agreement. So, too, one assumes, was the listing of the principals, which also reflects their salaries (save that Joan Roberts is promoted). Later publicity also credited Ralph Riggs and the principal dancers, although here they are subsumed under "a cast of sixty." Lawrence Langner precedes Theresa Helburn, which would change for New York.

Helene Hanff, its addition was communicated by phone from Helburn in Boston to Joseph Heidt, the Guild's press officer, in New York, forcing the office to make manual alterations to ten thousand press releases and other publicity materials.[30]

Heidt and his colleagues may just have regarded that as par for the course. The Guild press office had maintained a steady trickle of information on *Green Grow the Lilacs* since its first official announcement reported on 23 July 1942, and the pace quickened from mid-January 1943 on, as the show became a reality and interest had to be stirred up. Photographs started to appear (dancers in *PM* on 27 January; Celeste Holm in the *New York Herald Tribune* on 10 February), and factual information (on work in progress, casting, and so on) shifted in favor of statements of intent concerning what was tagged in advertisements as the "greatest musical show since *Show Boat*" (*Christian Science Monitor*, 6 March 1943). Not all the interest may have been welcome: a flurry of articles in the Boston press toward the end of February 1942 dealing with the casting of Sherry Britton as Lotta focused prominently on the fact that this "sometime charmer at the Old Howard and Globe Theatre here in Boston" was well known as a burlesque star, and was one of a number seeking to enter the "legitimate theatre." (Gypsy Rose Lee is cited as the prime example.)[31] Even if this was Hammerstein's intention with the character—and echoes of Will's experience in the "burleeque" in Kansas City are irresistible—this is probably not quite the tone wanted by the Guild. Helburn had already provided press notes for *Oklahoma!*: she wished to draw attention to the facts that the play appealed by virtue of its "American quality," that she wanted a "new and different music from the kind of music and the period in American history with which GG [*Green Grow the Lilacs*] is associated," that she was eager to secure Richard Rodgers (a Guild discovery in *Garrick Gaieties*) for this "revolutionary Guild production," that Hammerstein was an ideal collaborator because he cared about music, that in casting the Guild had sought a fresh, unjaded cast who would be actors first and musical performers second, and that the twenty-eight-piece orchestra was unusual for Broadway shows.[32] All this started to appear piecemeal in newspapers (it seems that the *New York Morning Telegraph* on 19 February was the first to mention "one of the largest orchestras of recent seasons—28 pieces"), and was taken over wholesale in *PM* on 31 March, as we have seen. Heidt also devised and enabled interviews with the key figures in the show: Rodgers and (especially) Hammerstein were quoted extensively in the *Christian Science Monitor* on 3 March, the *Boston Herald* on the

13th, the *Boston Morning Globe* and *Boston Post* on the 14th, and the *New York Post* on the 29th.[33]

Privately, however, Hammerstein seems to have been concerned about the likely reception of the show, at least to judge by a letter of 27 February from his son, Bill (in the navy), to whom he regularly reported progress:

> Your talk of rehearsals makes me homesick. About Jake [Schwartzdorf]—I thought you were dissatisfied with his job on *Sunny River*. You said so at the time. I think your analysis of his condition of mind is quite accurate and if he could get used to thinking in terms of big time he'd be a much better conductor—because I do believe he's capable and a good musician—altho his taste and judgement are not to be relied on.
>
> Your diatribe against present day audiences is completely justified—but I do believe it's at least partly the fault of the producers, writers, composers and publishers, who deliberately have lowered the standard. And your present collaborator has been one of the worst offenders—that string of empty, bawdy minstrel shows that have netted him so much success in the past few years have set the pace for the rest of them. Perhaps it will be his judgement that will serve as a balance and insure you a financial success with the show—not that I would not rather see you have your own way from a standpoint of the finer things. But whatever happens with it I wish you heartily a great hit and hope it's one you will enjoy to be proud of.[34]

However, Rodgers and Hammerstein were confident enough to have the Marlo Music Corporation go ahead with printing the sheet music of the songs from the show thought likely to be most successful in bookstores. The following were registered for copyright purposes on 12 March 1943: "Boys and Girls Like You and Me" (EP 112380), "The Surrey with the Fringe on Top" (EP 112381), "Oh, What a Beautiful Mornin'" (EP 112382), "People Will Say We're in Love" (EP 112383), and "Many a New Day" (EP 112384).[35] The Guild received a royalty of two cents per copy according to the agreement signed with Chappell and Co. on 4 February 1943.

New Haven

Out-of-town tryouts were a norm for Broadway (and also for the Theatre Guild) as ways of fine-tuning a show, or even rewriting it completely, of gauging likely box-office success (a failing show could be pulled before reaching New York), and of garnering pre-Broadway publicity. The Guild had used the Shubert Theatre in New Haven and the Colonial Theatre in Boston before, but in the case of *Oklahoma!* the out-of-town engagement may also have been facilitated by the fact that Lee Shubert (owner of the St. James Theatre on Broadway, where *Oklahoma!* would open) owned the New Haven theater and indirectly (through his professional relationship with another *Oklahoma!* investor, Marcus Heiman) held a lease on the Boston one. Presumably both Shubert and Heiman would have had some influence on whether *Oklahoma!* made it to New York: the Guild had to impress more than just its audiences and the critics.

The fact that posters, programs, and the like had to be printed in advance meant that they did not necessarily reflect the actual state of the show at a given performance; as we shall see, there was also a resistance to change in the programs, given the tendency to typeset new ones from old copy, with the result that information often became confused. (For example, when new singers or dancers replace old ones, their names appear where the old ones did, rather than in alphabetical order.) We have the New Haven program, two for Boston (one rather shoddily put together), and a regular series from the New York premiere on.[36] The differences between them reveal just how far things still had to go.

The show that opened in New Haven on 11 March — for three evenings and a matinee — cannot have been much different from what had been fixed by the end of the New York rehearsals: too much time would have been spent on getting used to the costumes, sets, and orchestra to permit significant rewriting. We have various accounts of last-minute changes to the costumes before the New Haven opening, mostly to simplify them (in particular, for the dancers), and Helburn and others relate how Mamoulian had decided to include a flock of pigeons to liven up "Boys and Girls Like You and Me," at least until they refused to follow the orders of their trainer.[37] Agnes de Mille's memoirs also suggest that tempers were frazzled and tantrums rampant. In terms of the songs, Jud's "Lonely Room" was omitted from both the New Haven and Boston programs, although it seems to have been reinstated in Boston. However, a number of cuts appear to have been made the morning after the New Haven opening, too late for incorporation in the Boston program, although they may have been enacted in Boston nevertheless. According to George Church, at a meeting of the cast that morning, Mamoulian announced that he needed to cut ninety minutes from the show, which may be an exaggeration but is still indicative of a problem.[38] Act 1 was fairly stable, so Langner said: "Indeed, except for a certain amount of cutting, it opened in New Haven very much as it is played today."[39] Act 2, however, remained problematic, despite all the work that had already been put into reshaping it during the rehearsals. Langner made the point clear in his description of events on the first night:

> As the crowd of managers, backers, friends of the actors, the composer and author chatted on the stage after the play was over, a well-known musical comedy producer who seldom talks in tones quieter than a resounding shout, informed everybody present that Oscar would have to rewrite the second act completely. Another important musical comedy producer called me on the telephone the next day and spent twenty minutes arguing with me that the perverted farm hand Jud should not be killed in the second act, because, in his experience of twenty-five years of producing musical comedies, there had never been a killing in one of them! I stated gently but firmly that this was essential to the play, and we would have to let it go at that. So pessimistic were the reports that came out of New Haven regarding the second act, that we decided to sell some additional interest in the play in order to be prepared for staying out of New York longer, if that were necessary, to take care of losses in New York.[40]

It was decided that "Boys And Girls Like You And Me" disrupted the flow, and that its choreography was too limited.[41] Other problems concerned the two male specialty dancers who had joined the cast early in rehearsals but had still not yet found their place. As Langner explained: "It was the custom of the time for all musical plays to have so-called 'specialty' dance numbers, and the original manuscript called for one or more dancers to appear in what were called 'spots' in the play to interrupt the action with a dance." But "as the style of the play evolved, it became apparent that no place could be found for such 'spots' either in the play action or the choreography."[42] George Church lost his central tap dance episode in "Oklahoma" on the grounds that it was too similar to the dancing in "The Farmer and the Cowman." He requested permission (in Boston, he said) to leave the show but was persuaded to stay on for the New York opening, given that he played Jud in the dream-ballet. He was later allowed to bow out gracefully (replaced as dream-Jud by Vladimir Kostenko on 1 June 1943) with a press release noting that "George Church, one of the featured dancers of *Oklahoma!* has left the cast of the musical hit to volunteer for overseas duty as an entertainer for the United Service Organizations."[43]

The case of Eric Victor was more acrimonious. Langner remembered him as "a weird-looking individual . . . who, long, lean and bearded, practiced leaping goat-like from the stage at unexpected moments, and scaring the lights and liver out of anyone he happened to take unawares."[44] During the rehearsals, a routine was developed in "The Farmer and the Cowman" in which, according to Paul Shiers, a chorus member, there was "a little solo for Eric Victor who did it with Bambi [Linn]. He did a tap step, not a conventional one, and Bambi caught on to the sound he was making. It was that sound which fascinated her, so she followed him around, as if he were the Pied Piper. Charming number; it was a show-stopper. But once we had opened in New Haven, they realized this number wasn't advancing the plot at all. Even though the audience responded to it, out it went."[45] Langner noted that although Victor fractured his wrist in New Haven, he was briefly given a "spot" in Boston at the end of "It's a Scandal! It's a Outrage!" jumping out of a barrel in cowboy costume and performing "his anti-gravitational antics," but "his appearance was so unexpectedly frightening, that it took ten minutes before the audience would laugh again, and moreover it so hurt the production stylistically, that we paid off his contract." In fact, Victor threatened legal action, and the Guild had to agree to pay him ten weeks' salary ($1,250) if he did not secure another role elsewhere. He does not appear in the New York program, where only Marc Platt is credited with dancing in "The Farmer and the Cowman."[46]

The uncertain status of act 2 is also reflected in the programs. The New Haven one lists four separate scenes, but only three in the list of musical numbers; the Boston one has four scenes (in a different order) but only two in the list of numbers; and the New York program (and also one for 18 July 1943) has three scenes and, again, only two in the list of numbers (table 4.2); such confusions continued in subsequent programs. The musical contents of these scenes also changed (table 4.3). In the New Haven program scene 2 ("Stable Shed") contained "Boys and Girls Like You and Me" and then "All er Nuthin'"; scene 3 ("A Meadow") had "Oklahoma"; and (presumably) scene 4 ("Laurey's Farm") had the finale ("Oh, What a Beautiful Mornin'"). In terms of the handling of the plot, in New Haven the Jud-Laurey exchange, where his assault prompts Laurey to admit her love for Curly and then Curly's marriage proposal (hence their love duet), probably took place in the stable, and then the shivaree (following "Oklahoma") and Jud's attempted murder of Curly (and Laurey?) adopted some version of the haystack scene in the play and in *Draft2* (so Laurey was not locked in the farmhouse, as in *Draft3*) before the show trial back at the farmhouse leading to the finale. In Boston the locations of scenes 2 and 3 were reversed, as was the running order: here, "All er Nuthin'" (now in the meadow) pre-

Table 4.2. List of scenes in the New Haven, Boston, and New York programs

New Haven	Boston	New York
Time: Just after the turn of the century	Time: Just after the turn of the century	Time: Just after the turn of the century
Place: Indian Territory, Oklahoma	Place[:] Indian Territory, Oklahoma	Place: Indian Territory (now Oklahoma)
Act I	Act I	Act I
Scene 1: Laurey's Farm House	Scene 1: Laurey's Farm House	Scene 1: The Front of Laurey's Farm House
Scene 2: The Smoke House	Scene 2: The Smoke House	Scene 2: The Smoke House
Scene 3: A Grove on Laurey's Farm	Scene 3: A Grove on Laurey's Farm	Scene 3: A Grove on Laurey's Farm
Act II	Act II	Act II
Scene 1: The Skidmore Ranch	Scene 1: The Skidmore Ranch	Scene 1: The Skidmore Ranch
Scene 2: Stable Shed	Scene 2: A Meadow	Scene 2: Skidmore's Kitchen Porch
Scene 3: A Meadow	Scene 3: Stable Shed	
Scene 4: Laurey's Farm	Scene 4: Laurey's Farm	Scene 3: The Back of Laurey's Farm House

ceded "Boys and Girls Like You and Me" (presumably, in the stable; and to be replaced—for the Broadway opening, if not before—by the reprise of "People Will Say We're in Love"), which was then followed by "Oklahoma" (presumably, at Laurey's farm); this explains the additional scene-change music linked to the materials for "Boys and Girls Like You and Me."[47] If the meadow was a full-stage set (as seems required by the six dancers used at one point), then this must have created problems with the change from scene 1. The new sequence from scene 3 to scene 4 also seems to have involved a relocation of the attempted murder (whether Jud setting fire to the farmhouse, as in *Draft3*, or his simply intervening in the wedding celebrations following "Oklahoma," as in the final version) and therefore to a somewhat easier staging; whatever the case, it meant that the sequence of the wedding through the shivaree to the fight and show trial took place more conveniently on a single set.

At the end of the New Haven run, almost all those involved in the production still seemed to have doubts about the success of the show: Celeste

Table 4.3. Musical numbers in act 2 according to the New Haven, Boston, and New York programs

New Haven	Boston	New York	Printed libretto
Scene 1 (Skidmore ranch)	Scene 1 (Skidmore ranch)	Scene 1 (Skidmore ranch)	Scene 1 (Skidmore ranch)
The Farmer and the Cowman (Fred, Aunt Eller, Will, Curly, Ado Annie, Carnes, and Ensemble); danced by Marc Platt and Eric Victor	The Farmer and the Cowman (Fred, Aunt Eller, Will, Curly, Ado Annie, Carnes, and Ensemble); danced by Marc Platt and Eric Victor	The Farmer and the Cowman (Carnes, Aunt Eller, Curly, Will, Ado Annie, Fred, and Ensemble); danced by Marc Platt	The Farmer and the Cowman
Scene 2 (Stable shed)	Scene 2 (Meadow)	[Front of traveler?]	Front of traveler
Boys and Girls Like You and Me (Curly and Laurey)	All er Nuthin' (Ado Annie and Will); danced by Katharine Sergava, Marc Platt, Kate Friedlich, Ray Harrison, Joan McCracken, Jack Dunphy	All er Nuthin' (Ado Annie and Will); danced by Joan McCracken and Kate Friedlich	All er Nuthin' (with two dancers)
	[Scene 3 (Stable shed)?]	Scene 2 (Skidmore's kitchen porch)	Scene 2 (The kitchen porch of Skidmore's ranch)
All er Nuthin' (Ado Annie and Will)	Boys and Girls Like You and Me (Curly and Laurey)	Reprise: People Will Say [We're in Love] (Curly and Laurey)	Reprise: People Will Say We're in Love
			(Front-of-traveler scene for Ado Annie, Peddler, and Will)
Scene 3 (Meadow)	[Scene 4 (Laurey's Farm)?]	[Scene 3 (Back of Laurey's farm house)?]	Scene 3 (Back of Laurey's farm house)

continued

Table 4.3. Continued

New Haven	Boston	New York	Printed libretto
Oklahoma (Curly, Aunt Eller, Ike, Fred, Laurey, and Ensemble); danced by George Church	Oklahoma (Curly, Aunt Eller, Ike, Fred, Laurey, and Ensemble); danced by George Church	Oklahoma (Curly, Laurey, Aunt Eller, Ike, Fred, and Ensemble)	Oklahoma
[Scene 4 (Laurey's farm)?]			
Finale: Oh, What a Beautiful Mornin' (Laurey, Curly, and the Entire Ensemble)	Finale: Oh, What a Beautiful Mornin' (Laurey, Curly, and the Entire Ensemble)	Oh, What a Beautiful Mornin' (Laurey, Curly, and Ensemble)	Oh, What a Beautiful Mornin'
		Finale (Ensemble)	

Note: NH*b* TG 123/17 has a different program for Boston that has in "Scene 3" "Boys and Girls Like You and Me," "Oklahoma," and the "Finale." This program also lists no dancers for "All er Nuthin'."

Holm was asked to sign a run-of-play contract but refused, doing so only on 29 March, and there were rumors that Mamoulian was to be replaced by George Abbott. Audience reaction was varied. Philip Barry Jr. was "absolutely entranced" and tried to persuade his father, Philip Sr., to invest some of his Guild royalties (for *The Philadelphia Story* and other plays) in the show: he decided against, mainly, it seems, because he did not like Riggs's play. De Mille reported Kurt Weill's response to the New Haven tryout: "He doesn't think it's good (It's not but it may succeed)"; he was only a little less begrudging a year later. Rodgers, on the other hand, claimed that the New Haven reception was "phenomenal."[48] The opinions of the New York critics and their representatives who traveled up for the opening were famously mixed, and the telegram sent to the feared syndicated columnist Walter Winchell—"No legs, no jokes, no chance"—soon entered the mythology.[49] But the local press reviews were entirely favorable. The *New Haven Journal-Courier* of Friday, 12 March, noted that this "lusty, swashbuckling musical play . . . about love and life in the early West" had a "good premiere"; "many of the players are well known and there are many who are not well known who will be soon," and "the excitement of the present can be laid aside for three hours while one enjoys the excitement of the past in this lively, sparkling show." The review predicted some slow spots would be removed by the next performance. According to the *New Haven Evening Register*, this "rollicking musical comedy" was "jammed to the hilt with tuneful melodies" and was "ideal escapist entertainment": "It is an excellent theatrical tonic to greet the approach of spring." As for the *Waterbury American*, "This show blows in with all the rigor and refreshing qualities of a strong wind across Oklahoma": "This entire creation is close to the soil," and "The Farmer and the Cowman" is "one of the best numbers in the show." Farther afield, Cecil Smith in the *Chicago Tribune* on 16 March noted of the New Haven performances that the show "will not be an unqualified success unless a great deal of revision does take place, despite its attractive decors and hummable score"; Smith felt that the show was too insecure in terms of style and tone, particularly in act 1 (he does not discuss act 2 on the grounds, he says, that it was to be heavily revised), and that the dream-ballet ("a la *Lady in the Dark*") lacked the "solidity of structure" apparent in *Rodeo*. On 17 March, however, *Variety* noted that the show had taken $10,000 in New Haven, and Harold Bone praised the Guild for "offering a package of nostalgia neatly wrapped in a talented cast and tied up with a blue-ribbon score"; the show "should stretch into a sizable stay on Broadway," and "film possibilities are bright."

Boston

"Away We Go!" opened at the Colonial Theatre, Boston, on Monday, 15 March. Hammerstein was somewhat upbeat, enclosing the New Haven press clippings in a letter to his son Bill: "I think I have something this time. These are *all* the notices. The work is to pull Act II together."[50] Agnes de Mille later claimed that the whole second act was reworked on the train from New Haven to Boston, including the addition of a small three-minute dance (another version of "All er Nuthin'"?). She also said that by the end of the two-week run in Boston (27 March), the entire play had been reorganized.[51] Although that seems an exaggeration, Langner refers to nightly conferences after each Boston performance between him, Helburn (in bed with the flu), Rodgers, Hammerstein, and Mamoulian: "By a rearrangement of the material in the second act, and with very little rewriting, within ten days of the opening of the play in Boston, it was in excellent shape, and in practically the exact condition in which it opened in New York." Langner also notes the changes to the lighting: "In the beginning, the scenery was lit in accordance with current so-called 'musical comedy lighting,' but as the play progressed in Boston, it was supplemented with the kind of lighting which is used in the dramatic theatre."[52] Mamoulian, on the other hand, claimed in a later interview that "for the last two weeks before we opened *Oklahoma!* on Broadway, no one even spoke to me. Rodgers thought I was destroying his music. He couldn't accept the singers having their backs to the audience. Everyone wanted me to restage it as an ordinary musical comedy. I refused, and they didn't even invite me to the opening night party."[53] Settling in to one theater for two weeks clearly had advantages in terms of bedding down the show and fine-tuning its weak points. One wonders, too, whether Rodgers and Hammerstein took time out to hear the Von Trapp family singers, who performed in Boston on 21 March.[54] One main difficulty, however, was coping with an outbreak of German measles that had been incubating in the cast since the rehearsals: Agnes de Mille recounts how she took the place of successive dancers forced into bed. Helburn, too, fell ill from stress, forcing Langner to come up to supervise.

One decision for Boston had already been made in New Haven, it seems. Jud's "Lonely Room" had been cut just before the first tryout. However, Alfred Drake tells how he gave Howard da Silva some emergency singing lessons in his New Haven hotel:

> At the New Haven opening . . . for some reason or other the producers had decided to cut Jud Fry's second-act [scene] solo, "Lonely Room." Perhaps it was because Howard Da Silva wasn't singing it too well; after all, he was an actor first, not a singer. But they felt it didn't work.
>
> Next day I went to Dick Rodgers and I said, "This is all wrong, that song is very important; it illuminates Jud's whole character. If you'd let me work with Howard on it I think I may be able to help him."
>
> So he agreed, and Howard and I went off by ourselves into one of those little public meeting rooms off the lobby of the Taft Hotel and we worked together on that song. . . . I did my best to coach him so that it would be a dramatic solo. That he could do. When they heard him do it again, they decided to put it back into the show. And in Boston it worked![55]

This also no doubt explains the several different attempts to find an appropriate key for the music. The addition in Boston of the song for da Silva ("which clarifies the character of the villain which he portrays") was noted in the *New York Times* on 29 March 1943. However, Drake, not da Silva, sang it on the original-cast recording (the second volume of which was done after da Silva had left the cast).

The Boston programs could not keep up with the changes. They omitted

"Lonely Room" (now restored, it seems), and included "Boys and Girls Like You and Me" (now deleted). One of the oddities is the allocation of "I Cain't Say No" to "Ado Annie and the Boys," suggesting that at some stage (if not necessarily in Boston itself) Rodgers and Hammerstein briefly reverted to the plan in *Draft2* to have a dance episode following the song. According to Celeste Holm, "I Cain't Say No" also gained one other addition in Boston, its encore stanza. For "All er Nuthin'" one of the Boston programs lists six dancers (Katharine Sergava, Marc Platt, Kate Friedlich, Ray Harrison, Joan McCracken, and Jack Dunphy), whereas none is listed in the New Haven or other Boston ones, and the New York program has only two (Kate Friedlich and Joan McCracken), as in the printed libretto and score.[56] This suggests some reorganization of the choreography, and also of its theme, in the light of changes already being considered during the rehearsals. We do not know how "All er Nuthin'" first appeared in Boston, although Kate Friedlich later recalled rehearsing the two-dancer version in the foyer of the Colonial Theatre after a matinee performance (Thursday, 18 or 25 March, or Saturday, 20 or 27 March).[57] This also suggests that the arrangement in the Boston program did indeed create staging difficulties (the shift from scenes 1 to 2), solved by having "All er Nuthin'" done in front of the traveler, where there would be room for two dancers, but not six.

The most obvious rearrangement, however, occurred in the song that provides the most enduring, and endearing, story associated with *Oklahoma!* —the title song itself. As we have seen, during the rehearsals "Oklahoma" was given a central tap sequence for George Church. However, the dance was cut, and when the show went to Boston, the question remained of what to replace it with. Celeste Holm credits a member of the chorus, Faye Smith, with the idea of singing it in harmony, a claim which Langner seems to support: "One of the chorus girls remarked to Rodgers, 'Why isn't there more chance for us singers to use our singing voices? We have a wonderful chorus, and not very much to do.' At that time, the number 'Oklahoma!' was being sung mainly by Curly and Laurey, and we were all calling for more excitement at this part of the play. Dick immediately conceived the idea of using the entire chorus for the number with explosive effect." Robert Russell Bennett was summoned from New York, and he reworked the chorus in a spectacular harmonization, supposedly while on the train to Boston.[58] The new version was tried out on the cast's Sunday off (21 March), first around a piano in the theater foyer, and then on stage, when Agnes de Mille came up with the "flying wedge," a V-shaped formation as the cast moved from the rear of

12. "Yeow!" The "flying wedge," where the cast moved en masse from the back to the front of the stage, soon became a trademark of the song "Oklahoma" that was reworked during the Boston tryout as a grand choral number and show-stopper. Lemuel Ayers's set for act 2, scene 3, with its receding haystacks (and Laurey's house moved from the stage left of act 1, scene 1 to stage right), provides a fine backdrop. (Uncredited)

the stage to the footlights. The reworking was used in the show for the second week in Boston and was a show-stopper: at long last, and even without Lotta's "barbaric Spanish song," Rodgers and Hammerstein had found their eleven o'clock number.[59]

Bennett, however, was not one to waste material, and traces of the original version of "Oklahoma" remain, if where one might not expect (or at least, recognize) them. According to Jay Blackton, the overture used in New Haven was "a little improvised thing that Robert Russell Bennett pasted together in time for that first performance"; the final overture was then written "when we got to Boston," by which he must mean during the Boston run (given the revisions to "Oklahoma").[60] The "little improvised thing" is presumably the "Temp[orary] Overture" for which there is a set of parts (incomplete) held by the Rodgers and Hammerstein Organization: its introduction (twenty-two measures) presents motives from "Boys and Girls Like You and Me" and then "People Will Say We're in Love" under swirling strings, linking to complete play-throughs of "Many a New Day," "Out of My Dreams," and "People Will Say We're in Love." However, the cutting of "Boys and Girls Like You and Me" forced the writing of a new overture, or at least significant parts thereof. The final version is much more rambunctious, starting with "The Farmer and the Cowman" (the opening sixteenth-note flourishes in the violins owe something to the New Haven overture) and ending with "Oklahoma"; this sandwiches "Pore Jud Is Daid" and then the three songs (in the same order) of the temporary overture. The bookend songs in the new overture emphasized the theme of community in ways that may have been prompted by the development of the show with the Boston expansion of "Oklahoma."[61] The version of this song in the overture, however, is not quite the same as the final version of the song in the show, precisely because Bennett pasted in portions of the score of the first (New Haven) version.

Next-day local reviews of the Boston performance were, again, generally favorable. Helen Eager in the *Boston Traveler* made the connection to Riggs's play: "When *Green Grow the Lilacs* had its first performance at the Tremont in 1930, Philip Hale observed in his review in the *Boston Herald* that the play might serve as the libretto for an opera. His judgment was proved sound last night." According to Elinor Hughes in the *Boston Herald*, the show opened "before a packed and enthusiastic audience": "Though there may be a few lifted eyebrows—the Guild promoting song and dance antics (tsk, tsk!)—the results were so satisfactory that I can't think of any reason why they shouldn't keep right at it. Big, handsome, picturesque and generally entertaining, the production isn't quite ready yet for Broadway, being as yet on the lengthy side and having some first[-]act doldrums, but the virtues are numerous and the failings can be remedied." Hughes also praised Agnes de Mille's dances, "which are an outstanding feature of the show and at one point come close to turning *Away We Go!* into dance drama rather than musical comedy." For the rest, "The Theater Guild has made no mistake with the production, and Broadway has a very agreeable experience in store for it." Peggy Doyle in the *Boston American* noted that the show "has freshness, vitality, wit, grace, elegance, lovely colors, lovelier girls, the most distracting tootsie-tossing of the year and a flagrantly irresistible score." L. A. Stoper in the *Christian Science Monitor* (16 March) had more criticisms:

the show was too long and had "too much rural humor and homely senti-
ment," the songs were too simple, the first scene dragged on, the death-scene
was problematic, and the whole production needed cutting and tightening
(as indeed occurred in Boston). However, he liked "Pore Jud Is Daid," "I
Cain't Say No," "Oklahoma" (which he calls a "chorus"), and the dream-
ballet. Rumors were already circulating about the change of title: Hughes
noted that it "could be improved on," and Stoper said, "It is reported that
when the production arrives in New York it will be called 'Oklahoma.' That
will help, too." Leo Gaffney in the *Boston Record* felt that the Guild needed
to decide whether it was presenting a musical comedy or a play with music,
and Elliot Norton in the *Boston Post* felt that "being shiny new, it is not yet
perfect. It is pretty nearly half an hour too long and some of its actors are
not yet slick in their roles." "Even so," he wrote, "this is one of the best shows
of its kind some of us have ever seen."

Members of the audience also recorded their reactions. On 16 March
one Edward W. Curtin of Massachusetts sent his comments to the Guild
office in New York: he liked "People Will Say We're in Love," in particular
the line "Don't you sigh, you sigh too much like me," but he felt that there
was too much dialogue in act 1, scene 1, wanted more comic punch lines for
Will Parker and Ali Hakim, thought Joan Roberts and Celeste Holm were
fine, and suggested cutting act 1, scene 3 (including the dream-ballet?). In
general, he felt that the dancing was too dominant ("I will admit it is very
good but too much of anything . . ."). Finally, "George Abbott took my advice and added a brassiere to *Kiss and Tell*. You could add a dozen of the
same to *Away We Go*. As the show stands, it is the hit of the season,—when I
see it later in the week I hope it will be the hit of many seasons." More realistic, perhaps, was Dorothy Hammerstein's account to Bill Hammerstein, her
stepson. On Saturday (probably 20 March) she began her letter, "I am going
to see the show tonight so will finish this tomorrow so that I can give my
personal reactions to the cuts and changes—It is running normal time now.
. . . Won't it be wonderful if the show is a smash hit?" She then added the
next day:

> The show played to capacity last night. Dick [Rodgers] says it is the first
> musical to make a profit the first week—it has paid travelling expenses[,]
> rehearsals and everything so if they do get any unexpected set backs in the
> form of bad notices they have a surplus to keep going while the public hears
> about it from Guild subscribers etc. Last night the show went well but I
> didn't like the performance. Celeste Holm had such a bad throat that she

couldn't sing but still made a hit and the cast have been so busy learning new lines that they have not been rehearsed in them and it was jerky to me. The score and lyrics are wonderful and the ballet is unsurpassed.

She did not like Betty Garde as Aunt Eller ("She gives me a pain in the neck"); "Joan Roberts is good but I would say Alfred Drake and Celeste Holm and Agnes De Mille's dancing dept are the stand outs. A girl in the ballet called McCracken is wonderful. Stands out and one finds oneself watching her all the time she is on the stage."[62]

The box-office receipts in Boston were indeed respectable: on 16 March the *New York Times* announced advance sales of $25,000, and on 29 March gross receipts of more than $50,000. On 20 March, Sara (Sadie) Greenspan, assistant business manager in the Guild office in New York, wrote to Helburn and Langner in Boston: "Glad business is so good in Boston. We'll be able to make a profit on the Boston engagement if next week is as good as this." On 26 March, Joseph Heidt, the Guild's press officer, cabled Lynn Riggs asking for biographical details for a press release: "Play looks swell Boston business very good." As the show packed up in Boston on Sunday, 28 March, after its last performance on the 27th, those involved must have felt that prospects were good.

In-house feelings, however, remained mixed. Hammerstein wrote to his son Bill on 25 March:

> I said I would write to you after the opening in N.Y. and I will. But the show is in such fine shape that I find myself with sufficient leisure and repose to write to you from here. This is Thursday. Last Monday we suffered a relapse. The show was slow and low-keyed because of the cast, concentrating on changes had lost the pace of the unchanged scenes. So we gave them a good drilling and the result was so successful that in one night we suddenly took on the aura of a hit. People have come up from N.Y. and are swooning. I now believe that here is the nearest approach to *Show Boat* that the theatre has attained. I don't believe it has as sound a story or that it will be as great a success. But it is comparable in quality, and may have a very long life. All this is said in the hope that a handful of beer-stupefied critics may not decide that we have tried to write a musical comedy and failed. If they see that this is different and higher in its intent, they should rave. I *know* this is a good show. I cannot believe it will not find a substantial public. There! My neck is out.

He also told Bill, "The name of the show is now *Oklahoma!*, a good, honest title." But Hammerstein was more reserved with his wife: "I don't know what to do if they don't like this. I don't know what to do because this is the only kind of show I can write."[63] On 29 March, Helburn wrote to Warren Munsell, the Guild's business manager, now in the army and based in London: "*Green Grow*, now entitled *Oklahoma!*, opens Wednesday night and I'll add a p.s. to this or send you a further note after it opens. It did very well in New Haven and Boston, with rave press and is really a lovely show, but I still don't dare count my chickens before they're hatched. Everyone who came up from New York was very much impressed. If we could skip the first night I know we'd be on Easy Street." Helburn also told Munsell that the Boston business meant that the show was financially secure, and that she had even been turning down late investors. Langner conveyed a similar general message to S. N. Behrman on 30 March: "Everyone seems to think the show looks good and I hope to God, for all our sakes, the boys here will recognize its difference and charm and loveliness, but I have weathered so many first-night agonies that I dare not look ahead." Both Helburn and de Mille also claimed (after the fact) to have been on tenterhooks, and Joseph Buloff told his wife that he was less than optimistic about the chances for the show's having a long run. Only Rodgers maintained (again in retrospect) that he had every confidence from the rehearsals through the tryouts, and even in Boston he predicted to Jay Blackton that the show could last six months on Broadway. Langner, however, was concerned:

> When we were in Boston, a musical play called *Dancing in the Streets*, produced by Vinton Freedley with the adorable Mary Martin in the lead, and with scenery and costumes by Robert Edmond Jones, was playing against us, and there was quite a question as to whether we should not try to race in to New York ahead of this play. Rudolf Krommer, Max Reinhart's shadow . . . came to Boston and saw both *Oklahoma!* and *Dancing in the Streets*, and he was as loud in his praises of the latter as he was pessimistic about the fate of *Oklahoma!* I myself had been worried as to what would happen in New York, because *Oklahoma!* was so different from any of the musicals which were running at the time. Many of the New York musical producers were either graduates of the burlesque, or produced slick musical shows, done with great professionalism, which by this time had hardened into a formula. Except for *Show Boat*, there was absent from them any of the poetry or mood of Americana which characterized *Oklahoma!*[64]

New York

When *Oklahoma!* opened at the St. James Theatre on Wednesday, 31 March 1943, *Lady in the Dark*, with Gertrude Lawrence, was in revival (its second) at the Broadway Theatre (eighty-three performances from 27 February to 15 May) before going on tour; the *Ziegfeld Follies* opened on 1 April at the Winter Garden; and *By Jupiter* was still playing at the Shubert Theatre. Broadway theatergoers could also see Michael Todd's revue *Star and Garter*; Fred K. Finklehoffe's revue *Show Time*; Cole Porter's *Something for the Boys*, chiefly a vehicle for Ethel Merman; Thorton Wilder's play *The Skin of Our Teeth*; S. N. Behrman's still popular *The Pirate*, with Alfred Lunt and Lynn Fontanne; Clifton Webb in Noël Coward's *Blithe Spirit*; F. Hugh Herbert's hit comedy *Kiss and Tell*; or Chekov's *The Three Sisters*. Johann Strauss's *Rosalinda* (a version of *Die Fledermaus*, with Shelley Winters as Fifi) ran from 28 October 1942 to 22 January 1944 (611 performances); and the revue *Sons o' Fun* was in its second year, having just transferred to the 46th Street Theatre. This was quite a distinguished list.

While *Oklahoma!* was playing in New Haven and Boston, the Guild Press Office in New York was busy drumming up business for the Broadway opening. On 16 March the *New York News* contained the report that if "Away We Go" was successful, the Guild would produce two musicals per season. On 18 March the *New York Times* noted that the show would open on 31 March and that it "is in such good shape that it does not need any more time on tour for polishing." Given the changes currently under way in Boston, this was grossly untrue. All this was presumably a result of the regular series of press releases issued from the Guild's press office. One received on 16 March noted the change of title from "Away We Go!" to "Oklahoma" (no exclamation point)—so it was also announced on that day in the *New York Times* and elsewhere (such as the *Chicago Tribune*)—and Heidt reiterated it in another release dated 19 March:

> *Oklahoma*, new Theatre Guild musical comedy formerly known as *Away We Go!* which is currently playing at the Colonial Theatre, Boston, will have its Broadway premiere at the St. James Theatre on Wednesday evening, March 31.
>   *Oklahoma* has music by Richard Rodgers with book and lyrics by Oscar Hammerstein 2d, and is based on the Lynn Riggs stage comedy, *Green Grow the Lilacs*. Rouben Mamoulian is directing, and the cast is headed by Betty

Garde, Alfred Drake, Joseph Buloff, Joan Roberts, Lee Dixon, Howard da Silva and Celeste Holm.

Designating *Green Grow the Lilacs* a "stage comedy" seems to have been an attempt to assuage fears of something too serious. On 22 March, Heidt issued another release for "Oklahoma" (again, no exclamation point), which "features a most unusual cast in that all its principals are actors as well as singers and dancers." Here the information is mostly factual concerning the cast (Eric Victor is mentioned among the dancers), although Heidt notes yet again that a twenty-eight-piece orchestra is large for musicals. On 26 March, Heidt issued a briefer information sheet for *Oklahoma!* when sending out complimentary opening-night tickets to critics. (Victor is not included among the dancers.) All this seems to have paid off in the report issued in *PM* on 31 March.

Neither Rodgers nor Hammerstein was unused to having a premiere at the St. James Theatre: *Pal Joey* and *Sunny River* were both done there. But they cannot have imagined the consequences of the New York opening of *Oklahoma!* The first night was not sold out, and the cold weather and snow did not help matters; nor did Marc Platt's having to dance on a severely injured ankle. But accounts of that opening now take on a legendary quality. According to de Mille: "I stood at the back. . . . Rodgers held my hand. The curtain went up on a woman churning butter; a very fine baritone came on stage singing the closest thing to lieder our theater has produced. He sang exquisitely with his whole heart about what a morning in our Southwest is like. At the end, people gave an audible sigh and looked at one another—this had seldom happened before. It was music. They sat right back and opened their hearts. The show rolled." Langner gives a similar impression:

> When the fateful day arrived for the opening of *Oklahoma!* in New York, we refused to allow anyone to be seated during the singing of the opening number, "Oh, What a Beautiful Morning," and it was apparent to me from the beginning of the play that it had started off on the right foot. I wondered how a New York audience would respond to the fact that for nearly forty-five minutes, not a single chorus girl appeared on the stage. But as one beautiful song followed another, the audience took the play to its heart, and there was the most tremendous outburst of applause at the end of the ballet, as the curtain fell upon the first act. During the intermission, I noted there was that electric thrill which passes through an audience when it feels that it is attending something of exciting import in the theatre.

During the second act, after the gaiety of the "Cowman and the Farmer" songs and dances, there was no doubt about the outcome. At the end of the play, the applause was overwhelming. A lump came into my throat, for not many years had any play of ours received such an ovation from its opening-night audience. The next day the newspaper critics wrote column upon column of praise for Rodgers, Hammerstein, Mamoulian and De Mille; there was not a single bad newspaper notice. And then the legend of *Oklahoma!* began to grow.

Sitting in a box, and cheering along with the rest, was Lorenz Hart, who had also seen the tryout in New Haven.[65]

Helburn claimed that the first notices of the performance, heard on the radio at midnight, were dismissive, but as she also notes, the immediate reaction of the newspapers (on 1 April 1943) to *Oklahoma!* (more often styled *Oklahoma*), ranged from positive to wildly enthusiastic (with just one somewhat cool exception).[66] Lewis Nichols in the *New York Times* was captured by the show's "infectious gayety, a charm of manner, beautiful acting, singing and dancing, and a score by Richard Rodgers that doesn't do any harm either, since it is one of his best." Burns Mantle (*New York Daily News*) called it "the most thoroughly and attractively American musical comedy" since *Show Boat* and extolled the integration of the dancing, although he felt that the show flagged somewhat in act 2; on the other hand, Wilella Waldorf, who wrote the coolest review (in the *New York Post*), thought that the show started slow but warmed up considerably as it progressed. For Burton Rascoe (*New York World-Telegraph*), too, Agnes de Mille deserved credit for making the dream-ballet "the biggest hit of the show." He was full of praise for Celeste Holm and thought that "Pore Jud Is Daid" would become a "barflies' lament" overnight. However, he ended somewhat bitingly: "the plot is allegedly derived from Lynn Riggs' *Green Grow the Lilacs*. What plot?" Howard Barnes (*New York Herald Tribune*) also picked up on the "theatrical Americana" and felt that despite the slow start, the show was a great success. He followed the Theatre Guild line on the casting: "There are no particularly well known performers in the piece, but that is all to the good in a show which has inherent theatrical excitement." Ward Morehouse (*New York Sun*) felt that "*Oklahoma!* has great charm. It is fresh and diverting. It is inclined to undue slowness at times and monotony creeps in, but it recovers, and by the time they're singing the lusty title song near the finish you're under the spell of it." John Anderson (*New York Journal-American*) was unequivocal: "In *Oklahoma*, the Guild has a beautiful and delightful show, fresh and imaginative, as enchanting to the eye as Richard Rodgers' music is to the ear." He felt that the show needed cutting in act 1 but accepted that such cuts would never happen. After the premiere, and as the queues at the box office lengthened day by day, the praise became still more fulsome. On 11 April, Lewis Nichols of the *New York Times* compared *Oklahoma!* with the *Ziegfeld Follies*; although he did not dismiss the latter, he preferred *Oklahoma!* for its experimental adventurousness, for its artistic qualities, and for its wholesomeness. By May and June the press was waxing even more lyrical.

Members of the audience were also quick to send their comments to the Guild. In early April, William Lockwood, a New York attorney, wrote suggesting the removal of the death scene. Helburn (it seems) replied on 9 April:

> We seriously considered the elimination of the death scene but, talking it over, we ultimately felt that as this was a play to music, we should stick to the true story line, and there is really no excuse for the entire threat of Jud if something doesn't come of it in the end. Furthermore, it was Jud's death that permitted Aunt Eller to give her speech about being tough, which seemed to us part of the essential pioneer quality of the play. Therefore, after much consideration we felt it wisest to keep this ending in.
>
> In the long run it's all a matter of opinion.[67]

She even took the trouble to forward Lockwood's letter to Hammerstein on 15 April, perhaps in fun, given that she had already replied: "Here's your chance to defend your principles—and ours. How about your sending a word to the meddling old gentleman—or tell me what you'd like me to say and I'll quote you." More typical, however, was the eulogy sent on 8 April by Myron Galewski addressed "To Everyone Concerned with the Production of *Oklahoma*":

> This is just to thank you for producing one of the most beautiful and exciting musical plays ever produced in the American theatre. *Oklahoma* is the kind of musical I have dreamed of but never hoped to see, and is an instance of what a musical can be when fine craftsmanship and artistry go into its making, and its source material is as happily chosen as *Green Grow the Lilacs*.
>
> I hope the Rodgers–Hammerstein–Mamoulian–De Mille combination gets together on another musical play in the not too distant future, so that

they can pass another miracle like *Oklahoma*, although as I said before that is almost too much to hope for.[68]

Galewski was a theater aficionado and amateur playwright, who therefore may have been trying to curry favor with the Theatre Guild. But clearly his opinion was widely shared.

CHAPTER 5

Reading *Oklahoma!*

A S WITH THE CONTEMPORARY REVIEWS, LATER ACCOUNTS OF OKLA-
homa! have tended to focus not just on its content but also on its
design and apparent intent. Rodgers and Hammerstein's (and, if we
are to believe his self-publicity, Mamoulian's) presumed search for a "new"
type of musical integrating drama, song, and dance comes high on a critical
agenda cemented early in the show's reception history, and oft repeated in
later studies.[1] So, too, does the virtuous simplicity and seeming artlessness
of the result—whether as praise or, in more sophisticated quarters (especially those lamenting the loss of the pungent wit of 1930s Rodgers and
Hart), as blame. It is also easy to ignore the complex collaborative processes, and even crisis management, that led, haphazardly or not, to so seemingly well-rounded a result. The "artless" trope could, of course, backfire: in
the months after the premiere, both Hammerstein and, still more, Rodgers
seemed anxious to explain just how much hard work and strong theatrical
experience had gone into the show, counterbalancing earlier press accounts
of the ease and routine nature of their collaboration.[2] "Integration," too, was
a loaded term, and one easier to assert than to prove: in newspaper interviews in the months after the premiere, Mamoulian played the "integration"
card quite strongly in terms of his production style—Hammerstein also gave
him such credit in an interview in the *Boston Post* on 14 March 1943—and
both Rodgers and Hammerstein used it when it suited them, if not with great
clarity. However, no one seems to have tired of the claim that in *Oklahoma!*
and then *Carousel* they had consciously and consistently escaped the typical
conventions of Broadway musical comedies to produce a much worthier art

form, the "musical play." Much hinged on the generic label to be applied to *Oklahoma!* On 7 January 1943 the *Daily News* reported, "The immediate problem is how to tag the show. It falls into the category of 'American folk opera' but the Guild doesn't want to call it an opera." The *New York Times* on the 19th quoted Rodgers as saying that *Oklahoma!* was "neither an opera nor an operetta," although he does not offer a better term. In an article in *PM* on 4 February 1942, Agnes de Mille used the term "folk opera." The show appears to have been called a "musical comedy" in the materials associated with the New Haven and Boston tryouts (and in the sheet music printed for "Away We Go!"), although at least some Boston reviewers called it a "musical play," the label generally used in the New York materials and later strongly associated with the show in public, if not always by the Guild.[3] It promised much more than the usual Broadway musical fare.

Kurt Weill resented these claims. On 13 April 1944 he wrote to Ira Gershwin that *Oklahoma!* was "definitely designed for a very low audience . . . and that, in my opinion, explains the terrific success." He also later remarked to Lotte Lenya on what seems to have been a report on *Carousel*: "So Rodgers is 'defining a new directive for musical comedy.' I had always thought that I've been doing that—but I must have been mistaken. Rodgers certainly has won the first round in that race between him and me. But I suppose there will be a second and a third round."[4] Jerome Kern also dismissed the music for *Oklahoma!* as "condescending."[5] Weill may have been grouchy because of his own former plans for *Liliom*, but one can understand his complaint, given that his own musicals of the late 1930s and early 1940s, not least *Lady in the Dark* (1941, an earlier "musical play"), had pushed further the boundaries of Broadway. It is also true that not all 1930s musicals were as dramatically feeble, or as focused on long-legged chorus girls, as later eulogists of Rodgers and Hammerstein would have us believe.[6] Moreover, any argument for serious drama in *Oklahoma!* is weakened, to say the least, by the seeming superficiality of a plot that focuses primarily, we might think, on who gets to take Laurey to the Box Social. There is not much action in *Oklahoma!* and its concerns do not seem to be particularly great. No one expects Shakespearean tragedy in a Broadway musical—at least before *West Side Story* (1957)—but one is left wondering whether *Oklahoma!* can bear the weight of its reception history.

Perhaps we should not ask too much. When war broke out in Europe, Theresa Helburn wrote to Eugene O'Neill (from whom she had long been expecting a series of plays) about the role of the theater, claiming that there

13. In addition to designing the sets for *Oklahoma!* Lemuel Ayers also did the poster (once the show's title had been fixed), for which he was paid an additional $100. He presents the show as a cheerful Wild West romp—even the "postcard" girl is tamed—although there is in fact a great deal more under the surface.

was still a need for serious drama: "Apart from the escape comedies and musicals, and the release of laughter, I believe that people will need greatness and beauty and emotional lift intensely." O'Neill, in return, was more realistic:

> Later on, after the victory in the war which must be won is won, and the reaction to the realities behind the surface of the peace sinks in, there will again be an audience able to feel the inner meaning of plays dealing with the everlasting mystery and irony and tragedy of men's lives and dreams; plays which are propaganda only for life as the artist attempts to illuminate it and transmute it into Art. People are too damned preoccupied with the tragedy of war now—as they should be—to want to face such plays. And I don't blame them. I'd rather spend an escapist evening with legs and music myself—or with pipe dreams that were treated as truth.[7]

Oklahoma! may not have had many "legs," but there were music and pipe dreams galore.

The casting is quite compact. There are twenty-three named characters in the New York program (see table 2.2), which may seem high compared with twenty in *Pal Joey* and thirteen in *By Jupiter*, but twelve of them are chorus members or dancers who required or deserved up-front credit in the cast list. Of the remaining eleven, Ike Skidmore and Cord Elam are bit parts (although Cord Elam comes into his own at the end as the Federal Marshall), leaving nine main roles. These roles are distributed quite neatly in terms both of the plot and of standard casting conventions on Broadway (and for that matter, of much opera). In effect, there are two separate "love" triangles, one comprising the lead boy and girl (Laurey and Curly, plus Jud), and the other the secondary, comic roles (Ado Annie, Will Parker, Ali Hakim). The triangles make for a more dynamic drama than do the couples conventionally found in musical comedies.[8] Each of them is overseen by an authority figure, a matriarch (Aunt Eller) for the first, and a patriarch (Andrew Carnes, Ado Annie's father) for the second. The ninth character, Gertie Cummings, became increasingly important after the disappearance of Lotta Gonzales, given that someone needed to be paired off with Ali Hakim, but she remains essentially also a bit part.

These two triangles stand apart, which in principle should have made things easier for rehearsal. Laurey and Ado Annie are friends (and have a long exchange in act 1, scene 1), but Will Parker comes into only minimal contact with Curly (in act 2, scenes 1 and 3) and Laurey (act 2, scene 2), and not at all with Jud, who, in turn, never interacts with Ado Annie or Andrew Carnes. Aunt Eller has some contact with Will (they dance together in "Kansas City"), and Carnes emerges somewhat improbably as the *deus ex machina* to resolve the Curly/Laurey/Jud plot. Although for much of the show Carnes is the querulous, and comic, shotgun-bearing father figure seeking to marry off his daughter, he suddenly gains stature as the federal judge who can try the case of Jud's death and pronounce Curly innocent. This grouping of characters is also reflected in their music. The songs for Laurey, Curly, and Jud are noticeably weightier than those for Ado Annie, Will Parker, and Ali Hakim. Ali Hakim is the most mobile character, moving freely between these various groups, although his music, such as it is, is distinguished chiefly by being nonmusic. *Oklahoma!* may well have sought to promote an agenda of community, but its own community of characters remains fractured along various dramatic and musical fault lines that, in turn, have some significance for the messages the show may have sought to convey.

"Sing it, Andrew!"

Act 2 of *Oklahoma!* begins with "The Farmer and the Cowman," representing a square dance at the Box Social. As the dance collapses into a fight—farmers and cowmen trading insults, then blows—Aunt Eller fires a gun into the air, points it at Andrew Carnes (a nice twist on his own attempts at a shotgun wedding for Ado Annie), and revives the music ("Sing it, Andrew! Dum tiddy um tum tum—"; p. 89), forcing him to pick up the refrain and achieve a different wedding between the two camps.[9]

Singing is an integral feature of the musical theater; it is also problematic in terms of verisimilitude. What is it, apart from the genre itself, that prompts and justifies song? And how might such songs insert themselves into the dramatic action? While many might feel these issues to be lost causes—we should just accept that musicals (and for that matter, operas) have music—they come to the fore in cases where the musical theater appeals to notions of naturalness, and also integration. The songs in *Oklahoma!* are fairly conventional in terms of the genre, ranging across the gamut of Broadway styles from comic patter to Romantic lyricism, along with two of Rodgers's "signature" waltzes ("Oh, What a Beautiful Mornin'" and "Out of My Dreams"). The chief omission is of songs based on jazz styles (with the slight exception of the bridge of "All er Nuthin'"), which Rodgers and Hammerstein presumably felt would be out of character for the time period. As Rodgers later said, "Oscar and I were both careful in writing the score and lyrics to make the songs sound natural when sung by cowboys, ranchers and farm girls living in Indian Territory at the turn of the century."[10] But for the moment, the question is whether these songs are anything more than interludes that stand entirely apart from the "play."

"The Farmer and the Cowman" illustrates one means of integration: it is presented as a "real" song (and dance) that is diegetic within the action, and therefore verisimilar (so, when Aunt Eller threatens Carnes with the gun, she orders him to "sing"). Two other songs in *Oklahoma!* are similarly diegetic: the opening "Oh, What a Beautiful Mornin'," which Curly comes "a-singin'" (p. 4) to Aunt Eller (having the voice unaccompanied at the start makes it more realistic still); and "Pore Jud Is Daid," presented by Curly as an example of what people might "sing like their hearts ud break" (p. 64) at Jud's funeral.[11] The latter builds on a speech for Curly in *Green Grow the Lilacs*, scene 3 (p. 63): "The folks ud all gether around and sing. *Sad* songs, of course. And some of 'em ud say whut a good man you was, and others ud say what a pig-stealer and a hound dog you was, and you'd orter been in the penitentiary long ago, fer orneriness." But while the other songs are mostly inverisimilar in such diegetic terms (as is much more often the case in musical theater), they are at least plausible in the manner of their introduction: as Jerome Kern pointed out in an interview around the premiere of his *Oh, Boy* (1917), "Plausibility and reason apply to musical plays as to dramas and comedies, and the sooner librettists and composers appreciate this fact the sooner will come recognition and royalties."[12] For the most part, the songs serve to create and emphasize a rhetorical point (for example, "I Cain't Say No," "Many a New Day," "All er Nuthin'"), to focus a narrative ("The Surrey with the Fringe on Top," "Kansas City"), or to lead into some kind of other world ("Out of My Dreams"). They are usually prompted by what one might call "I"-moments (sometimes "you" or "we") — "I got a beautiful feeling," "When I take you out tonight with me," "I got to Kansas City on a Frid'y," "I'm jist a girl who cain't say no" — as a character is allowed to articulate a position.

Even in such cases, a vestigial sense of verisimilitude may be achieved by subsequent lead-ins to dancing, as with Will Parker's illustration of the different types of dances he has encountered in Kansas City, or with the girls' "All right, boys! Revolve!" at the end of "It's a Scandal! It's a Outrage!" It also helps that with just one exception, all the songs in *Oklahoma!* are

sung to one or more other characters who, one assumes, are expected to re-
act (witness the frequent spoken interjections and physical gestures specified
in the libretto); it is symptomatic that, according to Lawrence Langner, the
songs were directed by Mamoulian rather than by the dance director as was
customary, which, he said, aided in integrating them into the show.[13] The
only true soliloquy (with a character left alone onstage), and therefore a very
striking one, is Jud's "Lonely Room." In fact, only rarely do Hammerstein
and Rodgers need to rely solely on convention to justify a song, as with the
"expected" act 1 love duet for Laurey and Curly, "People Will Say We're in
Love," or "Oklahoma" as an eleven o'clock number. Hammerstein made his
position clear: "There are few things in life of which I am certain, but I am
sure of this one thing, that the song is the servant of the play, that it is wrong
to write first what you think is an attractive song and then try to wedge it
into a story."[14] This is presumably why "Boys and Girls Like You and Me"
eventually disappeared from act 2.

"People Will Say We're in Love" also illustrates another technique used
by Hammerstein to locate the songs within the action. Songs that start or
end scenes (or scenes within scenes) are easier to manage than those that
appear in their middle: start-songs do not require a dramatic cue to begin,
while end-songs use the final applause to create an exit (with or without an
encore) and then allow a change in pace (as with "Many a New Day" and
"All er Nuthin'"). When a character who has just delivered a song stays on
stage (for example, after "Kansas City" and "I Cain't Say No"), it can create difficulties in terms of staging, while in all cases other than start-songs,
there must be some lead-in to ease the transition from the preceding speech.
Long orchestral introductions are not helpful in this regard. Rodgers (or perhaps better, Bennett) avoids them in *Oklahoma!* often starting more or less
straight in with the voice, even if this creates additional problems in terms
of the singer finding the right pitch; the orchestrations reveal a number of
changes to the introductions to the songs, including shortening them or even
discarding them completely.[15] Moving from speech to song can also be aided
by continuing the theme and tone of the preceding dialogue, or even, in
some cases, by delivering the first line(s) "half spoken" (as the libretto directs
for "Lonely Room," and the vocal score for "All er Nuthin'"). Immediately
prior to "People Will Say We're in Love" (pp. 56–57), Laurey and Curly are
bickering over the local gossip about their relationship. Laurey points out,
"Most of the talk is that you're stuck on me," the orchestra (soft strings) enters
as the speech continues with Curly's spoken "Cain't imagine how these ugly

rumors start" (just as the song itself is about to "start") and Laurey's "Me neither." The verse follows this two-measure introduction, with hardly a shift of rhetorical gears despite the move from speech to song. The illusion is aided still further by Hammerstein's use of long, proselike lines, even as the regular rhythms and rhymes both internal and external make it clear that we are in verse:

LAUREY

Why do they *think* up stories that *link* my name with yours?

CURLY

Why do the *neigh*bors gossip all *day* behind their doors?[16]

LAUREY

I know a *way* to prove what they *say* is quite untrue,
Here is the *gist*, a practical *list* of "don'ts" for you.

Only with the chorus do we move to shorter lines (hexameters to trimeters) to mark a change of musical pace:

Don't throw bouquets at me—
Don't please my folks too much,
. . .

The shift to trimeters is also an issue of musical form and was what Rodgers would have expected. "People Will Say We're in Love" uses the standard pattern of mid-twentieth-century popular song: a verse sets up a situation, and the chorus (or refrain, as it is often called in the vocal score) is the lyrical expression, and usually the melody that listeners associate with the song's title (which in turn generally derives from a catchphrase or hook in the chorus). The chorus is usually in one of two forms, the first involving parallel periods (ABAB or ABAC) and the second what has been called (not entirely helpfully) "lyric binary" (AABA or AABC), with an eight- or sixteen-measure phrase (A) then repeated, a middle eight-measure phrase (B; called the "middle eight," "release," or "bridge"), and then some kind of return to the first phrase, which may, however, be altered to provide a more climactic conclusion.[17] The second form tends to be the more common and is clearly outlined in both text and music of "People Will Say We're in Love": Laurey's "Don't throw bouquets at me" is the first A section (sixteen measures), and Curly's "Don't sigh and gaze at me" the second (another

sixteen), then an eight-measure bridge for both characters ("Don't start col-
lecting things") leading to a modified A section (eight measures) for the hook
("Sweetheart they're suspecting things—/People will say we're in love!"). In
such songs, the verse-chorus, or just the chorus, can then be repeated to extend the form, with or without a contrasting episode before the repeat (as
the "trio" in "I Cain't Say No"). Other straightforward lyric-binary songs are
"The Surrey with the Fringe on Top" and "Oklahoma." "All er Nuthin'" is a
lyric binary with no repeat of the initial A section, as is "Many a New Day"
with its rather odd twelve-measure A.

The three explicitly diegetic songs in *Oklahoma!* deviate from the lyric-
binary model, perhaps precisely to emphasize their diegetic status. "Oh,
What a Beautiful Mornin'" is laid out more as a simple strophic song with refrain (which is what it is meant to represent).[18] "Pore Jud Is Daid" is strophic
in the manner of a hymnlike dirge. (Spoken passages with underscoring separate the strophes.) And "The Farmer and the Cowman" has a more complex
sectional form with three strains ("The farmer and the cowman should be
friends," "Territory folk should stick together," "I'd like to say a word for the
farmer") in various combinations, reflecting the typical repetition and variation schemes of square dances. "Kansas City," an at least partly diegetic song
(Will sings of his exploits in the city, leading to a dance), likewise avoids the
model, with parallel periods in the chorus, as do "It's a Scandal! It's a Outrage!" (after a fashion) and "Out of My Dreams" (which has what Rodgers
called a "trio"—"Make up your mind . . ."—in his penciled score), although
the latter song is hard to categorize, perhaps because it was designed to lead
into the ballet rather than stand alone. But the most unusual piece in *Oklahoma!* is, of course, "Lonely Room," which, though linked to the ABAC
model, is extended in a manner that makes it appear through-composed.

The song forms in *Oklahoma!* taken both individually and collectively,
are by no means as regular as those who dismiss the genre might care to assume. It is not clear whether this variety is because of a deliberate wish to
break the mold (and therefore enhance the "natural" feel of the result) or
because Rodgers was often responding to preformed lyrics. Hammerstein's
poetic structures undoubtedly had some influence on the musical settings,
as Rodgers himself noted: "It helped me a good deal to have a completed
lyric in front of me. It also offered me the opportunity to break away—even
more than I had in the recent past—from the generally accepted 'AABA'
thirty-two-bar song construction."[19] Hammerstein must also have been involved in the decision to achieve further variation, and a greater degree of

cohesion, by extending these forms to include spoken or half-sung dialogue over underscoring. Again, this is not unusual in the repertory (particularly in film musicals), but it makes an effect. In "The Surrey with the Fringe on Top," Curly has a verse ("When I take you out tonight with me") then a chorus ("Chicks and ducks and geese better scurry"); Aunt Eller, Curly, and Laurey share a verse ("Would y'say that fringe was made of silk?"); Curly has a chorus ("All the world'll fly in a flurry"); the music continues under a long spoken dialogue (starting with Aunt Eller's "Yo'd shore feel like a queen settin' up in *that* carriage"); then Curly has the final chorus ("I can see the stars gittin' blurry"). In "All er Nuthin'," the verse (which starts with Will's "half spoken" "You'll have to be a little more standoffish") proceeds as sung dialogue between Will and Ado Annie, then shifts to measured speech over music (a vamp) as Will states his claim for having sown his last wild oat and wanting to know Ado Annie's intentions. Only then do we get the chorus ("With me it's all er nuthin'").

The most striking examples of in-song speech (unmeasured, measured, or half-sung) are in "It's a Scandal! It's a Outrage!" and "Pore Jud Is Daid." The former was almost certainly influenced by perceptions of Joseph Buloff's singing abilities, although it enhances the invective of Ali Hakim's opening diatribe, even while alienating him from the "singing" community. As for "Pore Jud Is Daid," the design is particularly complex. We have seen that this is established as a diegetic song and therefore is stanzaic, in the manner of the hymn it represents. Each stanza begins with "Pore Jud is daid/Pore Jud Fry is daid." Curly delivers two stanzas (". . . Oh, why did sich a feller have to die?" ". . . His fingernails have never b'en so clean"). Jud has an echo "And serene" in the second stanza; the stage direction is "Touched and carried away, he sings a soft response."[20] Curly then invents what the minister might say: the music distinguishes between Curly's speech ("'Nen the preacher'd git up and he'd say") and the minister's ("Folks! We are geth-ered here to moan and groan over our brother Jud Fry . . .") by having the latter chanted on a monotone over sustained chords, shifting into melody (at "But the folks 'at really knowed him") to allow Jud to echo the senti-ment ("Repeating reverently like a Negro at a revivalist meeting"). As the invented speech of the minister continues ("He loved the birds of the for-est . . ."), Curly moves from chant to speech, grandiloquence now granted by the hymnlike writing in the orchestra. We then have a third stanza of the song (". . . Becuz pore Jud is underneath the ground") that seems to shift even more into Curly's own voice, rather than that of a fictive congregation;

Jud again has an echo ("Miles around"). Jud, in turn, takes up a fourth stanza that breaks the opening pattern ("Pore Jud is daid,/A candle lights his haid . . . And now they know their friend has gone fer good"). According to the stage direction, "JUD is too emotionally exalted by the spirit of CURLY's singing to be analytical. He now takes up a refrain of his own," appropriating the song in a manner that is both bathetic and pathetic. The piece ends with a fifth stanza ("Pore Jud is daid/A candle lights his haid . . . But it's summer and we're running out of ice") that starts with both Curly and Jud singing together (no longer in the imagined voice of the congregation), leading to a final cadential "Pore Jud" (twice) in harmony. The shifts of rhetorical register are striking and produce a particularly ambivalent piece.

Such extended forms clearly serve to maintain musicodramatic continuities for longer than just a moment of lyrical expression. Again, "People Will Say We're in Love" provides a good example. After Curly's repeat of the chorus there is a pause (for applause), then the music continues under spoken dialogue as Curly tries to persuade Laurey to go with him, not with Jud, to the Box Social, and announces his exit to go and see Jud in the smokehouse (all this over the first sixteen measures of the chorus).[21] Laurey, left alone, picks up the repeat of the A section ("Don't sigh and gaze at me") but breaks down in tears before its end; the orchestra continues the melody to and through the B section under spoken dialogue between Laurey and Aunt Eller, then Laurey's hurried exit; and Aunt Eller is left alone on stage humming the final A section, "happy and contented, as lights dim and the curtain falls." A fair amount of action has taken place over forty-eight measures of music that also serve to close the scene.

Such cohesion is also clear on a more extended scale, if somewhat obviously, by virtue of the oft-noted use of reprises in *Oklahoma!* These are not unusual in terms of the genre but can still serve a dramatic purpose. After Curly's opening entrance to "Oh, What a Beautiful Mornin'" and his spoken dialogue with Aunt Eller, Laurey also announces her presence from offstage by singing the refrain of Curly's song; Hammerstein is careful to have Laurey make clear that she has "heared someone a-singin' like a bullfrog in a pond" (p. 7). This fixes a clear connection between Curly and Laurey. "The Surrey with the Fringe on Top" is reprised after "Kansas City" as the conversation returns to Curly's having hired a surrey to drive to the Box Social. (It also provides exit music for Curly.) The "trio" of "I Cain't Say No" reappears as Will presses his suit with Ado Annie ("S'posin' 'at I say 'at yer lips're like cherries")—even though he was not on stage to hear the original song—then leading into "Oh, What a Beautiful Mornin'" for the entrance of Curly and Gertie (waltzing) and the ensemble; the reprise of "I Cain't Say No" again forges a connection between a couple not yet together but bound to be so.[22] While some of these reprises are just functional (for example, to cover entrances and exits), others are not, and even when they are, some further dramatic point can be made, as when "Oh, What a Beautiful Mornin'" becomes the community song. The same applies to the change-of-scene music (supplied by Bennett). The shift from act 1, scene 1 to scene 2 is covered by an orchestral repeat of the song ending scene 1, "People Will Say We're in Love," while the one from scene 2 to scene 3 (after the smokehouse scene) reintroduces a feminine space by reference to "Many a New Day" (the all-girl song and dance in scene 1): Bennett must also have realized the dislocating tonal effect of moving *attacca* (so the score is marked) straight from the end of "Lonely Room" (in B minor) into "Many a New Day" (in E flat major). At the end of act 2, scene 1 (before Will and Ado Annie's scene in front of the traveler), Aunt Eller cues the change-of-scene music ("The Farmer and the Cowman" as the characters dance off) with "Pick 'at banjo to pieces, Sam!" and the same music recurs to lead into scene 2, emphasizing the illusion that the dance has still been going on elsewhere.

The most striking reprise in *Oklahoma!* however, occurs in act 2, scene 2. This is where, in Hammerstein's original design, Laurey and Curly were to have "the best song in the show, when it is written," which became (at least for New Haven) "Boys and Girls Like You and Me." In the final version, Curly proposes to Laurey, she accepts, and the contract is sealed with a kiss over the beginning of a reprise of "People Will Say We're in Love," with the melody played by a solo violin, often a marker of "romance," at least if we are to believe conventional representations of candlelit dinners. The dialogue continues over the music until Curly breaks into song at the cadence: "Let people say we're in love!" Laurey and Curly pick up the repeat of the A section ("Who keers what happens now?") and run through the B section ("Starlight looks well on us") and then the return to beginning ("Who cares if they tell on us?/Let people say we're in love"), ending in triumphant two-part harmony (with Laurey on a top a''), the first time they actually sing together, and therefore the first time this love duet becomes a love *duet*, fulfilling its potential only after Laurey and Curly have cemented their relationship. The technique is corny enough, the symbolism obvious, and the words are not Hammerstein's best, but there is no harm in playing to the gallery. And by now, "People Will Say We're in Love" has clearly become emblematic: it provides the change-of-scene music both before and after the next front-of-traveler scene for Will, Ado Annie, and the Peddler (with the "Persian goodbye" and "Oklahoma hello"), presumably because Ado Annie and Will have now finally declared their love, and it appears in the "Finale ultimo" after the community singing (again) of "Oh, What a Beautiful Mornin'." This replaced Hammerstein's original idea of ending with the "Surrey Song," which instead appears at the end of the outmarch (that begins again with "People Will Say We're in Love") for the curtain calls. What is most surprising, however, is that what was to emerge as the most obvious "communal" song in the show, "Oklahoma," does not return at the end; either there was no more time (or desire) to make further changes to the end of the act, or it was felt that it had done sufficient duty.

Shortly after the opening of *Oklahoma!* Hammerstein explained some of the musical problems he and Rodgers had faced:

> When *Green Grow the Lilacs* was first produced, it had songs, real American folksongs from the cow country—good ones, too. They were not part of the play's texture. They were delivered incidentally, sung by the characters at a party and by a cowboy chorus to cover scenic changes. The songs we were to write had a different function. They must help tell our story and delineate characters, supplementing the dialogue and seeming to be, as much as possible, a continuation of dialogue. This is, of course, true of the songs by [sic] any well-made play.
>
> Our problem in this case was to write words and music that would convey the flavor of the West and the feeling of the period, and yet not be slavish imitations of the Western songs that had been interpolated in the original. We didn't want to write second-hand hillbilly ballads. They wouldn't be as good as the real ones. What we aimed to do was to write in our own style and yet seem "in character" with the background and substance of the story.[23]

In fact, Hammerstein does something of an injustice to the folk songs (and their ubiquity) in Riggs's play, where they are more than just incidental. He also, if inevitably, overemphasizes the notion of integration. It is easy to exaggerate the case for musicodramatic cohesion in *Oklahoma!* even if, as we have seen, there is a strong tendency to do so. However, its songs do somehow belong in the show in ways perhaps less common in, say, a musical by Rodgers and Hart, where the best-known melodies soon became, and remain, entirely divorced from their original theatrical environment. (Who knows the contexts of "Bewitched, Bothered, and Bewildered," "There's a Small Hotel," or "With a Song in My Heart"?) Hammerstein himself was

aware of the point: "I don't believe that either Dick or I would be very successful essentially as popular songwriters—writers of songs detached from
plays. We can write words and music best when they are required by a situation or a characterization in a story."[24] *Oklahoma!* may or may not be "integrated," but its elements certainly fit together.

"There's a bright, golden haze on the meadow"

No less compelling than the songs of *Oklahoma!* are the broader messages
of the show, cocooned within the overall feel-good factor noted as being
so powerful even, perhaps especially, in 1943. Rodgers and Hammerstein
seemed to have pressed all the right buttons: nostalgia, idealism, community
spirit, and patriotism. Sentimental the work may be, but in America, at least,
it takes a cynic not to care about Laurey, Curly, and their world near Claremore in the Indian Territory (now Oklahoma): Hammerstein even drew
them his own special map to locate them in some kind of "real" space.[25]

    In part, the context is the search for an American identity that we have
already seen in Riggs's *Green Grow the Lilacs*, and that was also a prominent
feature of the later 1930s. Roosevelt's establishment of the Works Progress
Administration in 1935 (from 1939, the Work Projects Administration) may
have been to meet an immediate Depression need to create employment,
but it also led to the founding under its umbrella of the Federal Arts Project,
the Federal Music Project, the Federal Theatre Project, and the Federal
Writers' Project. These projects sought to broaden mass interest in the arts
by notions of their relevance to particularly American concerns: painting
(Thomas Hart Benton, Grant Wood), literature, theater, opera, and film all
had their part to play in focusing on Americana and hence in cementing
national identities. Even European exiles caught the enthusiasm: Benjamin
Britten's "choral operetta" *Paul Bunyan* (staged at Columbia University in
May 1941) paid homage to the folk heritage (and music) of the composer's
temporary home. *Paul Bunyan* was something of a failure and seems to have
had little broader impact; certainly, it does not get mentioned as a predecessor of *Oklahoma!* in the same way, if for different reasons, as *Show Boat* and
Porgy and Bess. But although, as we shall see, *Oklahoma!* had more immediate wartime concerns, its broader themes sit squarely in this environment:
indeed, it is a virtual poster for the New Deal, or perhaps better, a response
to its opponents. The New Deal's detractors advocated populism and isola-
tionism; Hammerstein instead brought small-town America into a broader

left-wing yet still wholesome vision, while also demonstrating (through Jud) the consequences of an isolationist position and its counterpart, closet Fascism.[26] Rodgers said that Helburn and Langner had been urging him to do something "American" since well before *Oklahoma!* Hammerstein played up the issue of national character even more strongly in his prepremiere interviews: "Well, as a result we've got what we think is a lusty, American kind of musical, a glorification of the American ability to invent its own musical forms and rhythms, its own songs and styles of singing. It's about time America stopped being in awe of other nations' music, and started appreciating the natural, spontaneous music of its pioneer localities, and the modern compositions inspired by that native music."[27]

The argument here can best be read in terms of the pastoral, perhaps inevitably given America's special relationship with its geography. Right from the start of *Oklahoma!* with "Oh, What a Beautiful Mornin'"—which Rodgers claimed could only be "pastoral in inflection"—Curly is shown to be a child of the land, in harmony with a nature ("All the sounds of the earth are like music") that is, in turn, sympathetic to him ("And a ol' weepin' willer is laughin' at me!") and even romantically inclined ("But a little brown mav'rick is winkin' her eye"); we may also suspect that he is a farmer already. Bennett's orchestration makes the point still clearer, with its Copland-like gestures (birdcalls, horn fifths) that reinforce the tendency of the expansive melody to evoke wide-open spaces.[28] Curly's musical abilities—accentuated still more in Riggs's play, where he not only sings but also plays the harmonium—are not such as to threaten his masculinity, for we know that all cowboys sing (and dance), but these special gifts mark him out for prominence, at least in wise old Aunt Eller's eyes and, we know from the outset, in Laurey's. The Indian Territory is established as a pastoral Arcadia, a land of milk and honey where song is in the air, a prelapsarian paradise of the Age of Gold. The trope is well established within Western literature, stemming back to the pastoral poets of the ancient Greeks (Theocritus) and transmitted to the modern age via the theatrical works of the Italian Renaissance (Torquato Tasso's *Aminta*; Battista Guarini's *Il pastor fido*) and by Shakespeare (*As You Like It* is an obvious example). This is not to say that Riggs or Hammerstein must have known their Tasso or Shakespeare—the pastoral trope is standard—although equally, there is no reason to deny them some knowledge of classical and similar sources. For example, Riggs makes at least one strong reference to mythology by way of Laurey's report (in scene 2; p. 31) of picking flowers in the meadow and seeing a snake with its tail in its mouth. This clearly links her to Eurydice, and hence the musical Curly to Orpheus, and Jeeter to Orpheus's rival, Aristaeus, another pastoral myth and also one with strong musical overtones. In the pastoral, simple country-folk live a life of bliss and innocence supported by bountiful nature, at one with their lives and with the world. They sing as if music were a natural language; they dance to celebrate the harmony and cohesion of the body politic.

It is typical of pastoral that in contrast to nature, and always explicitly or implicitly opposed to it, is the city, where civilization is merely a snare to trap the unwary into depravity and destitution. "Ev'rythin's up to date in Kansas City," sings Will Parker, "They've gone about as fur as they c'n go!": tele-phones, motorcars, skyscrapers ("seven stories high"), radiators, and indoor bathrooms. But Will is also taken by the "big theayter they call a burleeque" where for fifty cents one can see a stripper peel off her clothes: "She went about as fur as she could go!" Will demonstrates new dances he has learned there, first the two-step and then ragtime ("Seen a couple of colored fellers doin' it"): as far as he is concerned, "the waltz is through," which was prob-ably true enough of an American urban environment around 1900. The city is a place of untold riches—Will has earned his fifty dollars as first prize in a steer-roping contest—although it is also a place where a fool, good-hearted or not, can lose his money: Will splashes his prize on presents for Ado Annie. It is a place of awe but populated by city slickers open to ridicule (as in an episode in *Rodeo* involving, precisely, an outsider from Kansas City). All in all, it is better to stay safe in the country.[29]

Claremore is not so "up to date" as Kansas City, but nor is it "wild." Here the waltz is certainly not "through" if we are to believe the communal role (as both song and dance) of "Oh, What a Beautiful Mornin'," or Laurey's wistful "Out of My Dreams"; rather, it becomes just one of several emblems of good, old-fashioned country values. The land is cultivated ("The corn is as high as an elephant's eye"), and its inhabitants stand by principles as wholesome as their food (sweet-potato pie, cold duck with stuffing, lemon-meringue pie, and custard with raspberry syrup; pp. 99–105). The commu-nity is close to the railway, is about to build a school (the purpose of the Box Social auction), and is based on farmers who are "good and thrifty" citizens. True, the rule of law has not yet fully been established, although Cord Elam (the Federal Marshall) at least has the decency to realize that something is not quite right with Curly's trial, even if he is outvoted (and in the case of Jud's death, no one is going to feel that an injustice has occurred). But in

essence, Claremore mediates between the city and its not so different oppo-
site, the wilderness, by presenting a rose-tinted picture of rural America. As
Ado Annie asks Will in "All er Nuthin',"

> Would you build me a house,
> All painted white,
> Cute and clean and purty and bright?

—big enough for a family, and surrounded, one assumes, by a picket fence.
New Yorkers may not have known much about the real Oklahoma, but surely
they sensed in their hearts that this was a place that Americans could call
home.

In classical and even Christian terms, the pastoral Age of Gold may be
threatened from the outside by the city and its trappings of civilization, but
it also always contains within itself two sources of danger. When gold muta-
tes to iron, weapons, and therefore death, enter the land. Curly renounces
his gun, selling it at the auction. Jud, however, keeps his weapons to hand:
he is polishing his pistol at the start of act 1, scene 2; he tries to buy a "frog-
sticker" (a long knife) from the Peddler later in the same scene; and he twice
attempts to kill Curly, once with the "Little Wonder" in act 2, scene 1, and
again with a knife in scene 3, causing his own death. The "Little Wonder"—
a kaleidoscope containing lewd images and a hidden switchblade—is an im-
port from the city (Will brings it back with him), and only the two outsiders
to the community, Jud and the Peddler, know its real dangers. The knife
is more familiar, but no less underhand: real men shoot it out, but Curly
has already established (in 1.2) that he is a better shot than Jud. Jud's violent weapons, no less than his sociopathic tendencies, set him apart from
the "good" farmers of Arcadia.

But that, too, is part of the pastoral ethos. Every Arcadia contains its
satyr, the lust-filled half-man/half-beast who is a source of fear and a butt of
jokes. Every Garden of Eden contains its snake, which tempts evil but also,
and not entirely paradoxically, offers access to the fruit of knowledge. Curly
likens Jud precisely to a snake, and one refusing to enter the pastoral light
of day, in act 1, scene 2 (p. 71) in a speech taken directly from the equivalent
scene in the play (p. 75):

> In this country, they's two things you c'n do if you're a man. Live out of
> doors is one. Live in a hole is the other. I've set by my horse in the bresh
> some'eres and heared a rattlesnake many a time. Rattle, rattle, rattle!—he'd
> go, skeered to death. Somebody comin' close to his hole! Somebody gonna

step on him! Git his old fangs ready, full of pizen! Curl up and wait!—Long's
you live in a hole, you're skeered, you got to have pertection. You c'n have
muscles, oh, like arn—and still be as weak as a empty bladder—less'n you
got things to barb your hide with. (*Suddenly, harshly, directly to* JUD) How'd
you git to be the way you air, anyway—settin' here in this filthy hole—and
thinkin' the way you're thinkin'? Why don't you do sumpin healthy onct in
a while, 'stid of staying shet up here—a-crawlin' and festerin'!

For Laurey, however, Jud is more complex. This Caliban-like figure—the
parallels with Shakespeare's *The Tempest* are clear—is terrifying but also not
a little fascinating. As Olin Downes noted in his account of *Oklahoma!* in
the *New York Times* on 6 June 1943, "There are those who dislike, and with
some reason, the rather raw and Freudian interpolation, as the present book
makes it appear, of the figure of the sinister and lascivious Jud." Later critics played still more into the pastoral trope: Otis Gurnsey Jr., writing in the
Herald Tribune (1951), noted that the show's "single realistic character, Jud
Fry, is a terror in this ideal setting, and he is conveniently ditched after he
has served his purpose of accenting the rosiness around him."[30] Laurey fears
him and his nightly prowling outside her bedroom window, but at one time
at least, she was moved to compassion, nursing him through sickness (so Jud
recounts in act 2, scene 2). His lust is threatening, but his passion is powerful, and both offer something that Laurey can use to grow from a girl into a
woman. Just as the satyr often, and necessarily, exposes the (female) inhabitants of Arcadia to an earthy, physical sexuality that is then to be directed
and contained within social and ethical norms (marriage to the "right" man
produces legitimate—in both senses—children), so does Jud open Laurey's
eyes to a sexual life that will find its "proper" fulfillment in wedlock with
Curly. Jud may be her nightmare, so we discover in the dream-ballet, but
he also enables her to see things clearly.

Pastoral is the product of an urban culture (and of urbane authors), even
as it idealizes the nonurban Other. Whether the tone is nostalgic or polemi-
cal (or both), it is never as "natural" as it constructs itself to be, and it does
not require authenticity above and beyond what an urban audience might
(reasonably or not) believe life to be like in a "real" countryside that is, in
fact, a fiction. The situation is similar with pastoral's close relatives, exoti-
cism and orientalism. The apparent authenticity of *Oklahoma!* was a matter
for discussion in contemporary reviews—contributing to the argument over
its notional realism—and has remained so in the critical discourse. Thus it is

often noted that Miles White drew his costume designs from an "authentic" 1904–5 Montgomery Ward catalogue.[31] Rodgers, however, was more honest. In an article on *The King and I* in the *New York Herald Tribune* on 25 March 1951, he, too, focused on the issue of authenticity:

> It seems more likely that if one were to attempt to reproduce with accuracy the court of the King of Siam in the year 1860, he might have to show the king as an individual quite unattractive (physically, at least) to the Western eye. . . . Continue this technique . . . and it seems probable that you would end up completely repelling the Western eye, ear, nose and sense of touch. . . . In 1942 I had never been to the state of Oklahoma and I suppose it may be truthfully said that *Oklahoma!* doesn't contain a single bar of authentic Southwestern music. It doesn't seem to have hurt the overall effect.[32]

He went further in his autobiography, noting in the case of *Oklahoma!*:

> I remember that shortly before beginning the score Oscar sent me an impressively thick book of songs of the American Southwest which he thought might be of help: I opened the book, played through the music of one song, closed the book, and never looked at it again. If my melodies were going to be authentic, they'd have to be authentic on my own terms.
>
> This is the way I have always worked, no matter what the setting of the story. It was true of my "Chinese" music for *Chee-Chee*, of my "French" music for *Love Me Tonight*, and later of my "Siamese" music for *The King and I*. Had I attempted to duplicate the real thing, it would never have sounded genuine, for the obvious reason that I am neither Chinese, French, Siamese, nor from the Southwest. All a composer—any composer—can do is to make an audience believe it is hearing an authentic sound without losing his own musical identity.[33]

Rodgers's claim for a higher-level authenticity ("genuine" music that is authentic to the identity of the composer, or for that matter, to some kind of emotional truth) is a typical, even harmless, deception. Hammerstein had his feet more firmly in the theatrical ground: "Deriving from a source that is real, the whole production is lifted a plane above literal reality. There are authentic figures and genuine hoe-down steps in the dancing, but it is better dancing, more excited and varied than you would actually find in a barn or on a moonlit meadow. . . . To thus heighten reality is almost an obligation for a musical production. To accomplish it without becoming completely false is difficult. In this play the trick seems to have come off."[34] No one seeing

Oklahoma! will be fooled into thinking that it just paints a natural, warm-hearted picture of how people really lived in the Indian Territory around 1900. No one, too, will deny the theatrical artifice involved. But as with all theater, the question arises of just what messages are being conveyed.

"Plen'y of air and plen'y of room"

Clearly, *Oklahoma!* embraces that set of political, social, and cultural beliefs and practices known as the "American way." Good-hearted country folk forge a new life and a new future by virtue of hard work and core values. More immediately relevant in time of war, however, was a no less important subtext of the show, the claims of Manifest Destiny established in the 1840s as America's birthright to extend the boundaries of freedom "from sea to shining sea" (and even beyond).

Converting a Depression-era play about the struggles of a harsh life in the Southwest into a patriotic hymn to Manifest Destiny seems to have been a gradual process. The song that finally achieved the transition, "Oklahoma," came quite late in the creative process, as we have seen, and in its early version, it was more a character piece (with a central tap dance episode) than a stirring anthem to a state (in turn becoming in 1953 a state anthem). As Laurey and Curly emerge as newlyweds, Aunt Eller proclaims, "They couldn't pick a better time to start in life." The Indian Territory is about to become a "brand new state," and Laurey and Curly's wedding immediately becomes symbolic of an impending "marriage" with the Union, and of mankind with the earth. As a result, the glorified land will become still more beneficent, with "barley, carrots and pertaters" and "spinach and termaters," plus "plen'y of room to swing a rope" and "plen'y of heart and plen'y of hope." For wartime New Yorkers jaded by brownouts and food rationing—and with little space to "dig for victory" in backyard vegetable plots—the promised cornucopia must have been tempting indeed. Still more potent were the canonic notions of the "room" available in the open prairies of the "wild" West, and of the courageous optimism ("plen'y of heart and plen'y of hope") that made one proud to be an American: "We know we belong to the land,/And the land we belong to is grand!" The expansive, stirring melody makes the message clearer still. None of this is present in *Green Grow the Lilacs*, where Laurey and Curly's marriage remains a domestic affair. Nor does it bear much relationship to the realities of life in the Oklahoma dustbowl of the mid-1930s documented by John Steinbeck's *The Grapes of Wrath*, a geo-social crisis caused precisely by the new farming techniques extolled in the verse to "Oklahoma." Clearly, myth outweighs reality.[35]

No less bound up in *Oklahoma!* and closely linked to ideas of Manifest Destiny, is the notion of the frontier as a unique place where "American" values were forged. In his well-known lecture "The Significance of the Frontier in American History" presented before a meeting of the American Historical Association at the World's Columbian Exhibition in Chicago on 12 July 1893, Frederick Jackson Turner, a future professor of history at Harvard, laid down the premises of his "frontier thesis" precisely at the moment when, according to the 1890 census, the frontier had ceased to be a reality because of continuous settlement across the country. The frontier, Turner argued, "promoted the formation of a composite nationality for the American people. . . . In the crucible of the frontier the immigrants were Americanized, liberated, and fused into a mixed race." It demonstrated the interdependence of the different parts of the United States, and of towns and rural areas, in terms of economic production, an interdependence that in turn fostered federal government, a sense of national citizenship, and, so the argument inevitably went, the triumph of democracy. But for Turner, the frontier went still further in establishing an identifiable American character that became less and less European the more the frontier moved westward:

> The result is that to the frontier the American intellect owes its striking characteristics. That coarseness and strength combined with acuteness and inquisitiveness; that practical, inventive turn of mind, quick to find expedients, that masterful grasp of material things, lacking in the artistic but powerful to effect great ends; that restless nervous energy; that dominant individualism, working for good and for evil, and withal that buoyancy and exuberance which comes with freedom — these are the traits of the frontier, or traits called out elsewhere because of the frontier.[36]

But the question remained of who might best inhabit this land that is "grand." Both Riggs and Hammerstein clearly embrace this frontier ideology (as would most Americans of their period), but Hammerstein develops further the issue of land rights. The range wars of the last quarter of the nineteenth century between farmers and cowboys over access to the prairies were a well-known part of American history; they were also enshrined in countless B-Westerns of the 1930s and 1940s, often starring Roy Rogers (whom Helburn originally proposed as a possible Curly) or Gene Autry. *Oklahoma!* refers clearly to the range wars in "The Farmer and the Cowman," where the argument is that people of different kinds—be they farmers and cowboys or even, perhaps, wartime Americans and Russians—should "stick together" and "all be pals."

The farmer came out west "and made a lot of changes," says Carnes, to which the cowboys Will and Curly retort, "He come out west and built a lot of fences!/And built 'em right across our cattle ranges!" Yet in *Oklahoma!* it is clear which side has already won, just as it was by the 1890s. Carnes claims that "The farmer is a good and thrifty citizen," whereas all Aunt Eller can say for the cowboy is that he deserves sympathy because "The road he treads is difficult and stony." The cowboys in *Oklahoma!* are open to ridicule: Will Parker is clearly short on brains (given the time it takes him to figure out how not to spend the fifty dollars he needs to marry Ado Annie), and even the hero Curly admits (with some pride) that he is "bow-legged from the saddle" such that, according to Aunt Eller, he "couldn't stop a pig in the road" (p. 6). Yet the community near Claremore is close to integration: Curly is well known at the Williams household, and Cord Elam has married a farm woman (p. 88). Curly also knows where his future lies, so he tells Laurey in act 2, scene 2 (p. 123; following *Green Grow the Lilacs*, scene 6, p. 157):

> I'll be the happiest man alive soon as we're married. Oh, I got to learn to be a farmer, I see that! Quit a-thinkin' about th'owin' the rope, and start in to git my hands blistered a new way! Oh, things is a changin' right and left! Buy up mowin' machines, cut down the prairies! Shoe yer horses, drag them plows under the sod! They gonna make a state outa this, they gonna put it in the Union! Country a-changin', got to change with it! Bring up a pair of boys, new stock, to keep up 'th the ways things is going in this here crazy country! Now I got you to he'p me—I'll 'mount to sumpin yit!

He has already sold his saddle, horse, and gun to win the auction for Laurey's hamper at the Box Social. Curly and Laurey instead have a very different future ahead of them.

"I know I mustn't fall into the pit . . ."

". . . But when I'm with a feller—I fergit!" sings Ado Annie in "I Cain't Say No." Thus far, the heroes of the land that is grand would seem to be male farmers and cowmen: farmers' daughters and ranchers' gals are good only for dancing. The treatment of the opening of the song "Oklahoma" is revealing. Aunt Eller blesses the married couple ("They couldn't pick a better time to start in life"), Ike joins in ("It ain't too early and it ain't too late"), then Curly ("Startin' as a farmer with a brand-new wife"), then a triumphant Laurey ("Soon be livin' in a brand-new state"), to which all respond: "Brand new state/Gonna treat you great!" Or at least, that is how it goes in the libretto. In fact, the vocal score switches Curly and Laurey: it is for a man, not a woman, to make a public proclamation of statehood ("Soon be livin' in a brand-new state"), whereas it is for a woman, not a man, to celebrate domesticity ("Startin' as farmer with a brand-new wife"). However the switch occurred, it is disappointing in the context of a show that might seem, on the face of it, to reflect the empowering of women in wartime America.

Two of the lead female roles in *Oklahoma!* Laurey and Ado Annie, are each of a type.[37] Riggs's Laurey was "a fair, spoiled, lovely young girl about eighteen in a long white dress with many ruffles" (p. 12), and his Ado Annie "an unattractive, stupid-looking farm girl, with taffy-colored hair pulled back from a freckled face. Her dress is of red gingham, and very unbecoming" (p. 44). Neither, expressed thus, would suit conventional musical expectations, and Hammerstein avoids describing them altogether. But the audience knows where things stand. We learn from Mozart's *Die Zauberflöte* (*The Magic Flute*) that every Tamino needs a Pamina (and every Pamina a Monostatos, another Caliban-like figure), but also that every Papageno deserves a Papagena. In the (musical) theater, the pure, noble hero and heroine usually have their counterparts lower down the scale, who may not achieve greatness but nevertheless stand for Every(wo)man. We may all have the capacity to become a Tamino or Pamina, but few of us will want to scale such heights: there are benefits to being an average Joe, Will, or Annie.

The issue became enshrined in typical casting strategies for Broadway shows. While Laurey is the romantic female lead, Ado Annie is what in an earlier repertory would be called a *soubrette*, the clever but impertinent servant girl who comments wryly on the behavior of her betters. The soubrette is a no-nonsense, down-to-earth sort who is worldly wise and, so it is always made titillatingly clear, sexually aware, taking a significant degree of pleasure in being unable to "say no." Sex, however packaged, had always been part of the Broadway musical, often very explicitly so in the case of Rodgers and Hart. Indeed, Langner was concerned that *Oklahoma!* was "too clean": "It did not have the suggestive jokes, the spicy situations, the strip-teasers and the other indecencies which too often went with a successful musical of those days."[38] There is, of course, a dark side to sexual behavior in *Okla-*

14. The "shotgun wedding" between Ali Hakim (Joseph Buloff) and Ado
Annie (Celeste Holm) urged by her father Andrew Carnes (Ralph Riggs)
cannot, in fact, be a plausible outcome in *Oklahoma!* given the racial and
ethnic issues involved. (Uncredited)

homa! both for Ado Annie and for Jud. Sex and its consequences were also of
prime concern during wartime, both at the front and at home: statistics show
large increases in the divorce rate, the birth of illegitimate children, and
sexually transmitted diseases. Ado Annie may be a typically liberated good-
time girl with perfectly healthy urges ("Them stories 'bout the way I lost
my bloomers—Rumors!"), but she, too, needs to be reined into domesticity.
Her fascination with the exotic Ali Hakim clearly cannot be consummated,
even though he promises her "paradise" upstairs in the hotel in Claremore
(p. 37). We know, and Ado Annie comes to realize, that Will Parker is the
only man for her. It is a moment of capitulation forced by the genre, and by
social conformity, that Ado Annie can half-resist only by virtue of her own
feistiness at the end of "All er Nuthin'": "There's no use waitin' up for me,"
a late addition in Boston.

Laurey is not so innocent as she might appear—she knows full well what the Peddler wants from Ado Annie (p. 30)—and, so we learn from "Many a New Day," she, too, has dallied with men:

> Never've I chased the honey-bee
> Who carelessly cajoled me.
> Somebody else just as sweet as he
> Cheered me and consoled me.

She, too, will be forced "upstairs" in the dream-ballet (in the saloon with Jud's postcards).[39] But her status within the cast means that she must appear more virginal. The concerns are clear in the fact that Rodgers (over)compensates for Hammerstein's somewhat forthright lyrics for "Many a New Day" by strongly feminizing Laurey's music to contrast with Ado Annie's more aggressive two-step; the strategy is taken further in the film version of *Oklahoma!* by setting this song and its subsequent dance in Laurey's bedroom, with the all-female singers and dancers in their underwear. But if Ado Annie is an example of wartime sexual liberation, Laurey's empowerment seems, on the face of it, to be of a different sort. Orphaned as a child (we assume), she has been brought up by Aunt Eller, both of them running a farm with only the help of a hired hand (for the moment, Jud). As did many women in wartime America, she has taken on a male role, and while Laurey is no Rosie the Riveter, she is sufficiently strong-willed and independent that cowboy Curly, locked into a more traditional male view of gender, cannot quite cope with the result. She is "healthy and strong" and will not "blubber like a baby" when her man goes away: good advice for wives left at home by soldiers leaving for the front. It may seem inevitable, or at least a social requirement, that some day a "real" man will come along to assume the responsibilities of the household. But Laurey will need more than just an "Oklahoma hello" to convince her to marry Curly.

Both Ado Annie and Laurey represent in different ways the "new women" that gained status, power, and independence during, and because of, the war. It takes some effort to tame them by the end of the show, a concern that extended through the rehearsals to the tryouts (to judge by the repeated adjustments to the last two scenes) and even beyond. The issue would be paralleled in the real world as the "new" women's forcible return to domesticity during postwar demobilization was to create significant social and other difficulties. However, both reassurance and a sense of continuity are provided by the matriarch who benignly oversees the fates of all in her charge. Aunt Eller was the lead role in *Green Grow the Lilacs* (played by Helen Westley, who was also Parthy Hawkes in the 1936 film of *Show Boat*), and Betty Garde was the highest-paid cast member in *Oklahoma!* Although Aunt Eller hardly sings, she is a forceful stage presence. Again the type is familiar from Westerns: the strong senior woman no longer able to bear children but somehow acting as an earth mother to all, binding the community by taming its wildness. Not for nothing is Aunt Eller granted the speech (p. 81) that contains what Helburn claimed (in her letter to William Lockwood of 9 April 1943) "seemed to us part of the essential pioneer quality of the play": "Oh, lots of things happens to folks. Sickness, er bein' pore and hungry even—bein' old and afeared to die. That's the way it is—cradle to grave. And you can stand it. They's one way. You gotta be hearty, you got to be. You cain't deserve the sweet and tender things in life less'n you're tough." In *Green Grow the Lilacs*, scene 6, Aunt Eller's speech was more strongly gendered in terms not just of its speaker but also of its content: "Oh, lots of things happens to a womern . . ." (p. 146).[40] In *Oklahoma!* however, the themes are more universal, and here, at least, was a message that wartime audiences could take to heart. As Rodgers later said: "People could come to see *Oklahoma!* and derive not only pleasure but a measure of optimism. It dealt with pioneers in the Southwest, it showed their spirit and the kinds of problems they had to overcome in carving out a new state, and it gave citizens an appreciation of the hardy stock from which they'd sprung. People said to themselves, in effect, 'If this is what our country looked and sounded like at the turn of the century, perhaps once the war is over we can again return to this kind of buoyant, optimistic life.'"[41]

"Hambushed"

The one male who can move comfortably between these different social spaces in *Oklahoma!* is the Peddler, Ali Hakim. Of all the characters in the show, he interacts most fully with the rest; he is as comfortable selling garters to Aunt Eller as he is trading naughty postcards with Jud. In part, that is his profession. In part, however, it is due to what he represents.

In *Green Grow the Lilacs*, the unnamed Peddler (originally played by Lee Strasberg) is described as "a little wiry, swarthy Syrian." Hammerstein first designated him an "Armenian" and named him Kalenderian Kalazian (*Draft1*, *Draft2*), although this may have been felt inappropriate once Rouben Mamoulian (an actual Armenian) had come on board. By New Haven the character was billed as Ali Hakim (although the cues in the printed libretto are always labeled "Peddler," as in the drafts), and he is identified by other characters as "Persian." Contemporary audiences, however, would have been clear on the meaning. On 4 September 1945 one Richard H. Roffman (writing from the editorial office of *This Month*) complained to the Guild that the Peddler (still being played by the role's creator, Joseph Buloff) should not "talk with what can be considered a type of Jewish accent. . . . At this time in our international history, it might have been better to have given this character a Continental European accent. What do you think of the possibility of a change at this point?" Helburn's assistant replied on 14 September: "We can only say that Mr Buloff is trying to be as un-Jewish as possible. As the dialogue emphasizes the fact that he is Turkish as well as the program, we feel that 'any resemblance etc. is purely coincidental!'"[42] The notion of him being "Turkish" is somewhat disingenuous and does not appear in any program I have seen. And while the name "Ali Hakim" may seem Arabic, those in the know would have spotted the reference to the Yiddish and Hebrew *hacham*, a "clever man."[43] The ethnic twist cannot have been far from Langner's mind when he was pursuing Groucho Marx for the role in January 1943.

Buloff was a prominent player in New York Yiddish theaters and also had a reputation on Broadway for playing comic roles, often Jewish, middle-European, or otherwise exotic.[44] In Hammerstein's rendition (and in contrast to Riggs), Ali Hakim is much more careful with his syntax, and his articulation, than the Oklahomans; his speeches do not have the typical dialect markers, although Hammerstein does give him a tendency toward phonetic gutturals ("Hoodblinked! . . . Hambushed! . . .").[45] Buloff's inflections in the original-cast recording of "It's a Scandal! It's a Outrage!" may be typically Yiddish or generically Middle Eastern, but even without the linguistic cues, the role of the Peddler is stereotypically that of a wandering Jew, or of his counterpart, the "lonely gypsy" (as Ali Hakim refers to himself in act 2, scene 2; p. 125). He joins a long list of comic roles on Broadway played by Jewish actors and vaudeville performers who made a virtue of their ability to appear as exotic Others while also retaining the potential for assimilation in the ethnic melting pot of America. The results are both funny and painful.

Ali Hakim is certainly exotic: he offers the community all sorts of knick-knacks and gewgaws not normally available to them. He is also "Other," even down to his original costume (an outrageously gaudy checkered suit and a large fedora). No less typical of the exotic character type is the fact that he is in sexual overdrive, and is rather good at it, too. But that does not make him a complete outsider. He visits the Williams farm often; is viewed by Andrew Carnes as a suitable (or at least, convenient) husband for Ado Annie (although the audience knows better); is addressed by the men as a "friend" in "It's a Scandal! It's a Outrage!" even if they also volunteer him to be "the first man to be shot" in the male revolution against women; and in act 2, scene 1, he saves Curly from Jud's first attempt to kill him with the "Little Wonder." Of course, his sexual allure is more for the likes of Ado Annie than for Laurey, whose dramatic fate is such that she cannot be allowed to fall prey to such charms. But Ali Hakim manages to charm Laurey in other ways, inspiring in her a feminine eloquence that offers us the first glimpse of something more behind her initial mask of hard-headed dispassion. When the peddler asks Laurey if she wants to buy anything, she starts "working up to a kind of abstracted ecstasy": "Want a buckle made outa shiny silver to fasten onto my shoes! Want a dress with lace. Want perfume, wanta be purty, wanta smell like a honeysuckle vine! . . . Want things I've heard of and never had before—a rubber-t'ard buggy, a cut-glass sugar bowl. Want things I 'cain't tell you about—not only things to look at and hold in yer hands. Things to happen to you. Things so nice, if they ever did happen to you, yer heart ud quit beatin'. You'd fall down dead!" (pp. 33–34; compare *Green Grow the Lilacs*, pp. 49–50). And it is Ali Hakim who sells Laurey the "Elixir of Egypt" which enables her to see things clearly and, in the dream-ballet, to "make up her mind."

Richard Rodgers (of German-Jewish descent) was Jewish, albeit more, he said, "for socioethnic reasons rather than because of any deep religious conviction."[46] Oscar Hammerstein's family was also Jewish (from Russia), even if he, technically, was not (his mother was a Scottish Presbyterian). Both were also involved in pro-Jewish causes. But Hammerstein in particular seems to have identified with Ali Hakim, advertising himself as "Mister Ali Hakim-stein" on the invitation to the first-anniversary party for *Oklahoma!* on 1 April 1944.[47] Presumably, his intentions for the Peddler were playful rather than denigrating, but he must have realized the danger of going too far. At the beginning of act 1, scene 3 in *Draft2*, Ali Hakim mimics the blackface performance of so-called coon songs in "Peddler's Pack": the reference is clearly to the Jewish vaudeville performers well known for appearing in blackface, such as Al Jolson (memorialized in *The Jazz Singer*) and Eddie Cantor.[48] Whether or not this was just nostalgic coloring of the times, clearly it cut too close to a bone and was eliminated. Hammerstein also seems to have sought to make amends for the faux pas by giving Ali Hakim's story a satisfactory ending.

Ali Hakim must always remain on the margins. He does not sing in the communal hymn "Oklahoma," and for that matter, at least in the performance by Buloff, he hardly "sings" at all in the show: although Rodgers's original manuscript gives him the melody in the chorus of "It's a Scandal! It's a Outrage!" Buloff delivered it in rhythmicized speech instead—so it appears from the cast recording—and this is how it gets represented in the vocal score.[49] Elsewhere, even the slightest tendency for him to sing is repressed: the front-of-traveler scene between act 2, scenes 2 and 3 for Will, Ado Annie, and the Peddler (with the "Persian goodbye" and "Oklahoma hello") includes just a snatch of a song for the Peddler, beginning "One goodbye . . ." that is repeated as he exits. (There is some evidence in *Draft3* that Rodgers and Hammerstein intended an actual song here.) Yet by the time he relinquishes Ado Annie to Will (when he turns almost into a paternal figure, "giving away" the bride), he can claim to be a "friend of the fambly." And Hammerstein has already made the agenda clear by Ike Skidmore's words toward the end of "The Farmer and the Cowman" (my emphasis):

> And when this territory is a state,
> And jines the union jist like all the others,
> The farmer and the cowman *and the merchant*
> Must all behave theirsel's and act like brothers.

Although the original plan was to have Ali Hakim end up with Lotta Gonzales—another sexually active exotic Other—the final version made a better point. In the last scene (p. 135), he enters "dejected, sheepish, dispirited, a ghost of the man he was," worn down by his four-day-old marriage to Gertie Cummings. Gertie has fixed his future: "Ali ain't goin' to travel around the country no more. I decided he orta settle down in Bushyhead and run Papa's store." Having completed the transition from peddler to merchant, and from playboy to husband, he leaves the stage—again denied participation in a communal chorus, the final "Oh, What a Beautiful Mornin'"—only to return for the curtain call.[50] But his life has worked out as best it could in 1940s America.

"Oh, why did sich a feller have to die?"

"Pore Jud" Fry is the other "outsider" in *Oklahoma!*—as he was in *Green Grow the Lilacs*—but unlike the refashioned Ali Hakim, he lacks the sophistication, adaptability, and for that matter the character to be assimilated into the community. His burden is still greater than in the play given the evident shift from the domestic to the universal embodied in the song "Oklahoma," while his sociopathic isolation is accentuated by the fact that the community near Claremore in *Oklahoma!* is far tamer and more law-abiding (more American, in fact) than the rough-and-ready territory folk evoked by Lynn Riggs.[51] Jud's death has an inevitability born of necessity, even though this was the reason for the seemingly widespread feeling that Riggs's play could not be turned into a musical. A hired hand from Tulsa by way of Quabush on Laurey and Aunt Eller's farm, he, too, does not belong. His pursuit of Laurey is not so violent as is Jeeter Fry's in the play—which comes close to rape in scene 4 at the play-party (the Box Social in the musical)—and Jeeter's dubious past, linked darkly to vengeful fire-raising and murder, is more clearly articulated than Jud's. Similarly, Jeeter's attempted murder of Laurey and Curly by setting fire to the haystack in which they have been hoisted during the postwedding shivaree colors him more strongly than Jud's drunken intervention in the wedding party leading to his fight with Curly, although Hammerstein tries to redress the balance by having Jud previously (2.1) attempt to kill Curly with the "Little Wonder." However, Jud remains an object of fear (for Laurey), of disgust (for Curly), and, worst of all, indifference (from the rest). Save for his strange funereal duet with Curly ("Pore Jud Is Daid"), he cannot sing with, or to, anyone else, an isolation rendered still more complete as Hammerstein moved from his drafts to the final libretto: we have already seen that he lost his act 2, scene 2 reprise (before Laurey) of his original act 1, scene 2 song ("All That I Want"), and although the lyric sheet for "The Farmer and the Cowman" involves him in the spoken dialogue, he is absent in the libretto, appearing only later.[52] Jud's eventual death does not even merit the decency of a proper trial.

In *Green Grow the Lilacs*, Jeeter lives in the smokehouse but eats his meals with Aunt Eller and Laurey "like one of the fambly" (so Curly says; p. 20). He is denied that comfort in *Oklahoma!* In both the play (p. 20) and the show (p. 21), however, he is described as a "bullet-colored growly man" (Riggs also gives him "bushy eyebrows"), living in squalor and surrounded by dubious pin-ups. In the preamble to scene 3 of the play (pp. 59–60), Jeeter

15. The concluding fight between Jud (Howard da Silva) and Curly (Alfred Drake), and Jud's death, set the seal on the message of *Oklahoma!* by isolating and ultimately removing the sociopath who threatens its community. The death scene was one reason why many felt that *Green Grow the Lilacs* could not make a good musical; Hammerstein, however, felt that Jud was "the bass fiddle that gave body to the orchestration of the story." (Uncredited)

is also described as having "a curious earth-coloured face and hairy hands." The coloring, and also the simian attributes ("hairy hands"), could serve as any number of different racial and social markers, while the consistent association of words such as "black" and "nigger" with Jeeter in the play, and having Jud repeat Curly's pronouncements in "Pore Jud Is Daid" "reverently like a Negro at a revivalist meeting," create further ambiguities.

Hammerstein claimed in his "Notes on Lyrics" (1949) that Jud was "the bass fiddle that gave body to the orchestration of the story," preventing "this light lyric idyll from being so lyric and so idyllic that a modern theater audience might have been made sleepy, if not nauseous, by it."[53] Ali Hakim's exotic subversiveness may in the end be tamed by a reduction to a norm. Jud is far less easily contained. In the context of Frederick Jackson Turner's view of the frontier, the opposition of Curly and Jud would presumably be viewed as two sides of the same coin, the "dominant individualism working for good and for evil." For Gerald Mast and others, Jud represents the Fascism that was currently the enemy at war, to be countered by the integrative version of the American dream celebrated in the show; for Raymond Knapp, he is perhaps an Indian, perhaps a white outsider, or perhaps even Riggs himself.[54] For Andrea Most, he is the "bad" Jew (in contrast to Ali Hakim's "good" Jew) unable or unwilling to conform to the contemporary social and other mores imposed upon immigrant communities in America, and therefore refusing to integrate with the predominant "white" culture, whether of Claremore, Oklahoma, or, by extension, of mid-twentieth-century New York. (In this context, Jud's name, with its obvious etymological resonances, remains disturbing.)[55] For Bruce Kirle, Jud is a combination of all the above, melded with the isolationist opponents of the New Deal who also argued against American intervention in the war. But whichever way one reads the character, Jud does not seem open to redemption. This makes him very difficult to play.

Hammerstein also said in his "Notes on Lyrics" that as a result of "Pore Jud Is Daid," Jud "becomes, then, for a while, not just wicked, but a comic figure flattered by the attentions he might receive if he were dead. He becomes also a pathetic figure, pathetically lonely for attentions he has never received while alive. The audience begins to feel some sympathy for him, some understanding of him as a man."[56] The "comic" reading of "Pore Jud Is Daid" seems to have been preferred by contemporary reviewers, perhaps because they did not know what else to say. These reviewers, however, were entirely silent about Jud's other song, "Lonely Room." Again in his "Notes on Lyrics," Hammerstein gave his own view of how Jud "paints a savage picture of his solitary life, his hatred of Curly and his mad desire for Laurey. This is self-analysis, but it is emotional, not cerebral. No dialogue could do this dramatic job as vividly and quickly as does the song. When Lynn Riggs attended a rehearsal of Oklahoma! for the first time, I asked him if he approved of this number. He said, 'I certainly do. It will scare [the] hell out of the audience.' That is exactly what it was designed to do." While we cannot be sure whether Hammerstein intended the double meaning of "savage," his claim that Jud's self-analysis is "emotional, not cerebral" again reduces the character to a primal state. Langner seems to have captured a similar sense in his instructions to Reggie Hammerstein, stage manager of the national touring company, after seeing the show's opening in Washington, D.C.: "Tell Jud to lift his line, 'I don't want anything out of a peddler's bag.' This is his springboard for everything. He must be angry and carry this anger right through into the song."[57] Much will hinge on whether "Lonely Room" should "scare" the audience, as Riggs, Hammerstein, and Langner appear to have intended, or somehow attract its sympathy. But that, in turn, raises one of the paradoxes of music in the theater.

In his "Notes on Lyrics," Hammerstein regularly associates music with notions of ecstasy, when a character moves beyond thinking to feeling. By definition, then, a song should be "emotional, not cerebral." But what happens in the case of a character who is not allowed to think in the first place? Or to put the question more simply, can music do its job too well? Certainly, this helps explain some of the ambivalences within "Lonely Room," which is arguably the most powerful song in *Oklahoma!* It is unique within the show: the only soliloquy, and the only song in a minor mode, which Rodgers famously associated with Cole Porter's opportunistic appropriation of "'Jewish' music."[58] Its relatively free form is also unusual. At the opening, the dissonant accompaniment and the monotone-based vocal line is untypical for Rodgers (it has echoes of Kurt Weill), and the subsequent narrow range of the melody (within a seventh) and its carefully structured ascent to the final top note, $c\sharp'$ (on a ninth chord on B) is a finely judged representation of repression and release. Clearly, the song is marked out for "otherness" in the musical environment of *Oklahoma!*—indeed, it breaks significantly the bounds of musical decorum in and for the show—just as Jud is isolated from the rest of his world. But it also brings a clarity, and even power, to the character that he would otherwise lack. Omitting "Lonely Room" from the 1955 film of *Oklahoma!* was a mistake.

As for Jud's death, Hammerstein claimed, "I have never had the slightest squeamishness or hesitation about this scene. I think to have left it out might have made the second act a very feeble mate for the virile first act. Much of the flatness commonly found in musical comedy books is due to erroneous ideas of what you can't do in a musical play. It has been proved again and again that if the background is bright, and gayety surrounds the story, the events of the story can be as dramatic or tragic as anything found in a play without music."[59] But it was as problematic as Lynn Riggs found ending his play, and as we have seen, at least one member of the audience asked for it to be rewritten. The other option for persistent social outcasts, exile (whether self-imposed or not; compare Porgy in *Porgy and Bess* and

Joey Evans in *Pal Joey*), was hardly a feasible choice for a show that had no intention of leaving unanswered questions in its wake. Both Jeeter and Jud had to die because they cannot find room in the brave new world of the state of Oklahoma. In one sense, however, Jud's voice did indeed ring beyond his grave. As Rodgers and Hammerstein were to show in *Carousel*, even the antihero has his place in the theater, and even Billy Bigelow can enter the backyard of heaven.

"Ev'rythin's up to date . . ."

By the mid-1940s, various issues concerning *Oklahoma!* began to enter the discourse even of relatively "highbrow" critics concerned with the theater. One was whether *Oklahoma!* somehow contributed to the emergence of a contemporary "American" art form that could vie on equal terms with such European imports as "serious" spoken drama on the one hand, and opera on the other. Here the connections drawn with Gershwin's *Porgy and Bess* (encouraged in part by the Theatre Guild's association with both works) formed part of a broader agenda. *Oklahoma!* and *Porgy and Bess* each dealt with an American (and equally important, a non-European) subject, each drew on American popular song, and each appeared in Broadway theaters rather than in the iconic institutions of high culture. The demotic overtones are obvious: "American" art was to be by the people, for the people.

What *Porgy and Bess* and *Oklahoma!* specifically offered, however, were models for a new type of "American" (folk) opera. Olin Downes, the music (not theater) critic for the *New York Times*, saw the show toward the end of May 1943: on the 28th he wrote to the Guild, "I found it, as I had been told I would, a fascinating show and I am going to write about it pretty soon, in a Sunday issue." He went into more detail the same day with Hammerstein: "I am going to write a Sunday article about the show, probably for Sunday week, because I do think it's an extraordinarily interesting bit of musical theatre done in an original and American way. And I wish to heaven the Metropolitan and other American agencies of serious opera could muster half as much brains and originality as are evident in this piece."[60] He pursued the argument in his Sunday-supplement article of 6 June 1943, headlined "Broadway's Gift to Opera: *Oklahoma!* Shows One of the Ways to an Integrated and Indigenous Form of American Lyric Theatre." He had done the same for *Porgy and Bess*, using much the same arguments, in a text no less provocatively entitled "Roots of Native Opera: Popular Theatre May Prove Forerunning of Native American Style" (*New York Times*, 27 October 1935).[61] But by 1943, Downes thought that *Porgy and Bess* was "not important at all"; *Oklahoma!* instead took its place in the line from *Show Boat* through Gershwin's *Of Thee I Sing* (1931) in offering "a compellingly native art of the lyric theatre." .

As we have seen, the "American" character of *Oklahoma!* in terms of its subject matter and even musical style was not much in doubt. Downes, too, played up the show's adherence (in the words, music, stage sets, and dancing) to "genuine things that lie deep in the people and the soil": "Under the comedic mask and the convention of spurs, revolvers and ten-gallon hats we recognize an ancestral memory, echo of an experience that went deep, a part of the adventure that has made us ourselves." Here, the dance has a special part to play as "an irrefutable and indispensable fundament of a national esthetic, including a national music." But the issue of *Oklahoma!* being somehow "operatic" was trickier. *Porgy and Bess* seemed closer to the genre, both in its original entirely sung version and even in the 1941–42 revival with spoken dialogue. However, Downes was now inclined to dismiss Gershwin's work ("which survives by its melodies and not by the dramatic appositeness of the score"), and of course, only in his *Oklahoma!* headline did he use the magic word "integrated." He also resorted to a different argument of some historical sophistication: *Oklahoma!* fell into the mold of those comic-opera forms that had challenged the supremacy of serious opera in the eighteenth century: *opera buffa*, *opéra comique*, and the *Singspiel*, the last two being especially close because they mixed songs with speech. Thus *Oklahoma!* might equally offer an alternative to the international grand opera, one more strongly rooted in nationalist styles, and based on comedy rather than tragedy. Downes's points for comparison were Pergolesi's *La serva padrona*, Rousseau's *Le Devin du village* (leading to Bizet's *Carmen*), *The Beggar's Opera*, and Mozart's *Die Zauberflöte* (leading to Weber's *Der Freischütz*). Even Beethoven's "tragic and great (though manifestly imperfect)" *Fidelio* was brought into the frame, a comparison that, in turn, prompted John Gassner, the Guild's play reader, to suggest with some enthusiasm the idea of liaising with Virgil Thomson on staging a modern adaptation of Beethoven's *Singspiel*, with a rewritten book and added comedy.[62]

The dance critic George Beiswanger developed various threads of Downes's argument in 1944–45: "There is one stage today on which all the theatre arts unite in happy combination to produce theatre that is sheer, ample, and without inner tension or quarrel. I refer again to the musical stage, to such natural triumphs of the American theatre imagination as *Lady in the Dark* and *Oklahoma!* Grant that these are not Shakespeare nor Euripides nor Dante. But they come close to being Aristophanes or Molière. Increasingly they approach opera. And they are our own, genuine outpourings of American temperament, honest mirrorings of what we are."[63] Beiswanger saw a trajectory from vaudeville and burlesque through musical play to (American) opera, but then upped the stakes still further: the integration of drama, music, and dance in shows such as *Oklahoma!* did not just produce something more "operatic" in nature, but it also enabled *Oklahoma!* to approach the Wagnerian *Gesamtkunstwerk*, uniting all the arts in the service of dramatic expression. And although Richard Wagner (1813–83) was known for his grand operas based on myth (*Der Ring des Nibelungen*), romance epic (*Tristan und Isolde*), and sacred mystery (*Parsifal*), Beiswanger was careful to note that he, too, had produced a comic masterpiece, *Die Meistersinger von Nürnberg*. If comparing *Oklahoma!* to *Fidelio* was a stretch, *Die Meistersinger* was a leap too far. But Wagnerism had already become a hot topic in interwar American critical discourse, and its influence on the "integrated musical" had been proclaimed early on in the reception of *Show Boat*.[64] In part, the aim was to grant the genre something of the status of high art; in part, however, it was also to glorify American achievement.

This was like a red flag to a bull for the literary theorist Eric Bentley, who quotes Beiswanger extensively in his highly influential *The Playwright as Thinker* (1946). For him, the problem was not so much that the comparison with Wagner was absurd but that it was symptomatic of a more fundamental issue facing a modern theater in which "art and commodity have become direct antagonists":

> Perhaps Mr. Oscar Hammerstein is a fair specimen. His work *Oklahoma!* (the exclamation mark is his own) has been "hailed" as establishing a new genre, praised in at least one literary quarterly, awarded a Pulitzer Prize by special dispensation, and compared, not unfavorably, with *The Magic Flute*. It was the outstanding theatrical success of the war period; and it is entirely representative of current trends. In fact, it belongs with the "new Americanism" in being folksy and excessively, ostentatiously wholesome; also in being trite, cocksure, sentimental, and vacuous. On the stage it is decked out in gay color and from time to time enlivened by tricky dancing. But in all drama (I do not say in all *theatre*, for ballet and opera are theatre) color and

dancing are only an embellishment; in this case they are the embellishment of a scarecrow.[65]

To read this as the commonplace rant of an elitist, anti-Broadway stick-in-the-mud—even though Bentley was all that and more—is in fact to miss an argument of some subtlety. It emerges that the attack is not on Hammerstein per se, nor even on commercial Broadway theater (although that comes in for some opprobrium), but, rather, on the "theatricalists" who have subverted the cause of true drama. And for Bentley, the archtheatricalist—and the one who injected its poison into the dramatic vein—was, precisely, Wagner. According to Bentley, Wagner's music-dramas were not, in fact, dramas, and his idealized merging of the arts in the *Gesamtkunstwerk* did not create some kind of higher synthesis but, rather, mere confusion: each art form lost, rather than gained, from the enterprise. Wagner's works claimed high-minded ideals but in fact celebrated petit bourgeois values: "Nietzsche found out that Wagner was the spokesman of the new age in its most negative aspects. *Tristan* is grandiose illusion; *Die Meistersinger* is incarnate *gemütlichkeit*, the middle-class substitute for serenity."[66] The composer pretended to be a naturalist but was antinatural; he pretended to be literary but was antiliterary. And Wagner's insistence on total control of the theater (through the institutionalization of Bayreuth) led to the pernicious cult of the director. Bentley dissects Beiswanger's praise of *Oklahoma!* in unequivocal terms—"Here is a revived and jazzified Wagnerism which does not omit Wagner's nationalism and praise of the soil nor his belief in the historical inevitability of his success": "Mr Beiswanger's way of looking at things is symptomatic. His remarks remind us of the fact that popularized Wagnerism is probably the most widespread dramatic theory—or the most widely held preconception—of our day. The assumption is that theatre is primarily a musico-visual art, an art of spectacle, movement, and melody. It is ballet, it is opera. But it is not drama."[67] But the argument then becomes more loaded still. Bentley's anti-Wagnerism was motivated by the cause of anti-Fascism, given Wagner's appropriation by Hitler: "As Wagner grew older his nationalism took on the color of the times and he became a Reich-German, anti-French, anti-Semitic, and 'proto-Nazi.'"[68] Bentley's sideswipes at the proto-Wagnerian "nationalism," "praise of the soil," and "historical inevitability" in Beiswanger's account of *Oklahoma!* are also strongly coded. But here Bentley is acting as the mouthpiece of a better-known anti-Fascist, and in his view (expressed in *The Playwright as Thinker* and in numerous other of his publications) the only potential savior of modern drama, Bertolt Brecht. Bentley did not object to art for the people, but in his view, the much-needed re-unification of art and commodity could be achieved only by way of Brecht's politically engaged "epic theater."

In this light, one cannot rescue *Oklahoma!* from Bentley's accusation of its being "trite, cocksure, sentimental, and vacuous" by any Wagnerian ap-peal to the *Gesamtkunstwerk*, or even to the integration of music and drama. This is precisely because these qualities are a consequence both of "popu-larized Wagnerism" and of the paradoxes involved in the integrative model: "When drama takes on the abstract character of pure music or pure dance it ceases to be drama; when, as a compromise, it tries to combine the ab-stract with the concrete, it is invariably the drama, the words, that suffer. The words are the weakest element in *Oklahoma!* They are the weakest in-gredient in the Wagnerian brew." [69] The problem with *Oklahoma!* — Bentley seems to suggest — was not so much that it was no real opera but, rather, that it was not Brecht. It was a sop to the masses rather than a rallying to the cause of political awareness. And to extrapolate further (but only slightly), its patriotic celebration of America opened the door to Fascism. *Oklahoma!* was no solution: it was part of the problem.

Justifications for bringing Broadway into the musicological canon have gone down predictable lines: to deny artistic status to popular culture or to commercial success is to countenance an elitist double standard rooted in mere intellectual snobbery; Broadway musicals do indeed offer a wholly (in both senses) theatrical experience; and their music, at its best, can be pro-foundly dramatic. Such apologias are inherently conservative, even Roman-tic: by this reading, the better Broadway shows are scarcely different from, say, much nineteenth-century opera and therefore deserve equality of treat-ment. "Integration" clearly suits this agenda, however easily it might be ex-posed as a sham. But Bentley's position on the modernist crisis might better be countered by looking not backward but forward, and with a degree of postmodern self-awareness. *Pace* Bentley, any theatrical work will play on its own theatricality, even while pursuing the illusion that it does not exist within a stage. An audience will always be aware that it is watching a play (a musical, an opera) even as it "suspends disbelief" and pretends that it is not. Indeed, preserving a delicate balance between our awareness of what a the-atrical work is and what it represents is essential to any aesthetic judgment or emotional response: we are no less aware of, and moved by, the art and craft of the theater than of, and by, what happens to its characters. Thus to praise *Oklahoma!*—or any dramatic work—for its "realism," or to blame it for its lack thereof, is to miss a point: nothing in the theater is ever "real," nor do we expect it to be so.

Similarly, in musicals (and for that matter, in opera) music always draws attention to itself as music even when it pretends to be emotional articulation; thus it will be diegetic to the genre even if it is not diegetic within the drama in terms of verisimilitude. Songs (arias, duets, ensembles) can perfectly well contribute to a drama, reveal a character, or even just entertain an audience, without having greater burdens placed upon them. Studying Broadway shows brings home the issues with particular clarity. It is not that the Broadway musical is, in the end, like opera; rather, it is that opera is, in the end, like the Broadway musical. And both reveal the nature of what it is to work in the musical theater.

CHAPTER 6

From Stage to Screen

THE DAY AFTER THE PREMIERE OF OKLAHOMA! THE CONGRATULA-
tory telegrams rolled in, including one from Joshua Logan regretting
his lack of involvement. Early April was a time for celebration. The
Guild delivered to Rodgers and Hammerstein each a quart of champagne,
for which Hammerstein sent thanks on 3 April: "Isn't it wonderful for all of
us that they came through?" Theresa Helburn and Lawrence Langner also
sent their thank-you letters to the cast and crew. Langner wrote to Margot
Hopkins, the rehearsal pianist: "Now that all the clouds have blown away,
and the sun is shining, please let me say how much I appreciate your hard
work and the splendid job you did."[1] Helburn was even more effusive in her
letter to Robert Russell Bennett of 7 April:

> May I tell you how tremendously I enjoyed [your] symphonic treatment of
> *Porgy and Bess* when I heard Reiner play it. It was a thrilling experience! I
> now feel that you are tied up with both of the Guild's musical achievements.
> May I take this opportunity of telling you again how profoundly I appreci-
> ate your extraordinarily fine contribution to the success of *Oklahoma*[!]? It
> seems to be one of those rare miraculous occasions in the theatre when all
> one's dreams come through a hundred percent and more. I sit on the stairs
> at the St. James often with my eyes closed, and enjoy your orchestration
> more than I can tell you. (And isn't it nice I can't get a seat!)
> I hope you'll be working with us again before too long.[2]

She also wrote on 9 April 1943 to Cecil Smith in Chicago: "We did a lot
of work in a short time on *Oklahoma!* and New York gave it a rousing welcome. It seems to be the biggest hit in town at the moment and we hope it

THE THEATRE GUILD

presents

Oklahoma!

A Musical Play Based on the play
"GREEN GROW THE LILACS" by LYNN RIGGS

Music by

RICHARD RODGERS

Book and Lyrics by

OSCAR HAMMERSTEIN 2d

Production directed by

ROUBEN MAMOULIAN

Dances by

AGNES de MILLE

Settings by LEMUEL AYERS   Costumes by MILES WHITE

W i t h

BETTY GARDE · ALFRED DRAKE · JOSEPH BULOFF
JOAN ROBERTS · LEE DIXON · HOWARD da SILVA
CELESTE HOLM · RALPH RIGGS · MARC PLATT
GEORGE CHURCH · KATHARINE SERGAVA
Orchestra directed by JACOB SCHWARTZDORF
Orchestrations by RUSSELL BENNETT

Production under the supervision of
THERESA HELBURN & LAWRENCE LANGNER

16. Souvenir programs for Theatre Guild productions were sold by Al Greenstone, who also invested in *Oklahoma!* This is an early example: George Church (the first dream-Jud) is listed in the cast—but after Marc Platt (he is before Platt in the 31 March 1943 program, which presumably was typeset before Church lost his tap sequence in "Oklahoma")—and Jacob Schwartzdorf has not yet adopted the Americanized form of his name. Theresa Helburn now appears before Lawrence Langner (compare the Boston flyer for "Away We Go!" in figure 11), as on the 31 March program and in all subsequent publicity. The image draws on Lemuel Ayers's backdrop for the dream-ballet.

will continue that way for a long time to come. We are all very happy about it. It is so rare when one can combine one's most cherished dreams with a big popular success, as we have been able to do in this." Langner, on the other hand, said later that it took a while for the Guild's achievement to sink in: "It was only as the enthusiasm grew month by month with the impact of the play upon the American public . . . that we began to realize that we had produced a theatre classic." He also noted the dignitaries who later insisted on seeing the show, including Mayor Fiorello La Guardia, Mrs. Roosevelt, and the Duke and Duchess of Windsor, who saw the show "half-a-dozen times" and visited the cast backstage. (The duke was particularly taken with Joan McCracken, it seems.)[3] Meanwhile, Agnes de Mille, on the verge of marriage (14 June 1943), was busy receiving, and turning down, offers from MGM and Paramount.[4]

Now it was time to get back down to business. The Guild needed to plan its next season—Mamoulian was soon sent new scripts to vet—and as for *Oklahoma!*, business arrangements needed to be put in place.[5] On 9 April, Langner notified Rodgers and Hammerstein of the Guild's intention to exercise its option to buy the film rights for *Green Grow the Lilacs* from MGM for $50,000 (they would have saved $10,000 had they done it up to two days before the premiere), presumably to control a bidding war.[6] The sums involved could be large: for example, on 11 February 1943, the *New York Times* reported that Twentieth Century–Fox had upped its bid for Cole Porter's *Something for the Boys* to $300,000 (the owners were holding out for $350,000), and on 4 May it announced the rumor that the Guild had set a price of $500,000 for *Oklahoma!* (plus 25 percent of gross on a seven-year lease, according to the *Boston American* on 5 May). It seems that this was more to discourage offers than to solicit them. Meanwhile, the Guild, Rodgers, and Hammerstein made plans to capitalize on their success by forming a company to be called Theatre Guild Musical Productions—to last five years in the first instance—wherein Rodgers and Hammerstein would write one musical play per season for the Guild and produce musical plays by others by mutual agreement: "It is further hoped to affiliate with musical studios for the training of voice and acting for this type of play, with Agnes de Mille and/or others in the training of dancers."[7] In a separate negotiation, Hammerstein also invited Agnes de Mille on 7 June to choreograph *Carmen Jones*, although she turned it down because of her commitment to Kurt Weill's *One Touch of Venus*, even though "the show has no story."[8] Nothing formal came of the idea of a company, however, and the Guild's subsequent involvement in musicals remained fairly limited: the revue *Sing Out, Sweet Land* (opened 27 December 1944), billed as "A Salute to American Folk and Popular Music," then Rodgers and Hammerstein's *Carousel* (19 April 1945) and *Allegro* (10 October 1947).

Rodgers and Hammerstein were also being solicited for other projects. Offers started pouring in even as *Oklahoma!* started to prove itself near the end of the Boston tryout. Hammerstein wrote to his son Bill on 25 March that Ludwig Bemelmans had asked him and Rodgers to adapt his novel *Hotel Splendide*, and that "the rumble of attractive offers is already echoing from Broadway and Hollywood, but I am going to be very careful about my next venture." On 2 May 1943 he noted that he and Rodgers had been given a choice of three film treatments for musical adaptation, including one for Judy Garland for (he wrote on the 17th) MGM. By 1 June, Hammerstein told Bill that plans were firming up for them to work on *State Fair* for Darryl F. Zanuck at Twentieth Century–Fox, news he repeated on 12 June (when he also sent Bill a copy of Olin Downes's 6 June article on *Oklahoma!*): "Dick and I are writing a screenplay and score for a picture. We will do all the work here in the east, with no supervision. For this we each receive fifty grand, of which the government will allow us to keep about five! That's the penalty for writing *Oklahoma*[!]" On 14 July he reported that he had been in Hollywood to sign the contract for the film (which was released on 29 August 1945). Hammerstein also had his own irons in the fire. In May 1943 he yet again revived the plans of the previous year for a revival of *Show Boat* produced by MGM, first at the Lewisohn Stadium and then on Broadway before moving to the silver screen. He told Bill on 17 May that he had recruited Mary Martin as Magnolia but was still having problems finding an appropriate Cap'n Andy Hawks (as in 1942) and so had dropped his plans, somewhat to his relief. However, Arthur Freed was still writing to Hammerstein about a film of *Show Boat* in October 1943, even though he admitted that it would take a while to bring it to the boil. (In fact, MGM released *Show Boat* only in 1951, with Kathryn Grayson, Ava Gardner, and Howard Keele.) By summer 1943 Hammerstein was also preoccupied with the preparations for *Carmen Jones*, in which Freed also expressed periodic interest, in particular after the *Oklahoma!* premiere.[9]

The Guild still had decisions to make regarding *Oklahoma!* At the top of the agenda was a proposal (first made on the day of the Broadway opening) from Louis Dreyfus of the London office of Chappell and Co. to bring the show to London, opening in May. The liaison was Warren Munsell, the Guild's business manager, now in the army and based in London. On 7 April, Helburn told Munsell, obviously in response to a request for a libretto and the songs, "Oscar has been bringing the script up to date so we haven't been able to mail it to you yet. I'll send it as soon as it is ready (possibly Monday) with copies of the music that has been printed." She notes, however, that Rodgers did not want the show to be done in England unless with an American cast. That opinion had firmed into a definite no by 29 April, again for casting reasons, although Munsell continued to try to persuade the Guild otherwise, and the matter seems to have been kept in play.[10] On 17 May the Guild bought the British rights to the show from Rodgers and Hammerstein by paying a series of advances on royalties.[11] On the 21st, however, Rodgers, Hammerstein, Helburn, and Langner held a meeting at the Dorset Hotel, where they reached agreement on a number of issues, including deferring the English production.[12] Helburn informed Munsell of that decision on 27 May, noting likely tax problems and the fear of loss of control:

> We all feel this is a very special production. The success of it was due to a combination of talents involved and unless it can be directed under the supervision of the authors or directors or producers or all six, it might turn out very badly and none of us are in a position to go over even if we could get priorities. Dickie and Oscar keep saying, "Well, let them tell us whom they have suggested for the parts." If you or Dreyfus have anyone in mind let me know but I still don't want you to be put to the trouble of lining up a tentative cast only to have them decide to wait.

The issue also got mixed up with a proposal to take *Porgy and Bess* to London, which had foundered at the last minute (but it is unclear when) because, it seems, of difficulties over the dialect. Langner also temporized in a letter to Munsell of 14 June: "On the English situation, we don't want to commit ourselves on anything although we favor the Dreyfuss proposition. One idea which Hammerstein and Rodgers seemed favorable towards was to take the Drury Lane [Theatre] with a contract for three months after the war was over. What do you think of this proposition? Can it be repaired in time? Is there any other better theatre available? We had bad luck there with *Porgy and Bess*. It is a pretty big theatre and not to[o] well located." Munsell pursued the case in July 1943, when the Guild also received another offer for London from the Hyams brothers.[13] But *Oklahoma!* was not to cross the Atlantic until 1947.

On 3 May 1943 Langner reported to Munsell that "Mark [Heiman] and Shubert will go on backing the Guild now that *Oklahoma!* has brought in the bacon. There is talk of a second company, but we will not talk about it until next Fall."[14] Other issues decided at the meeting at the Dorset Hotel on 21 May were not to release any "grand rights" on the show—that is, for non-Guild dramatic performances ("In fact, it was felt it would be more valu-able to release these after the run of the play")—and, precisely, not to set up a touring company just yet. For the rights, Langner made the position on *Oklahoma!* clear to Munsell in his letter of 14 June: "I regard it as a sort of meal ticket for the Guild for the next ten years if stretched out properly because it has the same kind of interest that *Life with Father* has, but in addi-tion to that, it has the musical angle, and if the Shubert operettas like *Stu-dent Prince* and *Blossom Time* are any criterion, we can have an *Oklahoma!* department at the Guild and run it all our lives."[15] Thus the Guild seems to have made no response to Sandor Ince's approach to Howard Reinheimer on 4 June 1943 offering to act as agent for European rights for *Oklahoma!* and to arrange translations and adaptations.[16]

A touring version of the show, however, was more of a live issue. Helburn had already floated the idea by Munsell on 29 April: "We're thinking of the possibility of organizing a company for Chicago and the road next year, if this one proves as solid a New York resident as it seems to be now—it leads all others at the moment, and seems to be growing steadily in popularity. Isn't it a grand bit of luck to have come at this moment?" Despite Langner's claim to Munsell on 3 May that there would be no discussion of touring until after the summer, rumors soon circulated that *Oklahoma!* would in fact go on tour in fall: Vail Scenic Construction Co. wrote to the Guild on 19 May commenting on a report to that effect in the *New York Times* and suggested that sets should be built immediately given the increasing shortage of ma-terials due to wartime exigency.[17] John Haggott seems to have acted upon the suggestion, recording (on 29 May) ideas for a reduced touring set and informing Helburn on 3 June that Vail was quoting $5,500 for the construc-tion; the final estimate (2 August 1943) was $5,850.[18] By 6 June the *New York Times* was reporting on the likelihood of a touring company for *Oklahoma!* starting in October (with Harry Stockwell as Curly), that Langner was not eager to sell the film rights to the show, and that the Guild was even contem-plating making its own film version. The *Chicago Daily Tribune* suggested

17. The popularity of *Oklahoma!* led to numerous advertising spinoffs, as in this unidentified press cutting from April 1943 selling Lux soap powder with photos of the original cast. "'We Lux scores of costumes and stockings in this show,' says Hallye Clogg, wardrobe mistress [shown at the ironing board]. 'It's a real economy!'"

on 4 July 1943 and confirmed on 1 August that the city would be one of the
early beneficiaries of the tour: in effect, the Guild had little choice, given
its commitment to non–New York subscribers.

Langner also seems to have had other ambitions. In July 1943 he was
seeking a permanent relationship with Joshua Logan to direct three works
per season.[19] His thank-you letter to Agnes de Mille of 2 April 1943 also
offered some hint of discussions in play concerning his long-term interest in
ballet: "I cannot say in words how much I appreciate and admire the work
you have done in *Oklahoma!* I am really quite serious about the ballet and
wonder if you would like to try to give me a budget at your convenience."
His intentions become still clearer in a letter to de Mille written on 20 April:

> After seeing a program of the Ballet Theatre consisting of *Romeo and Juliet*,
> *Dark Elegy*, your own piece, and a piece of nonsense called *Helen of Troy*,
> I am more convinced than ever that there is room for a theatre ballet suited
> for theatre presentation in which there will be some theatre sense, as well
> as mood, music and modernity, which describes almost everything on the
> program except your number, and yet the Opera House was crowded with
> people (most of the men being effeminate) who raved over some of the most
> boring ballet it has ever been my ill fortune to witness.[20]

There is also a cryptic reference to "another ballet play in the offing" in
a note from Langner to Jerry Whyte of 12 June 1943; here Langner notes
two female dancers at the Ballet Russe whom he wishes to interview and
says "I am watching the picture closely."[21] Again, nothing came of this, but
the idea kept bubbling away. On 12 April 1944 Helburn (it seems) told Elia
Kazan that for the 1944–45 season, and in addition to *Carousel*, the Guild
was planning "two or three ballet plays."[22] She referred to the Ballet Theatre ("Langner's long-time dream!") in her account of the twenty-fifth birthday of the Theatre Guild in the *New York Times* on 16 April 1944, where
she also mentions plans for *Liliom* with "those incomparable craftsmen,
Rodgers and Hammerstein."[23] Helburn also approached Aaron Copland in
May 1944 with a scenario for a ballet; he turned it down.[24] On 16 July 1944
the *Chicago Daily Tribune* reported that future Guild projects included
the foundation of a company akin to the D'Oyly Carte and an American
operetta series entirely by Rodgers and Hammerstein, starting with *Liliom*,
which had been "thoroughly Americanized" and would appear in the fall.
Clearly Langner had been giving out interviews during a recent trip to Chicago (*Oklahoma!* was still playing there), one of which also appeared on

6 August 1944 in the *Chicago Sunday Times*: "Langner was full of plans.
Quoth he: 'The Rodgers-Hammerstein musical version of Molnar's *Liliom*
is now getting itself down on paper and will be ready sometime in the fall.
. . . We are also negotiating for a regular Theatre Guild radio program, we
are organizing a Ballet Theatre and we aim to do a movie a year in Hollywood. The first one [will be] taken from *Anna and the King of Siam*, a novel
by Margaret Langdon [Landon] that is about to become a best-seller. We
have bought the rights.'"[25] In fact, the Guild had been pursuing an association with a film production company from the second half of 1943, first
with United Artists (November 1943), then with David O. Selznick (December 1943), then with Columbia Pictures (August–November 1944).[26] As for
Rodgers and Hammerstein, the *New York Times* published on 26 May 1943
the story that they would soon be approached to provide the music and lyrics
for "an untitled comedy with music" to be produced and directed by Kazan.
Rouben Mamoulian, on the other hand, soon went back to Hollywood with
plans for a film of *Porgy and Bess*.[27]

Others in the Theatre Guild were concerned with the dangers of becoming too closely identified with Rodgers and Hammerstein. On 29 June
1943, for example, John Gassner, the Guild's play reader, wrote to Helburn
and Langner, "I think we ought to consider the problem of finding one
or two other composers and librettists, in order not to have to rely solely
on Dickie Rogers. How about Jerome Kern, Irving Berlin, Aaron Copland,
Earl Robinson, Harold Rome, Marc Blitzstein, Kurt Weill, Elie Siegmeister
and—for something sophisticated—Cole Porter. With *Oklahoma*[!] so successful, I think we have [an] entrée to all of these—and I think this is the
most opportune time to establish the best contacts with all these people."
He repeated the warning on 31 July 1943: "And again let me state that we
shouldn't depend entirely on Rogers [*sic*]. After *Oklahoma*[!] it should be
possible to get Irving Berlin, Jerome Kern, and others. And for something
really bright we might turn to Cole Porter and bring out the best in his talents just as the Guild brought out the best in Rogers." Gassner went on to
discuss Brecht's *The Good Woman of Setzuan* (with music to be provided
by Weill) and added a list of sixty-five "Recommendations for Musicals" (including Elmer Rice's *Street Scene* and Molnár's *Liliom*). At the top of the
list was William Saroyan's *The Time of Your Life*, to be set by Jerome Kern:
"act quickly. Strongly recommended."[28]

For the moment, however, the die was cast. As Langner noted to Munsell
on 30 September 1943: "We've never had a hit like *Oklahoma!* The line has

been unbroken since April. *Show Boat* is nothing by comparison. In my estimation it can play ten weeks in a city which ordinarily plays one week. The
cast is inexpensive, and it averages $7,500 in New York and should average
about $6,000 on the road. It's one of those things which come once in a
lifetime. Knock on wood, etc., etc.!" Helburn, Langner, Rodgers, and Hammerstein held weekly lunches of what they called the "Gloat Club" at Sardi's
restaurant to discuss business and casting problems throughout much of the
long run of *Oklahoma!*[29] Certainly they could "gloat" over their achievement, but as the show turned into a business, it required extensive management and maintenance in order to keep the wheels turning smoothly and
the profits rolling in.

Rewards and Recognition

As the Broadway production of *Oklahoma!* settled into routine, the Sunday
supplements maintained a steady stream of interest in the show. In the *New
York Times* alone, John Martin produced effusive praise of de Mille's choreography, and of the psychological realism of the dream-ballet, in a special
article on 9 May 1943; Hammerstein wrote his own account of the creation
of the show on 23 May; on 6 June, Olin Downes produced his extended discussion of "Broadway's gift to opera"; and on 1 August, Rodgers himself took
up his pen to show that "it ain't luck" that *Oklahoma!* was such a success.
The critics continued the rhetoric of the Guild's preopening press releases,
now reinforced by the show's artistic and commercial success, and gradually
set in stone the claims for a revolution in the Broadway musical to match
the impact of *Show Boat* some sixteen years before. The inclusion of the
libretto in Burns Mantle's anthology of "best plays" of 1942–43 was also a
sign of significant kudos.[30]

On the stage, the usual problems, and some unusual ones, arose. Lee
Dixon was regularly plagued by his alcoholism, forcing his understudy, Paul
Shiers, to be constantly in the wings, while Howard da Silva had a near-fight
with the stage manager in early November 1943: "This is one of a number
of unpleasant incidents which started when we were in rehearsal in February."[31] Da Silva was also known for clowning around in performances and
ad-libbing: "He has kidded through different performances and resents criticism for this." Offstage, too, tempers could run high. Langner and Mamoulian had a shouting match over the phone on 16 June 1943, prompting Langner, Helburn, Rodgers, and Hammerstein each to write to the director on

19 June.[32] The complaint hinged on an article in the *Daily Mirror* of 13 June ("Mamoulian Broke Rules in Stage Hit"), wherein Mamoulian had claimed credit for the quiet opening of the show, the location of the first two songs, and the casting of Drake and Roberts (although as the Guild notes, "these two players were already picked and their contracts signed, long before you ever came into the picture"). Articles favorable to Mamoulian, and claiming that *Oklahoma!* owed a great deal to his philosophy of musical theater, had also recently appeared, they said, in the *New York Times* (29 May), the *Christian Science Monitor* (4 June), and the *New York Post* (7 June).[33] Mamoulian seems to have learned his lesson: the article on him in the *New York Times* on 25 July was much more restrained, crediting him only with the strongly rhythmic nature of the production and the decision to have brightly colored costumes. But this was to be the first of many spats within the production team as Mamoulian, Riggs, and, later, Agnes de Mille argued over not getting the recognition they felt they deserved. Riggs thought that he was not given sufficient credit on the cover of the published edition of the libretto, writing to his attorney, Howard Reinheimer (who also acted for Hammerstein) on 10 June 1944:

> But one of the remarkable things about this show is how very hard someone—let us call it some idle and floating and malicious devil—has worked to keep what small credit is due me from being given me.
>
> Mr. Leverton will tell you the absurd and continuous violations of contract—leaving my name out of newspaper releases about waived royalties for overseas productions, mentioning everyone's name but mine in monthly magazine ads, leaving my name off the two most conspicuous hoardings in the theatre marquee, etc. etc.
>
> This is just another one of those cases . . .

The arguments with de Mille were particularly bitter, building up to a climax in 1947–48 which led to her gaining a percentage royalty (0.5 percent). Even Helburn was sensitive to the issues: on 23 April 1946 she wrote to Joseph Heidt, the Guild's press officer, from Connecticut, where she was ill, asking that he ensure that she get sufficient acknowledgment for *Oklahoma!* at its Los Angeles opening, for in Chicago everyone had given the credit to Langner and Marshall.[34]

The cast of *Oklahoma!* was in high demand for individual benefit appearances, which the Theatre Guild limited to one per week on 21 May 1943.[35] The success of the show was also used as leverage for salary increases.

Joan Roberts went from $250 per week in her initial contract to $265 on 5 April 1943, $315 on 5 July, and $365 on 30 August; Celeste Holm from $275 (an increase on her initial Standard Minimum Contract at $225) to $350 on 27 May; Bambi Linn from $70 to $90 on 12 July (and to $140 on 4 July 1944); and Katharine Sergava from $100 to $125 on 3 September (and $175 on 27 June 1944). Jay Blackton's weekly salary was increased from $200 to $250 on 28 May. Even the humble chorus members and dancers petitioned for an increase on their average of $50 per week because *Oklahoma!* was "a tremendous hit"; their salaries were raised to $52.50 on 1 July 1943 or thereabouts.[36] This was a period of quite high inflation. The *New York Times* of 23 June 1943 noted that the average American monthly salary was $85.03, while advertisements for positions around this time suggest that a sales assistant could expect to earn around $30 per week and a midlevel accountant $2,600 per year.

Clearly, *Oklahoma!* was on a high. The escalating costs during the rehearsal period must have been scaled back slightly, to judge by the fact that on 9 June 1943 Langner informed Charles Riegelman, the husband of one of the investors, that the production had cost $83,378.15 plus an Actors Equity Bond of $10,110, and in other documents around this time $82,000 is given as a ballpark figure.[37] According to Guild accounts, by 5 June 1943 the show had turned a profit of $64,430 on the basis of gross receipts of some $30,000 per week. This was about average for a successful musical: for example, the *New York Times* of 16 March 1943 reported gross receipts for the previous week of *Ziegfeld Follies* (Philadelphia) at $38,500, *Sons o' Fun* at $30,200, *Lady in the Dark* at $27,400, and the play *The Patriots* at $13,094. In September 1943 *Oklahoma!* was bringing in between $8,000 and $9,000 profit per week to the Guild (that is, after royalties and costs had been paid); and for the week ended 25 December, the Guild made an operating profit of $6,793.31 on the New York production (it would have been almost $8,000 were it not for Christmas gifts), plus $8,038.70 from the national touring company (currently in Chicago), to which was added income from the souvenir books in New York ($1,003.25) and royalties for the sheet music. For the last, in fall 1943 the sheet music of "People Will Say We're in Love" was selling nine thousand copies per day, and "Oh, What a Beautiful Mornin'" four thousand, with the Guild earning two cents a copy.[38] In this Christmas week author's royalties on the production (for Rodgers, Hammerstein, and Riggs) totaled $2,445.17 for New York and $2,382.56 for Chicago, which works out to $2,112 each for Rodgers and Hammerstein; for the investors, a

1 percent share in the show (purchased for $1,500) would have produced a return of $148 that week, giving an average of about $7,500 for the year. Relatively high ticket prices helped: in April 1943 seats at evening performances ranged from $1.10 to $4.40, whereas one could see Gertrude Lawrence in *Lady in the Dark* for $1.10 to $2.75 (up to $3.30 on Saturday evenings).

The financial consequences were obvious. Hammerstein, for example, was estimated to be earning a tidy $35,000 per year from royalties on pre-*Oklahoma!* material.[39] His attorney Howard Reinheimer predicted on 16 July 1943 that his income that year for tax purposes would be roughly $80,000 and recommended that half the New York royalties be placed in a special account to cover the tax liability. (Hammerstein religiously deposited $500 per week.)[40] Once the touring company came on stream, his income just from the performances of *Oklahoma!* must have averaged about $100,000 per year, to which would be added royalties from sheet music and recordings. Lynn Riggs's 1 percent of gross receipts in 1944 (from the two concurrent productions in New York and Chicago) evened out at about $500 per week after Samuel French and Co. had deducted its 20 percent commission. In public, and with his investors, Langner remained dour: on 2 November 1943 he wrote to S. N. Behrman that "*Oklahoma!* has arrived too late, for the government takes practically all." On 30 August 1944 Guild attorney William Fitelson, commenting on the proposed financing of *Carousel*, warned Helburn that *Oklahoma!* was "in the nature of a freak": "I need not direct your attention to the substantial financial risks involved in the production and presentation of musicals, as well as the great amount of time and attention necessary." But clearly the financial picture looked bright. The New York company's gross reached one million dollars in its thirty-third week of operation, on 13 November 1943; by the end of its first year almost 700,000 people had seen the show, and receipts were up to $1,600,000. It had grossed more than $7,000,000 when the New York run closed in May 1948; the national company reached its $9,000,000 gross on 23 September 1948. Agnes de Mille, who had an axe to grind, cited a Theatre Guild estimate that *Oklahoma!* had grossed $45,000,000 in its first ten years, and that its world earnings over fifteen were $60,000,000. What produced such large returns was not so much the weekly receipts—which as we have seen were comparable with other musicals (and were constrained by the size of the theater)—but, rather, the show's unusual longevity. Rodgers and Hammerstein's $2,000 per week in 1944 would have gone up and down in subsequent years depending on box-office takings and the number of active productions, but they must each have gained well over a million dollars for the first ten years of the show. As for Riggs, by 8 November 1947 he was estimated to have received a total royalty of $144,501.86 on the American companies, and $3,900.00 on the English one. When the Broadway run closed on 29 May 1948, *Oklahoma!* had paid off its backers by some 2,500 percent according to one estimate, and the returns continued until the sale of the show to Rodgers and Hammerstein in 1953: Helburn said that those who invested $1,500 in the show made $50,000 on their investment (presumably, after the apportionment of the sale), while *Variety* on 9 January 1980 reported that the return was 5,000 percent (that is, $75,000 on a $1,500 investment).[41]

The Guild, and for the most part Rodgers and Hammerstein, retained their concern to limit the rights to *Oklahoma!* so as to protect the profits of the Broadway production. Langner regularly refused film offers for the show in September 1943, January 1944 (starring Jimmy Cagney), February 1944, and May 1945 (Ginger Rogers). Newspapers ran rife with speculation, but as Langner told William Cagney on 19 January 1944: "The profits from the theatre are so good that it is foolish for us to talk about anything else right now." Similarly, he wrote to Harry Sherman on 22 June 1944: "We have no interest in having a picture made of *Oklahoma!* for many years to come. We are making a net profit of between $750,000 to $1,000,000 a year out of the stage rights and expect to do so for a number of years to come. So why bother with a picture until, let us say, 1950!"[42]

There was more of a dispute over performances of *Oklahoma!* songs on the radio. On 17 May 1943 Hammerstein wrote to his son Bill:

> You said you were listening in on the hit parade for *Oklahoma*[!] music. You won't hear it. We are not plugging any number enough for that. We are letting the score grow on a gradual incline, in the hope that it will have more lasting quality that way, as the non-plugged scores used to have. Further, we are not concentrating on one number. We are advancing slowly on a wide front with four songs: "Beautiful Morning" [*sic*], "People Will Say We're in Love," "Oklahoma," and "The Surrey with the Fringe on Top." Of these the leader is, at the moment[,] "People." My bet over the long route is "Mornin'." Actually if all performances of all four numbers were concentrated on one number, it would be well up on the list. But, like all overplugged songs it would be done for in two or three months. We have higher ambitions. I hope the experiment is successful. This is an ideal chance to make it because the show needs no exploitation through song-plugging. The line at the box-office remains unbroken. They are selling way into the summer. The advance is about $100,000. It is like a dream.

He wrote much the same on 1 June (Hammerstein tended to repeat himself in letters to Bill, in part because of fears that mail was not reaching members of the armed forces), adding "As a long-pull proposition this will, I think, become an important score—as has *Porgy and Bess* and *Show Boat*, which were treated in the same way." A playlist of *Oklahoma!* songs on the radio for the first half of July (with about fifty entries) confirms that these four songs were indeed the ones most reaching the public, whether in programs or in advertising, but also suggests that the plan to restrict their exploitation was not having much success. Hammerstein admitted defeat in a letter to Bill of 15 August 1943: "I once promised that *Okla[homa!]* would never get on the hit parade because we wouldn't high pressure it. But it got out of hand and 'People Will Say We're in Love' is in its sixth week on the parade and is now number three. I believe it is the most played on the air at the moment. 'Surrey' and 'Oklahoma' are in the first 30. 'Morning' is still my bet for the most important song in the long run—wait and see. The score [the sheet music]—this means much more—has already sold over 200,000 copies and is going at the rate of more than 20,000 per week." On 13 October he noted, "The music sales here have passed the half million mark, and getting, if anything, stronger. The Crosby and Sinatra records (made with vocal accompaniment, orchestras banned by Petrillo) are selling phenomenally. Petrillo has made a deal with Decca and they are proceeding immediately with a 12[-]side album."[43]

Frank Sinatra recorded "People Will Say We're in Love" (arranged by Alec Wilder) with the Bobby Tucker Singers on 7 June (never released), 22 June and 5 August 1943 (when he also recorded "Oh, What a Beautiful Mornin'"). Both songs were also recorded by Bing Crosby, again with vocal backing. Such choral accompaniments were a consequence of the 1942–44 dispute between recording companies and the American Federation of Musicians (of which James Caesar Petrillo was president), which led, in effect, to a strike in recording studios by instrumental musicians. As Helburn wrote to Warren Munsell in London on 12 August:

> There are no records of *Oklahoma!* that we can send you. As you know, the Petrillo ban on the union musicians still holds. They cannot play for broadcasting so the only record that has been made is a singing of "People Will Say We're in Love" with Frank Sinatra, which if it sounds anything like his radio singing of the same must be terrible. E.N.S.A. made a recording for the British armed forces—a half hour of all the songs. There should be a copy in

the London office. It has to be played with a special needle, etc. but if you can get access to their records they might let you hear it. It is also choral. The cast here volunteered to make it but the musicians refused, and they couldn't afford to pay the $500 needed for the orchestral accompaniment.[44]

In the second half of 1943 Langner engaged in a heated debate with Rodgers and Hammerstein about the broadcasting of songs from *Oklahoma!* —Langner regarded it as an infringement, whereas Rodgers and Hammerstein were now in favor of the publicity—and he made frequent attempts to stop their use in New York nightclubs. As he wrote to Rodgers on 2 November 1943, "I certainly feel that if we are as conscientious as you feel we are about the show, you really should cooperate with us. There is no sense in your left hand cutting off your right hand. I have heard only one good rendering of *Oklahoma!* music on the radio, and the rest of it stinks." According to Munsell, Louis Dreyfus in London was also having problems controlling bootleg orchestrations and recordings.[45] But Langner, too, must have been playing a double game, supporting the proposed original-cast recording for which Petrillo had permitted an exemption. Volume 1 (Decca Album DA 359) was recorded on 20 and 25 October 1943 and released on 2 December 1943; vol. 2 (DA 383; including "It's a Scandal! It's a Outrage!" "Lonely Room" [sung by Alfred Drake; da Silva had left the show], and "The Farmer and the Cowman") was recorded on 24 May 1944 and released on 3 January 1945. On 8 December 1943 Langner (it seems) wrote to Jack Kapp, president of Decca, "May I tell you how very much I appreciate the taste and care with which you have reproduced the *Oklahoma!* music. I can only tell you that we who have been super-critical of all interpretations on the air, feel that you have done us proud."[46]

In December 1943 Langner entered into a lawsuit with Republic Pictures Corp. over the film *In Old Oklahoma* (starring John Wayne and released on the 6th) because of its too similar title; they settled on the 20th, and the film was reissued in 1945 as *War of the Wildcats.* On 25 January 1944 Charles Riegelman, the husband of one of the investors in *Oklahoma!* expressed to the Guild his concern for competition between *Oklahoma!* and the Yiddish *A Wedding in Oklahoma* then playing at the Douglas Park Theatre in New York: Sam Weller saw it and said that the music bore no relation to *Oklahoma!* and that the subject was the Jewish diaspora fleeing the Nazis to Oklahoma, although he admitted that he was hampered because he did not understand the language. Langner regularly refused requests from professional and amateur companies to stage the show. And in 1945, Langner once again took Republic Pictures to court over a film with the proposed title *The Oklahomans*.[47]

Clearly, *Oklahoma!* had entered the public consciousness, becoming part of an American mainstream. The award of a special Pulitzer Prize on 2 May 1944 helped: Rodgers later claimed that he was to have received the Pulitzer Prize for music but that he indicated that he could not accept it without Hammerstein, which explained the compromise "special" award.[48] As Lewis Nichols wrote in the *New York Times* on 7 May 1944:

> *Oklahoma!* is more than a show, it probably is even more than an institution, although the proof of that will lie in whether it gets through the hot summer of 1944. Its success has given heart to producers, to composers of musical shows, to librettists who have not learned the repertory of double entente [*sic*], to dance directors. After offering *Oklahoma!* the directors of the Theatre Guild found they could walk on the sidewalks again without being nudged off to the streets, and the Guild, too, is a good thing to have around. It is wayward at times, but perfection makes no permanent home on Broadway. And finally, and what is undoubtedly the most important phase of the matter, *Oklahoma!* during its thirteen months here and less time on the road, has restored to a huge public a faith in the theatre and a feeling that it might be fun to go there again.

Nichols went on to note the regular (and regularly reported) clamor for seats for the show on Broadway and on tour. Audiences often paid premiums to ticket scalpers or "diggers"—despite efforts by the Guild to prevent the practice—and would write begging letters to the Guild for tickets, calling in favors and friendships, or even just telling heartrending stories. Radio on the one hand and sheet music sales on the other must have played a part in the show's reputation, while the issuing of the complete vocal score (registered for copyright purposes on 1 December 1943, EP 118496) and the cast recording in December further aided the show's dissemination.[49] In terms of the sheet music, seven songs from the show were available: "Oh, What a Beautiful Mornin'," "The Surrey with the Fringe on Top," "I Cain't Say No," "Many a New Day," "People Will Say We're in Love," "Out of My Dreams." and "Oklahoma." By 9 November 1943 sales had reached 600,000, with 41,000 copies sold that week; by the end of January 1944 the sheet music was at a total of 1,153,000, and 225,000 copies of the Decca recording had been sold (at five dollars each).[50] By the end of 1944 (after the resolution of the American Federation of Musicians dispute), further recordings of *Oklahoma* songs were made by singers more familiar in the opera house, including James Melton and Eleanor Sterber with Al Goodman's Orchestra ("Oklahoma," "The Surrey with the Fringe on Top," "People Will Say We're in Love," "Out of My Dreams," "Kansas City," "Oh, What a Beautiful Mornin'"), and John Carter Thomas with Victor Young's Orchestra and the Ken Darby Chorus ("Oh, What a Beautiful Mornin'," "Kansas City"). In 1944 Robert Russell Bennett's "symphonic suite" based on *Oklahoma!* was also recorded by the Los Angeles Philharmonic Orchestra, conducted by Alfred Wallenstein.[51] Accounts of *Oklahoma!* and its creators in popular magazines (such as *Life* on 24 May 1943), usually with photographs or imaginative illustrations, also served a purpose, while the surprising flurry of beauty products and jewelry marketed under an *Oklahoma!* umbrella suggests how the show developed a life offstage.[52] So, too, does the music at the Democratic Party Convention in Chicago in 1944 (nominating Roosevelt and Truman). The governor of Oklahoma, Robert S. Kerr, gave the keynote speech: he was introduced by an orchestra (presumably the one currently performing in Chicago) playing "Oklahoma," while "Oh, What a Beautiful Mornin'" celebrated the nomination, and the dawning of a new political day.[53] Only later, however, did "Oklahoma" become the state's anthem: there seems to have been a first attempt in the Oklahoma legislature in the mid-1940s—scuppered by a female member who claimed that "Every night my honey lamb and I" was indecorous—but the official statute was eventually passed by the Oklahoma State House of Representatives on 28 April 1953 (House Bill no. 1094), and ratified by the Oklahoma Senate on 6 May. It is clear that *Oklahoma!* had become what de Mille wrote to Lawrence Langner on 14 April 1947: "not only our pride and joy: it's a kind of national institution."[54]

On Tour

The Guild had initially been reluctant to commit to touring *Oklahoma!* although as we have seen, plans for the so-called National Company were under way by May 1943, and after a tryout in New Haven on 14 October, it opened in Washington on the 18th, the day before the first tryout of Hammerstein's *Carmen Jones* in Philadelphia. The new company then toured briefly (Baltimore, Cleveland) before settling in for a sixty-week run in Chicago (opening on 15 November for what would turn out to be 532 performances).[55] Langner was anxious for the press to realize that the national company was not inferior to the New York one, that the cast and dancers had been carefully selected by Rodgers, Hammerstein, de Mille, and the Guild (and that many had had experience in the New York production), and that Mamoulian's production was being faithfully reproduced by Jerome Whyte. In 1944 there were also plans to set up an "Oklahoma Pacific Coast Corp." to stage *Oklahoma!* on the West Coast for three years, but the project foundered over issues related to the capital gains tax.[56] On 8 January 1945 the national company began its grueling schedule of tours: mostly one-week runs in major theaters on the East Coast and in the Midwest (starting with Guild subscription cities)—with occasional trips to the West Coast (thirteen weeks in San Francisco from 8 February 1946, then twelve weeks in Los Angeles from 6 May) and Southwest—that continued until 2 May 1953. The high point of the tour was when *Oklahoma!* opened to fanfares and festivities in Oklahoma City on 25 November 1946, even if bad weather put a damper on a proposed parade; on this occasion, Helburn, Langner, Rodgers, Hammerstein, and Mamoulian were made honorary members of the Kiowa Indians.[57] When the New York run closed on 29 May 1948, the Guild constituted the so-called First Company, which toured smaller theaters until 21 May 1949, carefully avoiding geographical competition with the national company. All this involved a massive logistical operation. But the national company made huge profits: on 29 March 1953 the *New York Times* reported that it had grossed $15,000,000 by the show's tenth anniversary.

Shortly after the New York premiere, requests came in for international tours of *Oklahoma!* in particular to England and Australia, presumably because of American troops stationed there. The Guild was reluctant, not just out of its desire for exclusivity but also, one assumes, because of the difficulties of international transport during wartime. For the moment, nothing was done internationally save the version of *Oklahoma!* that toured military bases under the auspices of the United Service Organizations (U.S.O.) from 26 February 1945 for nine months, specifically excluding England, Australia, and New Zealand.[58] Quite apart from the patriotic impulse, this was presumably part of the Guild's ongoing strategy to maintain favorable treatment from the draft board on the grounds that *Oklahoma!* made an essential contribution to the war effort. The company had already done a special performance at West Point on Sunday, 31 October 1943, and from 6 June 1944 until early March 1945 there were Tuesday matinees of *Oklahoma!* at reduced prices (from $0.60 to $2.10) for members of the armed forces.[59]

Shortly after the war ended, discussions began with the London impresario Prince Littler to take *Oklahoma!* to the Theatre Royal, Drury Lane. Sets, properties, and some of the cast shipped out on the freighter S.S. *Malancha* in early 1947, while the rest of the cast, together with Langner and Helburn and trunks of costumes, took the *Queen Elizabeth*, which ran aground in the Solent, threatening to delay the opening. The show first reached English audiences in Manchester, starting on 18 April, opening in London on Wednesday the 30th.[60] Langner noted other difficulties in London, including fitting the set into the theater, the outdated lighting system, the raked stage (causing problems for the dancers), and lackadaisical British stagehands. Postwar Britain was still in depression, with rationing and regular power cuts; the Americans had severe difficulties living on their salaries, prompting the Guild to send regular care packages of food and other luxuries; and reconciling income taxes was a perpetual headache. The Guild was also concerned that Rodgers and Hammerstein were in effect competing with themselves by also taking to London their production of Irving Berlin's *Annie Get Your Gun* (it opened on 7 June 1947). On 29 January, Langner had sternly reminded them, "I know that your heart is with *Oklahoma!*, but that you no doubt feel a duty to Irving Berlin. However, I do think that in this instance Berlin should recognize that but for the fact of *Oklahoma!*, his own show would never have been done."[61] The London opening of *Oklahoma!* however, was the predictable triumph, precipitating what many English critics described as the "American invasion" of the West End that awakened the British theater from its torpor of Noël Coward preciosity and Ivor Novello escapism. It played 1,548 performances (figures vary slightly) in London before going on tour.

The London *Oklahoma!* started with an all-American cast—including a good number of veterans of the Broadway and national companies—with British standbys undergoing training to take over roles as original cast members left. London took the show to its heart, revisiting and reworking the claims promulgated in the Broadway reception of the show while also reifying America as (in jaded British eyes) a young land of energy and opportunity. According to Lionel Hale in the *Daily Mail* (1 May 1947), *Oklahoma!*

> is simplicity so artfully staged that it goes from beginning to end with a superb swing. A swing. The whole evening is very much like a happy child on a swing. It tells of Oklahoma as a young State of America. Its company is youthful. Some of the ballets are not so nearly well danced as they are

designed, but the communal zest carries them over. . . . But this smash-hit evening is not an evening of stars—it is colour plus music, plus wit, plus dancing, put together with a sort of inspired single-mindedness to re-create on the stage the young people of a youthful part of the earth.[62]

While the "American invasion" was not as pronounced as its reception would have us believe, *Oklahoma!* and *Annie Get Your Gun* clearly made their mark. Not for nothing did the British Broadcasting Corporation present a radio broadcast of an abbreviated version of *Oklahoma!* (both dialogue and songs), using the Drury Lane cast, on 28 May 1949.[63] West End shows soon found it essential to cultivate the new vitality, "realistic" plotlines, and the integration of music, drama, and dance presumed now to be essential to Broadway. English models followed the trend, whether as commonsense commercialism, in homage, or occasionally as parody, as with the comic dream-ballet in the British comedian Arthur Askey's *Bet Your Life* (1952). The Ruritanian chorus in Ivor Novello's *Gay's the Word* (1951) may have complained with skittish zest:

> Since *Oklahoma!*
> We've been in a coma
> And no one cares for us.
>
> . . .
>
> Though some people feel
> That Agnes de Mille
> Is brainy, we are *sure* that we are brainier
> In Ruritania!

But the influence could hardly be resisted.[64]

By 1951, so Lawrence Langner noted in his autobiography, *Oklahoma!* had been performed in England, Sweden (it opened on 26 November 1948), South Africa (23 December 1948 to 12 November 1949), Australia (19 February 1949, for eight months), and Norway (7 June to 30 September 1949), to which he should have added Denmark (30 March 1949 to 19 March 1950) and New Zealand (as part of the Australia tour).[65] Certainly, the Guild at one point considered performances in other countries and languages: there is an undated "List of writers in this country who might prepare *Oklahoma!* for productions in foreign countries," including Kurt Weill and Bertolt Brecht for Germany, Ferenc Molnár for Hungary, and other names for Czechoslovakia, France, Italy, Poland, Russia, Scandinavia, Spain, Portugal, and Latin America. However, a request for a performance in Buenos

Aires in May 1944 was turned down, as were similar requests in 1947–48 for Austria, Germany, Holland, Hungary, and Switzerland. In October 1951 Hammerstein was keen on a production in Israel, although this never came to fruition; nor did proposed performances in Mexico (October 1950), Bombay (June 1951), and France (November 1951), or a rather odd request (26 October 1950) to stage a performance in Yiddish in New York.[66] All amateur performances—whether in the United States or elsewhere—were still rigorously forbidden. And Langner must have completed his autobiography before the chief triumph of *Oklahoma!* in 1951, its stage and televised performance during the September Festival in Berlin as part of the American offerings (also including Gian Carlo Menotti's opera *The Consul* and Euripides' *Medea*). Celeste Holm once again reprised the role of Ado Annie; the rest of the cast was drawn from the national company. According to the *New York Times* (13 September 1951): "All that *Oklahoma!* has to offer of melody and zest and color captivated Berlin tonight [12 September] as definitely as it has scored with spectators in the United States and England. . . . For the popular American production it represented a triumph over the barriers of language and unfamiliarity with the folklore on which it is based." Not only was *Oklahoma!* truly a badge of Americana; it was also in distinguished artistic company.

The *Oklahoma!* Family

Lawrence Langner's prediction that the Theatre Guild would need an entire office permanently devoted to *Oklahoma!* fell not far short of the truth. On 1 September 1943 both the Broadway and the touring companies of *Oklahoma!* came under the management of Jerry Whyte, the original stage manager, who liaised with Helburn and Langner on matters of casting and production; on his return from the army, he became production manager of all Guild musicals.[67] Helburn and Langner periodically attended the show to see what shape it was in, as did Rodgers, Hammerstein, Mamoulian, and de Mille, making notes on the performance which would be passed on to Whyte for attention. For example, on 25 April 1945 Hammerstein reported that Evelyn Wyckoff (Laurey) and Harry Stockwell (Curly) were too stodgy, and that he disliked Edna Skinner as Ado Annie: "The deviations from the original direction that occur in several spots are irritating but I am inclined to think not terribly important. What is important is that they should be nipped in the bud before more of the same creep in."[68] Whyte also supervised the London production, eventually staying in England to manage a separate production company for Rodgers and Hammerstein (principally, for the London *South Pacific*).

Inevitably, those involved in the original production of *Oklahoma!* moved on. Alfred Drake went to Hollywood, although he returned to Broadway to star in the Guild's *Sing Out, Sweet Land* (opened 27 December 1944) and later was the first Petruchio in Cole Porter's *Kiss Me Kate* (1948).[69] On 12 February 1944 Jay Blackton gave six weeks' notice to move to a weekly show on RCA Radio. Celeste Holm opened in Howard Arlen's *Bloomer Girl* on 5 October 1944; *Bloomer Girl* also had other *Oklahoma!* connections, including Joan McCracken, now as a principal dancer, choreography by Agnes de Mille, sets by Lemuel Ayers, and costumes by Miles White. A good number of female chorus members and dancers left to return to the home as their husbands came back from the war: this was Kate Friedlich's reason for giving notice on 13 August 1944. Blackton was replaced briefly by William Reddick, who was then fired at the end of March 1944 because he could not get on with the cast and despite, he claimed (on 29 March), the endorsement of José Iturbi: "I would like to point out that whether you engage Mr. Toscanini or Mr. Bruno Walter or a Broadway conductor, your performances for a considerable time cannot possibly be a photographic reproduction of the more than four hundred preceding ones. Your cast will inevitably go through a period of readjustment with *anyone* who takes over." Of the principals, Joseph Buloff remained longest in place (until August 1946); he was replaced by David Burns, who had played Ali Hakim in the national company. Meanwhile, a succession of new players entered the stage.[70]

It is hard to keep track of the cast members moving in and out of the show, but the most distinguished alumni of *Oklahoma!* on Broadway include Bonita Primrose and Shelley Winters as Ado Annie (Winters from September 1947 to January 1948); Mary Hatcher, Betty Jane Watson, and Evelyn Wyckoff as Laurey; Howard Keel, Jack Kilty, and Harry Stockwell as Curly; and Murvyn Vye as Jud.[71] Some of the original chorus members and dancers graduated through the ranks, but only rarely did they become Broadway principals: thus Nona Feid and Vivian Smith joined Jud's postcards, and Paul Shiers moved up the cast list from Mike to Fred. Dorothea M(a)cFarland is perhaps the chief exception: originally in the chorus, she took the role of Gertie in July 1944, then got her chance to play Ado Annie on tour (from March 1945) and then on Broadway (from December 1946) and in the first London cast. Several Gerties, in fact, became Ado Annies,

18. The many distinguished graduates from the *Oklahoma!* "family" included Shelley Winters, who played Ado Annie from September 1947 to January 1948. Although costumes were replaced, the tendency was to reproduce the originals as closely as possible (compare Celeste Holm's dress in figure 14), as was the case with the production as a whole. (Vandamm)

including Patricia Englund (Gertie on Broadway, then Ado Annie on tour and as a replacement in London) and Vivienne Allen (both roles on Broadway). Others of the cast went on to different careers—such as Barry Kelley (the first Ike Skidmore), who had significant success in the cinema from the late 1940s through the 1960s—or even just to different Rodgers and Hammerstein shows. The original cast of *Carousel* (1945) included a number of *Oklahoma!* graduates, including John Raitt as Billy Bigelow (he had understudied Harry Stockwell as Curly in Chicago, replacing him in May 1944), Murvyn Vye (a Broadway Jud) as Jigger Craigin, and Bambi Linn as Louise.[72] Similarly, *Me and Juliet* (1953) included Joan McCracken in the lead. And sometimes the direction went the other way: Patricia Northrop, one of the later Laureys, had made her Broadway debut in the chorus of *South Pacific*.

The movement between the Broadway and national companies (and also the international troupes) was quite typical, and it made obvious sense as lesser cast members and understudies on Broadway gained higher-ranked roles on tour, while principals on tour might eventually get a chance on Broadway. Harry Stockwell, Evelyn Wyckoff, and Pamela Britton (the first Curly, Laurey, and Ado Annie in the national company) had acted as understudies for Alfred Drake, Joan Roberts, and Celeste Holm, respectively, whether or not they were being deliberately groomed. Stockwell and Wyckoff then returned to Broadway when Alfred Drake left the show in June 1944, and Joan Roberts in July. Other original members of the national company who moved up the lists include Jack Kilty (Fred; he eventually played Curly on Broadway), Alfred Cibelli (Sam; later a distinguished touring Jud, who, it seems, was the first to both sing and dance the role), and the dancer Gemze de Lappe. Bonita Primrose, who started in the chorus on tour, played Ado Annie in the U.S.O. troupe (1945), then on Broadway (October 1945 to December 1946), and later took the role to South Africa (1948–49). Mary Hatcher, a popular Laurey, is a similar example, while Isabel Bigley started in the chorus of the Broadway company, played Armina (now a singing role) in the first London cast, and eventually took the role of Laurey there, before starring as Sarah Brown in *Guys and Dolls* (1950–53) and returning to Rodgers and Hammerstein with *Me and Juliet*.

Rodgers and Hammerstein insisted on auditioning all the principals in either company, and Mamoulian could also be involved in major casting decisions. On 16 July 1947 the Guild sent a telegram to Queenie Smith (a Los Angeles theatrical agent, and presumably the actress who had played Ellie

Mae Shipley in the 1936 film of *Show Boat*), asking her to "engage Sherry O'Neill beginning chorus $75 New York to be groomed for Ado Annie national company salary $125. Will tell her after four weeks grooming whether she capable of playing part." Pamela Britton is another case in point, being yet another Gertie (on Broadway from August 1943) who joined the national company as Ado Annie. However, she then had other plans: on 26 February 1944 she received a stern admonition from Jerry Whyte on proposing (threatening?) to sign a Hollywood contract with MGM: "I sincerely hope you know what you are doing because, as I told you in Chicago, you are not yet equipped to go out and attempt to create a new role. You have not had the experience or the seasoning to cope with the problems that will confront you in Hollywood." Whyte was wrong: Britton played the "Girl from Brooklyn" falling in love with Frank Sinatra in *Anchors Aweigh* (1945), and was Barney Lee in *A Letter for Evie* (1946). By 1947, however, she was back on Broadway, starring in *Brigadoon*.[73]

Whyte's treatment of Britton is somewhat typical of the rather paternalistic approach to members of the *Oklahoma!* casts, especially the women. Those who committed themselves to the show would be fully supported, up to a point, but recalcitrants could be cast out of the "family" and even into professional exile. According to Agnes de Mille, the Theatre Guild released Diana Adams, one of the original dancers, to perform in Kurt Weill's *One Touch of Venus* (also choreographed by de Mille) only after weeks of negotiation, and they took a dim view of such "incest." Betty Jane Watson joined the Broadway cast as Gertie in November 1943, then the national company as Laurey in July 1944, returning to Broadway as Laurey in October 1945. She then joined her male lead, Howard Keel, in the London cast of *Oklahoma!* that opened on 1 May 1947. However, she did not disclose that she was pregnant, which led to her dismissal from the cast and, as a result, a threatened lawsuit, although Watson eventually withdrew. She was back on the Broadway stage in June 1948 (in *Sleepy Hollow*) and landed a role in the moderately successful *As the Girls Go* in November 1948. (It ran, with a break, through to January 1950.) However, she never again worked for the Guild or for Rodgers and Hammerstein.[74]

But the *Oklahoma!* family also generated significant loyalty. Owen Martin played Cord Elam on Broadway throughout the entire run (also standing in as Ali Hakim in September–November 1947), then in the national company, then in the New York 1951 revival, finally shifting to Andrew Carnes in the New York City Center production in 1953. Some of the dancers seem to have been particularly faithful, whether out of commitment or out of necessity. Two of the original 1943 dancers were involved in subsequent tours: Vivian Smith did the choreography for the U.S.O. tour in 1945, while Erik Kristen eventually played dream-Curly in London (1947) and in the South Africa production of *Oklahoma!* in 1949 (which also included Bonita Primrose repeating her Broadway Ado Annie), which he supervised. Gemze de Lappe offers a similar case: she started as a dancer (Aggie, the Bambi Linn role) in the first national company and ended up as dream-Laurey on Broadway (July 1946) before taking the same role in London, then supervising the choreography for the Australian production in 1949. In the case of the dancers, the reason for these continuities was simple: Agnes de Mille's choreography was never notated—although it appears that it was filmed—and so could be passed on only from dancer to dancer until the oral tradition broke down.[75]

Transferring cast members between companies clearly supported the desire to maintain a consistent production style for *Oklahoma!*: the original sets and costumes were carefully reproduced as needed, and both Mamoulian's blocking and de Mille's choreography were faithfully preserved. The practice extended even to the publicity photos: on 14 November 1944 the *Chicago Daily Tribune* included a photo of the national company (Curly and Laurey in the surrey, surrounded by the other characters) that reproduced almost exactly an original publicity photo for the Broadway premiere, and a good number of other *Oklahoma!* poses became standard. This was not unusual for touring shows: it made for economies of scale and also gave regional audiences the impression that they were seeing a Broadway-quality production. However, it becomes more striking in the context of the length of the *Oklahoma!* run. The show became strongly resistant to change—alterations to the original were severely frowned upon by the Guild and by Rodgers and Hammerstein—whether because of its iconic status or because there was no need to change the formula once it had been proved to work so well: Rodgers used the term *frozen*, in a positive sense.[76] The issue had some impact on the 1955 film version: Bosley Crowthers in the *New York Times* (16 October 1955) noted that it was (somewhat inevitably) tied to the stage production. The film, in turn, given its own iconic status, had its influence on subsequent stage revivals, not least Trevor Nunn's at London's Royal National Theatre (1998), which introduced numerous elements from the film, such as staging "Kansas City" at a train station.

Changing Fortunes

In his autobiography (1951) Langner proudly ended his comments on *Oklahoma!* by saying that "unless present signs are deceptive," the show would continue on the stage "for many years to come."[77] He was both right and wrong.

The Guild's relationship with Rodgers and Hammerstein had already become fractured. Langner does not devote nearly as much space in his autobiography to *Carousel* as to *Oklahoma!* even though he considered it "the finest American musical play of our time."[78] It is not clear whether his neglect is because it could not be regarded as a landmark, because it was not a happy collaboration, or because it was less of a hit than *Oklahoma!*: it had 890 performances on Broadway (at the large Majestic Theatre) from 19 April 1945 until it closed on 24 May 1947. But there was no doubt about the Guild's third collaboration with Rodgers and Hammerstein, *Allegro*, which opened on 10 October 1947, also at the Majestic. Although Helburn and Langner regularly professed their enthusiasm for the show, at least in public, it was a disaster behind the scenes, not least because Agnes de Mille proved herself a failure at directing: as Helburn wrote to Langner on 5 June 1947, "We are supposed to be having an *Allegro* meeting right now. I'm worried to death about Agnes as a general. She doesn't seem to have any realization of her responsibilities." This made the Guild doubly annoyed at de Mille's repeated complaints about her treatment over *Oklahoma! Allegro* closed on 10 July 1948 after 315 performances, a respectable number for most shows but an ignominious one for the supposed magic touch of Rodgers and Hammerstein (it did better on tour), and the Guild later claimed to have lost $54,000 on it.[79] The duo made the split, forming their own production company for *South Pacific* (which opened at the Majestic on 7 April 1949); the problems with de Mille may also be one reason why *South Pacific* did not have any significant choreography.[80] The Guild did not entirely abandon its involvement in musicals: it produced Morton Gould's *Arms and the Girl* (1953; based on Lawrence Langner and Armina Marshall's play *The Pursuit of Happiness*); was involved—somewhat disastrously, it turned out—in the early plans for Lerner and Loewe's *My Fair Lady* in 1951–53; and had a good run (924 performances) with Jule Styne's *Bells Are Ringing* (opened 29 November 1956). But the momentum was lost. On 10 May 1956 Helburn suggested to Rodgers and Hammerstein Owen and Donald Davis's play *Ethan Frome* (1936) for their next musical (Hammerstein declined), but this seems not to have been associated with any Guild venture.[81] By now, *Oklahoma! Carousel*, and *Allegro* had been sold, and the formal relationship between the Guild and Rodgers and Hammerstein was dissolved.

Already by the time *Oklahoma!* opened in London in April 1947, there were signs that the show's popularity on Broadway was heading toward its natural decline: on 29 March 1946 Langner instructed Jerry Whyte, "Now that *Oklahoma!* is past its peak, and business is falling off, it is essential that we do not increase the salary list."[82] No other musical had run as long, fashions were changing, and market saturation had set in. In April 1947 the Guild ran a survey of its Broadway audience to determine the likely future of the show.[83] On 30 March, Rodgers wrote a puff in the *New York Times* on the show's fourth birthday, praising in particular the Theatre Guild for having had the courage to mount *Oklahoma!* and the skill to maintain it in production. But box-office receipts were on the decline, and the Guild faced the consequences of contractual decisions made somewhat casually before it was realized just what a success *Oklahoma!* might be. In particular, the agreement to pay royalties on gross receipts to Rodgers, Hammerstein, Riggs, Mamoulian, and, after April 1947, de Mille, was disadvantageous given that whether the show made a profit or loss, these royalties would still fall due. Accordingly, the Guild periodically asked the beneficiaries to waive royalties in the interest of keeping the show on the stage. (The same would later occur for the London production.) The contract with Lee Shubert allowed him to remove *Oklahoma!* from the St. James Theatre if weekly gross receipts went below $18,000, a clause he invoked on 22 December 1947, although the Guild argued the evidence and managed to stave off closure for a while, at least.[84] But things had not been going well for some time. In October and November 1947 Langner successfully persuaded the leading parties to waive their royalties once more, noting to Garrett Leverton (of Samuel French, acting for Riggs) on 20 November, "Certainly we as a management have spared no efforts on our part to keep the show in wonderful shape. It would have been dead two years ago but for what we have done." The Guild also tried to stop the rot by seeking to bring Alfred Drake and Celeste Holm back into the cast for the 2,000th performance on 4 December, with Rodgers conducting and Gene Kelly as Will Parker "if we can secure him." Other proposals for the pre-Christmas performances included having de Mille dance in the ballets, and casting Danny Kaye or Jimmy Durante as the Peddler— although only Holm returned in the end. This was ostensibly to capitalize on the Christmas market, although as Langner explained to Riggs on

19. Richard Rodgers conducted the 2,000th performance of *Oklahoma!* on
4 December 1947, as he did for other special occasions. The Theatre Guild
had hoped to bring back Alfred Drake and Celeste Holm, and to recruit Gene
Kelly as Will Parker; however, only Holm agreed. By now, the show's fortunes
were on the wane, and the Broadway run closed on 29 May 1948. (Ben
Mancuso, Cosmo-Sileo Associates)

28 November, there were other concerns: "They are making a great effort
not to fall below the stop clause during the first three weeks of December
so that we don't get kicked out of the theatre. That is why there will be all
the doings with Celeste."[85] On 15 March 1948 the Guild attempted to get
Judy Garland to take a brief turn as Laurey (then Kathryn Grayson on the
22nd, and Deanna Durbin on the 24th). The fifth-anniversary performance
on 31 March 1948 was planned as a big gala, so it was reported in the *New
York Times* on 7 March 1948, although the article also noted, "This, to be
sure, will be the last party for *Oklahoma!* on Broadway. The champion, in its
present incarnation, is on the way out." In early May the Guild press office
was making plans for what Joseph Heidt claimed would be the world-record

(for a musical) 2,239th performance on 30 June, beating *Chu-Chin-Chow* in London at 2,238 performances; the previous longest-running musical on Broadway had been the revue *Hellzapoppin* with 1,404 performances (surpassed by *Oklahoma!* on 1 July 1946). Heidt suggested Bing Crosby, Mickey Rooney, Perry Como, Frank Sinatra, or Gene Kelly as a guest Curly, and for Laurey, Judy Garland, Betty Grable, Shirley Temple, Ginger Rogers, or Dorothy Lamour, among others.[86] But the writing was on the wall: *Oklahoma!* closed on 29 May 1948 after 2,212 performances (some accounts give 2,202, and others 2,248).

The British run had a similar trajectory, with huge success in London, then a tailing off of profits by early 1950, then significant receipts on tour and, again, a decline. The net pretax operating profits on the British production per fiscal year (which in England runs from April to April) were as follows: to 5 April 1948, $151,497.87; to 5 April 1949, $276,469.75; to 5 April 1950, $69,816.23. The total net posttax profit for the three years was $233,569.05. The net pretax profit for the year ending 31 March 1952 was $50,185.27, and for 31 March 1953, $4,829.32.[87] This was the nature of show business. But the situation in America had other consequences. If the Guild did not run seventy-five performances of *Oklahoma!* in first-class theaters each year (as well as meet other requirements, including no longer than a six-month layoff), the rights would revert to Rodgers and Hammerstein. Not all theaters being toured by the national company counted, and all was not well here, either: the national company had its first summer layoff in 1950. This is presumably why the Guild engineered a New York run for the national company from 29 May to 28 July 1951 (at the Broadway Theatre) before the Berlin Festival in September. That run was well received, but sales dropped sharply in the summer and the Guild closed it early, moving *Oklahoma!* to the so-called subway circuit (that is, New York suburban theaters), for which producer George Brandt rented the scenery and costumes and employed some of the company.[88] As the national company resumed touring on its return from Berlin, its profits declined severely and costs spiraled, causing an exchange of increasingly worried memoranda between Helburn and Langner. Then in mid-March 1952 the costumes and sets were destroyed by fire. Lemuel Ayers was immediately contracted (on 28 March) to supervise the re-creation of the originals: the new sets cost $22,400 (three times as much as in 1943), and the company was laid off until August. The bad luck continued: one of the new backdrops (the barn) was soon damaged by a collapse caused by rotting ropes in the Grand Theatre, Calgary, in late November

1952, which prompted a prolonged insurance claim.[89] The touring company sputtered out in 1953 with final performances in Washington in March and April—including a celebration of the show's tenth anniversary—and Boston in late April and early May.

The March 1952 layoff triggered contractual questions from the attorneys. The hardheaded Howard Reinheimer (acting for Rodgers and Hammerstein) moved quickly to approach the Guild attorneys (Fitelson and Meyers) claiming a reversion of rights to his clients. However, it seems that this was less a direct threat than a prelude to a discussion of the sale of these rights (and separately, those for *Carousel* and *Allegro*) by the Guild. The haggling began, with meetings between the interested parties and their attorneys on 20 March, 23 May, and 12 June 1952. Armina Marshall was suspicious, writing to Langner on 17 April: "I do not understand why Howard Reinheimer is so eager to buy these three plays. . . . I feel that we should not release our rights on these unless we were paid a pretty penny and I am sure that any kind of deal they are making with us, they expect to benefit by it."[90] The Guild set their price at $1,690,000 for *Oklahoma!* (but was willing to settle at $1,000,000); Rodgers and Hammerstein began at $350,000, raising their offer to $650,000, then $700,000. In mid-1952, the Guild thought it had a strong case because of unspecified tax problems facing Rodgers and Hammerstein. In turn, however, the Guild had taken serious losses on the 1951–52 season ($104,792.31) and clearly needed an injection of capital.[91] On 19 November 1952 Langner instructed his attorneys to keep pitching for $800,000, and Fitelson and Meyers eventually did better, in part, one suspects, because of reports of the film production. The Guild also started backing other horses, including (at least until May 1953) plans for working with another musical team, Alan Lerner and Frederick Loewe, on a musical adaptation of George Bernard Shaw's *Pygmalion* (which the Guild had staged in 1926–27, and which Weill had considered in 1937, and Rodgers and Hammerstein in the mid-1940s, although Hammerstein abandoned the idea because of difficulties in adaptation).[92] On 8 June 1953 the Guild granted the rights to *Oklahoma!* to a new L&H Company (Langner and Helburn), presumably so as to protect both the Guild and the *Oklahoma!* investors from any disadvantageous action arising from the forthcoming sale. The deal was signed on 6 August 1953 for $851,000, which Rodgers and Hammerstein paid in various installments ending on 1 March 1957.[93] The Guild had mixed feelings: according to the *New York Times* (31 July 1953), Helburn's view was that the deal "worked out well for everybody," although Langner was more reticent. Rodgers, however, could also afford to be generous, writing (on 1 September 1953) in response to Helburn, Langner, and Armina Marshall's congratulatory telegram on the opening of the show under the new production team: "I don't want to get maudlin about this but I think it can't do any harm to express in writing the enormous debt that this present operation of *Oklahoma!* owes to you three people. Without your careful ministrations over all these years, the material itself would surely have deteriorated and you have turned over to us, not only a first rate physical production, but a theatre piece in completely first class emotional shape." Hammerstein expressed similar sentiments on 3 September, writing to Helburn: "Thank you for your nice telegram. You have turned over a very well brought up child, and we will try to see that she continues worthy of her early training."[94]

The Guild paid its investors for the last time. Meanwhile, Rodgers and Hammerstein set the seal on their new possession by staging a three-week (expanded to five) limited engagement of *Oklahoma!*—using a good number of the principals from the former national company and the ever-faithful production manager, Jerry Whyte—at the New York City Center, starting on 31 August 1953 to mark what Mayor Vincent Impellitteri had designated Rodgers and Hammerstein Week. (It then toured until 1 May 1954.) At that point, as the newspapers were eager to point out, there were four Rodgers and Hammerstein shows playing concurrently in New York. (The others were *The King and I*, *Me and Juliet*, and *South Pacific*.) *Oklahoma!* had a run at the New York City Center Light Opera from 15 December to 2 January 1966, then a silver anniversary performance (conducted by Rodgers) at New York's Lincoln Center on 26 March 1968 (with Howard da Silva as Jud); for the latter, the orchestrations were revised (so annotations in the scores reveal). But *Oklahoma!* did not return to the Broadway stage until 13 December 1979 (to 24 August 1980; directed by William Hammerstein, with de Mille's choreography re-created by Gemze de Lappe), then again in the London Royal National Theatre 1998 production (directed by Trevor Nunn, with new choreography by Susan Stroman) that opened in New York on 21 March 2002, closing on 23 February 2003.

The Silver Screen

It is clear that while the sale of *Oklahoma!* was triggered by the collapse in the number of first-class performances in 1952, there was another item on the agenda. The main reason why the Guild held on to *Oklahoma!* for much longer than seemed commercially viable—and was in the end able to put significant pressure on Rodgers and Hammerstein—was the anticipation of a Hollywood deal. As we have seen, various offers to make a film of *Oklahoma!* had been made in as early as 1943 and 1944: all were turned down by the Guild because of the profitability of the show on Broadway, yet rumors of filming sporadically resurfaced through the 1940s. On 23 February 1949 *Variety* reported that Rodgers and Hammerstein wanted never to make any film of *Oklahoma!* given their huge income from stage royalties. Likewise, they regularly refused permission to use songs from the show in other films: as Hammerstein noted to Rodgers on 28 March 1949 (in response to a request from MGM for permission to use "Out of My Dreams" in the sequel to *Mrs. Miniver*), "I don't see how we can start giving any releases on *Oklahoma!* By the time it is sold for a picture, the music will be used up on the screen."[95]

Things soon changed. Joshua Logan claimed that Rodgers and Hammerstein had decided in 1950 to form a company to produce film versions of their musicals based on the stage productions, starting with Fred Zinnemann directing *Oklahoma!*[96] On 11 June 1952 Cinerama expressed an interest in filming the stage version of *Oklahoma!* but again the offer was declined. In March 1953, however, Rodgers and Hammerstein became members of the board of directors of the newly formed Magna Theatre Corporation, created by Joseph M. Schenk of Twentieth Century–Fox and Michael Todd, who were promising to begin the output of films in the new Todd-AO widescreen process (a rival to Cinerama), with Arthur Hornblow Jr. as producer (he had produced the Kern-Hammerstein *High, Wide, and Handsome* of 1937). Rumors that the first such film would be of *Oklahoma!* were denied, but none too convincingly: in the *New York Times* of 29 March 1953 Schenk is quoted as saying, "We have no commitment at this point with Rodgers and Hammerstein for any film including *Oklahoma!* but they did not join our company as directors without the thought of contributing to its success." Given the outcome, it seems clear that the Zinnemann idea from 1950 had now been put into effect; Hornblow, too, was working on behalf of a new company called Rodgers and Hammerstein Pictures, Inc. The screenwriters Sonya Levien (who had worked on *State Fair*) and William Ludwig began a project called "Operation Wow!" in early 1953, if not shortly before, producing a complete draft script dated 27 April 1953: this was none other than *Oklahoma!* Agnes de Mille had also completed her scenario for the dream-ballet by early April. On 29 March 1953 the *New*

York Times had said that "the Guild doesn't think the time is ripe yet for a movie"; on 26 April it reported that auditions for the cast were under way.[97]

The plan was to go into production in spring 1954 and release the film later that year. However, there were the usual delays, caused in part by the need to identify a site for the location shooting—eventually, the San Rafael Valley near Nogales, Arizona—and to plant a cornfield with time to grow "as high as an elephant's eye" (the planting was done in January).[98] A final script was prepared by 1 June 1954, subsequently amended through to 14 September; and the cast was announced in the *New York Times* on 19 June. The script follows the original libretto quite closely, as does the film (unlike the case of *Carousel*). However, there were a number of proposed and actual alterations, including, perhaps inevitably, still more changes to the penultimate scene, which brings back the haystack fire from *Green Grow the Lilacs* (as appears in the April 1953 and June 1954 scripts). In the smokehouse scene, "Lonely Room" appears before "Pore Jud Is Daid" in both scripts, with a subsequent reprise at its original location: presumably this was thought to give a better introduction to the character of Jud Fry.[99] However, "Lonely Room" and the reprise were cut on 14 September 1954, as was "It's a Scandal! It's a Outrage!" meaning that neither Jud (Rod Steiger) nor Ali Hakim (Eddie Albert Sr.) got to sing (save Steiger briefly in "Pore Jud Is Daid"), even though they both had singing voices, Steiger having trained in opera. However, the film did make some capital of having Steiger also play dream-Jud in the ballet, a practice that had been instituted, it seems, by Alfred Cibelli in the national company.

The bulk of the materials on the making of the film seems to have been transferred to the Rodgers and Hammerstein Organization in New York, including production reports, payment records, invoices, and tax records.[100] The film orchestrations are also deposited there. In terms of curiosity value, the most intriguing document is an inventory of film reels (but not the reels themselves) containing screen tests for the main roles:

> Curly: Keith Andes, Russell Arms, Ridge Bond, Vic Damone, James Dean, Paul Newman, Danny Scholl, Robert Stack
> Laurey: Joan Evans, Mona Freeman, Florence Henderson, Piper Laurie, Betty Lynn, Joanne Woodward
> Will Parker: Bob Fosse, Jack Russell
> Ado Annie: Barbara Cook, Debbie Reynolds
> Ali Hakim: Jack Carter, Lee Cobb, Kurt Kaznar, Jerry Mann, Eli Wallach
> Jud: Gene Evans, Rufus Jones, Jason Robards Jr., Rod Steiger, Murvyn Vye

For Curly, Laurey, and Jud, actors who had played the roles on stage were screen-tested (Ridge Bond, Florence Henderson, and Murvyn Vye, respectively), although this may have been just out of kindness: the only transfers from stage to screen were Marc Platt (now just one of the dancers, with a bit part) and Bambi Linn (dream-Laurey), working to Agnes de Mille's new choreography. However, other connections were maintained to the original show: Jay Blackton conducted and Robert Russell Bennett did some of the orchestrations before withdrawing from the project because of concerns over the background music.[101] (He was replaced chiefly by Adolph Deutsch.)

Of those screen-tested here, only Rod Steiger—fresh from his triumph in *On the Waterfront*—made it to the final cut. Rodgers had himself suggested Phil Silvers for the role of the peddler and thought that Frank Sinatra would be an ideal Curly (he was a better Nathan Detroit in the film of *Guys and Dolls*, released three weeks after *Oklahoma!* on 3 November 1955).[102] But instead the cast was made up of actors relatively well known in film-musical roles, including Gordon McCrae (Curly), Gene Nelson (Will), and the favorite Eddie Albert Sr., and also the trusty old-timers Charlotte Greenwood (Aunt Eller), Jay C. Flippen (Ike Skidmore), and Roy Barcroft (Cord Elam). Gordon McCrae had already performed excerpts from *Oklahoma!* with Florence Henderson (from the national company) on television in the *General Foods 25th Anniversary Show: A Salute to Rodgers and Hammerstein* (1954). He also starred in the film musicals *On Moonlight Bay* (1951), *About Face* (1952), and *By the Light of the Silvery Moon, The Desert Song*, and *Three Sailors and a Girl* (all 1953). Gene Nelson, too, was in *Three Sailors and a Girl*, as well as starring in *Lullaby of Broadway* (1950), *She's Back on Broadway* (1953), and (second to Tony Curtis) *So This Is Paris* (1955). Shirley Jones, who had started out in the chorus in *South Pacific*, made her film debut as Laurey; she also played the role in the production staged in Paris in June 1955 as part of the U.S. "Salute to France." Jones then shared the lead with McCrae in the film of *Carousel* (1956) and had a distinguished career in Hollywood (an Oscar for Best Supporting Actress in *Elmer Gantry* [1960]; Marian Paroo in *The Music Man* [1962]) before becoming a television icon in *The Partridge Family*. The oddest casting was Gloria Grahame as Ado Annie, since she was primarily known for her recent sultry film noir roles (although she also played Angel in Cecil B. DeMille's *The Greatest Show on Earth* of 1952). Other cast credits went to James Whitmore (Andrew Carnes), Barbara Lawrence (Gertie Cummings), and James Mitchell (dream-Curly). Mitchell had worked with the American

20. "And that's about as fur as she c'n go!" Will Parker (Lee Dixon) teaches the newfangled two-step to Aunt Eller (Betty Garde) in the 1943 staging of "Kansas City." Lemuel Ayers's spectacular design for act 1, scene 1 is clear, with Laurey's house stage left, a picket fence, and a homely quilt. Locating "Kansas City" at a railway station in the 1998 Royal National Theatre production stemmed from the 1955 film. (Wide World Photos)

Ballet Theatre and also took specialty dance roles in musicals such as *Deep in My Heart* (1954).

This was director Fred Zinnemann's first musical, and the filming was made problematic by the decision to shoot each scene twice, once in 35 mm (to be shown in CinemaScope) and once in 65 mm (for Todd-AO): the dual format is one reason why the film came in way over budget at $6,800,000.[103] The outdoor scenes were shot on location for seven weeks from 14 July 1954 in the San Rafael Valley and elsewhere in Arizona and New Mexico. The interior and dance sequences were shot later at MGM studios, with filming completed on 6 December 1954. The Todd-AO version (the first in the new process) was released on 11 October 1955 and played at the Rivoli Theatre, New York, for more than a year before the film had its general release in CinemaScope on 1 November 1956. The two versions look and sound significantly different, and they have different openings: the opening credits in the Todd-AO version play as if in a theater, with stage curtains drawn back to reveal the scene, while the CinemaScope version begins with Curly riding through cornstalks. Bennett felt that the widescreen format was inappropriate for such a "darling little show of vignettes of little people," and Rodgers was even less enthusiastic: "Visually, parts of the film were impressive, with some stunning shots of elephant-eye-high corn, the surrey ride, and the cloud-filled Arizona sky. But the wide-screen process was not always ideal for the more intimate scenes, and I don't think the casting was totally satisfactory. At any rate, from then on — except for *South Pacific* — Oscar and I left moving pictures to moving-picture people and stayed clear of any involvement with subsequent film versions of our musicals."[104] However, the film was a box-office smash and received Academy Awards for Best Music and Best Sound Recording.

Although the Theatre Guild had no further rights to *Oklahoma!* it insisted acrimoniously and at some length on being properly acknowledged in the title credits to the film.[105] Peace was soon restored, however. On 12 October 1955 Helburn wrote to Rodgers: "It was really a very moving experience for me to see *Oklahoma!* again in its latest and most sumptuous garb! It brought back infinite memories of our struggles eleven [*sic*] years ago and an awareness of all that has eventuated since then for you both. What a fortunate coming together of talents that was for the American theatre — the two of you and Agnes and Reuben and Russell and Lem and Miles — certainly the all American team for the decade!" Rodgers replied the next day:

> Oscar and I are so grateful for your kind and generous letter about the *Oklahoma!* film. We will never stop being grateful to you and Lawrence for having started this whole thing going.
> It was good to see you the other night and as soon as we get *Pipe Dream* off our shoulders let's get together and have some fun.
> Much love from all of us.
> Affectionately.[106]

It had been a long journey for "Helburn's Folly," and one that finally reached a new home.

Appendix A

A Time Line for *Oklahoma!*
5 May 1942 to 31 March 1943

This chronology lists all precisely or approximately datable events pertaining to *Oklahoma!* up to the New York opening, chiefly from documents in *NHb* TG (to which all document citations refer unless otherwise stated), the *New York Times*, and related materials. For further details of these sources (and the *sigla* by which I refer to them), see Appendix B. Events described in personal reminiscences and the like are not included unless their dates are reasonably secure. Other newspaper articles (mostly from the clippings in *NHb* TG Pressbook 197) are mentioned only if they preempt, or differ from, the *New York Times*.

Abbreviations

GGtL	*Green Grow the Lilacs* (play)
OH	Oscar Hammerstein 2nd
TH	Theresa Helburn
LL	Lawrence Langner
NYT	*New York Times*
RR	Richard Rodgers

5 May 1942 (Tu)	Warren Munsell (Guild business manager) outlines shared financing of 1942–43 season with Marcus Heiman and Lee Shubert, including their willingness to fund a musical based on *GGtL*; 97/"W. Munsell Memos 1939–42."
15 May (F)	TH reports *GGtL* project at Guild meeting; 97/green folder "Munsell."
18 May (M)	Russel Crouse turns down offer to adapt *GGtL* and is unable to attend meeting that afternoon; 37/"Russel Crouse." TH informs Riggs of plans for play as a musical; 113/"Lynn Riggs" no. 2. TH prepares notes on adapting play; 118/8 (dated 18 May but no year).
27 May (W)	John Gassner (Guild's chief play reader) suggests Aaron Copland for *GGtL* if TH no longer wishes to pursue Kurt Weill, and asks whether TH has heard Earl Robinson play for her; 52/"Gassner Memos 1942–3."
29 May (F)	Gassner suggests that TH should write to Earl Robinson, having heard his music; ibid.
12 June (F)	Gassner suggests Roy Harris and Ferde Grofé for *GGtL*, or Earl Robinson to write stirring numbers; ibid.
16 June (Tu)	RR sends script (of *GGtL*?) to Joshua Logan; 118/8 (reproduced in Wilk, *Ok!* 108).
14 July (Tu)	Munsell pursues negotiations with MGM over film rights for *GGtL*; 97/"W. Munsell Memos 1939–42."
16 July (Th)	Garrett Leverton writes to Guild re film rights; Wc TG 2.
17 July (F)	TH sends a copy of *GGtL* to Dorothy Hammerstein; 58/"Oscar Hammerstein" (pink tab).
20 July (M)	Munsell continues negotiations with MGM; 97/"W. Munsell Memos 1939–42."
22 July (W)	Guild announces that RR, OH, and Lorenz Hart will soon begin work on a musical version of *GGtL*; *NYT*, 23 July 1943. RR seeks contact with John O'Hara, author of book for *Pal Joey* (1940); 124/"O."
28 July (Tu)	OH hopes to write a lyric for Artie Shaw, even though he is now juggling three shows at once; Wc HC 5 of 9/"1942/S."
30 July (Th)	Howard Reinheimer writes to Guild re contractual arrangements for *GGtL*; Wc TG 2.
early August	Contract prepared for RR, OH, and Riggs; Wc TG 1 (dated by month only).
9 Aug. (Su)	*NYT*: *GGtL* will not be ready "until about Christmas"; OH plans to open *Carmen Jones* on Broadway in October; *Show Boat* is ready for a Broadway revival sponsored by MGM; the Harbach–OH–Kern "musical play" *Hayfoot, Strawfoot* is in preparation.

12 Aug. (W)	OH approaches John Charles Thomas about role in musical play with RR; *Wc* HC 5 of 9/"1942/T."
20 Aug. (Th)	Munsell continues discussions with MGM, but MGM is unwilling to finance musical to extent of $25,000; 97/ "W. Munsell Memos 1939–42." OH turns down request (3 Aug.) to read a cowboy play by E. P. Conkle, Department of Drama, University of Texas at Austin, because of potential conflicts with *GGtL*; *Wc* HC 5 of 9/"1942/C."
23 Aug. (Su)	*NYT*: Lynn Riggs is now a private in the army and will write no new plays for the duration of his tour.
24 Aug. (M)	OH refuses invitation to a cocktail party from Victor Roudin on the 27th because he will go to Doylestown on Wednesday for a week of solid writing; *Wc* HC 5 of 9/"1942/R."
27 Aug. (Th)	OH tells Louella Parsons that he is working on *GGtL* with RR and Hart; *Wc* HC 6 of 9/loose papers.
31 Aug. (M)	*NYT*: over the weekend OH, RR, and Hart began work on *GGtL* at RR's home in Connecticut; production planned for fall.
2 Sept. (W)	OH offers to meet Dorothea MacFarland (chorus singer in *Oklahoma!*) on his return from California; *Wc* HC 5 of 9/ "1942/Mc."
5 Sept. (Sa)	*NYT*: OH has gone to Hollywood for ASCAP meeting, also to audition actors and singers for *Carmen Jones*, *GGtL*, and Broadway revival of *Show Boat*.
17 Sept. (Th)	*NYT*: OH has postponed *Carmen Jones* to work full-time on *GGtL*; it will not involve Hart, contrary to previous Guild announcement; RR and OH are now completing work at OH's farm in Pennsylvania; Hart is in Mexico gathering local color for "a sort of good-will musical" planned for the present season, "Muchacho." Leo Kerz writes to TH asking to do set design for *GGtL*; 118/7. OH writes to Louis Dreyfus (London) saying that he is working with RR on a show for the Theatre Guild, plus *Carmen Jones* and the *Show Boat* revival, while also considering an MGM contract; *Wc* HC 6 of 9/loose papers.
18 Sept. (F)	*NYT*: TH has returned from California previous day and announces that *GGtL* should go into rehearsal some time in December; Hart is not in Mexico but in the Doctors' Hospital, New York, being treated for "undulant fever" contracted while in Mexico doing research for "Muchacho."
23 Sept. (W)	Richard Halliday, Mary Martin's husband, says that Martin is not interested in the *Show Boat* revival but wishes to know more of *GGtL*; Leighton Brill requests news of progress on *GGtL*; *Wc* HC 5 of 9/"September 1942." Max Gordon promises OH to help raise money for a show (probably *GGtL*); *Wc* HC 5 of 9/"October 1942."

24 Sept. (Th)	Agnes de Mille writes to TH asking to do choreography for *GGtL*; 39/"Agnes de Mille" (yellow tab). Dorothy Johnson asks OH for audition; *Wc* HC 5 of 9/"1942/J."
26 Sept. (Sa)	*Daily Mirror*: Rouben Mamoulian is in New York to discuss directing *GGtL*.
28 Sept. (M)	TH informs Riggs of progress on act 1 (which should be finished by mid-October, although RR has been called out of town); 113/"Lynn Riggs" no. 2.
30 Sept. (W)	LL writes to RR about de Mille and suggests he go see *Rodeo*; 125/"Ra" (transcribed in Wilk, *Ok!* 114).
1 Oct. (Th)	Auditions with OH (including Alfred Drake; Lee Dixon also invited but probably did not appear); 123/1.
2 Oct. (F)	Letter of agreement from RR and OH to Guild to provide book, lyrics, and music for *GGtL*; $200 advance royalty; play to be completed by 31 Dec. 1943 [1942?]; Guild to have fifteen-day option to accept; *Wc* TG 4. Jessica Dragonette suggested for Laurey; *NHb* TG 123/1; *Wc* HC 5 of 9/ "October 1942."
3 Oct. (Sa)	Munsell reviews contract sent by Reinheimer and asks for later date of performance; 97/green folder "Munsell" (compare the contract in *Wc* TG 4 dated [blank] October but not signed).
4 Oct. (Su)	*NYT*: OH has postponed *Carmen Jones* to next January, and revival of *Show Boat* to next summer, to work on *GGtL*. Lou Calhern has heard rumors of Rouben Mamoulian directing, but suggests Robert Ross; 118/7. John M. Furhman asks OH for audition; *Wc* HC 5 of 9/"1942/F."
6 Oct. (Tu)	Auditions with OH, including Alfred Drake reading Curly; 123/1.
8 Oct. (Th)	Onstage auditions, including Ruth Weston for Aunt Eller; TH suggests that RR and OH attend Madison Square Garden rodeo; 123/1.
12 Oct. (M)	Auditions with OH, TH, RR; 123/1.
14 Oct. (W)	OH turns down requests for audition for *GGtL* by Ruth Ives and Millicent Hoyt McKean (in the latter case, because he is too busy writing the script); *Wc* HC 5 of 9/"1942/I," "1942/Mc." Leighton Brill requests news of progress and casting; *Wc* HC 5 of 9/"October 1942."
16 Oct. (F)	Premiere of Copland's *Rodeo* attended by OH, TH, RR. OH tells Mrs. Michael Moldow that there are no parts for children in his new show; *Wc* HC 5 of 9/"1942/M."
18 Oct. (Su)	LL forwards to OH a letter from Oliver Smith (designer of *Rodeo*) asking to do set design for *GGtL*; 118/8 (dated 18 Sept. but probably Oct. given that it refers to LL having missed *Rodeo*).

23 Oct. (F)	Suzanne Foster (singer) suggested for cast; 123/1.
26 Oct. (M)	TH cables Bretaigne Windust perhaps re directing *GGtL*; 118/8. Frank Sheil of Samuel French and Co. writes to Riggs re contractual arrangements and says that OH has completed act 1; *NHb* Riggs 5/113.
28 Oct. (W)	OH tells Laurence Schwab that when he finishes *GGtL* "next week," he will send a copy of the script to quell Schwab's skepticism about the project; *Wc* HC 6 of 9/loose papers. OH tells Len Mence that no part is suitable for him in *GGtL*; *Wc* HC 5 of 9/"1942/M."
3 Nov. (Tu)	Paul Porter asks to stage-manage *GGtL*; *Wc* HC 5 of 9/ "1942/P."
6 Nov. (F)	OH's secretary defers request from Arthur List (made on 30 Oct.) to be considered as conductor for *GGtL*; *Wc* HC 5 of 9/"1942/L." Jacob Steisel recommends Oliver Smith as designer for *GGtL* (OH responds favorably on the 12th); *Wc* HC 5 of 9/"1942/S."
7 Nov. (Sa)	Laurence Schwab tells OH that he is willing to read script of *GGtL*; *Wc* HC 5 of 9/"November 1942."
12 Nov. (Th)	OH tells Schwab he will send script next week when copies have been made; *Wc* HC 5 of 9/"1942/S."
15 Nov. (Su)	*NYT*: LL writes (on the twenty-fifth-anniversary season of Guild) that *GGtL* is going into rehearsal; Alfred Drake is being considered for lead; show is to be penultimate offering of season (final one yet to be chosen from two comedies).
16 Nov. (M)	Copies of OH's script start to be distributed by Guild; 118/8.
17 Nov. (Tu)	TH informs Munsell that she is awaiting the contract from Reinheimer, that Max Gordon may persuade Columbia Pictures to invest, but that the film rights are causing delay; 97/"Munsell Memos to T.H. 1941." OH's secretary notifies George Irving of potential audition on 24 Nov.; *Wc* HC 5 of 9/"1942/I." OH tells Charles Ruggles of possibility of a musical by OH and RR for Ruggles, Charles Winninger, and Vera Zorina, although a scenario is not yet ready given the work on Theatre Guild show; *Wc* HC 5 of 9/"1942/R."
19 Nov. (Th)	OH registers "Oklahoma" at Library of Congress for copyright; *Wc* TG 1.
20 Nov. (F)	Felicia Sorel requests meeting with OH to discuss choreography for *GGtL* (meeting arranged for 25 Nov. by OH's secretary on 23 Nov.); *Wc* HC 5 of 9/"1942/S."
21 Nov. (Sa)	TH arranges for Elia Kazan to collect script; 118/8 (reproduced in Wilk, *Ok!* 109).
25 Nov. (W)	Sara Greenspan asks about reserving a theater, which is pressing if opening is to be February; 161/"1942." OH meets with Felicia Sorel to discuss choreography; *Wc* HC 5 of 9/

	"1942/S." OH invites Dorothy Johnson for audition before RR on 1 Dec. (she had requested an audition on 24 Sept.); *Wc* HC 5 of 9/"1942/J." OH refuses Mrs. Brock Pemberton's invitation to co-chair the opening of American Theatre Wing Merchant Seaman's Club because of work on *GGtL*; *Wc* HC 5 of 9/"1942/P."
26 Nov. (Th; Thanksgiving)	Kazan cables TH turning down *GGtL*; 118/8 (reproduced in Wilk, *Ok!* 110).
27 Nov. (F)	OH writes to Arthur Freed turning down MGM contract and informing him of progress on *GGtL*; *Wc* HC 6 of 9/loose papers. LL writes to OH introducing Maria Gambarelli (actress and dancer) for cast; 123/1.
1 Dec. (Tu)	*Daily News*: OH wants Charlotte Greenwood for cast. RR and OH sign agreement with Riggs to adapt play; *Wc* TG 1.
2 Dec. (W)	TH sends script and play to Rouben Mamoulian; 118/8 (reproduced in Wilk, *Ok!* 110).
3 Dec. (Th)	*NYT*: OH has completed book for *GGtL* and is "wrestling" with lyrics; rehearsals to begin late December or early January for a February opening; Joan Roberts will probably be one of the leads (Laurey); *Carmen Jones* is still a possibility for spring, despite reports of its being held over to next season.
4 Dec. (F)	Gassner suggests Valentine Grenville for cast; 52/"Gassner Memos 1942–3."
7 Dec. (M)	OH tells his Hollywood agent, Frank Orsatti, that he has no role for Ilona Massey; *Wc* HC 5 of 9/"1942/O." OH says he has no time to advise Josephine Shelton on handling new songs because he is too busy finishing *GGtL*; *Wc* HC 5 of 9/ "1942/S."
8 Dec. (Tu)	LL writes on inability to cast "Andzia" (last name unknown) and says that RR and OH have total control of casting; TH cables Nate Blumberg of Universal Pictures to recruit Deanna Durbin for Laurey; 123/1.
9 Dec. (W)	Mildred Webber of the William Morris Agency suggests Joseph Buloff for Peddler; 123/1.
10 Dec. (Th)	Universal Pictures says that Durbin is unavailable due to filming commitments; 123/1.
11 Dec. (F)	Contract negotiations with Alfred Drake; 123/1.
14 Dec. (M)	OH promises Dorothea MacFarland to let her know when chorus auditions will be held (rehearsals will probably begin latter part of January); *Wc* HC 5 of 9/"1942/Mc."
15 Dec. (Tu)	Frank Sheil of Samuel French and Co. tells Riggs that agreement is finally closed, that OH has completed the book, and that work is under way on music and lyrics; *NHb* Riggs 5/113.
17 Dec. (Th)	*Daily News*: Elizabeth Patterson to take the lead.

21 Dec. (M)	*NYT*: Max Gordon has dropped *Carmen Jones* for current season because of commitments in Hollywood; OH is still seeking a spring production; *GGtL* will go into rehearsal around 20 Jan. and is due in New York in March; Joan Roberts is set for the cast. Alfred Drake signs Standard Minimum Contract; 118/16. Francis Feist repeats request made "a number of weeks ago" to design costumes for *GGtL* and *Carmen Jones*; Wc HC 5 of 9/"1942/F."
22 Dec. (Tu)	Joan Roberts signs Standard Minimum Contract; 118/16.
29 Dec. (Tu)	TH meets with David Lowe about fund-raising; 85/"David Lowe." TH reports to Munsell on difficulties with MGM and the failure of Max Gordon to deliver Columbia investment; 97/"Munsell Memos to T.H. 1941."
31 Dec. (Th)	Lowe writes to TH outlining fund-raising plans; Wc TG 12.
1 Jan. 1943 (F)	*NYT*: Jerome Whyte to be stage manager.
4 Jan. (M)	Lowe meets with TH and agrees to act as fund-raiser for $50 per week; 85/"David Lowe."
5 Jan. (Tu)	LL tries to interest Bertram Bloch as investor and invites him to audition on 8 Jan.; 124/"B." Lowe outlines fund-raising strategy to TH; Wc TG 12.
6 Jan. (W)	Adelaide Klein suggested for Aunt Eller; 123/1.
7 Jan. (Th)	*Daily News*: *GGtL* to go into rehearsal 25 Jan. to open early March; problems of labeling the work; cast is made up of unknowns; it is hoped to be another *Show Boat*.
8 Jan. (F)	TH informs Munsell that she has to raise $100,000; 97/"Lieut. Colonel Munsell." Audition for investors, Studio 520, Steinway Hall, 4 P.M.
10 Jan. (Su)	Guild prepares list of possible investors; Wc TG 12.
11 Jan (M)	OH writes to Leighton Brill noting casting difficulties, given that to date only Drake, Roberts, and Garde are committed; Wc HC 2 of 9/"Selections."
12 Jan. (Tu)	TH notes that de Mille, Mamoulian, Drake, Roberts, Robert Russell (for Jud?), Holm, and Garde are committed; 118/7 (another copy in 123/7).
14 Jan. (Th)	J. E. Brulatour Inc. invests $5,000 in show; Wc TG 12.
15 Jan. (F)	Audition at apartment of Natalie Spencer; 85/"David Lowe."
mid Jan.	TH cables for meeting with Miles White; 118/8.
16 Jan. (Sa)	Sylvia Hahlo (agent) renews recommendation for Buloff (and Romney Brent) as Peddler and seeks news of decision on Robert Russell; 123/1.
17 Jan. (Su)	*New York Herald Tribune*: *GGtL* to start rehearsals on 1 Feb., and to open on 8 Mar.; contains twelve songs "in a more-or-less popular ballad style"; Mamoulian will probably direct; Drake and Roberts are cast; Holm has been mentioned. *Sunday Journal*: casting is virtually complete; rehearsals will start within two weeks. "This musical brings the split, at least

	temporary and probably permanent, of Richard Rodgers and Lorenz Hart"; Garde signed yesterday; Drake and Roberts are cast.
19 Jan. (Tu)	NYT: GGtL to start rehearsals on 1 Feb. and be staged in New York late in March, but not at Guild Theatre; Mamoulian will produce; RR says it is "neither an opera nor an operetta"; Alfred Drake and Joan Roberts have been cast; Betty Garde and Celeste Holm recently added; "Two other important roles, one a peddler and the other a new character recently added, are yet to be filled"; rehearsals to last four or five weeks; tryouts to be in New Haven and Boston; Broadway theater not yet selected. Guild holds auditions for Will Parker (Walter Donohue, Danny Drayson, Fred Barry, Hie Thomson, Jack Blair, "Mark" [Marc] Platt), Lotta (Lorraine de Woods), Peddler (Joseph Buloff, Zero Mostel), and Ado Annie (Shirley Booth, and perhaps Eugenia Rawls, Georgette Starr, and Ann Terry); TH attempts to recruit Shirley Temple; LL attempts to recruit Groucho Marx for Peddler; 123/1.
21 Jan. (Th)	Lemuel Ayers negotiates over fee for sets but wishes to sign contract soon; White cables TH to say that he will be back in town Monday; 118/8. TH informs Munsell of MGM agreement to secure option to retain film rights on Riggs's play, and of the fact that she has raised $65,000 from investors; 97/"Lieut. Colonel Munsell."
22 Jan. (F)	OH tells Laurence Schwab that he has no time for reading, with six numbers still unwritten for his show; Wc HC 5 of 9/ "1942/S."
23 Jan. (Sa)	RR, OH, and Guild sign agreement with MGM to secure option to obtain film rights on Riggs's play; Wc TG 1. RR and OH sign contract with Guild to write book, lyrics, and music; Wc TG 1.
24 Jan. (Su)	NYT: MGM has offered the film rights on GGtL (which the Guild "is converting into an elaborate musical") for $40,000.
25 Jan. (M)	Auditions with de Mille for "tap dancers and ballet boys and girls" at Guild Theatre; New York Post, Brooklyn Citizen, Women's Wear Daily, New York World-Telegram, Daily Mirror, 21 Jan; NYT, 22 Jan.
27 Jan. (W)	Photo of tap and ballet dancers auditioning appears in PM. Groucho Marx turns down Peddler; 123/1.
28 Jan. (Th)	LL attempts to get Anthony Quinn for Jud; John Haggott, production manager, makes queries about Ward Bond's voice (for Jud?); 123/1. Audition at apartment of Jules Glaenzer; 85/"David Lowe."

29 Jan. (F)	NYT: further auditions today for "tap and ballet boys and girls" at Guild Theatre (see also *Brooklyn Citizen* and *New York Post*, 27 Jan.; *Brooklyn Eagle*, *New York Journal-American*, *Newark Star-Ledger*, 28 Jan.). Standard Minimum Contract drafted for Betty Garde; 118/16. LL seeks roping act (Montie Montana); 123/1. Letter of engagement sent to de Mille; Wc TG 2. Herbert Langner invests $1,000; Wc TG 12.
30 Jan. (Sa)	Ayers signs contract; Wc TG 2. Ayers invests $1,000 of his fee in show; Wc TG 12. TH informs Munsell that she believes she has raised all the money needed, and that the show will go into rehearsal in a week; 97/"Lieut. Colonel Munsell."
31 Jan. (Su)	NYT: Guild has canceled plans for final comedy of season (Peggy Lamson's *Respectfully Yours*) thereby causing problems over its subscription guarantees.
1 Feb. (M)	NYT: Mamoulian has signed contract (but letter of agreement prepared only on 5 Feb.). *Brooklyn Citizen*: GGtL goes into rehearsal on Tuesday; Mamoulian will direct; show will open in New Haven on 11 Mar., then have two weeks in Boston from the 15th. White signs contract; Wc TG 1, 2 (with additional bonus agreed; 118/16). Haggott cables Ward Bond, Paul Guilfoyle, Arthur Hunnicut, and Anthony Quinn (and Howard da Silva?) re Jud; 123/1.
2 Feb. (T)	NYT: Joseph Buloff to play in GGtL; rehearsals to start next Monday. OH apologizes to Carl E. Weininger for not having looked at songs he sent on 11 Jan. because he has been in the country finishing the script of GGtL; Wc HC 5 of 9/ "1942/W."
3 Feb. (W)	Shirley Temple's mother turns down part on her behalf; rehearsal call issued for 8 Feb.; 123/1. Holm signs Standard Minimum Contract; 118/16. Guild Associates Inc. invest $15,000, Al Greenstone $1,250, Sherman and Marjorie Ewing $1,000 each; Wc TG 12.
4 Feb. (Th)	Chappell and Co. agree on sheet music royalties (two cents per copy to Guild); Wc TG 2. TH notes casting suggestions (for what?); Haggott cables da Silva saying that RR and OH are prepared to rewrite Jud's songs; Mary Pickford (in Hollywood) cables TH confirming the "definite no" from Mrs. Temple; 123/1. Guild distributes copies of script, including one in "blue and silver covers (with new last scene)"; 118/8.
5 Feb. (F)	NYT: Guild issues another emergency call for chorus boys and girls. Letter of agreement prepared for Mamoulian; Wc TG 2.
6 Feb. (Sa)	TH writes to Jack Hickisch for details of square-dance calls; 118/8. Negotiations with Joan Roberts's agent over salary increase when production costs paid off; 118/16.

7 Feb. (Su)	*NYT*: *GGtL* to be staged at Forty-sixth Street Theatre.
8 Feb. (M)	*NYT*: Lemuel Ayers (sets) and Miles White (costumes) are to work on *GGtL*; rehearsals begin today; Lee Dixon is in cast. Riggs asks TH for information about progress on show; 118/8. Brooks Costume Co. agrees to reduce cost of costumes by $5,000 as investment in show; *Wc* TG 12. TH cables Lee Shubert re putting show in St. James Theatre but wants the seats re-covered; 118/8 (reproduced in Wilk, *Ok!* 151). Standard Minimum Contract prepared for Howard da Silva as Jud; Alfred Drake signs run-of-play contract; 118/16. TH writes to Drake's agent, Edith van Cleve, about increased fee (to $500 per week) when production costs are paid off; Jerome Whyte, stage manager, cables Juanita Juarez (Lotta?) to come to theater; 123/1. Eric Victor signs Standard Minimum Contract; 125/"U–V" (reported in the *New York Post*, 15 Feb.). First rehearsal call; 58/"Oscar Hammerstein, *Oklahoma!*: Costumes and Correspondence."
9 Feb. (Tu)	Haggott prepares preliminary salary list for show; 123/7. George Church called for rehearsal; 123/1. Guild prepares letter of engagement for Jacob Schwartzdorf (Jay Blackton) to conduct; *Wc* TG 2.
10 Feb. (W)	*NYT*: *GGtL* to open in New Haven on 11 Mar., then two weeks in Boston from 15th. Haggott writes to Office of Price Administration for permission to purchase shoes; 118/8 (another copy in 58/"Oscar Hammerstein, *Oklahoma!*: Costumes and Correspondence"; concerns are also noted in the *New York Post*, 15 Feb.). Katharine Sergava signs Standard Minimum Contract; 118/16. Da Silva called for rehearsal; 123/1. Various singers and dancers removed from cast (for no-show at first call?), including Jane Lawrence (but see below, 20 Feb.); 123/1 (dated 10 Jan. 1943 but must be Feb.).
before 11 Feb.	White has prepared list of costumes (which has a penciled annotation dated 11 Feb. and also references to sketches); 58/"Oscar Hammerstein, *Oklahoma!*: Costumes and Correspondence."
11 Feb. (Th)	*NYT*: *GGtL* to open in St. James Theatre (no date given). *New York Herald Tribune*: Whyte has signed contract as stage manager. Contract agreed with Shuberts to open at St. James Theatre on 31 Mar.; *Wc* TG 4.
13 Feb. (Sa)	TH(?) responds to Riggs's request for information on progress, discussing the title ("Away We Go!"), cast and production, and the fact that the song "Oklahoma" has just been written; 118/8 (partly reproduced in Wilk, *Ok!* 197).
14 Feb. (Su)	*Sunday News*: shortage of men for chorus. Henry Vincent offers himself as understudy; 125/"U–V."

15 Feb. (M)	NYT: show to be called "Away We Go!" Barry Kelley (Ike Skidmore) called for rehearsal; 123/1. Ongoing negotiations with Shubert re St. James Theatre and the payment of stagehands and musicians; 118/8. Guild receives notice that George Church has been drafted; 58/"Oscar Hammerstein, *Oklahoma!*: Costumes and Correspondence."
16 Feb. (Tu)	NYT: all roles in "Away We Go!" now filled by the engagement of Howard da Silva; Guild is uncertain whether to keep the show in Boston for a third week to avoid competition with *Ziegfeld Follies* (to open 1 Apr.). Brooks Costume Co. provides estimate for costumes ($15,000); 58/"Oscar Hammerstein, *Oklahoma!*: Costumes and Correspondence." Jack Harwood ("fancy roper") called for rehearsal; 123/1.
17 Feb. (W)	David Lowe submits report on prospective investors; Wc TG 12. Contract settled with Vail Scenic Construction Co.; 58/"Oscar Hammerstein, *Oklahoma!*: Costumes and Correspondence." Sherry Britton (Lotta) and Owen Martin (Cord Elam) called for rehearsal; 123/1.
19 Feb. (F)	*New York Morning Telegraph*: Jacob Schwartzdorf has signed contract and will conduct a twenty-eight-piece orchestra. *New York Herald Tribune*: Marc Platt, Katherine Sergava, Kate Friedlich, and Eric Victor will have specialty dancing numbers in "Away We Go!" I. Miller and Sons submits invoice for shoes ($1,538.60); 58/"Oscar Hammerstein, *Oklahoma!*: Costumes and Correspondence."
20 Feb. (Sa)	NYT: Platt, Sergava, Friedlich, and Victor will have specialty dancing numbers; Jacob Schwartzdorf will direct twenty-eight-piece orchestra. Jane Lawrence (Gertie and understudy) called for rehearsal; 123/1.
21 Feb. (Su)	Guild prepares production timetable for New Haven; 118/8 (reproduced in Wilk, *Ok!* 165).
22 Feb. (M)	Possible run-through of show; de Mille, *"Dance to the Piper" and "Promenade Home,"* 1: 325.
23 Feb. (Tu)	*New York Herald Tribune*: Barry Kelley has joined cast.
24 Feb. (W)	NYT: Ralph Riggs and Barry Kelley have joined cast; "Away We Go" to open on Broadway in first week of April but may yet stay in Boston a third week to avoid conflict with *Ziegfeld Follies*. Guild acknowledges investment of $15,000 from Columbia Pictures Corp.; Wc TG 2. Brooks Costume Co. asks about the additional five outfits (capes and hats) for dancing girls in ballet; 58/"Oscar Hammerstein, *Oklahoma!*: Costumes and Correspondence." Last rehearsal call for new cast members; 123/1. Run-through held, on which TH makes notes, including suggestions for cuts; 118/8.

25 Feb. (Th)	*New York Sun*: Edwin Clay has joined cast (also *NYT*, 27 Feb.). TH informs Munsell of progress; 97/"Lieut. Colonel Munsell."
26 Feb. (F)	*Boston Daily Record*: Sherry Britton signed to play Lotta. Understudy sought for Joan Roberts; 123/1. LL writes to Selective Service System in support of Alfred Drake's appeal against being drafted; 120/17. LL sends script to Jed Harris (possible investor?) after both had attended a rehearsal (run-through?) that afternoon; 124/"Ha."
2 Mar. (Tu)	TH asks Riggs for advice on title; 118/8 (reproduced in Wilk, *Ok!* 197). Max Dreyfus (Chappell and Co.) assumes one-third of orchestration costs up to New York opening; Wc TG 19. I. Weiss and Sons submits invoice (c. $550) for cloth material for sets; 58/"Oscar Hammerstein, *Oklahoma!*: Costumes and Correspondence." Ayers paid $100 for an additional backdrop; Wc TG 2. A "dress rehearsal" held (but without sets or costumes); 87/"McA–McZ" (LL writes to Evelyn Walsh McClean, 6 Mar., apologizing for not attending a dinner party because of a dress rehearsal of *Oklahoma!* "last Tuesday").
4 Mar. (Th)	Dress parade at Brooks Costume Co.; 118/8 (reproduced in Wilk, *Ok!* 165). I. Weiss and Sons submits invoice ($295) for cloth material for additional drop; 58/"Oscar Hammerstein, *Oklahoma!*: Costumes and Correspondence."
5 Mar. (F)	Production schedule (costs) prepared; 118/7 (another copy in 122/10; reproduced in Wilk, *Ok!* 104).
6 Mar. (Sa)	Account sheet prepared showing receipts and expenses; 118/7. Vail Scenic Construction Co. submits invoice for sets ($6,772.19; of which $4,234 has already been paid in two installments on 17 and 27 Feb.); 58/"Oscar Hammerstein, *Oklahoma!*: Costumes and Correspondence." Load-out of Guild Theatre; 118/8 (reproduced in Wilk, *Ok!* 165).
7 Mar. (Su)	Stage crew travels to New Haven; 118/8 (reproduced in Wilk, *Ok!* 165).
8 Mar. (M)	*Boston Traveler*: tickets for Boston run on sale from this morning. Stage setup in Shubert Theatre, New Haven (–9 Mar.). Joan Roberts signs run-of-play contract; 118/16.
9 Mar. (Tu)	Company travels to Shubert Theatre, New Haven, with reading rehearsal on set at 10 A.M., and walk-through rehearsal in evening; 118/8 (reproduced in Wilk, *Ok!* 165; see also the report in the *Daily News*, 9 Mar.). Bambi Linn signs run-of-play contract; 118/16. TH(?) writes to Hickisch explaining that his square-dance calls are not being used; 124/"Ha." S. N. Behrman invests $5,000; Guild agrees "pool" (with Lee Shubert and Marcus Heiman) to invest $25,000 and guarantee $15,000 bond; Wc TG 12.

10 Mar. (W)	Orchestra and company rehearsal(s?), 10–6, then dress rehearsal without orchestra at 7 P.M.; 118/8 (reproduced in Wilk, *Ok!* 165). Guild requests funds from "pool"; *Wc* TG 12.
11 Mar. (Th)	Finish lighting in morning, then company rehearsal with orchestra, 12–3; 118/8 (reproduced in Wilk, *Ok!* 165). "Away We Go!" opens 8:30 P.M.; runs to Saturday.
12 Mar. (F)	Sheet music of five songs from "Away We Go!" registered for copyright; *Wc* HC 6 of 9/"O.H. Songs 1920–45."
14 Mar. (Su)	Company and crew travel to Boston.
15 Mar. (M)	"Away We Go!" opens at Colonial Theatre, Boston. Lilian Riegelman and Ralph Friedman each invest $2,500 in *Oklahoma!* *Wc* TG 12
16 Mar. (Tu)	*NYT*: "Away We Go!" to be called "Oklahoma" on its New York opening; had advance sales of $25,000 in Boston (compare press release from Joseph Heidt, Guild press officer, in *NYp* MWEZ/+/n.c./25609, folder 5). *New York News*: if "Away We Go!" is successful, Guild will produce two musicals per year. Brooks Costume Co. sends note about additional costumes (including one for George Church "for specialty in wedding"); 118/7. Edward Curtin sends comments on Boston performance; 124/"Ca."
17 Mar. (W)	*Variety*: "Away We Go!" took in $10,000 in New Haven. New Haven and Boston notices sent to Harry Cohn (Columbia) noting impending change of title to "Oklahoma"; 120/11. Boston notices sent to S. N. Behrman; 124/"B." William Rose II invests $2,500; *Wc* TG 12.
18 Mar. (Th)	*NYT*: "Oklahoma" [*sic*] to open on Broadway on 31 Mar.; according to Heidt, the show "is in such good shape that it does not need any more time on tour for polishing."
19 Mar. (F)	Heidt issues press release with details of "Oklahoma"; *NYp* MWEZ/+/n.c./ 25609A, folder 1.
20 Mar. (Sa)	"Sadie" (Sara Greenspan) in Guild office in New York writes to LL in Boston asking about seat allocations for New York opening, says she is pleased about Boston success, discusses allocation of complimentary seats in New York, notes investments from Mrs. Riegelman and Ralph Friedman, and asks LL's intentions for the Rose investment; 118/7.
22 Mar. (M)	Heidt issues further press release with details of "Oklahoma"; *NYp* MWEZ/+/n.c./ 25609, folder 1.
24 Mar. (W)	Display advertisements for *Oklahoma!* (so styled) start to appear daily in the *NYT*, etc.
25 Mar. (Th)	*New York Herald Tribune*: tickets go on sale today for Broadway opening. OH writes to his son Bill about Boston success; *Wc* HC 6 of 9/"1944."

26 Mar. (F)	Heidt asks for biographical details from Riggs; *NHb* Riggs, 6/120. Heidt sends out press tickets (plus information sheet) for New York opening; *NYp* MWEZ/+/n.c./25609, folder 2.
28 Mar. (Su)	*NYT*: 13 Apr. performance of *Oklahoma!* will be for benefit of Child Education Foundation.
29 Mar. (M)	*NYT*: *Oklahoma!* made almost $50,000 in Boston; de Mille had measles and Platt injured a toe; revisions of script were made; title song was restaged; a new song added for da Silva ("which clarifies the character of the villain which he portrays"); Eric Victor has withdrawn. Holm signs run-of-play contract; 118/16. TH informs Warren Munsell of Boston success; 97/"Lieut. Colonel Munsell." Sheet music of "Oklahoma" (song) registered for copyright purposes; *Wc* HC 6 of 9/"O.H. Songs 1920–45."
30 Mar. (Tu)	LL informs S. N. Behrman of Boston success; 6/"Behrman" no. 1.
31 Mar. (W)	*Oklahoma!* opens at St. James Theatre, New York. Louis Dreyfus of Chappell and Co., London, proposes bringing show to England to open in May; 97/"Lieut. Colonel Munsell."

Appendix B

Archival and Other Sources

The following offers an overview and description of the archival materials on which the present study of *Oklahoma!* is based.

The Theatre Guild

The main Theatre Guild materials now reside in the Yale Collection of American Literature, Beinecke Rare Book and Manuscript Library, Yale University (Uncat. MSS ZA; NHb TG). There is also a collection of Theatre Guild documents (20 folders) concerning contractual, financial, and other details pertaining specifically to *Oklahoma!* in the Library of Congress, Washington, D.C. (Wc TG); this was purchased from Lionheart Autographs Inc., New York, in November–December 1994 by the Leonore and Ira Gershwin Trust (a typescript inventory on Lionheart paper is dated February 1993).

Of the Beinecke materials, Series I ("Theatre Guild Correspondence")—to which all citations refer unless otherwise noted—consists of 159 boxes with folders organized quite systematically in alphabetical order of individual names, with subgroupings by show, to which additional boxes are being added as Theresa Helburn's personal files are sorted into the collection. These folders contain letters, memoranda, invoices, and accounts, plus whatever else a conscientious secretary thought to put in a filing cabinet; there are twelve boxes (115–26) of documents under "Rodgers and Hammerstein," with subsidiary sequences for *Allegro*, *Carousel*, *The King and I*, *Oklahoma!* (the largest), and *South Pacific*. Series II consists of larger silver-colored boxes organized by show, containing program books, photographs, and other production materials (boxes 41 and 42 relate to *Oklahoma!*). There are additional boxes of press clippings and photographs (boxes 11–13), and a further set of pressbooks with clippings pasted in (the Broadway *Oklahoma!* is covered chronologically beginning with press book 197, and the touring company with book 201).

Given the role of the Theatre Guild in producing *Oklahoma!* it is not surprising that the Guild collections contain the bulk of the surviving administrative materials pertaining to it, at least for the show's first ten years. (There were few records to keep after it was sold to Rodgers and Hammerstein in 1953.) Most of the *Oklahoma!* documents in the Beinecke materials are filed together under Rodgers (boxes 118–25), although others are located under Hammerstein (in box 58), or elsewhere in the overall alphabetical sequence according to the individuals involved (for example, folders for de Mille, Mamoulian, Riggs, and so on). This ordering is surely the result of one or more filing systems at some time somewhere in the Guild's offices. However, it must have been created after March 1943, for there are no folders labeled (for the musical) "Green Grow the Lilacs" or "Away We Go!" The Guild materials on *Oklahoma!* in the Library of Congress must derive from the same source, but it is not clear when they were removed. The Beinecke boxes contain at least two empty folders (118/3, "*Oklahoma!* Investors"; 122/7, "*Oklahoma!* Motion Pix"), each with a note dated 5 April 1947 by Marion Hubbell, secretary to Lawrence Langner, indicating that the contents had been handed over to Warren Caro, then the Guild's executive secretary; these may have entered the folders later sold to the Library of Congress (as Wc TG 12 and 16 or 17, although all these folders also contain material dating from after 1947). A memo from Caro of 6 December 1946 (*NHb* TG 30/"Interoffice—Warren Caro") also suggests that he pulled out *Oklahoma!* files in preparation for a pending trip to Europe to finalize arrangements for the opening of the show in London: this memo notes contracts, correspondence, and memoranda of the type now in the Library of Congress. Thus it seems likely that the two collections stemmed from different offices within the Guild, the Beinecke folders coming from Lawrence Langner's and Theresa Helburn's, it seems, and the Library of Congress ones from a business manager; this is confirmed, broadly speaking, by their different scopes. Fortunately, it was in the nature of office administration even before the age of the photocopier that multiple copies tended to be made of important (and not so important) documents which would therefore find their way into different files within one or more filing systems; thus if something cannot be found in a file where it might be expected, a copy is sometimes in another. Unfortunately, it was, and is, also in the nature of office administration that filing systems develop haphazardly over time, that original classifications schemes are forgotten or superseded, that materials dealing with two or more separate matters create obvious filing problems, and that documents are easily misplaced or lost. For example, in terms of the various collections studied here, letters that should survive in two copies—the original and a carbon depending on their sender and recipient—often do not. Similarly, information pertaining to the British production of *Oklahoma!* (1947–53) is distributed across very different types of Theatre Guild files in a manner that is not entirely illogical but is scarcely systematic.

These materials range widely in terms of their function and therefore formality, from contracts and financial statements (invoices and the like), through business and personal letters, to office memoranda, personal notes, and even idle jottings on scraps of paper. The more formal a document, the more reliable it might seem to be (up to a point), although of course the less formal ones—for example, when ideas were being tried out—are often more illuminating. In a period when the telephone had a limited role in serious business, a great deal was written down. But while contracts, accounts, memoranda, and letters might seem straightforward, more casual notes can be very cryptic, such that their association with *Oklahoma!* is apparent only by their having been placed (correctly or not) in an *Oklahoma!* file. Documents (particularly carbon copies and personal notes) do not always contain evidence of date or authorship, although that can sometimes be construed by way of subject and tone. It is clear that although the various individuals in the Guild consulted with each other, they could nevertheless take action independently and not always consistently. It is also clear that although the Guild's offices worked reasonably efficiently, such that we still have a great amount of material on the show, some documents never entered the files, while other meetings, conversations, and decisions, even on matters of importance, were never recorded in the first place.

Oscar Hammerstein 2nd

The Oscar Hammerstein 2nd Collection in the Library of Congress (Wc HC) is arriving piecemeal: the initial deposit comprised a large collection of boxes (the *Oklahoma!* material is in green box 13) plus five red-bound scrapbooks; there have been more recent deposits received from the Hammerstein family in August 2003, containing boxes 1–9 plus additional "expansion space boxes" (for example, X box 7), for which the Library of Congress holds summary inventories prepared by Amy Asch in spring 2000 and winter 2002–3, although the material itself is not yet catalogued nor fully available for consultation (thus there is no guarantee that the reference system used here will remain in the future).

The Hammerstein Collection comprises personal notes, correspondence, press clippings, and programs, etc. For *Oklahoma!* it also contains sketches for the lyrics, and one partial draft libretto; furthermore, the Library of Congress holds in its main collection a complete draft libretto of *Oklahoma!* of November 1942, of which copies also survive elsewhere. These draft librettos have been particularly useful in determining the development of the show, and also changes in its conception up to and through the rehearsals. Reference is made to them as follows:

Draft1: Wc HC 13/7. Carbon-copy typescript of act 1, scene 1 (for the most part, minus lyrics), titled "*Green Grow the Lilacs*: Musical Version." This would seem to date from late summer 1942. The pagination in *Draft1* runs from 1-1-1 to 1-1-33; the paper and the typewriter then change as the pagination runs 34–40, with no act or scene number (and Aunt Eller is styled "Aunt Ella"). Thus it may conflate two different redactions of the text, or may just have been produced by two typists working concurrently (although the differently styled name is problematic).

Draft2: Library of Congress, ML50.R67.O4.1942 (but absent from the library's author and title catalogues). Bound carbon-copy typescript of the complete show (for the most part, minus lyrics) submitted by Hammerstein to the Library of Congress for copyright deposit on 19 November 1942. Wc TG 1 contains Hammerstein's certificate of deposit (dated that day) for the typescript, given the number "Class D unp. No. 83786"; the Library of Congress copy of *Draft2* is stamped with the date and the same Class D number. Typed title page: "*Oklahoma*/Book and Lyrics/by/Oscar Hammerstein 2nd/(Based on the Play *Green Grow the Lilacs*/by Lynn Riggs)/Music to be furnished/by/Richard Rodgers." Act 2 has a separate title page: "*Green Grow the Lilacs*/(Musical Version)/*Act Two*" (that is, the styling of

Draft1). There are two further carbon copies in New York Public Library for the Performing Arts at Lincoln Center, NCOF+, each titled "Green Grow the Lilacs (Musical Version)," one with a brown soft cover (marked "no. 8" in the top right-hand corner) and the other with a black hard one; they have different layouts but contain substantially the same text (some differences reflect penciled additions to the text which Hammerstein submitted for copyright purposes). Page references in the present text are to the Library of Congress copy.

Draft3: Library of Congress, Rouben Mamoulian Collection, box 11 (blue/silver cover). Complete libretto based on *Draft2*, with new version of act 2, scene 3 (although song list at beginning reflects the old version). Lyrics are included within the text for "Oh, What a Beautiful Mornin'," "The Surrey with the Fringe on Top," "Kansas City" (first verse and first chorus), "I Cain't Say No," "Many a New Day" (chorus only), "People Will Say We're in Love," "Pore Jud Is Daid," "When I Go Out Walkin' with My Baby," "Out of My Dreams," "The Farmer and the Cowman," "Together," and the act 2, scene 2 reprise of "People Will Say We're in Love"; other songs are cued as in *Draft2*. This is presumably the script "in blue and silver covers (with new last scene)" distributed by the Theatre Guild on or about 4 February 1943, and so was the text used when rehearsals began on the 8th. The new version of act 2, scene 3 in *Draft3* is also tipped in at the end of the black hardcover copy of *Draft2* in New York Public Library for the Performing Arts at Lincoln Center, NCOF+. The Rouben Mamoulian Collection contains two additional copies of *Draft3* (box 11, blue/silver cover; box 15, black binder—perhaps the one seen in figure 3), each in some disarray, with multiple inserts, paste-overs, and deletions reflecting subsequent revisions through the rehearsals and tryouts, eventually leading to the final text.

The New York Public Library for the Performing Arts also holds two librettos of *Oklahoma!* again with the call number NCOF+, each with blue hard covers. These are mimeographed copies, one of which seems to be identical to the mimeographed libretto bound into a scrapbook in the Hammerstein Collection: they appear to be post-premiere prompt texts or the like and include the lyrics, with only minor differences from the printed libretto that appeared in 1943.

For the lyrics, the Hammerstein Collection includes a separate folder (recently deposited by Hammerstein's biographer, Hugh Fordin) of sketches for a good number of songs intended for (if not always used in) *Oklahoma!* (cited as Wc HC "*Oklahoma!* sketches"). In addition, we have song-by-song lyric sheets that Hammerstein somehow transmitted to Rodgers, if not always in the current format, and that also seem to have formed the basis of additional copies for rehearsal and production purposes; in almost all cases, the relevant sheet is included in each of Rodgers's voice-piano manuscripts (Library of Congress, Richard Rodgers Collection, box 12). All but four are mimeographed, one ("The Surrey with the Fringe on Top") is typed, and three ("Lonely Room," "All er Nuthin'," "Boys and Girls Like You and Me") are carbon copies; those three contain pagination cues to a script (none squares with the surviving copies of *Draft1*, *Draft2*, or *Draft3*). Many of these match the (mostly) mimeographed lyric sheets prepared for Jerry Whyte, the stage manager, and also distributed to Lynn Riggs and Theresa Helburn.

While the lyric sketches and drafts are in Hammerstein's hand or done, it seems, on his typewriter, most if not all of the copies of the drafts and final scripts were prepared by the Rialto Bureau, a typing and mimeographing service at 1501 Broadway which Hammerstein and/or the Theatre Guild seem to have used regularly (the Rialto label is stuck on the covers of several of the texts listed here). The Rialto copies are typically paginated by act-scene-page, either with the numbering restarting in successive scenes (so, 1-1-1, 1-2-1) or continuing (so 1-1-40, say, is followed by 1-2-41); the two systems are used variously and inconsistently, although restarting would allow whole scenes to be rewritten and retyped without disrupting the pagination. Copies were made by way of carbon paper (for the most part we do not have the originals), which explains the different layouts of substantially the same text: one could produce only a limited number of copies by this means, so additional copies required retyping from scratch. This appears to have been cheaper and more effective than mimeographic reproduction, at least until a final text was set.

Richard Rodgers

The Richard Rodgers Collection at the Library of Congress (Wc RC), deposited in stages from 10 November 1954, is almost entirely musical. For *Oklahoma!* box 12, folders 1–15 contain his voice-piano scores (plus the lyric sheets noted above), and boxes 34–37 (23 folders) the orchestrations by Robert Russell Bennett; both are arranged in alphabetical order of song title. They are catalogued in the library's online finding aid (http://www.loc.gov/rr/perform/special/rodgers.html). The status of these manuscripts is somewhat problematic, as are their chronology and (later) ordering: an annotation on Rodgers's copy of the song "Oklahoma" says that it was presented to the Library of Congress by the composer on 31 December 1958 (or perhaps 1953; the final figure is unclear), and the others appear to have arrived there later. A thorough account of these sources would be possible only in a (much needed) critical edition.

All the *Oklahoma!* songs are written by Rodgers on the twelve-stave manuscript paper (with "CHAPPELL PROF[essional]" at the bottom right of each right-hand page, and "Printed in the U.S.A." at the bottom center) that he had used at least as far back as for *Pal Joey* (1940). They are laid out as if for publication in sheet music format, with a centered title and credits for the lyrics and music on left and right, respectively; they are also reasonably complete in musical terms, with fully functional (and well-harmonized) piano parts—if not quite the same as those in the published vocal score. Presumably these copies were made for the purpose of printing the sheet music—songs known to have been late additions (in particular, "Oklahoma" and "All er Nuthin'") are indistinguishable from those thought to have been composed early on (for example, "Oh, What a Beautiful Mornin'")—but must have been done so prior to the definitive version of the show achieved by the premiere. They are very "clean," with few corrections save for obvious copying mistakes and no signs that they were used for rehearsal (although of course they or their exemplars could have provided the basis for rehearsal copies). However, Rodgers also adopts standard notational shortcuts: in some cases, measures for the verse are numbered in arabic and those for the chorus in roman, with later passages with the same accompaniment cued by number to save writing out the piano part again. In general, the songs are notated with only the minimum music required, such as one verse and one chorus, the assumption being that the copyist (and the orchestrator) would be able to work out what was needed to set the complete text: this prompts some rather cunning labeling for "The Farmer and the Cowman," with its three sections (A, "The farmer and the cowman should be friends . . .̣"; B, "Territory folk should stick together . . ."; C, "I'd like to say a word for the farmer . . .") that recur in various orders. Some songs also lack introductions that, it seems, were added during the orchestration process (or even after, as staging needs became apparent). As one would expect, too, there is no music in Rodgers's hand for the entrances, exits, scene links, reprises, and so on, nor for the overture and dream-ballet.

There are a few sketches, either included with individual songs or, when more than one song is sketched on a page or sequence of pages, in a separate folder (Wc RC 12/16). Sketch material is contained in the folders for "Boys and Girls Like You and Me," "I Cain't Say No," "Out of My Dreams," "People Will Say We're in Love," and "Pore Jud Is Daid"; Wc RC 12/16 contains sketch material for "I Cain't Say No," "Many a New Day," "Oh, What a Beautiful Mornin'," and "The Surrey with the Fringe on Top," mixed with other unidentified melodies (plus "Wait Till You See Her" from By Jupiter, which is odd unless Rodgers was just reusing old paper).

The orchestral scores are in separate fascicles (often headed "Lilacs") and were al-most entirely prepared by Robert Russell Bennett himself—his careful ink manuscript is distinctive—although a few additions late in the show's genesis are in pencil in a different hand. In addition to the individual songs, the scores include the overture, dream-ballet, reprises, music for scene changes, entrances, and exits, and other "utili-ties," all of which were arranged by Bennett. There are some minor differences from the published vocal score, and evidence of alterations during rehearsals (particularly in terms of song introductions). The scores contain various layers of annotations and additions (performance instructions and the like), plus some later revisions to the orchestration; some apparently relate to the use of this material by the New York Phil-harmonic Orchestra at the Rodgers and Hammerstein Night at Lewisohn Stadium on 7 August 1948 (with extracts from Allegro, Carousel, Oklahoma!, South Pacific, and State Fair) and in subsequent summers.

There are additional orchestral materials in the archives of the Rodgers and Ham-merstein Organization (NYrh), including parts for the original overture, for "Pore Jud Is Daid" in F major, for "Lonely Room" in D minor, and for "Boys and Girls Like You and Me" in G major (with the final chorus in A flat major) and the following scene change, plus a few choral harmonizations.

Other Sources

The Beinecke Library also holds the Lynn Riggs papers (YCAL MSS 61; NHb Riggs), organized into series (I, Correspondence; II, Writings; and so on) by boxes and folders, each numbered sequentially through the entire collection (so 1/1–27 leads to 2/28–53); and the Lawrence Langner papers (MSS Za; NHb Langner), in boxes and in some disarray. As one would expect, the Riggs papers contain material relating both to Okla-homa! (insofar as Riggs was involved) and to the original Green Grow the Lilacs. There are further Oklahoma! materials in the New York Public Library for the Performing Arts at Lincoln Center, including librettos, press releases, newspaper clippings, a small collection of letters from and to Richard Rodgers (NY*p* RC), and some film and video material; and in the archives of the Rodgers and Hammerstein Organization, New York. Alas, I have been able to take only brief account of the Rouben Mamoulian Collection, newly arrived at the Library of Congress and in the process of being catalogued.

Editorial Principles

I cite the *Oklahoma!* materials listed above by collection, box, and folder—thus Wc RC 12/1—using where possible the folder numbers provided by the library concerned. In the case of the Beinecke Theatre Guild collection, the folders in the boxes retain just their original file tabs and are identified accordingly (for example, NH*b* TG 113/green folder "Lynn Riggs" no. 2), although for the main *Oklahoma!* boxes, I have allocated folder numbers to allow a simple box/folder reference (see the list in the Bibliography). Within these folders, documents tend to be loose, unpaginated, and usually in disarray; they are also fragile and easily displaced. In my transcriptions, I have preferred to be faithful to original stylings, spellings, punctuation, and so on, even when inconsistencies ensue ("theatre" and "theater," for example), although abbreviations have been standardized, and there has been more intervention in the case of telegrams (which are normally all uppercase, with punctuation spelled out); also, titles, which are variously underlined, in uppercase, in quotation marks, or undifferentiated from the main text, have been treated consistently: italics for shows and other full-length works, and quotation marks for songs, other short works, and working titles. In the case of the draft librettos and lyrics, I have normalized the styling and layout: original character cues in lowercase are now in small capitals; stage directions originally in roman now in italic; underlined words in italic. In my own portions of the text, I consistently call the show *Oklahoma!* rather than attempting to preserve the chronology of its different titles, save where it is useful to do so. The endnotes provide references to primary sources save where they are listed elsewhere (for example, in the appendixes), and also to other relevant secondary material, using short-title forms in the case of published texts included in the Bibliography. However, I have not identified standard reference works both in hard copy and online, such as the excellent Internet Broadway Database (http://www.ibdb.com)—my main source for details of Broadway shows and their casting—and the Internet Movie Database (http://www.imdb.com), or the usual online sources for historical newspapers which I consulted for the *New York Times*, *Christian Science Monitor*, and *Chicago Daily Tribune*. (Other press quotations are taken from the clippings in the Theatre Guild press books in the Beinecke Library.) For the final texts of the play and the libretto, I have followed Lynn Riggs, *Green Grow the Lilacs: A Play* (New York: Samuel French, 1931) and *"Oklahoma!": A Musical Play by Richard Rodgers and Oscar Hammerstein, 2nd; Based on Lynn Riggs' "Green Grow the Lilacs"* (New York: Random House, 1943).

Notes

CHAPTER 1. Setting the Stage

1. For the Theatre Guild, see Langner, *Magic Curtain* (the passages relevant to *Oklahoma!* also appear in Block, *Richard Rodgers Reader*, 112–24); Helburn, *Wayward Quest*; D'Andre, "Theatre Guild," 72–100.

2. Helburn (*Wayward Quest*, 55) says that *Enter the Hero* was withdrawn during rehearsals.

3. Helburn, *Wayward Quest*, 62.

4. Quoted in the *New York Times*, 21 August 1959.

5. *NHb* TG 78/"Langner, Lawrence: Scenario of Western Play," dated 25 October 1934 (the play dealt mostly with property greed); Langner to J. P. McEvoy, 6 September 1928, 87/"McA–McZ" (ballet). Nothing seems to have come of the ballet proposal.

6. For de Mille, see Langner to Richard Rodgers, 11 August 1943, *NHb* TG 125/"Ra" (this was "the only other ballet the Guild has done"); Langner, *Magic Curtain*, 371. For *Valley Forge*, see Grant, *Rise and Fall*, 254.

7. Hamm, "Theatre Guild Production."

8. She also requested a similar position for Hammerstein's *Carmen Jones* on 2 July 1942 (Wc HC 5 of 9/"1942/J"), although in the end the choral director was Robert Shaw.

9. *NHb* TG 152/"Kurt Weill" contains the correspondence noted here. A good number (but not all) of these exchanges are discussed in D'Andre, "Theatre Guild," 4–52; see also Weill's reports to Lotte Lenya in Symonette and Kowalke, *Speak Low*, 208–37. Erik Charell, a sometime actor and film director, directed and coproduced *White Horse Inn*, which was currently playing on Broadway (223 performances from 1 October 1936 to 10 April 1937); Burgess Meredith was Crook-Finger Jack in the 1933 Broadway production of *The Threepenny Opera* and eventually played the title role in a revival of *Liliom* at the 44th Street Theatre, New York, in 1940; Francis (František) Lederer was currently taking lead roles in Hollywood.

10. D'Andre, "Theatre Guild," 5 n. 15.

11. Helburn, *Wayward Quest*, 293; D'Andre, "Theatre Guild," 168.

12. For O'Neill, see Helburn, *Wayward Quest*, 271. The Kern-Hammerstein project was based on Donn Byrne's book *Messer Marco Polo*, a plan dating back to the early 1930s; Fordin, *Getting to Know Him*, 125–26. Helburn (*Wayward Quest*, 271) wrongly links this to "Byron." *Wc* HC 6 of 9/loose papers contains details of a proposed production with Max Gordon in Christmas 1935, and also a letter from Hammerstein to Sigmund Romberg of 12 September 1938 saying that he and Kern were working on the show.

13. Helburn, *A Wayward Quest*, 159.

14. Symonette and Kowalke, *Speak Low*, 317 ff. (*The Pirate*); *NHb* TG 37/"Russel Crouse" (*Much Ado About Nothing*); 52/"John Gassner" (pink tab; *The Good Soldier Schweik*, 9 September 1943); 152/"Kurt Weill" (*Pursuit of Happiness*; 11 September and 12, 19 November 1943). Langner had also sent his play to George Gershwin for consideration as a musical on 12 November 1935; *NHb* Langner 130. It was eventually set by Morton Gould in 1953.

15. Van Wyck Brooks, *On Literature Today* (New York: Dutton, 1941), 28–29, quoted in D'Andre, "Theatre Guild," 158.

16. Borowitz, "'Pore Jud Is Daid'"; Riggs had already confirmed some of these associations himself in interviews.

17. This and the following two letters are in Braunlich, *Haunted by Home*, 81–82, 75–76, 77.

18. Riggs to Miss Morrison, *NHb* Riggs 4/81. Samuel French and Co. published a "reading version" of *Green Grow the Lilacs* in 1931. In 1932 it also issued *Cowboy Songs, Folk Songs, and Ballads from "Green Grow the Lilacs" by Lynn Riggs (as Produced by the Theatre Guild, Inc.)*, with the music (melody only) of the songs included within most scenes of the play (some are different from those in the printed text), and also the "Singing Interludes" (issuing of the music was suggested by Barrett Clark to Riggs on 12 January 1932; Riggs 1/16). According to the 1931 preface (p. vii), the printed text is "a little fuller, a little more complete" than the original, especially in scenes 5 and 6. *Wc* TG 15 includes an undated typescript of the play that seems to represent a later performing version (it includes the character Cord Elam, not listed in the cast of the play's premiere but present in the 1931 edition).

19. Womack, "Lynn Riggs as Code Talker." There is, however, a danger of turning Riggs into a victim, and he certainly was not as "closeted" as some have presumed (compare Knapp, *American Musical*, 133).

20. *NHb* TG 62/"Theresa Helburn" (pencil on tab). Other documents relating to the play are in *NHb* TG 113 (several folders marked "Lynn Riggs") and in *NHb* Riggs 1/15 (Barrett Clark's comments on the play to Riggs and reports on negotiations with the Theatre Guild), 5/108–13 (letters to Samuel French and Co., plus royalty statements), 6/120. The Guild contracts are in Riggs 28/483 (with a $500 advance against royalties).

21. Helburn, *Wayward Quest*, 162–68 (on "managers' rehearsals"), 247–50 (on rewriting).

22. *NHb* Riggs 6/120 (original); *NHb* TG 113/green folder "Lynn Riggs" no. 3 (carbon copy).

23. *NHb* TG 113/green folder "Lynn Riggs" no. 3.

24. Ibid. (Mamoulian, Abbott). Biberman's letters and Riggs's response are in *NHb* Riggs 6/120 (Riggs also relayed it with some amusement to Barrett Clark on 13 May; Riggs 1/15); see also Helburn's account of Biberman's general method in *Wayward Quest*, 220. His intention to go to the Southwest was also announced in the *New York Times*, 15 May 1930, reporting on his wedding to Theatre Guild actress Gale Sondergaard.

25. *Wc* TG 1 (on copyright registration; it was registered as D-unpub-7017); *New York Times*, 14 November 1930 (on rehearsals); Helburn to the Management Board of the Guild, 2 December 1930, *NHb* TG 113/green folder "Lynn Riggs" no. 2 (notifying them of the dress rehearsal the following Thursday).

26. For the first scene rewrite, see Herbert Farrar's telegram from Boston to Helburn, 13 December 1942, *NHb* TG 113/green folder "Lynn Riggs" no. 3. *NHb* Riggs 13/228 contains penciled notes for revisions ("Rewrite last scene . . .") on letterhead from the Ritz-Carlton Hotel in Boston; these seem to have brought the scene into a form close to the published text. Some of the letters of complaint (and one of approval) were summarized in a document in *NHb* TG 113/green folder "Lynn Riggs" no. 2.

27. Braunlich, *Haunted by Home*, 98.

28. *NHb* Riggs 5/112 (negotiations); *Wc* TG 1, 7 (contracts). The deal with RKO was announced in the *New York Times* on 10 August 1935, and the one with MGM on 18 June 1936 (dating the event "yesterday").

29. *NHb* Riggs 5/112 (Sillbar Productions proposes a New York revival in June–July 1939); 5/113 (radio); *NHb* TG 113/green folder "Lynn Riggs" no. 2 (Arthur Hopkins of the Plymouth Theatre complains of restrictions, 9 March 1944).

30. Braunlich, *Haunted by Home*, 140, 142 (Gershwin, Copland); *NHb* Riggs 1/18 (Barrett Clark to Riggs re Gershwin, 14 October 1936); 2/30 (Foss); Pollack, *Aaron Copland*, 419–21 (*Tragic Ground*), Riggs 1/21 (letters to Copland), 28/483 (*Tragic Ground* contract, dated 20 March 1945).

31. Carbon copies of the two letters (unattributed) to Hart are in *NHb* TG 59/"Larry Hart"; the tone of the 31 January letter suggests Langner, while the 2 February one would seem to be from Helburn, given her remarks in *Wayward Quest*, 217.

32. Langner, *Magic Curtain*, 368–69; for *Lysistrata* and Merman, see also Helburn, *Wayward Quest*, 217.

33. Rodgers, *Musical Stages*, 21.

34. *Wc* HC 5 of 9/"1931" (sequel), "1935" (notes on screen tests and revisions to the draft screenplay).

35. Wilk, *Ok!* 249.

36. Altman, *American Film Musical*, 298–316; Banfield, *Jerome Kern*, chap. 4. I am grateful to Stephen Banfield for drawing this film to my attention.

37. Fordin, *Getting to Know Him*, 174 (see also Nolan, *Lorenz Hart*, 286–87; Secrest, *Somewhere for Me*, 220). The idea was revived for Kern and Hammerstein in early 1942, and by Rodgers and Hammerstein in 1953 (Fordin, *Getting to Know Him*, 322).

38. For *Show Boat* (which opened on 5 January 1946), see Rodgers, *Musical Stages*, 250. Kern and Hammerstein were billed as producers, but Kern had just died.

39. *Wc* HC 6 of 9/loose papers. Hammerstein also refers to his (less than fruitful) efforts on the war song in a letter to Laurence Schwab of 9 March 1942.

40. *Wc* HC 6 of 9/loose papers (Brill, Freedley), yellow folder (Rossitto). For Rose and *Saratoga Trunk*, see also *New York Times*, 30 January 1942.

41. *Wc* HC 6 of 9/yellow folder (Gordon); box 2 of 9/loose papers, and *New York Times*, 3 May 1942 (Crawford); Irving Caesar to Hammerstein, 18 May 1942, *Wc* HC 6 of 9/yellow folder, and *New York Times*, 4 June 1942 (MGM); *New York Times*, 1 August 1942 (St. Louis).

42. *Wc* HC 5–6 of 9 contain numerous letters concerning the (arduous) task of casting and financing *Carmen Jones* going back to March–April 1942. On 25 June, Hammerstein told Hall Johnson that he had finished act 2 and was "hard at work on the third" (5 of 9/"1942/J"). By early July he was sending out copies of the lyrics to potential singers—for example, to Avis Andrews as Carmen Jones and to the agent Lester Schurr for a potential Husky Miller on 9 July (5 of 9/"1942/A"). On 2 July, Hammerstein told his Hollywood agent Frank Orsatti that he planned to complete *Carmen Jones* by 15 July (6 of 9/loose papers), and on the 21st he apologized to Peter Piper (a Chicago theatrical agent) for not replying sooner about casting possibilities because he had been concentrating on the job of finishing it (5 of 9/"1942/P"). He sent out finished scripts to Orsatti to give to Arthur Freed (of MGM) and to Laurence Schwab (a former producer and friend) on 4 and 7 August, respectively (5 of 9/"1942/O," "1942/S"). There are letters of 16 and 23 July to Max Gordon about producing the show (6 of 9/loose papers), but as we shall see, this collapsed.

43. Harriman, *Take Them Up Tenderly*, 198.

44. Oscar Hammerstein 2nd, "Voices versus Feet: With the Triumph of Head over Heels, Operetta Regains Its Popularity," *Theatre Magazine* 41, no. 5 (May 1925): 14, quoted in D'Andre, "Theatre Guild," 119. See also ibid., 120–22, for comparisons with opera.

45. Fordin, *Getting to Know Him*, 126.

46. Hamm, "Theatre Guild Production," 497 n. 8.

47. Symonette and Kowalke, *Speak Low*, 287 (Weill); *Wc* HC 2 of 9, undated folder (Hammerstein). Warren Munsell (business manager of the Theatre Guild) was less impressed on seeing it at Maplewood on 13 October, complaining of the sloppy production, the musical cuts, and the poor performance; see his note of 18 October 1941 in *NHb* TG 97/"Munsell Memos to T.H. 1941."

48. *NHb* TG 113/"Lynn Riggs." Garrett H. Leverton, a professor in the School of Speech at Northwestern University and director of the University Theatre, acted on Riggs's behalf at Samuel French and Co. Riggs had also introduced him to Helburn as a potential director of Theatre Guild productions.

49. See the poster in Wilk, *Ok!* 20; for the broader aims of Westport, see Helburn, *Wayward Quest*, 313–16.

50. Wilk, *Ok!* 25, 30–31; Secrest, *Somewhere for Me*, 223–24. Anderson married John Steinbeck in 1950.

51. Langner, *Magic Curtain*, 369; Rodgers, *Musical Stages*, 203.

52. Rodgers, *Musical Stages*, 216; Helburn, *Wayward Quest*, 282.

53. *NYp* MWEZ/+/n.c./25609, folder 1.

CHAPTER 2. Contracts and Commitments

1. *NHb* TG 125/"Ra" (Langner responding to Rodgers's apology for his article in the *New York Times* that perhaps did not sufficiently acknowledge Langner's contribution to *Oklahoma!*); Langner, *Magic Curtain*, 369; Hammerstein, "In memoriam [Theresa Helburn]," NY*p* Billy Rose Theatre Collection, cited in D'Andre, "Theatre Guild," 2–4 (compare the *New York Times*, 21 August 1959); *NHb* TG 90/"Mary Martin/Richard Halliday"; Helburn, *Wayward Quest*, 282 ("fulfillment of my dream"; "Helburn's Folly").

2. *New York Times*, 15 November 1942. The Guild celebrated its actual twenty-fifth birthday in April 1944; *New York Times*, 16 April 1944.

3. *NHb* TG 52/"Gassner Memorandums T.G.–L.L. Files," "Gassner Memos 1942–3."

4. *NHb* TG 118/8, reproduced in Wilk, *Ok!* 33.

5. Helburn, *Wayward Quest*, 121 (Theatre Guild press office).

6. Clark was also suggested on 28 January 1942 for Dogberry in a proposed Guild production of *Much Ado About Nothing*; *NHb* TG 52/"Gassner Memos 1942–3."

7. Woodward ("Tex") Ritter had played in the original *Green Grow the Lilacs*, and at some point had taken the role of Cord Elam, according to a cast list (but not that of the premiere) in *NHb* TG 113/green folder "Lynn Riggs" no. 6.

8. *New York Times*, 12 May 1942; May Gadd, mentioned here, eventually advised Agnes de Mille on some of the dancing in *Oklahoma!* There was a slightly cooler account in the *New York Times* on 17 May 1942, complaining that the festival was too theatrical to be "authentic," yet not enough to be real theater. The festival did not return to New York in 1943.

9. Helburn, *Wayward Quest*, 283; Rodgers quoted in Secrest, *Somewhere for Me*, 225; Rodgers, *Musical Stages*, 216. I have not found any evidence to support Hyland's claim (*Richard Rodgers*, 138) that Theatre Guild documents show Rodgers discussing *Green Grow the Lilacs* with the Guild in March 1942.

10. The note is marked in pencil at the bottom, "Green Grow the Lilacs." For Logan's response to an approach from the Guild, which he said took place at a party, see his *Josh*, 187–88.

11. Fordin, *Getting to Know Him*, 183–84. Taylor, *Some Enchanted Evenings*, 165, has Hammerstein reading the play aloud to Kern beside his swimming pool. Hammerstein left for California on 9 May and was back by 10 June. A later penciled note (undated, in an unidentified hand) on an otherwise unrelated letter from Hammerstein (at his farmhouse in Doylestown, Pa.) to Harry Ruby (in Beverly Hills) of 30 June (W*c* HC 6 of 9/loose papers), a semihumorous complaint on not being invited to a party, reads "May 18 Oscar in LA in talk w[ith] Jerry [Kern] re GGtheL and MITA [*Music in the Air*] ref. LA Civic Light Opera."

12. Hammerstein, "In re *Oklahoma!*" *New York Times*, 23 May 1943.

13. Wilk, *Ok!* 57–58, mostly following Taylor, *Some Enchanted Evenings*, 165, and Fordin, *Getting to Know Him*, 184. However, Wilk also places Hart in Mexico at this time, which seems unlikely, given that he had been away for a month, so Rodgers said (*Musical Stages*, 217), when he returned (in mid-September).

14. *Wc* HC 6 of 9/loose papers.

15. Fordin, *Getting to Know Him*, 174, quoting a letter from Rodgers to Hammerstein written in July 1941.

16. Rodgers, *Musical Stages*, 209; Fordin, *Getting to Know Him*, 184–85; Nolan, *Lorenz Hart*, 287, 290. We shall see that the idea reemerged for Rodgers and Hammerstein in 1943.

17. Secrest, *Somewhere for Me*, 220 (1938 or 1939); Nolan, *Lorenz Hart*, 290 (1941); Wilk, *Ok!* 58 (Gershwin quoted by Michael Feinstein).

18. Rodgers, *Musical Stages*, 216–17.

19. Logan, *Josh*, 188; Nolan, *Sound of Their Music*, 4.

20. "Muchacho" (styled *Muchacha*) was announced as dropped in the *New York Times*, 27 November 1942.

21. Rodgers, *Musical Stages*, 217 (stretcher); Nolan, *Lorenz Hart*, 300 (Guilford).

22. Harriman, *Take Them up Tenderly*, 181. Harriman dates the profile as being completed "shortly before Mr. Hart's death," although in fact it contains references to matters subsequent to it (such as the sale of 500,000 copies to date of the Decca cast album of *Oklahoma!*).

23. *New York Times*, 4 December 1942 (RKO purchases *Higher and Higher* for $15,000); 2 February 1943 (MGM purchases *Jumbo*).

24. Hammerstein, Harbach, and Kern released the amateur rights to *Hayfoot, Strawfoot* to the National Theatre Conference (for advertising to its members) from 1 September 1942 to 1 September 1943; *Wc* HC 6 of 9/loose papers. It was performed at Syracuse University in 1942; Fordin, *Getting to Know Him*, 157. John Gassner also suggested it to the Guild (under the title *Needle in a Haystack*) on 14 September 1942 ("Shuberts are interested, but I think we could get it, if we wanted it"); *NHb* TG 52/"Gassner Memos 1942–3."

25. Gordon spun the story differently in the *New York Times*, 21 December 1942: he had dropped the show because he needed to be in Hollywood from early March 1943. *Wc* HC 5–6 of 9 contain numerous letters re the casting of *Show Boat* and *Carmen Jones*; the cable to Freed is in 5 of 9/"1942/F," and the letter to Brackett in 6 of 9/loose papers. On 20 August 1942 Hammerstein also responded to Macklin Marrow's request to act as musical director of one of his shows: "Russell Bennet [*sic*] is going to conduct *Carmen Jones*. Later in the season when *Show Boat* is produced, Jerome Kern will, of course, have the decision on who will conduct his score" (5 of 9/"1942/M"). According to a letter from Frank Orsatti of 28 December 1942, Freed revived his interest in *Show Boat* about that time and was also pursuing a biopicture of Oscar Hammerstein's grandfather; 5 of 9/"December 1942." However, these may just have been attempts to revive Hammerstein's interest in an MGM deal.

26. For MGM, see Fordin, *Getting to Know Him*, 183, 196, 197. *Wc* HC 5–6 of 9 (various folders) has frequent letters and cables from Frank Orsatti dating from October and November 1942 seeking to persuade him to take a deal first mentioned by Hammerstein in August; Hammerstein's final refusal to Arthur Freed is in box 6 of 9, loose papers. See also Helburn, *Wayward Quest*, 286, which further notes that at the same time Rodgers was expecting a commission from the air force (compare Rodgers, *Musical Stages*, 210, and the ridiculing of the idea in Secrest, *Somewhere for Me*, 263–64). For Kern, see Rodgers, *Musical Stages*, 235; Fordin, *Getting to Know Him*, 217.

27. Fordin, *Getting to Know Him*, 231 (2 percent); Harriman, *Take Them up Tenderly*, 181 (Rodgers and Hart take 3 percent of the gross each when collaborating with one or more authors on a show, and more when they work alone). However, the contract specified only a small advance ($200 each to Rodgers and Hammerstein and a nominal $1 to Riggs).

28. Abbott, *Mister Abbott*, 198; Nolan, *Lorenz Hart*, 298. A similar arrangement with Rodgers, designed not to embarrass Hart, had been adopted with Abbott for *Best Foot Forward* (1941–42). Oscar and Dorothy Hammerstein also attended a performance of *Beat the Band* in Boston on 22 September: Johnny Green's letter of thanks of 23 September is in *Wc* HC 5 of 9/"September 1942."

29. Langner, *Magic Curtain*, 370; Helburn, *Wayward Quest*, 283 (late summer 1942).

30. Hanff, *Underfoot in Show Business*, 80.

31. *NHb* TG 87/"M." See also the profile on Mamoulian in the *New York Times*, 25 July 1943.

32. Helburn to Riggs, 1 May 1930, *NHb* TG 113/green folder "Lynn Riggs" no. 3.

33. Rodgers, *Musical Stages*, 221. Langner, on the other hand, seems to claim that the Guild wanted Mamoulian, "the hero of *Porgy and Bess*," from the outset; *Magic Curtain*, 371.

34. *NHb* 118/8. This cable is odd: although dated 26 October 1942, it reads "Would you be available to direct production starting sometime in September[?]" There is a pencil instruction to file this with "Green Grow."

35. The draft is in *NHb* TG 89/"Rouben Mamoulian" (white tab); the typed letter is in *Wc* TG 2. It is not clear on what basis the *New York Herald Tribune* on 17 January 1943 (and the *New York Times* on the 19th) could have reported that Mamoulian would direct *Oklahoma!* or the *New York Times* on 1 February (and numerous other papers around then) that he had signed his contract.

36. *NHb* TG 39/"Agnes de Mille" (yellow tab). Hammerstein also had Alton in mind for *Carmen Jones*; his letter requesting return of the script on 11 January 1943, and Alton's apology for slowness on account of being so busy with the *Ziegfeld Follies*, are in *Wc* HC 5 of 9/"1942/A."

37. Langner, *Magic Curtain*, 371. Helen Tamiris also wrote to the Guild asking to do the choreography; see her undated letter in *NHb* TG 145/"Taa-Taz."

38. Rodgers, *Musical Stages*, 194.

39. Helburn (*Wayward Quest*, 285) says that de Mille wrote to Langner, but she is somewhat cool about de Mille in her autobiography. For *Rodeo*, see Pollack, *Aaron Copland*, 363–74.

40. *NHb* TG 39/"Agnes de Mille" (yellow tab). On the latter letter, there is a penciled note, "talked about Ballet."

41. Wilk, *Ok!* 114.

42. *New York Times*, 1 August 1943; here Rodgers also attributes to Helburn the idea of using de Mille for *Oklahoma!* He says much less about the occasion in *Musical Stages*, 221, perhaps because of his subsequent experiences with de Mille.

43. *NHb* TG 39/"Agnes de Mille" (yellow tab).

44. De Mille, *"Dance to the Piper"* and *"Promenade Home,"* 1: 319. Internal evidence dates this just before Thanksgiving. The Ballet Russe toured *Rodeo* and other

ballets to the West Coast, then the Midwest, opening in Chicago on Christmas Day (*New York Times*, 3 January 1943). De Mille left the tour in Los Angeles to return to New York to work on *Oklahoma!* ("*Dance to the Piper*" and "*Promenade Home*," 1: 322).

45. *NHb* TG 16/"Lemuel Ayers" no. 1. Langner later claimed (*Magic Curtain*, 371) that Ayers and Miles White, who both worked on *The Pirate*, had been discovered by Alfred Lunt and Lynn Fontanne, who starred in it.

46. For the poster, see his invoice of 29 April 1943 in *NHb* TG 16/"Lemuel Ayers" no. 2.

47. For Whyte, see Rodgers, *Musical Stages*, 223 (noting that he was brought over from George Abbott's office); Secrest, *Somewhere for Me*, 217–19. Whyte's appointment was reported in the newspapers only later.

48. Wilk, *Ok!* 124.

49. Documents pertaining to Blackton's engagement are in *Wc* TG 2; for his apparent reluctance to sign, see Wilk, *Ok!* 147.

50. Clipping in *NHb* Riggs 30/518.

51. *NHb* TG 123/1 contains an undated four-page list of possible cast members. Franchot Tone and Alfred Drake are two penciled additions to a list of thirty-one names for Curly.

52. For Greenwood, see Fordin, *Getting to Know Him*, 190; *Wc* HC 5 of 9/"September 1942" also has an undated letter from her reiterating interest in the show, although she is uncertain about her imminent commitments (which might include joining the cast of Cole Porter's *Let's Face It!*). For Martin, see Fordin, *Getting to Know Him*, 190 (which also relays the "roses" comment without date). Helburn's interest in Martin is discussed in "Inside *Oklahoma!*" (*NHb* TG 118/4; *NYp* MWEZ/+/n.c./25609A, folder 6; it seems to date from 1948), and Helburn, *Wayward Quest*, 284; they were introduced at Westport by Cheryl Crawford (Helburn, *Wayward Quest*, 328). Halliday's letter is in *Wc* HC 5 of 9/"September 1942." For Dietrich and *One Touch of Venus*, see the *New York Times*, 27, 31 January 1943.

53. Rodgers, *Musical Stages*, 222.

54. Helburn, *Wayward Quest*, 284–85. For other audition stories, see Wilk, *Ok!* 127–42.

55. Wilk, *Ok!* 85. For Drake and *Beat the Band*, see the *New York Times*, 8 October 1942.

56. In his letter of 26 February 1943 in support of Drake's appeal against being drafted (*NHb* TG 120/17), Langner says that the Guild had been negotiating with Drake since early November. Roberts later claimed that she signed her contract only during the Boston tryout; Secrest, *Somewhere for Me*, 251.

57. On 6 January 1943 Helburn was still considering other possibilities for Aunt Eller, including Adelaide Klein, currently in *Uncle Harry*. Russell is included in the four-page undated cast list in *NHb* TG 123/1 as a possible candidate for Jeeter (Jud); a Robert Russell had played on Broadway in *The Jazz Singer* (1925) and *Whatever Goes Up* (1935).

58. Unlike the others, Rawls, Starr, and Terry are not linked to any specific character in the audition list. For Lotta, *NHb* TG 123/1 contains an undated memo noting a telephone conversation with the theatrical agent Sylvia Hahlo: "Miss Hahlo has found a spanish girl dancer—a show stopper named Anita. She would like you or someone to

see her, if possible at her studio 9 E. 59th St., where she has all her costumes, etc. I'll speak to Johnny [Haggott] about this."

59. Wilk, *Ok!* 140–41 (audition before Christmas); *NHb* TG 118/8 (Granville, etc.). Rodgers (*Musical Stages*, 222) said that Holm was one of the first to audition in fall 1942, but I have not found any evidence to support this.

60. Wilk, *Ok!* 142.

61. The approach to Temple as Laurey is noted in Helburn's "Inside *Oklahoma!*" that seems to date from 1948 (*NHb* TG 118/4; *NYp* MWEZ/+/n.c./25609A, folder 6). It was repeated in a press release issued by the Guild for the tenth anniversary of the show in 1953 (*NHb* TG 118/4; *NYp* MWEZ/+/n.c./25609A, folder 3), taken up in the *New York Times*, 29 March 1953. See also Helburn, *Wayward Quest*, 284; Rodgers, *Musical Stages*, 222. The Guild also seems to have approached Temple for an unknown role in June 1941; *NHb* TG 145/"Tea–Tez."

62. Mostel was sent the third of seven copies with pink and silver covers sometime after 16 November 1942; see the postcard in *NHb* TG 118/8. Otto Karlweiss, included as a possible peddler in an undated (yellow) list of casting suggestions in 123/1, had also been sent a script. A list of names made by Helburn dated 3 March 1943 (for what is unclear, but it is filed in the *Oklahoma!* papers) contains the well-known comedian Phil Silvers; 120/16, 123/1. Rodgers later considered him for the role of the Peddler in the film; *NYp* RC 8/11.

63. Secrest, *Somewhere for Me*, 250.

64. Helburn, *Wayward Quest*, 198 (donation); *NHb* TG 90/"Groucho Marx" (1942 letters, plus correspondence about another possible collaboration in 1946). The reference is to Eugene O'Neill's *Ah, Wilderness!* produced by the Guild in 1933. Marx said much the same about discarding his comic trademarks in the *New York Times*, 14 September 1941.

65. Secrest, *Somewhere for Me*, 251.

66. The cable does not specify the role, but *NHb* TG 123/1 contains a note scribbled on a postcard that links Guilfoyle with the other candidates for Jud.

67. *NHb* TG 123/1. The cable is undated but presumably is one of the batch Haggott sent out on 1 February.

68. De Mille, "*Dance to the Piper*" and "*Promenade Home*," 1: 322–23.

69. So he said in a 1993 interview for the Broadway Oral History Project (video in *NYp* MGZIC 9-5170). Also in this video are the husband-and-wife pair Paul Shiers and Vivian Smith (respectively a singer and a dancer in the original *Oklahoma!*), and Wally Peterson, who was in the 1947 Drury Lane production.

70. Church said he was recruited only after da Silva had been agreed upon for Jud (so only in early February); Wilk, *Ok!* 136–37.

71. *NHb* TG 58/"Oscar Hammerstein, *Oklahoma!* Costumes and Correspondence." In early 1944 Cunningham was being considered as a possible temporary understudy for Marc Platt; Helburn to Langner, 17 January 1944, 124/"Ha" ("Merce Cunningham could do Marc's part but has some back trouble so couldn't do the lifts").

72. Anderson is listed as Gertie in a salary list of 9 February; *NHb* TG 123/7.

73. *New York Times*, 31 January 1943 (Lawrence), 11 February 1943 (Equity). For the dancers' low salaries, see also Helburn, *Wayward Quest*, 286–87; and for Kate Friedlich negotiating something better, see Wilk, *Ok!* 133.

74. *NHb* TG 118/7 (week-ending account of 25 December 1943; reproduced in Wilk, *Ok!* 242); 123/6 (May 1944 estimate).

75. Langner to Alfred Tamarin in the Guild press office, 16 September 1943, *NHb* TG 123/17.

76. Helburn, *Wayward Quest*, 282.

77. *NHb* TG 97/"Warren Munsell" (pencil on tab); Helburn, *Wayward Quest*, 281.

78. See the undated memorandum on budget procedures in *NHb* TG 161/"1942." For Gordon, see also Wilk, *Ok!* 11–12.

79. Langner, *Magic Curtain*, 368; Hanff, *Underfoot in Show Business*, 75–85. Hanff's count of sixteen consecutive flops probably began with the next production after Saroyan's *The Time of Your Life* (1939).

80. *NHb* TG 97/"Lieut. Colonel Munsell"; *New York Times*, 24 January 1943 (Porter, noting that not all the money had been spent). Almost all the details of the *Oklahoma!* investors presented here are drawn from documents in *Wc* TG 12.

81. Rodgers, *Musical Stages*, 223–24; Fordin, *Getting to Know Him*, 197; Secrest, *Somewhere for Me*, 253–54.

82. Ferencz, "Broadway Sound," 185 (Bennett); Fordin, *Getting to Know Him*, 197 (taxi; see also the *New York Times*, 10 April 1949); Rodgers, *Musical Stages*, 226 (first-night party).

83. Langner, *Magic Curtain*, 370–71. Compare Rodgers, *Musical Stages*, 223–24, which says that seventy people were present but no one invested.

84. Helburn, *Wayward Quest*, 285.

85. The settlement documents are in *Wc* TG 19; see also *NHb* TG 85/"David Lowe."

86. *New York Times*, 23 July 1944.

87. According to Langner (*Magic Curtain*, 370), "We took a studio in Steinway Hall on several occasions."

88. The figure Helburn expected from MGM varies in Rodgers, *Musical Stages*, 224 ($75,000 for 50 percent of the profits plus an additional $75,000 for the film rights, which is implausible); Fordin, *Getting to Know Him*, 196 ($69,000 for 50 percent, and $75,000 to include the film rights).

89. For example, Wilk, *Ok!* 105, says that there were twenty-eight investors in *Oklahoma!* Presumably he derived this number from the (later) lists of investors in *NHb* 121/3, 123/15.

90. It is not clear whether to believe the claim (Rodgers, *Musical Stages*, 224; Fordin, *Getting to Know Him*, 196; Nolan, *The Sound of Their Music*, 16; Wilk, *Ok!* 10–11) that Cohn invested his own money out of bravado: all correspondence and payments were addressed to Columbia Pictures. Brulatour had been the first president of Universal Pictures and remained associated with what was left of the filmmaking industry in Fort Lee, N.J., until his death, aged seventy-six, in October 1946. A list in *Wc* TG 12 also links him to Max Gordon and Marcus Heiman. He later invested in other Guild plays (*The Iceman Cometh, Carousel, Jacobowsky and the Colonel, The Fatal Weakness, He Who Gets Slapped,* and *O Mistress Mine*).

91. *New York Times*, 19 November 1941, 10 October 1943 (*Venus*); *NHb* TG 26 (*Lucretia*; not a Guild production, although there was some association).

92. So Haggott says in a letter of 16 February 1946 (another refutation of David Lowe's claims) in Wc TG 19.

93. Langner, *Magic Curtain*, 370.

94. Helene Hanff (*Underfoot in Show Business*, 80) notes of the Guild, "During the next few weeks [after the opening of *The Russian People* on 29 December 1942] we heard they were holding backers' auditions, and that they had the promise of a third of the money needed, from Broadway's biggest single backer, though there were several ifs attached to his promise." By "biggest single backer" she seems to mean Max Gordon.

95. De Mille, *"Dance to the Piper" and "Promenade Home,"* 1: 324–25.

96. Nolan, *The Sound of Their Music*, 16; Wilk, *Ok!* 153–54. Holm called it the first run-through, although there also seems to have been one on 24 February and perhaps also the 22nd.

97. Guild to Dreyfus, 2 March 1943, Wc TG 19: "We appreciate your understanding of our problem and your generous gesture."

98. Wc TG 12 (Lowe); NHb TG 123/7 (Haggott); 118/7 (production schedule; reproduced in Wilk, *Ok!* 104).

99. Hanff, *Underfoot in Show Business*, 82–83. Compare the *Chicago Daily Tribune*, 21 May 1944, where Langner gets the credit for resisting Lee Shubert's demand to remove Jud's death and Max Gordon's advice to cut act 1, scene 2.

100. Wilk, *Ok!* 16 (New Haven). For the $25,000, see George Holland's column "Boston After Dark" in the *Boston Evening American*, 17 March 1943.

101. Wilk, *Ok!* 99 (Howard S. Cullman; see also the *New York Times*, 29 March 1953), 183–84 (playwright Philip Barry). A similar story appeared in the *Chicago Daily Tribune*, 16 April 1944.

102. *New York Times*, 16 February 1943. However, there was a rumor in the *New York Times*, 9 May 1943, that a sixth play would indeed be offered: Eugene Bryden's adaptation of Gogol's *The Inspector General*.

103. Compare Helburn, *Wayward Quest*, 199 (the theater, at 930 seats, was too small to be economical); Hanff, *Underfoot in Show Business*, 78 (it was to be sold to pay off Guild debts).

104. This is the capacity noted in the *New York Times*, 24 May 1942. Other sources give 1,509.

105. The link with the Colonial Theatre was by way of the United Booking Office (of which Lee Shubert was a director and vice president, with Marcus Heiman as president), which booked shows into the Colonial and a large number of other theaters across the country. Heiman held a lease on the Colonial Theatre first indirectly through his attorney (1932–43; as the Boylston Theatre Company), then directly (1943–52), until the owners (the Ames Estate) sold the theater to the Shuberts (who owned it until 1957, when prompted to sell it as a result of an antitrust suit); Stein, *Boston's Colonial Theatre*, 47, 81, 89. I am grateful to Maryann Chach, director of the Shubert Archive, for this information.

106. *New York Times*, 8 February 1943: *Sons o' Fun* would stay in the Winter Garden unless its takings dropped to $22,000 or $23,000.

107. Although the announcement in the *Christian Science Monitor* on 15 February referred only to two weeks, the *Chicago Daily Tribune* (16 March 1943) review of the New Haven tryout also refers to three weeks in Boston.

108. *NHb* TG 120/17.

109. Display advertisements for *Oklahoma!* began appearing on the 24th, and for the *Ziegfeld Follies* on the 27th. The third opening that week was Victor Wolfson's play *The Family*, on Tuesday the 30th (postponed from the 23rd).

CHAPTER 3. Creative Processes

1. Rodgers, *Musical Stages*, 227.

2. Ibid., 218; Hammerstein, "Notes on Lyrics," 8.

3. Hamm, "Theatre Guild Production." The 1941–42 Cheryl Crawford production also seems to have started with "Summertime."

4. The early origin of the song was reported in the 1943 souvenir booklet for *Oklahoma!* (photocopy in NYrh); see also Hammerstein, "Notes on Lyrics," 7–8.

5. Hammerstein, "Notes on Lyrics," 15–16. For their working practices, see also Fordin, *Getting to Know Him*, 190–91.

6. "In re *Oklahoma!*" *New York Times*, 23 May 1943.

7. *New York Times*, 1 August 1943 (sick with joy); Nolan, *The Sound of Their Music*, 11 (ten minutes; see also Fordin, *Getting to Know Him*, 189); *New York Times*, 14 May 1944, (Sardi's); 29 March 1953 (anniversary).

8. A single leaf of the printed play survives in Wc HC "*Oklahoma!* sketches." The one exception to my comment on the dialogue is ibid., no. 23, which roughs out an exchange between Laurey and Curly about Jud taking her to the Box Social.

9. *NHb* TG 118/8.

10. On their relative speeds of working, see also Helburn, *Wayward Quest*, 288. Hammerstein gave similar details of his method in the *New York Times*, 10 April 1949. His 1946 account of "Oklahoma," however, does not quite square with Robert Russell Bennett's (see page 94).

11. For example, Wc HC 6 of 9 contains a carbon copy draft script of act 1 of *Three Sisters* (1934) which looks very similar to the *Oklahoma!* drafts: lyrics are not included, but songs are described in terms of the intent and content (although there are no proposed song titles).

12. The equivalent line in the play (p. 16) is "She likes you—quite a little."

13. Wilk, *Ok!* 129.

14. The orchestration in Wc RC 34/5 still has an (unclear) cue to "Dancing Boys enter."

15. Ethan Mordden (*Rodgers and Hammerstein*, 33) suggests that the change was made because of the character Jeeter Lester in Jack Kirkland's *Tobacco Road* (1933), revived at the Forrest Theatre from 5 September to 3 October 1942. Riggs's play *The Domino Parlor* (1928; revised as *Hang On to Love*) included a villain called Jude Summers.

16. Mordden (*Rodgers and Hammerstein*, 34) and Nolan (*The Sound of Their Music*, 13) are wrong to claim that "When I Go Out Walkin' with My Baby" was eventually substituted by "Kansas City"; there are similar misprisions in Hyland, *Richard Rodgers*, 142. The song was eventually recycled in the 1995 stage version of *State Fair*.

17. Knapp, *American Musical*, 182 n. 1.

18. Riggs had made the fire-raising thematic by virtue of an earlier conversation

(scene 3, p. 71) between Curly and Jeeter concerning a disgruntled farmhand burning a farm. This conversation is retained in Hammerstein's act 1, scene 2 (p. 69), although it serves little point, given his alterations to the ending.

19. Rodgers, *Musical Stages*, 219.

20. "Eight Bars and a Pencil," *New York Times*, 8 June 1947, reprinted in Ferencz, *"The Broadway Sound,"* 301–4.

21. Harriman, *Take Them up Tenderly*, 191–92. For Rodgers and Hart, see Block, *Richard Rodgers*, 24; and compare Nolan's (*Lorenz Hart*, 273) description of their practice on *Pal Joey*, where in the case of love songs the music was written first, and for "situational numbers," the lyrics. Hammerstein ("Notes on Lyrics," 13) likewise claimed that the music for the chorus of "People Will Say We're in Love" came first.

22. Another line here, "No better [than] anybody else, but just as good," appeared in "The Farmer and the Cowman."

23. Both of these sketches might plausibly be associated with the verse for "Many a New Day": no. 12 has the right tone, while the "wear"/"hair" rhyme does indeed appear in the verse, if in a different context. Incidentally, I have found no evidence for the quite persistent story that "[This Was] A Real Nice Clambake" in *Carousel* derives from a song ("This Was a Real Nice Hayride") originally intended for *Oklahoma!*

24. Hammerstein, "Notes on Lyrics," 14–15.

25. Wc HC "*Oklahoma!* sketches," nos. 81 (various "Don't"s), 80 (complete stanza), 82 (Laurey's middle section). No. 107 is a sketch for the verse.

26. Banfield, *Jerome Kern*, chap. 4.

27. Wilk, *Ok!* 192 (Boston). Wc HC "*Oklahoma!* sketches," no. 27, gives the stanza "I'm just a girl who cain't say no/Kissin's my favorite food/. . ./I cain't resist a Romeo . . .")—that is, combining what became the beginning of the encore stanza with what became the ending of the second.

28. Carter, "In the Workshop." The lyric sheet in Wc RC 12/7, like just a few of the others here, is what seems to be an "original" carbon (possibly from the Rialto Bureau). Its page number, 1-2-54, does not match *Draft2* or the final typescript librettos in Wc HC and in Wc TG 10 and so must derive from a different typescript (and presumably one not paginated scene-by-scene). It begins with Jud's speech "Don't want nothin' from no peddler . . ." (as in the final version, p. 76), and ends with the stage direction "He tears the Police Gazette picture from the wall, kicks over the table and starts to tear up all his wo[r]n-out symbols, as the curtain falls."

29. The orchestration is numbered in pencil "#10A (13p)," which may relate to the numbering of the song "All That I Want" (no. 10) in the act 1 song list in *Draft2* (see table 3.2); "Lonely Room" is no. 15 in the final version.

30. De Mille, *"Dance to the Piper" and "Promenade Home,"* 2: 238.

31. Grant, *Rise and Fall*, 27–28 (although *pace* Grant, Laurey does go up to *a″* in the act 2 reprise of "People Will Say We're in Love"). *Oklahoma!* was not performed with microphones; ibid., 191.

32. Compare the analytical approach adopted in Forte, *American Popular Ballad*.

33. Rodgers's own much less analytical account of this song (*Musical Stages*, 219) focused on its response to the rhythms of the words and on "painting" its images.

34. Rodgers, *Musical Stages*, 108. However, the remark is made in the context of his refusing to make such a cut in *A Connecticut Yankee*.

35. *New York Times*, 14 May 1944; see also *New York Times*, 21 January 1945.

36. Rodgers, *Musical Stages*, 218 (no problems); Nolan, *Sound of Their Music*, 11 (five hours "flying time," quoting Rodgers); Secrest, *Somewhere for Me*, 304 (six days); *New York Times*, 14 May 1944 ("People Will Say We're in Love"; compare Hyland, *Richard Rodgers*, 145).

37. Wilk, *Ok!* 153.

38. More or less the same story appeared in the *New York Post*, 6 December 1979, and in the *New York Times*, 9 December 1979. I have not found it in any accounts (by de Mille or others) before 1979. De Mille seems to have repeated the "circus ballet" claim in an interview with Wilk (*Ok!* 118); it also appears in Secrest, *Somewhere for Me*, 252; Miller, *Rebels with Applause*, 45; Grant, *Rise and Fall*, 260.

39. De Mille, *"Dance to the Piper" and "Promenade Home,"* 2: 237.

40. Wilk, *Ok!* 148. Compare de Mille's quite precise musical instructions for *Rodeo*; Pollack, *Aaron Copland*, 367.

41. Note that from m. 159 (top of p. 120 of the vocal score) the given numbers are ten too low. There were also other problems here: the reprise of "Pore Jud Is Daid" at m. 381 is in E major in the orchestral score (E flat major in the vocal score), shifting abruptly to E flat major for m. 389.

42. Just three dance-hall girls get separate credit in the New York program.

43. Wc RC 35/4, p. 142. There are a number of such notes in the score, referring to actions from the dancers (in this case, George Church and Katharine Sergava) that cue the music.

44. Rodger W. Stuart, "The Joys and Headaches of Show's Uncrowned Hero—the Orchestrator." I am grateful to George Ferencz for drawing this article to my attention. It should be said, however, that Bennett's scores for the "end of Act I" and "new end Act I" are indistinguishable (in terms of paper, writing style, etc.) from the rest of his work on *Oklahoma!*

45. I am grateful to Stephen Banfield for this information.

46. There had been other New York performances of the "original" in 1932 and 1934–35. Sir Thomas Beecham conducted a more complete version at the Metropolitan Opera in 1942.

47. Block, *Richard Rodgers*, 30 (*Say It with Jazz*); Banfield, *Jerome Kern*, 201 (Kern to Hammerstein, 19 May 1933).

48. Wc HC "*Oklahoma!* sketches," nos. 6–8 (three carbon copies).

49. Wc HC "*Oklahoma!* sketches," no. 14. The first line has some resonance of the song originally planned for Laurey ("All That I Want") that eventually became "Many a New Day."

CHAPTER 4. Heading for Broadway

1. *New York Times*, 21 February 1943.

2. For document references here and below, see the time line in the appendix. Those dismissed included Harry Antrim, Jane Lawrence (rerecruited later in February to play Gertie Cummings), Robert Trout, Herbert Ross, Eugenia Delarova, Ferma Sironi, Frances Martone, Helen Rollins, Muriel Breunig, Helen Benner, and Dorothy Kell.

3. Langner, *Magic Curtain*, 372–73. As we have seen, a competing account has Helburn coming up with the idea for the song in a taxi ride shared with Hammerstein on the way to an audition for investors.

4. *NHb* TG 123/1 (rehearsal call); 124/"Ha" (ticket request). Church (Wilk, *Ok!* 156–57) located this "during the third week of rehearsal"; the 16th, when Harwood was called, was in the second week. Langner had also tried to recruit a roper, Montie Montana, on 29 January; 123/1.

5. Rodgers, *Musical Stages*, 223.

6. *NHb* 118/8 (6 February); 124/"Ha" (9 March; list of calls; request for donation); Wilk, *Ok!* 154 (Gadd).

7. Wilk, *Ok!* 146–47. The point is made strongly and repeatedly in the Broadway Oral History Project interview (1 April 1993) with, among others, dancers Marc Platt and Vivian Smith in *NYpl* MGZIC 9-5170 (video).

8. Wilk, *Ok!* 148–49; *NHb* TG 124/"Wa" (Wood on McCracken).

9. See the addition to the costume list in *NHb* TG 58/"Oscar Hammerstein, *Oklahoma!*: Costumes and Correspondence."

10. *NHb* TG 118/8 (Helburn notes); Wilk, *Ok!* 149–50 (Anderson); de Mille, "*Dance to the Piper*" and "*Promenade Home*," 1: 325.

11. Helburn, *Wayward Quest*, 286. For Rodgers, see Wilk, *Ok!* 146, 152, 158.

12. De Mille, "*Dance to the Piper*" and "*Promenade Home*," 1: 325–26.

13. See the costume list in *NHb* TG 118/8.

14. *NHb* TG 118/7. Church is not listed as one of the specialty dancers in the *New York Herald Tribune* on 19 February, or the *New York Times* on the 20th (Marc Platt, Katharine Sergava, Kate Friedlich, and Eric Victor).

15. *NHb* TG Helburn box 41 contains an empty folder marked "Lyrics—TH's copy," which presumably contained a similar set.

16. The omission of "Kansas City" from Riggs's set, however, may just be an accidental loss, given that these papers are in some disarray.

17. 2-2-11a–c also survive in *Wc* RC 12/1.

18. Wilk, *Ok!* 174.

19. Rodgers included this tag in a set of second-time measures for the chorus of the song in *Wc* RC 12/1.

20. Langner, *Magic Curtain*, 375.

21. See the lists in *NHb* TG 58/"Oscar Hammerstein, *Oklahoma!*: Costumes and Correspondence," and 118/8. *Wc* HC "*Oklahoma!* sketches," no. 25 (for "It's a Scandal! It's a Outrage!"), also contains a cryptic reference to a third act. There is no other evidence of a proposed three-act division, although it makes some sense, given the passage of time between act 2, scenes 2 and 3.

22. Church later recalled that he received the notice on the return from Boston and just before the New York opening—see Wilk, *Ok!* 209—but this seems inaccurate. After the premiere, audition notes often contained annotations pertaining to draft status; see, for example, those in *NHb* TG 120/14, from the second half of 1943. Langner's appeals are in 120/17.

23. The deferment was reported in the *New York News* on 28 March.

24. *Wc* HC 5 of 9/"June 1943."

25. On cast complaints see Wilk, *Ok!* 149 (quoting Alfred Drake).

26. Rodgers, *Musical Stages*, 225.

27. Langner, *Magic Curtain*, 373; compare Hanff, *Underfoot in Show Business*, 81 (Hanff overhears Langner asking for the dresses to be cut lower).

28. These and other titles are on separate postcards in *NHb* TG 118/8. For further attempts, see the reproductions in Wilk, *Ok!* 196, and for the general issue of naming, see ibid., 194, 205.

29. Although one letter in *Wc* TG 12 of 18 March 1943 styles it "Oklahoma! (Away We Go)."

30. Hanff, *Underfoot in Show Business*, 83–84. Hanff also claims (p. 80) that Helburn was using the title "Away We Go" in late December 1942.

31. *Boston Daily Globe*, 26 February 1942; see also the *Boston Daily Record*, 26 February, and *Boston Sunday Advertiser*, 28 February.

32. *NYpl* MWEZ/+/n.c./25609, folder 6: "TH on GREENGROW," undated. *NHb* TG 118/8 contains a list of "Personnel of the Orchestra for *Green Grow the Lilacs*," with eight first violins, two second violins, two violas, two cellos, two double-basses, one harp, one flute, one oboe (doubling English horn), two clarinets, two French horns, two trumpets, one trombone, one guitar, one banjo, and one percussionist. This adds up to twenty-nine, but presumably the guitar and banjo doubled. There is also some confusion in the orchestrations as to whether the oboe also doubled oboe d'amore (for "People Will Say We're in Love").

33. A press release of one such "interview" for Hammerstein survives in *NYp* MWEZ/+/n.c./25609, folder 1. There are similar materials for Rogers in 25609A, folder 6.

34. *Wc* HC 6 of 9/"1943."

35. These details come from a document prepared by the law offices of Fulton Brylawksi (Washington, D.C.) to Howard Reinheimer on 1 March 1965 concerning the copyrights of *Oklahoma!* materials (and other shows and songs by Rodgers and Hammerstein); *Wc* HC 6 of 9/"O.H. Songs 1920–45." For these five songs, see the reproductions in Wilk, *Ok!* 206. "Oklahoma" was registered on 29 March 1943 (EP 112749), "Out of My Dreams" on 27 April (EP 113472), and "I Cain't Say No" on 19 July (EP 115168).

36. The New Haven program is reproduced in Wilk, *Ok!* 178–79. There is a photocopy of the Boston program (from an original owned by Dan Dietz) in *NYrh*, which also has the New York programs from 31 March 1943 (the premiere) and for the week beginning Sunday 18 July 1943. There is a slightly different Boston program in *NHb* TG 123/17, which appears to have been produced quite hastily, to judge by the printing errors.

37. Helburn linked the pigeons with "Boys and Girls Like You and Me" and Boston in her interview for the 1959 radio show *Heartbeat of Broadway: The Story Behind "Oklahoma!"* (sponsored by the American Heart Foundation; there is a recording in the Library of Congress), but notes their being left in the rafters of the Shubert Theatre in New Haven (no song identified) in *Wayward Quest*, 288. The *New York Post* on 31 March 1943 linked the story with Boston. Nolan (*Sound of Their Music*, 20–21) associated the pigeon disaster with the dropping of "Boys and Girls Like You and Me"; George Church (Wilk, *Ok!* 175–76) connected them to the act 2 finale in New Haven.

38. Wilk, *Ok!* 185.

39. Langner, *Magic Curtain*, 373.

40. Ibid., 374.

41. Wilk, *Ok!* 186. "Boys and Girls Like You and Me" was sung by Judy Garland for the film *Meet Me in St. Louis* (1944), although the scene was cut; Rodgers then used it as dance music in the 1965 version of *Cinderella*, and it currently appears as a song (for the King and Queen) in stage versions of that show. Together with "When I Go Out Walkin' with My Baby," it was also recycled in the 1995 stage version of *State Fair*.

42. Langner, *Magic Curtain*, 372.

43. Wilk, *Ok!* 199 (permission to leave); *NHb* TG 123/17 (undated press release). Platt gives the impression (Wilk, *Ok!* 216) that Church left the show earlier, which is incorrect. Church returned to *Oklahoma!* in 1945.

44. Langner, *Magic Curtain*, 372.

45. Wilk, *Ok!* 139. Compare Vivian Smith (Shiers's wife and one of the dancers) ibid., 185: "It was a charming piece which Agnes had created, Bambi following Eric around, loving everything he did in the solo, and it ended up with a special finish, with Eric going up into a tree right there on stage!" There are widespread cuts in this number in the orchestration in *Wc* RC 34/3.

46. Langner, *Magic Curtain*, 372; *NHb* TG 125/"U–V" (legal action). The *Boston Record* on 22 March noted that Victor had broken his wrist in New Haven but would soon be back in the show. Church (Wilk, *Ok!* 185) says that Victor "settled for a small sum" before the move to Boston. His withdrawal is noted in the *New York Times*, 29 March 1943. De Mille (*"Dance to the Piper" and "Promenade Home,"* 1: 331) refers to Marc Platt rehearsing "Kansas City" in Boston around 26 March; this may be a mistake for "The Farmer and the Cowman" consequent upon the decision over Victor.

47. *NYrh* has conductor's score (single line) and two sets of parts (in G), numbered "new 15" then changed to "16" (so after "All er Nuthin'" was switched?). The parts have a final chorus in A flat, with an instruction to repeat for scene change; there are also additional parts (no. 16A) headed "Boys and Girls for Change."

48. Wilk, *Ok!* 182 (Holm), 184–85 (Abbott, quoting Alfred Drake), 183–84 (Barry); de Mille, *"Dance to the Piper" and "Promenade Home,"* 1: 329 (Weill); Rodgers, *Musical Stages*, 224. Elaine Anderson also seems to have had more confidence; see Langner, *Magic Curtain*, 373–74.

49. Wilk, *Ok!* 183 (Winchell), probably drawing on Hanff, *Underfoot in Show Business*, 82. The wording of the telegram (from Winchell's assistant, Rose, who left before act 2) varies in different tellings of the story, as does its source (some attribute it to Mike Todd).

50. *Wc* HC 6 of 9/loose papers; undated handwritten note on letterhead of the Ritz-Carlton Hotel in Boston.

51. Wilk, *Ok!* 192, 195; compare de Mille, *"Dance to the Piper" and "Promenade Home,"* 1: 329. For rewriting on the train, see also Helburn, *Wayward Quest*, 289.

52. Langner, *Magic Curtain*, 374–75. Langner credits the decision on the lighting to Mamoulian and notes the changes that had to be made to the St. James Theatre in New York as a result.

53. Hyland, *Richard Rodgers*, 146.

54. An advertisement for the Von Trapps' performance in the Copley Plaza Ball-

room is included in the Boston program in *NHb* TG 123/17. Of course, their story later inspired *The Sound of Music*.

55. Wilk, *Ok!* 186.

56. Unless the six-dancer listing is a mistake, and the performers were meant to be credited for the next item, "Boys and Girls Like You and Me," which, according to Alfred Drake, did have some minimal choreography; see Wilk, *Ok!* 186.

57. Wilk, *Ok!* 208.

58. Ibid., 200–203 (Holm on Smith; Blackton's account of Bennett's train ride); Langner, *Magic Curtain*, 375. Bennett gave a more mundane (and typically restrained) account in his essay "Eight Bars and a Pencil," *New York Times*, 8 June 1947, reprinted in Ferencz, "*Broadway Sound*," 301–4.

59. Alfred Drake also tells of his idea for taking the "encore" down a semitone (D flat major rather than D major); Wilk, *Ok!* 203. However, this seems unlikely, and Drake may be thinking, instead, of the decision, made before the orchestration, to have the solo chorus (m. 41) in D flat major. There is a fair amount of confusion in the orchestration (*Wc* RC 36/4), with additional marks for transposition, and apparently a twelve-measure cut before m. 101 (the scale beginning on B preceding the harmonized version of the chorus). The song also seems at one stage to have begun with a vamp for "Were you scared etc. LAURY [*sic*] I was skared Curly would back out on me" (not in the libretto, but drawn from the play).

60. Wilk, *Ok!* 174.

61. Miller, *Rebels with Applause*, 33, makes the point for "The Farmer and the Cowman."

62. *Wc* HC 6 of 9/loose papers. Holm described getting laryngitis in Boston in her interview for the radio show *Heartbeat of Broadway: The Story Behind "Oklahoma!"* (1959), saying that the more her voice cracked, the more the audience laughed.

63. Fordin, *Getting to Know Him*, 201.

64. Kadison and Buloff, *On Stage, Off Stage*, 136; Rodgers, *Musical Stages*, 225–26 (every confidence); Wilk, *Ok!* 200 (six months; Rodgers quoted by Jay Blackton); Langner, *Magic Curtain*, 376. *Dancing in the Streets* opened in Boston on 22 March 1943 but never made it to New York.

65. De Mille, "*Dance to the Piper*" and "*Promenade Home*," 1: 332; Langner, *Magic Curtain*, 376–77; Logan, *Josh*, 188, and Nolan, *Lorenz Hart*, 303–4 (Hart cheering).

66. Helburn, *Wayward Quest*, 289–90 (radio notices).

67. *NHb* 124/"La," which also contains the following unsigned note to Hammerstein.

68. *NHb* 124/"Ga"; *Wc* HC 5 of 9/"June 1943" [*sic*]. A play by Galewski survives in manuscript in the Columbia University Rare Books and Manuscript Library, Aaron Frankel Collection.

CHAPTER 5. Reading *Oklahoma!*

1. For example, Block, "Broadway Canon"; Evans, "Rodgers and Hammerstein's *Oklahoma!*"; Green, "*Oklahoma!*"; Mordden, *Beautiful Mornin'*, 70–79; Taylor, "Script and Score."

2. Hammerstein's "In re *Oklahoma!*" *New York Times*, 23 May 1943; "Mr. Rodgers Insists That It Ain't Luck," *New York Times*, 1 August 1943. For an earlier counterexample, see "Writing Music?—Just a Chore," *Christian Science Monitor*, 3 March 1943 (containing interviews with Hammerstein and Rodgers).

3. In his autobiography, for example, Langner sometimes refers to *Oklahoma!* as a "musical comedy," and rather dismissively so. For the emergence of the term "musical play" and the kudos attached to it in the late 1930s and early 1940s, see D'Andre, "Theatre Guild," 130–37.

4. Block, *Enchanted Evenings*, 136–37 (Weill to Gershwin); Symonette and Kowalke, *Speak Low*, 460 (Weill to Lenya, 18 May 1945).

5. Banfield, *Jerome Kern*, 65.

6. Roost, "Before *Oklahoma!*"

7. Helburn, *Wayward Quest*, 273 (Helburn to O'Neill, May 1940), 275 (O'Neill to Langner, 11 August 1940).

8. Miller, *Rebels with Applause*, 33.

9. Knapp, *American Musical*, 130.

10. Rodgers, *Musical Stages*, 219.

11. Miller, *Rebels with Applause*, 38–39 (realistic).

12. D'Andre, "Theatre Guild," 118.

13. Langner, *Magic Curtain*, 375.

14. Hammerstein, "Notes on Lyrics," 19.

15. For example, the orchestration of "I Cain't Say No" in Wc RC 34/5 has an eight-measure introduction, and that of "All er Nuthin'" (34/1) a four-measure one (both were cut). Part of the inventory of the *Oklahoma!* touring company properties sold to Rodgers and Hammerstein in 1953 (Wc TG 2) included a pitch pipe, which presumably solved some of the problems. There was also a pitch pipe in the London inventory; see Wc TG 11.

16. The vocal score has "chatter all day."

17. See the exhaustive treatment in Wood, "Development of Song Forms."

18. Mast, "As Corny as Kansas in August," 92.

19. Rodgers, *Musical Stages*, 220.

20. The stage direction in the typed lyric-sheet in Wc RC 12/13 is "Touched and suddenly carried away, [Jud] bellows out a response," and at the end, "JUD looks puzzled. CURLY doesn't give him much time to think it over." The lyric sheet in NHb 122/1 has an added line for Curly's speech (after Jud's "He loved his fellow man"): "And he loved the animals—And animals loved him. Even the cows 'at he used to milk at five o'clock on a winter mornin's with his ice-cold fingers!" In the orchestration, mm. 30–37 was originally eight measures longer.

21. During the spoken dialogue, the vocal score, but not the libretto, has the stage direction "JUD appears."

22. Miller, *Rebels with Applause*, 43–44.

23. "In re *Oklahoma!*" *New York Times*, 23 May 1943.

24. Hammerstein, "Notes on Lyrics," 14. However, he also notes (p. 27) the importance for songwriters of their songs having a reception outside of a show.

25. Wc HC "*Oklahoma!* sketches," no. 84.

26. Opposition to the New Deal is discussed in Kirle, "Reconciliation"; see also

Filmer, Rimmer, and Walsh, *"Oklahoma!"* which further hints at the pastoral tendencies which I explore in more detail. For the broader issues, see Donovan, "'Oh, What
a Beautiful Mornin''"; Jones, *Our Musicals, Ourselves*, 141–45; Rugg, "What It Used
to Be."

27. *New York Times*, 1 August 1943 (Rodgers); *New York Post*, 29 March 1943
(Hammerstein).

28. *New York Times*, 1 August 1943 (Rodgers); Knapp, *American Musical*, 128
(romantically inclined); Miller, *Rebels with Applause*, 37 (farmer); Sears, "Coming of
the Musical Play," 126 (wide-open spaces).

29. Most, *Making Americans*, 41–42.

30. Suskin, *Opening Night on Broadway*, 503. Compare William Hawkins in the
World-Telegram and Sun (ibid., 504): "Even more breathtaking was the use of an extremely serious neurotic person, and a realistically ugly situation, in a musical comedy."

31. Wilk, *Ok!* 120. The *Chicago Daily Tribune*, 4 July 1943, refers to White's use
of "an ancient mail order catalog" for the costumes.

32. Cited in Most, *Making Americans*, 187.

33. Rodgers, *Musical Stages*, 220. I have not managed to identify a likely candidate
for the book of songs.

34. "In re *Oklahoma!*" *New York Times*, 23 May 1943.

35. Knapp, *American Musical*, 132–33.

36. Turner, "Significance of the Frontier," 22–23, 37.

37. Goldstein, "I Enjoy Being a Girl."

38. Langner, *Magic Curtain*, 376; see also Edward W. Curtin's letter of 16 March
(after seeing the Boston opening) in chap. 4. However, Langner also reports Vincent
Freedley's comment on *Oklahoma!* (in Boston): "I think this play will be a tremendous success! And don't think it's so clean either." Langner adds, "There is, of course, a
certain amount of lusty humor in *Oklahoma!* but it is never lascivious."

39. Miller, *Rebels with Applause*, 45.

40. "You cain't deserve the sweet and tender things in life less'n you're tough" was
also Hammerstein's addition.

41. Rodgers, *Musical Stages*, 227.

42. *NHb* TG 125/"Ra." Gerald Mast ("As Corny as Kansas in August," 98) also
notes that Buloff played the role with a "Dutch" (that is, "Deutsch" = Yiddish) accent.

43. Most, *Making Americans*, 113, on which my reading of Ali Hakim relies significantly; see also Kirle, "Reconciliation," 265.

44. For example, Aaron Greenspan in Sylvia Regan's *Morning Star* (1940), Istvan
in Dan Goldberg's *The Man from Cairo* (1938; set in Budapest), and Zamiano in Ben
Hecht's *To Quito and Back*, set in Ecuador (1937). The same characteristics apply to his
numerous Hollywood roles, including one of the KGB commissars, Ivanov, in the film
Silk Stockings (1957).

45. Perhaps significantly, Hammerstein dropped one of his intended introductory
expletives ("Embellzed") that appears in Wc HC *"Oklahoma!* sketches," no. 18.

46. This comes from the very first paragraph of Richard Rodgers's autobiography,
Musical Stages, 4.

47. Wilk, *Ok!* 256; Most, *Making Americans*, 115. He and Rodgers appeared as

"The Territory's Peerless Singing & Dancing Team." Typically, Rodgers chose the more WASP-ish "Mister Will Parker Rodgers."

48. Most, *Making Americans*, 32–39, 54.

49. According to his wife, Buloff carried off the song "in his own peculiar half-singing, half-speaking style" that, in turn, was an influence for Rex Harrison in *My Fair Lady*, so Harrison claimed; see Kadison and Buloff, *On Stage, Off Stage*, 136. Most (*Making Americans*, 107) claims wrongly that Ali Hakim sings in "Oklahoma."

50. Photographs of the "finale" of *Oklahoma!* (for example, Most, *Making Americans*, 117) regularly include Ali Hakim, but according to the stage directions, he leaves before the shivaree, Jud's death, and the trial. These photographs all have the appearance instead of a staged photo call.

51. Kirle, "Reconciliation," 267–70.

52. Wc RC 12/3, with a line ("shouting over music, across at the cowmen") "Before the farmers come y'never had no fields full of growin' grain!"

53. Hammerstein, "Notes on Lyrics," 18.

54. Mast, "As Corny as Kansas in August" (compare Filmer, Rimmer, and Walsh, "Oklahoma!" 392); Knapp, *American Musical*, 133–34.

55. Most, "'We Know We Belong to the Land.'" Her article created a flurry of controversy: see *PMLA* 113 (1998): 452–53 (Sandra K. Baringer; arguing that Most's arguments concerning assimilation need to take into account Riggs's own pro-Indian agenda); 453–54 (Robert Hapgood; denying the "Negro" resonances—the issue is more Jud's refusal to change); 114 (1999), 97–99 (Michael Steig; objecting to the "Jewish" reading). This, in turn, seems to have prompted Most to tone down her reading, which is far less direct in *Making Americans*, 116–18. For the change of name from Jeeter to Jud, see chap. 3. The name on Howard da Silva's initial contract dated 8 February 1943 (*NHb* TG 118/16) is "Judson Fry," which scarcely alters the etymological problems ("son of . . ."). "Jud" as a first or last name is usually regarded as a contraction or pet form of Jude, Judah (or Judas), and Jordan; see Partridge, *Name This Child*; Smith, *Dictionary of American Family Names*. Partridge notes that although the name is associated with notions of praise, it is stigmatized by the association with Judas the Traitor. The English "Fry" or "Frye" comes from "free" in the sense of one free of obligations to the lord of the manor.

56. Hammerstein, "Notes on Lyrics," 19.

57. *NHb* TG 124/"Ha" (1 November 1943).

58. Rodgers, *Musical Stages*, 88; Magee, "Irving Berlin's 'Blue Skies.'"

59. "In re *Oklahoma!*" *New York Times*, 23 May 1943.

60. *NHb* 124/"Da" (Downes to Guild, 28 May 1943); this folder also includes a telegram (25 October 1943) from Downes asking for tickets to the show as a favor. Wc HC 5 of 9/"June 1943" (Downes to Hammerstein, 28 May 1943, also requesting tickets for Arturo Toscanini and Vladimir Horowitz and their wives to attend *Oklahoma!*).

61. D'Andre, "Theatre Guild," 128–29.

62. *NHb* TG 52/"Gassner Memos 1942–3" (7 June 1943).

63. Beiswanger, "Theatre Today," 25–26.

64. D'Andre, "Theatre Guild," 120–22.

65. Bentley, *Playwright as Thinker*, 6–7. For Bentley, see also Swain, *Broadway*

Musical, 6–7, although Swain is too willing to use him just as a foil for his own Wagnerian defense of the musical.

66. Bentley, *Playwright as Thinker*, 117, which does scant justice to Nietzsche's complex (and changing) views of Wagner.

67. Ibid., 282. The emergence of "star" directors was a matter of some concern in the 1940s, prompting extensive debate over drama's authorial voices; Beiswanger addressed the same issue in "Theatre Today."

68. Bentley, *Playwright as Thinker*, 110.

69. Ibid., 283–84.

CHAPTER 6. From Stage to Screen

1. *NHb* TG 124/"La" (Logan, 1 April 1943); 58/"Oscar Hammerstein" (pink tab); 124/"Ha" (Hopkins, 2 April 1943).

2. *NHb* TG 124/"B." Bennett's "symphonic picture" based on *Porgy and Bess* was first performed by the New York Philharmonic under Fritz Reiner on 31 March 1943 (Bennett was there, missing the premiere of *Oklahoma!*), and was repeated on 2, 3, and 5 April; see the notices in the *New York Times*.

3. *NHb* TG 125/"Sa"; Langner, *Magic Curtain*, 377. Langner also wrote to Abe Kurnit, the master carpenter, on 5 April, "In appreciation of all your help and hard work on this difficult production"; 124/"K."

4. De Mille, *"Dance to the Piper" and "Promenade Home,"* 1: 334.

5. *NHb* TG 89 (Mamoulian). Mamoulian also attended a Guild production conference in mid-June 1943; see Gassner's memo to Langner of 12 June in 52/"John Gassner" (pink tab). The Guild's 1943–44 season contained *Othello* (starring Paul Robeson), Paul Osborn's *The Innocent Voyage*, and S. N. Behrman's (after Franz Werfel) *Jacobowsky and the Colonel*. This was fewer plays than the norm, in part, so the *New York Times* explained (5 April 1944), because of the demands of *Oklahoma!*

6. *Wc* TG 2. Howard Reinheimer confirmed the purchase on 19 April 1943, also outlining the schedule for payment by installments; *Wc* HC 5 of 9/"April 1943."

7. There are several drafts of the (undated) contract in *NHb* TG 118/14, and one in *Wc* HC 5 of 9/"April 1943." The music-studio idea was revived in mid-1944 (with John Raitt and George Houston; D'Andre, "Theatre Guild," 222), and it later seems to have developed into a plan (again, unrealized) for the Guild to produce opera in English (see the report in the *Chicago Daily Tribune*, 1 October 1944, which also mentions Raitt and Houston).

8. *Wc* HC 5 of 9/"June 1943."

9. The letters to Bill are in *Wc* HC 6 of 9/"1944." The Bemelmans proposal seems to have revived plans first raised in September 1941. A letter from Arthur Freed of MGM of 14 October 1943 (*Wc* HC 6 of 9/"1944"; this letter also discusses *Show Boat*) suggests that one of the MGM projects was *The Belle of New York*, which in fact was released in 1952 as a vehicle for Fred Astaire and Vera-Ellen. However, the Judy Garland one may have been what became *Meet Me in St. Louis* (1944), which originally included Garland singing "Boys and Girls Like You and Me." (The scene was cut after the first preview.) Charles Ruggles (whom Hammerstein had approached several times in 1942) again turned down the part of Cap'n Andy on 4 May 1943; *Wc* HC 5 of 9/

"May 1943." Hammerstein's agent in Hollywood, Frank Orsatti, also asked for a copy of *Carmen Jones* for Freed on 2 April 1943; 5 of 9/"April 1943."

10. Helburn to Munsell, 7 and 29 April 1943, *NHb* TG 97/"Lieut. Colonel Munsell."

11. W*c* TG 11.

12. Summaries are in *NHb* TG 119/7 and 124/"Ca."

13. *NHb* TG 97/"Munsell Memos to T.H. 1941" (Helburn to Munsell, 27 May 1943); 124/"Ma" (Langner to Munsell, 14 June 1942); 97/"Munsell" (pink tab; William Morris Agency to Langner relaying Hyams offer, 19 July 1943). Langner repeated his plan to Munsell on 23 December 1943, 97/"Munsell" (pink tab): "My idea is that this is much more apt to be a play for Drury Lane than is *Porgy and Bess* which already failed in England."

14. This and the following letters to Munsell are in *NHb* TG 97/"Munsell" (pink tab).

15. Howard Lindsay and Russel Crouse's *Life with Father* opened on Broadway on 8 November 1939 and eventually closed on 12 July 1947 after 3,224 performances. Sigmund Romberg's *The Student Prince*, produced by the Shuberts, opened on 2 December 1924 and closed after 608 performances; it was revived in 1931 (42 performances) and 1943 (153 from 8 June to 2 October). The Shuberts' production of *Blossom Time* (with music by Franz Schubert adapted by Romberg) had a large number of performances in 1921–22 and 1924–25, and briefer revivals in 1926, 1931, 1938, and 1943 (4 September to 9 October).

16. W*c* HC 5 of 9/"June 1943."

17. I have not found any such report in the *New York Times*, although the *New York Telegraph*, *New York Herald Tribune*, and other papers reported on or about 17 May the signing of Harry Stockwell as Curly in the second company of *Oklahoma!* to be put into production the next season.

18. *NHb* TG 125/"U–V" (May–June); 118/17 (August).

19. *NHb* TG 85/"Joshua Logan."

20. *NHb* TG 124/"Da" (2 April); 39/"Agnes de Mille" (pink tab; 20 April). The American Ballet Theatre staged David Tudor's *Dark Elegies* and *Romeo and Juliet*, Agnes de Mille's *Three Virgins and a Devil*, and David Lichine's *Helen of Troy* at the Metropolitan Opera House on 13 April; *New York Times*, 14 April 1943.

21. *NHb* TG 156/"Jerry Whyte."

22. *NHb* TG 72/"Elia Kazan" (pink tab). There are notes (1943–44) on ballet-plays also in 52/"John Gassner" (pencil on tab [#1]). On 4 June 1944 the *Chicago Daily Tribune* reported that the Guild's 1944–45 touring season would include "a program of ballet plays called *American Dances.*"

23. Rodgers, Hammerstein, and the Guild prepared an agreement for *Liliom* in November 1943 and signed in February 1944; *NHb* TG 116/"Carousel" (yellow tab). A conference on adapting the play was held at Hammerstein's house on 7 December 1943, during which Rodgers seems to have suggested the idea of "Soliloquy."

24. *NHb* TG 35/"Aaron Copland."

25. The clipping was sent by Sam Weller to Langner also on 6 August; *NHb* TG 120/8. Langner refers (in very general terms) to the Guild's interest in entering film production, then television, in *Magic Curtain*, 430–36. Landon's book was first published

in 1944. The film *Anna and the King of Siam*, starring Rex Harrison and Irene Dunne, was released in 1946 by Twentieth Century–Fox; there is no indication that the Guild was involved. However, on 28 September 1944 Kay Swift wrote to the Guild offering to write the music for the Guild's rumored adaptation (for the stage?) of *Anna and the King of Siam* to be done by Philip Barry; 145/"Swa–Sz."

26. *NHb* TG 145/"Joseph E. C. Swan" (United Artists); 131/"David O. Selznick"; 131/"Myron Selznick"; 34/"Columbia Pictures." Langner noted to Munsell on 30 September 1943 that the Guild had established a Motion Picture Department with a view to negotiating two films per year.

27. *New York Times*, 25 July 1943.

28. *NHb* TG 52/"Gassner Memos 1942–3." For September 1943 suggestions of musicals with Weill (*The Good Soldier Schweik* and *The Pursuit of Happiness*), see chap. 1.

29. Helburn, *Wayward Quest*, 293. She initiated the lunches with a memo of 7 May 1943; *Wc* HC 5 of 9/"May 1943."

30. Mantle notified Hammerstein of his intention to include the libretto probably in June 1943; see his letter dated "Monday" in *Wc* HC 5 of 9/"June 1943."

31. Wilk, *Ok!* 252 (Dixon; compare Rodgers, *Musical Stages*, 222–23); *NHb* 124/"Da" (da Silva, reported by Elaine Anderson, assistant stage manager, to Langner, 9 November 1943). Da Silva had already asked for feature billing on 2 April 1943, according to a document in this same folder.

32. *NHb* TG 89/"Rouben Mamoulian" (white tab); *Wc* HC 6 of 9/yellow folder; see also D'Andre, "Theatre Guild," 215–17.

33. I cannot find any such *New York Times* article.

34. *NHb* Riggs 5/99 (Riggs); *NHb* TG 39/"Agnes de Mille" (yellow tab), 61/"Theresa Helburn," and *Wc* TG 11, 19 (de Mille; see also de Mille, "*Dance to the Piper*" and "*Promenade Home*," 2: 252–54); *NHb* TG 122/3 (Helburn). The Rodgers and Hammerstein Organization later offered some further redress to de Mille; see its newsletter *Happy Talk* 1–2 (Winter 1994): 1, 3.

35. So Helburn decreed in a circular memo; *Wc* HC 5 of 9/"May 1943."

36. *NHb* TG 118/16 (Roberts, Holm, Linn, Sergava); 123/7 (Blackton); 118/7 (undated petition; the signatories include George Church, which would place the document in April or May).

37. *NHb* TG 125/"Ra." Langner used the $82,000 figure in his various letters appealing draft notices for cast members; 120/17.

38. The accounts are mostly in *NHb* TG 118/7 (including the one for the week ending 25 December 1947, reproduced in Wilk, *Ok!* 242). See also 118/4 ("Celebrating the Tenth Anniversary of Rodgers and Hammerstein") for sheet music sales in fall 1943.

39. Harriman, *Take Them up Tenderly*, 198, and see chap. 1.

40. *Wc* HC 5 of 9/"July 1943"; folder "August 1943" here contains royalty checks for the New York *Oklahoma!* averaging $1,000 per week.

41. *NHb* TG 20/"S. N. Behrman" no. 1; 116/"Carousel" (yellow tab; Fitelson); *New York Times*, 30 March 1944 (first-year returns); 118/4 ("Celebrating the Tenth Anniversary of Rodgers and Hammerstein"; New York receipts to 1948); 120/13 (national company to September 1948); de Mille, "*Dance to the Piper*" and "*Promenade Home*," 2: 253–54; *NHb* Riggs 5/113–15 (Riggs royalty statements); *NHb* TG 120/13 (Jack

Koritzer [the Guild accountant] to Helburn, 13 November 1947, estimating Riggs's total royalties); 118/4 ("Celebrating the Tenth Anniversary of Rodgers and Hammerstein"; 2,500 percent; compare the *New York Times*, 19 May 1948); Helburn, *Wayward Quest*, 290 ($50,000; compare de Mille, *"Dance to the Piper" and "Promenade Home,"* 2: 252–53, which dates the $50,000 before the sale of the show); *Variety*, 9 January 1980 ("*Oklahoma!* At First *Away We Go*, but to Insiders, 'Terry's Folly'").

42. *NHb* TG 122/8. Rumor of a film with Jimmy Cagney as Curly (and directed by Rouben Mamoulian) appeared in the *Chicago Daily Tribune*, 22 December 1943.

43. The letters to Bill are in *Wc* HC 6 of 9/"1944." The rest of the letter of 17 May concerns the revival of *Show Boat* and the plans for a score for MGM. The one of 1 June also refers to *State Fair*. The July playlist is in *Wc* HC 5 of 9/"July 1943."

44. *NHb* TG 125/"Ta" (Sinatra); 120/18 (complaints by Sam Weller, director of publicity for the national company, about Sinatra and Crosby); DeVeaux, *Birth of Bebop*, 295–306 (1942–44 dispute); 97/"Lieut. Colonel Munsell" (Helburn to Munsell, 12 August 1943).

45. *NHb* TG 120/11, 122/4 (radio, clubs, theaters); 125/"Ra" (Langner to Rodgers, 2 November 1943; Rodgers disagrees in letter of 6 November, reporting a discussion with Hammerstein); 97/"Munsell" (pink tab; Louis Dreyfus).

46. *NHb* TG 38/"Decca Records." This was not the first complete original-cast recording of a musical, as is often claimed; see Grant, *Rise and Fall*, 203–4, for other precedents, including *The Cradle Will Rock* (recorded 1938) and *Porgy and Bess* (1942).

47. *NHb* TG 122/4, *Wc* TG 2 (Republic Pictures); *NHb* TG 113/"Charles Riegelman" (*A Wedding in Oklahoma*); 118/13 (*The Oklahomans*).

48. Rodgers, *Musical Stages*, 228.

49. Max Dreyfus at Chappell and Co. was thanked for a copy of the vocal score on 23 December; *NHb* TG 124/"Ca." Dreyfus had formed a partnership with Rodgers and Hammerstein, Williamson Music, which published *Oklahoma!* and subsequent Rodgers and Hammerstein musicals (as well as songs, etc., by other composers); *New York Times*, 25 June 1944. Williamson Music received the copyrights on the sheet music held by the original publisher, Marlo Music Corporation, on 30 August 1943. The name came from the fact that both Rodgers and Hammerstein had fathers called William; *New York Times*, 21 January 1945. Self-publishing (in effect) would, of course, increase royalties and income.

50. For the copyright registrations, see chap. 4. The other song published, "Boys and Girls Like You and Me," was of course dropped. For the sales figures, see Hammerstein to Bill, 9 November 1943, *Wc* HC 6 of 9/"1944" (also noting that "Decca is getting out a beautiful 12-side album"); Harriman, *Take Them up Tenderly*, 198 (figures for January 1944).

51. A good number of these recordings are available as bonus items on the Naxos rerelease of the original-cast recording (Naxos 8.120787, 2005).

52. Licensing agreements are in *Wc* TG 19.

53. Langner, *Magic Curtain*, 378–79, which also discusses the adoption of "Oklahoma" as a state anthem. Helburn reported the convention plans to Jerry Whyte on 5 July 1944; *NHb* TG 156/"J. Whyte" (yellow tab).

54. *NHb* TG 121/5; the comment is made in the context of de Mille's being upset at not having had a say in choosing new dancers for the London company.

55. The dates of these openings vary in some sources but are confirmed by the clippings (announcements and reviews) in *NHb* TG Pressbook 202.

56. *NHb* TG 123/11, 124/"Ca." There had been talk as early as late summer 1943 of taking *Oklahoma!* to Los Angeles; *Chicago Daily Tribune*, 5 September 1943. Later plans for a performance in the Hollywood Bowl in June–July 1948 also came to naught; 120/13.

57. Helburn, *Wayward Quest*, 292; Rodgers, *Musical Stages*, 228–29.

58. Contractual details from October 1944 survive in *NHb* TG 123/13 (and the tour had been rumored in the *New York Times* on 25 June 1944); there is a prop list, dated 23 February 1945, in 58/"Hammerstein: *Oklahoma!*" Ted Hammerstein (Oscar's cousin) managed the show; he was later involved in other touring productions of *Oklahoma!* including Australia. Another Hammerstein, Reginald (Reggie, Oscar's younger brother) supervised the two U.S. *Oklahoma!* companies in 1944–45, while Jerry Whyte was in the army.

59. *NHb* TG 125/"Wa" (West Point); 123/6, 123/8, *Wc* TG 19, *New York Times*, 22 May 1944 (matinees). Royalties were waived. Rodgers later claimed (*Musical Stages*, 229), erroneously, that these were free.

60. Some sources give the opening as 29 April, which was presumably a press preview; all the "good luck" telegrams in *NHb* TG 121/4 are dated 30 April. Langner (*Magic Curtain*, 381) refers wrongly to a two-week engagement in Manchester.

61. *NHb* TG 121/5.

62. Cited in Snelson, "West End Musical," 24.

63. The script and further details are in *NHb* TG 120/4.

64. Snelson, "West End Musical," 175 (*Bet Your Life*), 201 (*Gay's the Word*). Snelson (pp. 40–56) also discusses the more serious imitation of *Oklahoma!* in John Toré's *Golden City* (1950).

65. Langner, *Magic Curtain*, 383. A Swedish translation (by Eli Oftedal) of the libretto survives in *Wc* HC 13/4.

66. These requests are in *NHb* TG 118/17, 120/13, 121/17 (which also includes the list of writers), and *Wc* HC 2 of 9/"*Oklahoma!* documents 1949–51."

67. Whyte's new contract is in *NHb* TG 125/"Wa." His correspondence is in *NHb* TG 156, which also contains subsequent letters of reappointment. Langner noted his original appointment to Munsell on 30 September 1943; *NHb* TG 97/"Munsell" (pink tab).

68. *NHb* TG 58/"Oscar Hammerstein." For similar notes on the London performance on 17 July 1948 (a matinee) by Warren Caro, executive secretary of the Guild, see 30/"Warren Caro" (yellow tab).

69. On 22 June 1944, Langner wrote to Drake (in Hollywood) about using him for a forthcoming production of either *Romeo and Juliet* or *Hamlet*; *NHb* TG 40/"Alfred Drake." This folder also includes letters concerning Drake's authorial collaborations with lyricist Edgar Eager.

70. *NHb* TG 123/1 (Blackton, Reddick); 118/5 (Friedlich).

71. See the data on *Oklahoma!* in Green, *Fact Book*, although this cannot always be assumed to be accurate.

72. Raitt's impending role in *Carousel* was reported in the *Chicago Daily Tribune* on 28 May 1944.

73. NHb TG 120/13 (O'Neill, presumably the Sherry O'Neil who played in the film *Training for Trouble* [1947]); 129/9 (Britton). This folder also includes other notes on casting after auditions with Rodgers, Hammerstein, and Mamoulian.

74. De Mille, *"Dance to the Piper" and "Promenade Home,"* 2: 74–76 (Adams); NHb TG 121/5 (Watson). Already in December 1943 there had been rumors of Watson replacing Joan Roberts, and on the 10th, Alfred Tamarin, the Guild's press representative, accused Dorothy Ross, a New York theatrical agent, of manipulating a news item to that effect in that day's issue of the *New York Sun*; 125/"Wa."

75. Only the Scandinavian performances did not have a member of the *Oklahoma!* team on board. For the dancing, Vivian Smith refers to the problem in the Broadway Oral History Project interview on *Oklahoma!* (1 April 1993) in NYp MGZIC 9–5170 (video). In April–May 1944, arrangements were made to film the dream-ballet, "Many a New Day," and "The Farmer and the Cowman," plus, if there was time, "Kansas City" and the dance of "All er Nuthin'"; see Helburn's memo of 18 March in NHb TG 123/1, and also documents in Wc TG 2. After the August 1953 sale, Rodgers and Hammerstein requested and received a set of films in six containers (Langner to Sara Greenspan, 11 May 1954, NHb TG 122/11, Wc TG 16); this suggests that everything requested was filmed (with the ballet on two reels). It is not clear whether this is the source of the seven-minute clip of the original dream-ballet now in NYp (which I have not been able to see).

76. Rodgers, *Musical Stages*, 266; see also his comments (p. 264) on the troublesome modifications in the Drury Lane *South Pacific*. Agnes de Mille (*"Dance to the Piper" and "Promenade Home,"* 2: 239) said something similar of the dances for *Oklahoma!* which were "rooted into the score and dialogue and have become part of the flesh; that is why they are always reproduced no matter who stages the revivals."

77. Langner, *Magic Curtain*, 383.

78. Ibid., 391.

79. NHb TG 120/10 (Helburn to Langner); Wc TG 16 (losses on *Allegro* noted by W[arren] C[aro], 16 March 1950).

80. Despite the split, both Langner and Helburn invested in *South Pacific*; weekly summaries of profits for it (averaging over $10,000 per week) survive in NHb TG 126.

81. NHb TG 58/"Oscar Hammerstein."

82. NHb TG 118/15.

83. NHb TG 119/10.

84. NHb TG 118/15. There had already been rumors of this happening in October 1947; 120/10.

85. NHb TG 118/15 (Langner to Leverton; Langner proposing Kelly, 24 November 1947), 120/13 (other proposals), 123/14 (Holm's contract for December 1947; see also the *New York Times*, 1 December 1947); NHb Riggs 6/20 (Langner to Riggs).

86. NHb TG 118/15; Wc TG 19; *New York Times*, 19 May 1948.

87. NHb 123/2 (1948–50 statements from the Guild's New York accountants, Pinto, Winokur and Pagano), 120/10 (1951–52), 123/15 (1952–53).

88. *New York Times*, 28, 30 July 1951; Wc TG 20 (subway circuit contracts).

89. NHb TG 119/3 (declining profits); Wc TG 1 (contract for Ayers), 2 (details of costs); NHb TG 118/11–12 (other documents relating to the fire); 120/13, 123/15, Wc TG 6 (insurance claim).

90. *NHb* TG 122/10.

91. See the 1951–52 accounts in *NHb* Langner 127.

92. In *Wayward Quest*, 295, Helburn also notes her various approaches (at unspecified times and on unspecified projects) to Gian Carlo Menotti, Irving Berlin, Leonard Bernstein, Kurt Weill, Sigmund Romberg, and Cole Porter. Berlin and Porter were also candidates for the *Pygmalion* project; see D'Andre, "Theatre Guild," 242–57.

93. *Wc* TG 17, 18; *New York Times*, 31 August 1953 (price given as $840,000).

94. *NHb* TG 120/13 (Rodgers); 58/"Oscar Hammerstein."

95. *Wc* HC 2 of 9/"*Oklahoma!* documents 1949–51."

96. Logan, *Movie Stars*, 125.

97. Scripts survive in *Wc* HC 13/3 (27 April script); 13/5 (an earlier version of act 1 only, with amendments dated 14 April); 13/2 ("final script" dated 1 June 1954, with pages added up to 14 September 1954). De Mille sent an undated postcard to Hammerstein ("I've already completed the scenario for the Dream Ballet and I think it's good"), which he acknowledged on 14 April 1953. See also the *New York Times*, 10 August 1953, 17 August 1953 (announcing the firm agreement to make the film), 13 September 1953.

98. For the planting, see the *New York Times*, 11 July 1954, 12 September 1954.

99. The revised order had already been suggested by Olin Downes in the *New York Times*, 6 June 1943.

100. There are also budget details and schedules in *NYp* RC 8/11–13. A preliminary budget was prepared on 14 December 1953, and the next budget, already showing significant overspends, on 20 March 1954.

101. See his comments in his (1978) memoirs in Ferencz, "Broadway Sound," 218–20.

102. *NYp* RC 8/11.

103. In the Todd-AO process, the image took up sixty-five millimeters of the film and the six-channel sound occupied five; hence the apparent inconsistency of referring to Todd-AO film as 65 mm or 70 mm.

104. Ferencz, "Broadway Sound," 220 (Bennett); Rodgers, *Musical Stages*, 285. Rodgers had long been somewhat jaundiced about film versions of his musicals, based on his and Hart's experiences with Hollywood; see Hischak, *Through the Screen Door*, 4–9.

105. *Wc* TG 18.

106. *NHb* TG 120/13. *Pipe Dream* opened on 30 November.

Bibliography

DOCUMENTS

The bulk of the documents associated with the Theatre Guild and *Oklahoma!* are in *NHb* TG, Series I (Correspondence), 118–25 (eight boxes), and *Wc* TG 1–20 (twenty folders in two boxes). For *NHb* TG, the outline contents listed below are based on rationalized versions of the folder tabs, with editorial modifications in square brackets; for *Wc* TG they derive from the summary list of contents provided by Lionheart Autographs, Inc., included at the head of the collection. Inclusive dates, where given, are approximate.

NHb TG 118/1	*Oklahoma!*: 1951–52 [1950–53]
118/2	*Oklahoma!*: clippings [1951–52]
118/3	*Oklahoma!*: investors [empty]
118/4	Untitled [fact sheets and narratives for tenth anniversary]
118/5	Rodgers and Hammerstein, *Oklahoma!* [1944–49]
118/6	*Oklahoma!*: general [1948–54]
118/7	Business: *Oklahoma!* [1943]
118/8	Production: *Oklahoma!* [1942–43]
118/9	Ref: *Oklahoma!* [1946–47]
118/10	*Oklahoma!*: birthday party 1947 (4th)
118/11	*Oklahoma!*: USA 1952[–53]
118/12	*Oklahoma!* [1951–52]
118/13	Republic [Pictures] case [1943–45]
118/14	Rodgers-Hammerstein, *Oklahoma!*: contract
118/15	*Oklahoma!*: #1 [Broadway company, 1946–50]
118/16	*Oklahoma!*: 1943–44 [contracts]
118/17	*Oklahoma!*: #2 [national company] 1943–44 [1943–48]
119/1	*Oklahoma!*: actors; London situation [1947–50]
119/2	Amateur rights, *Oklahoma!* [1944–45]

NHb TG 119/3   *Oklahoma!*: American company [1951–52]
119/4   *Oklahoma!*: anniversary party [1947–48]
119/5   Anniversary party, 1944, *Oklahoma!*
119/6   *Oklahoma!*: birthday party, 1944
119/7   Rodgers and Hammerstein, *Okla[homa!]* [1943–44]
119/8–9   *Oklahoma!*: fifth anniversary party [1948]
119/10   Audience questionnaire, *Oklahoma!* [1947]

120/1   Benefits, *Oklahoma!* [1944]
120/2–3   *Oklahoma!*: Berlin [1951]
120/4   *Oklahoma!*: bdcst [BBC Broadcast, 1949]
120/5   Casting letters, *Oklahoma!*: 1944[–45]
120/6   Chicago, general corres[pondence], *Oklahoma!* [1944–45]
120/7   Chicago, correspondence, Herbert Farrar [general manager; 1943–
                   44]
120/8   Chicago, correspondence, S. M. Weller [director of publicity;
                   1943–44]
120/9   *Oklahoma!*: Chicago (casting) [1944]
120/10   *Oklahoma!*: English [and Australian] production [1947–49]
120/11   *Oklahoma!*: Columbia Pictures [1943]
120/12   A [misplaced from miscellaneous correspondence in *NHb* TG 124]
120/13   Rodgers and Hammerstein, *Oklahoma!* [1947–55]
120/14   Auditions [1943]
120/15   *Oklahoma!*: ballet
120/16   Casting letters, *Oklahoma!* 1943[–45]
120/17   Draft calls [into the armed forces], *Oklahoma!* [1943–46]

121/1   *Oklahoma!*: England; press, programs, billing, etc. [1947]
121/2   *Oklahoma!*: London company [1947–50]
121/3   *Oklahoma!*: England; financial matters (individual contracts,
                   investors letters, etc.) [1947–50]
121/4   *Oklahoma!*: England; opening at Drury Lane, London [1947]
121/5   *Oklahoma!*: England; general correspondence [1947–51]
121/6   *Oklahoma!*: England [1952]
121/7   *Oklahoma!*: England [yellow tab; 1952–53]
121/8   *Oklahoma!*: England; transportation, visas, travel information, etc.
                   [1947]
121/9   *Oklahoma!*: England; statements [1951–52]
121/10   *Oklahoma!*: England; Gillespie Bros. [chartered accountants; 1953]
121/11   *Oklahoma!*: England; Littler correspondence (except contract
                   matters) [1950]
121/12   *Oklahoma!*: England; contract file [1947–50]
121/13   *Oklahoma!*: England; ticket arrangements [1947]
121/14   *Oklahoma!*: England; production, cast; Jerome Whyte correspon-
                   dence [1948]
121/15   *Oklahoma!*: England, 1952

NHb TG 121/16   *Oklahoma!*: foreign rights, 1946[–50]
121/17   Foreign rights, *Oklahoma!* [1943–44]

122/1   Lyrics: J. Whyte's copy
122/2   Meyer, Max: daily reports, *Oklahoma!* [1943–44]
122/3   Los Angeles: Rodgers, *Oklahoma!*, L.A. opening [1946]
122/4   *Oklahoma!*: infringements [1943]
122/5   *Oklahoma!*: possible production in Mexico [1947–50]
122/6   *Oklahoma!*: Mexico [1951]
122/7   *Oklahoma!*: motion pix [empty]
122/8   *Oklahoma!*: motion pictures [1943–45]
122/9   *Oklahoma!*: national company [1950–51]
122/10   Hammerstein, *Oklahoma!* [1943, 1952–53]
122/11   Hammerstein, *Oklahoma!*: sale 1953[–54]
122/12   *Oklahoma!*: national company [1943–45]
122/13   *Oklahoma!*: national co[mpany; 1935–51; 1935 letter concerns film
                      rights to *Green Grow the Lilacs*]

123/1   Cast NY company [1942–45]
123/2   *Oklahoma!*: New York, summer 1951 [and United Kingdom, 1948–50]
123/3   *Oklahoma!*: New York company, 1945
123/4   *Oklahoma!*: Oklahoma City trip [1946]
123/5   *Oklahoma!*: radio [1943]
123/6   Special matinee, *Oklahoma!* [1944–45]
123/7   *Oklahoma!*: salary memos [1943–45]
123/8   *Oklahoma!*: special matinee for servicemen [1944–45]
123/9   *Oklahoma!*: statements [1951–53]
123/10   Tickets, *Oklahoma!* [1943–44]
123/11   *Oklahoma!*: tax situation [1944]
123/12   Vacations [1944]
123/13   U.S.O. camp shows, *Oklahoma!* [1944–45]
123/14   Out folder, *Oklahoma!* [lapsed contracts; 1944–48]
123/15   *Oklahoma!*: tour, 1952–53 [and 1954; plus U.K. details]
123/16   *Oklahoma!*: press and programs [1946–49]
123/17   Press, *Oklahoma!* [1943]

124   [Miscellaneous correspondence on *Oklahoma!* B–Q, mostly
                      1943–45; for "A," see *NHb* TG 120/12]

125   [Miscellaneous correspondence on *Oklahoma!* R–Z, mostly 1943–45]

Wc TG 1   Photostat contracts [1935–43]
2   Important contracts [for productions, royalties, principals; 1929–53]
3   Music and [a few] programs [1951–53]
4   Contracts and inventories [1942–53]

Wc TG 5   Los Angeles production of *Oklahoma!* [1951–52]
6   Insurance claim, Canada [1950–54; concerns damage to backdrop in
             Calgary in late November 1952]
7   *Green Grow the Lilacs* [production and film rights, etc.; 1929–36]
8   *Oklahoma!*: New York staging [undated; lighting and prop lists]
9   Foreign rights to *Oklahoma!*; foreign productions [1943–49]
10   *Oklahoma!*: script [two copies, plus two vocal scores]
11   London production of *Oklahoma!* [1945–54]
12   Investors in *Oklahoma!* [1943–54]
13   Berlin production of *Oklahoma!* [1951–52]
14   *Oklahoma!*: garnishee execution [re Alfred Cibelli Jr.; 1953]
15   *Green Grow the Lilacs*: script
16   *Oklahoma!*: film [1935–54]
17   "Confidential" file on *Oklahoma!*: motion picture rights [1952–53].
18   Sale of *Oklahoma!* [1952–56]
19   *Oklahoma!*: miscellaneous [1943–53]
20   *Oklahoma!*: subway circuit [that is, in New York outside Manhattan;
             1951]

LITERATURE

Abbott, George. *Mister Abbott*. New York: Random House, 1963.

Altman, Rick. *The American Film Musical*. Bloomington: Indiana University Press,
    1987.

Banfield, Stephen. *Jerome Kern*. New Haven: Yale University Press, 2006.

Beiswanger, George. "Theatre Today: Symptoms and Surmises." *Journal of Aesthetics
    and Art Criticism* 3, nos. 9–10 (1944–45): 19–29.

Bentley, Eric. *The Playwright as Thinker: A Study of Drama in Modern Times*. New
    York: Reynal and Hitchcock, 1946.

Block, Geoffrey. "The Broadway Canon from *Show Boat* to *West Side Story* and the
    European Operatic Ideal." *Journal of Musicology* 11 (1993): 525–44.

———. *Enchanted Evenings: The Broadway Musical from "Show Boat" to Sondheim*.
    New York: Oxford University Press, 1997.

———. *Richard Rodgers*. New Haven: Yale University Press, 2003.

Block, Geoffrey, ed. *The Richard Rodgers Reader*. New York: Oxford University Press,
    2002.

Borowitz, Albert. "'Pore Jud Is Daid': Violence and Lawlessness in the Plays of Lynn
    Riggs." *Legal Studies Forum* 27 (2003): 157–84.

Braunlich, Phyllis Cole. *Haunted by Home: The Life and Letters of Lynn Riggs*. Nor-
    man: University of Oklahoma Press, 1988.

Carter, Tim. "In the Workshop of Rodgers and Hammerstein: New Light on *Okla-
    homa!*" In *Music Observed: Studies in Honor of William C. Holmes*, ed. Susan Parisi
    and Colleen Reardon, 55–64. Warren, Mich.: Harmonie Park, 2004.

D'Andre, David Mark. "The Theatre Guild, *Carousel*, and the Cultural Field of Ameri-
    can Musical Theatre." Ph.D. diss., Yale University, 2000.

de Mille, Agnes. *"Dance to the Piper" and "Promenade Home": A Two-Part Autobio-graphy* (1952, 1958). New York: Da Capo, 1980.

DeVeaux, Scott. *The Birth of Bebop: A Social and Musical History.* Berkeley: University of California Press, 1997.

Donovan, Timothy P. "'Oh, What a Beautiful Mornin'': The Musical *Oklahoma!* and the Popular Mind in 1943." In *American Popular Music: Readings from the Popular Press,* vol. 1, *The Nineteenth Century and Tin Pan Alley,* ed. Timothy E. Scheurer, 161–72. Bowling Green, Ohio: Bowling Green State University Popular Press, 1989.

Evans, Larry James. "Rodgers and Hammerstein's *Oklahoma!* The Development of the 'Integrated' Musical." Ph.D. diss., University of California, Los Angeles, 1990.

Ferencz, George J., ed. *"The Broadway Sound": The Autobiography and Selected Essays of Robert Russell Bennett.* Rochester, N.Y.: University of Rochester Press, 1999.

Filmer, Paul, Val Rimmer, and Dave Walsh. "*Oklahoma!* Ideology and Politics in the Vernacular Tradition of the American Musical." *Popular Music* 18 (1999): 381–95.

Fordin, Hugh. *Getting to Know Him: A Biography of Oscar Hammerstein.* New York: Random House, 1977.

Forte, Allen. *The American Popular Ballad of the Golden Era, 1924–1950.* Princeton: Princeton University Press, 1995.

Goldstein, R. M. "I Enjoy Being a Girl: Women in the Plays of Rodgers and Hammerstein." *Popular Music and Society* 13, no. 1 (1989): 1–8.

Grant, Mark N. *The Rise and Fall of the Broadway Musical.* Boston: Northeastern University Press, 2004.

Green, Stanley. "*Oklahoma!* Its Origin and Influence." *American Music* 2, no. 4 (1984): 88–94.

Green, Stanley, ed. *Rodgers and Hammerstein Fact Book: A Record of Their Works Together and with Other Collaborators.* New York: Lynn Farnol Group, 1980.

Hamm, Charles. "The Theatre Guild Production of *Porgy and Bess.*" *Journal of the American Musicological Society* 40 (1987): 495–532.

Hammerstein, Oscar 2nd. *"Oklahoma!": A Musical Play by Richard Rodgers and Oscar Hammerstein, 2nd; Based on Lynn Riggs' "Green Grow the Lilacs."* New York: Random House, 1943.

———. "Notes on Lyrics" (1949). In Hammerstein, *Lyrics by Oscar Hammerstein II,* 3–48.

Hammerstein, William, ed. *Lyrics by Oscar Hammerstein II.* Rev. ed. Milwaukee: Hal Leonard, 1985.

Hanff, Helene. *Underfoot in Show Business* (1962). 3rd ed. Boston: Little, Brown, 1980.

Harriman, Margaret Case. *Take Them Up Tenderly: A Collection of Profiles* [from the *New Yorker*]. New York: Knopf, 1944.

Helburn, Theresa. *A Wayward Quest: The Autobiography of Theresa Helburn.* Boston: Little, Brown, 1960.

Hischak, Thomas S. *Through the Screen Door: What Happened to the Broadway Musical When It Went to Hollywood.* Lanham, Md.: Scarecrow, 2004.

Hyland, William G. *Richard Rodgers.* New Haven: Yale University Press, 1998.

Jones, John Bush. *Our Musicals, Ourselves: A Social History of the American Musical Theatre.* Lebanon, N.H.: Brandeis University Press, 2003.

Kadison, Luba, and Joseph Buloff, with Irving Glenn. *On Stage, Off Stage: Memories of a Lifetime in the Yiddish Theatre*. Cambridge: Harvard University Press, 1992.

Kirle, Bruce. "Reconciliation, Resolution, and the Political Role of *Oklahoma!* in American Consciousness." *Theatre Journal* 55 (2003): 251–74.

Knapp, Raymond. *The American Musical and the Formation of National Identity*. Princeton: Princeton University Press, 2005.

Langner, Lawrence. *The Magic Curtain: The Story of a Life in Two Fields, Theatre and Invention, by the Founder of the Theatre Guild*. New York: Dutton, 1951.

Logan, Joshua. *Josh: My Up and Down, In and Out Life*. New York: Delacorte, 1976.

———. *Movie Stars, Real People, and Me*. New York: Delacorte, 1978.

Magee, Jeffrey. "Irving Berlin's 'Blue Skies': Ethnic Affiliations and Musical Transformations." *Musical Quarterly* 84 (2000): 537–80.

Mast, Gerald. "As Corny as Kansas in August, as Restless as a Willow in a Windstorm." In Block, *Richard Rodgers Reader*, 87–112. First published in Mast, *Can't Help Singin': The American Musical on Stage and Screen* (New York: Overlook, 1987), 201–18.

Miller, Scott. *Rebels with Applause: Broadway's Groundbreaking Musicals*. Portsmouth, N.H.: Heinemann, 2001.

Mordden, Ethan. *Rodgers and Hammerstein*. New York: Abrams, 1992.

———. *Beautiful Mornin': The Broadway Musical in the 1940s*. New York: Oxford University Press, 1999.

Most, Andrea. "'We Know We Belong to the Land': The Theatricality of Assimilation in Rodgers and Hammerstein's *Oklahoma!*" *PMLA* 113 (1998): 77–89.

———. *Making Americans: Jews and the Broadway Musical*. Cambridge: Harvard University Press, 2004.

Nolan, Frederick. *Lorenz Hart: A Poet on Broadway*. New York: Oxford University Press, 1994.

———. *The Sound of Their Music: The Story of Rodgers and Hammerstein*. 2nd ed. New York: Applause, 2002.

Partridge, Eric. *Name This Child: A Dictionary of English (and American) Christian Names*. London: Methuen, 1936.

Pollack, Howard. *Aaron Copland: The Life and Work of an Uncommon Man*. Urbana: University of Illinois Press, 1999.

Riggs, Lynn. *Green Grow the Lilacs: A Play*. New York: Samuel French, 1931.

Rodgers, Richard. *Musical Stages: An Autobiography* (1975). 2nd ed. Cambridge, Mass.: Da Capo, 2002.

Roost, Alisa. "Before *Oklahoma!* A Reappraisal of Musical Theatre During the 1930s." *Journal of American Drama and Theatre* 16 (2004): 1–35.

Rugg, Rebecca. "What It Used to Be: Nostalgia and the State of the Broadway Musical." *Theater* 32 (2002): 45–55.

Sears, Anne. "The Coming of the Musical Play: Rodgers and Hammerstein." In *The Cambridge Companion to the Musical*, ed. William A. Everett and Paul R. Laird, 120–36. Cambridge: Cambridge University Press, 2002.

Secrest, Meryle. *Somewhere for Me: A Biography of Richard Rodgers*. New York: Knopf, 2001.

Smith, Elsdon C. *Dictionary of American Family Names.* New York: Harper and Brothers, 1956.

Snelson, John. "The West End Musical, 1947–54: British Identity and the 'American Invasion.'" Ph.D. diss., University of Birmingham (U.K.), 2002.

Stein, Tobie S. *Boston's Colonial Theatre: Celebrating a Century of Theatrical Vision.* Boston: Colonial 2000, 2000.

Suskin, Steven. *Opening Night on Broadway: A Critical Quotebook of the Golden Era of the Musical Theatre, "Oklahoma!" (1943) to "Fiddler on the Roof" (1964).* New York: Schirmer, 1990.

Swain, Joseph P. *The Broadway Musical: A Critical and Musical Survey.* 2nd rev. ed. Lanham, Md.: Scarecrow, 2002.

Symonette, Lys, and Kim H. Kowalke, eds. *Speak Low (When You Speak Love): The Letters of Kurt Weill and Lotte Lenya.* Berkeley: University of California Press, 1996.

Taylor, Betty Sue. "An Analysis of the Script and Score of *Oklahoma!* A Prototypical Musical Play." Ph.D. diss., City University of New York, 1985.

Taylor, Deems. *Some Enchanted Evenings: The Story of Rodgers and Hammerstein.* New York: Harper, 1953.

Turner, Frederick Jackson. "The Significance of the Frontier in American History." In *The Frontier in American History*, 1–38. New York: Henry Holt, 1920.

Wilk, Max. *Ok! The Story of "Oklahoma!" A Celebration of America's Most Loved Musical.* New York: Applause, 2002.

Womack, Craig S. "Lynn Riggs as Code Talker: Toward a Queer Oklahomo Theory and the Radicalization of Native American Studies." In *Red on Red: Native American Literary Separatism*, 271–303. Minneapolis: University of Minnesota Press, 1999.

Wood, Graham. "The Development of Song Forms in the Broadway and Hollywood Musicals of Richard Rodgers, 1919–1943." Ph.D. diss., University of Minnesota, 2000.

Permissions

Index

INDEX 315

book, 81; and Jay Blackton, 48; Joshua
Logan, 33; Robert Alton, 45
Byrne, Donn, 274

Caesar, Irving, 23, 276
Cagney, Jimmy, 6, 225
Cagney, William, 225
Cahill, Marie, 89
Caldwell, Erskine, 17
Calherne, Lou, 42
Campbell, Walter, 10
Cannon, Hughie, 90
Canova, Judy, 30; possible Ado Annie, 54
Cantor, Eddie, 201
Carmen Jones (Bizet and Hammerstein,
1943), 295; casting, 23, 36, 38, 39, 278;
choral director, 273; delayed premiere,
20, 38, 67, 215, 229, 276; finished July
1942, 34; and "Lotta," 92; melodrama,
106; Robert Alton, 279; Robert Russell
Bennett, 19, 48
Caro, Warren, 266, 298
Carousel (Rodgers and Hammerstein, 1945):
"A Real Nice Clambake," 285; film, 246,
247; less successful than *Oklahoma!* 239;
"Louise's Ballet," 124–25; more ambi-
tious vocal writing, 112; with *Oklahoma!*
graduates, 236; social outcasts, 206; sold to
Rodgers and Hammerstein, 240, 243; and
Theatre Guild, 7, 28, 215, 219–20, 224,
239; underscoring, 106
Carter, Jack, 246
Chappell and Co., 35, 153, 216, 297;
subsidizes orchestrations, 75
Charell, Erik, 6, 273
Chekov, Anton, 168
Chodorov, Jerome, 64
Church, George, 60, 125, 139, 213, 286, 288,
289, 296; drafted into army, 148; leaves
show, 155; in "Oklahoma," 142, 155, 162,
213
Cibelli, Alfred, 236, 246
Cinderella (Rodgers and Hammerstein,
1957), 18; 1965 version, 289
Clark, Barrett H., 11, 274, 275
Clark, Bobby, 30, 277
Clay, Edwin, 65, 262
Clement, Colin, 47

Clogg, Hallye, **218**
Clurman, Harold, 3
Cobb, Lee, 246
Cohen, Frederic, 60
Cohn, Harry, 70, 72, 282
Cole, Jack, 140
Collier, Buster, 56
Colonial Theatre, Boston, 4, 78, 153–54, 160,
162, 283
Colton, John, 36
Columbia Pictures, 67, 70, 220; investing in
Oklahoma! 71, 282
Columbia University, 19, 186
Como, Perry, 242
Congreve, William, 18
Conkle, E. P., 82
A Connecticut Yankee (Rodgers and Hart,
1927), 17, 37, 120, 285
Cook, Barbara, 246
Copland, Aaron: "American" ballets, 45; con-
sidered for *Oklahoma!* 31–32; and Lynn
Riggs, 17; pastoral, 187; Theatre Guild,
219, 220. See also *Rodeo*
Le Coq d'or. See *The Golden Cockerel*
Coward, Noël, 4, 168, 231
Crawford, Cheryl, 3, 22, 23–24, 280
Crosby, Bing, 226, 242
Crouse, Russel, 8, 36, 68, 295; considered for
Oklahoma! 29–30
Crowthers, Bosley, 238
Crump, John, 64
Cullman, Howard S., 283
Cunliff, Leo, 10
Cunningham, Merce, 60, 281
Curtin, Edward W., 165
Curtis, Tony, 247

da Silva, Howard (Howard Silverblatt), 138,
203, 227, 244; behaves badly, 221; drafted
into army, 148; prior career, 64; problems
with "Lonely Room," 115, 161; recruited,
58–59, 60, 281, 293
Damone, Vic, 246
Dante Alighieri, 208
Darby, Ken, 229
Davis, Donald, 239
Davis, Jetar (Jeeter), 10
Davis, Owen, 239